Contents

Use accepted formats and conventions when preparing
routine business documents • Standard formats and
conventions of business documents • Analyse, extract and
adapt information to meet a given purpose • Adaptation
and presentation of relevant information for use in business
documents/formats • Presentation of documents for ease
of use and to reflect purpose • Use English correctly

Contribute to the work of a team • Confirm own
responsibilities including working arrangements • Carry out
tasks allocated • Work with others to complete tasks
• Communicate effectively with others • Maintain effective
working relationships • Review your contribution to the
team activity • Review the overall performance of the team
• Present a positive image to customers • Follow company
procedures for communicating with customers • Interact
effectively with customers • Use appropriate tone and
manner • Convey information clearly and accurately
• Resolve difficulties using organisational procedures
• Record information accurately • Ensure customers'
requirements have been met

Describe and compare business organisations • Explain how
business organisations develop • Describe why an
organisation must have clear aims and objectives • Explain
how business organisations are structured • Describe how
activities are organised to meet the organisation's objectives
• Outline the roles of people at different levels of the
organisation • Managers and department heads • Identify
levels of hierarchy • Identify and evaluate the importance
of effective administration • Identify and explain effective
working practices • Explain the importance of organising

Level 2
OCR Certificate in
Business Administration

Diane Canwell
with Bernard Kane

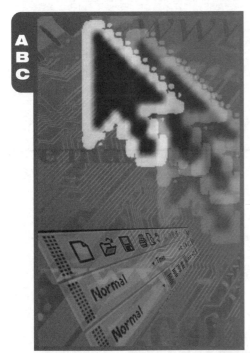

Published in 2004 by:
Nelson Thornes Ltd
Delta Place
27 Bath Road
CHELTENHAM
GL53 7TH
United Kingdom

04 05 06 07 08 / 10 9 8 7 6 5 4 3 2 1

A catalogue record for this book is available from the British Library

ISBN 0 7487 8531 0

Page make-up by GreenGate Publishing Services, Tonbridge

Printed and bound in Great Britain by Scotprint

Acknowledgements

Microsoft Office screenshots are reproduced with permission from Microsoft Corporation. Microsoft and its products are registered trademarks or trademarks of Microsoft Corporation in the United States and/or other countries.

The authors and publishers would like to thank the following for permission to reproduce material:

Giry Daniel/Corbis Sygma, page 158; DTI, page 162; PA Photos, page 163; Oxfam, page 155.

Every effort has been made to contact copyright holders and the author and publishers apologise if any have been overlooked.

Introduction

Above all, the OCR Level 2 Certificate in Administration is a practical qualification which aims to encourage and develop your ability to work without supervision. The first five units cover the majority of administrative tasks and activities and should provide you with the evidence to present to an employer that you are able to function in an administrative post.

There are five mandatory (compulsory) units which deal with working with colleagues and customers, written communication, office procedures, work practices in an organisation and the use of information communication technology. Collectively the Units 1 to 5 aim to give you a firm understanding of what is involved in an administrative job.

The five mandatory units have equal value and they each contribute 20% of the marks towards the final qualification. Different centres will tackle these five units in a different order. Some may choose to link the units, such as Units 2 and 4, or Units 1 and 2. The information technology skills, which are covered in Unit 5, will be particularly useful for Units 1 and 2.

This book has been written so that you can easily find information which directly relates to a unit's assessment objectives, or the knowledge, understanding and skills section of the specification. Each of the assessment objectives has a clear heading, as do all of the knowledge, understanding and skills. It is therefore easy to find exactly what you need as the information included in the book has been written in the same order as the specification.

Units 2 and 4 are assessed by your centre's own devised assignments. Your tutor will mark them and then OCR will check the marking. Units 1, 3 and 5 take the form of OCR examinations. Unit 5 is part of the Level 2 Certificate for IT Users (CLAIT Plus). If you already have this qualification you will able to use this as evidence to pass the unit of this qualification.

Units 1 and 3 require you to sit a two-and-a-half-hour examination. You will be given an additional 10 minutes reading time. You will need to achieve a minimum of 50% in order to pass these examinations. Both Units 1 and 3 have four tasks or questions, which may be broken down into sub-questions. In the examination for Unit 1 all the questions flow from one setting in which you are asked to adopt a particular role. This is done so that your ability to use business communications consistently in a range of different business documents is tested. Unit 5 is a three-hour examination and requires you to work around a scenario that will test your knowledge and understanding, as well as skills in being able to create, manage and integrate files.

Unit 2 requires you to show your ability to communicate with customers, meeting each of the eight assessment objectives. Your tutor will witness your performance and complete a Witness Statement on your behalf. OCR provides checklists to assist you and your tutor in making sure that you have covered all aspects of the assessment.

Unit 4 requires you to show an understanding of administrative procedures. This unit is ideally carried out during a period of work experience, although you may well be able to undertake these activities at your centre. Again, OCR provides Witness Statements and Candidate Evidence Sheets.

The purpose of this qualification is to provide you with the background, knowledge and skills in order to progress to the NVQ in Administration Level 2, which is the gateway to higher administration qualifications.

Diane Canwell
May 2004

Preparing business communications

Four key assessment objectives

- Use accepted formats and conventions when preparing routine business documents
- Analyse, extract and adapt information to meet a given purpose
- Use appropriate tone and style for different purposes
- Use English correctly

Each of these broad objectives covers a number of specific skills relating to preparing business communications.

In this unit you will learn how to:

- recognise and use standard formats for business documents
- recognise and apply conventions for routine documents
- prepare letters
- prepare e-mails
- prepare faxes
- prepare memos
- prepare forms
- prepare agendas
- prepare business notes
- prepare business reports
- prepare and present articles
- create job descriptions
- create leaflets, notices and advertisements
- understand the relevance and context of information when presenting it
- identify information not appropriate for inclusion
- identify and extract relevant information
- check instructions and sources
- adapt information for specific formats and contexts
- adapt and present information for various business documents
- present documents which are easy to use
- select and use vocabulary to suit specified context
- use style to reflect business context
- use tone to reflect the needs of the recipient
- adapt tone to meet non-standard situations
- use tact, diplomacy, persuasion and technical style

- appreciate the use of appropriate tone and style to reflect context and purpose
- accurately spell common words
- ensure punctuation is accurate and consistent
- correctly structure complex sentences
- organise information into paragraphs.

In working for any business or organisation you will routinely handle what may appear to be complex information. You will need to be able to read through the information and take from it any relevant information. You will also need to be able to present information in an accurate way, using what is known as a standard format. Sometimes you will need to design your own formats. You will also need to write communications, both straightforward and complex, and learn how to use the correct tone and style.

Business communications rely on people understanding the information that is sent to them, as well as being able to send clear information to others. You will need to develop your business English skills and apply what you have learned to different business situations.

Use accepted formats and conventions when preparing routine business documents

Even the simplest memo or letter must follow a particular format and set of conventions. These are the rules which a person should follow when creating a document and which determine the way the document will look. Different types of business communication, or document, follow different sets of formats and conventions. If you follow these formats and conventions, those receiving and reading your communication will have a much better chance of understanding the information contained in it.

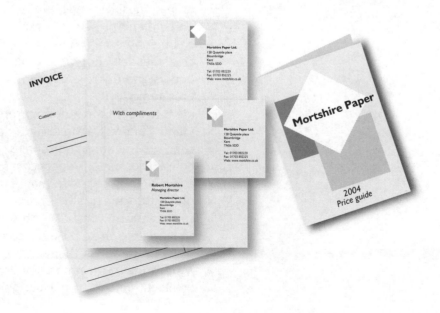

Figure 1.1

Standard formats and conventions of business documents

Because each type of business document has a different format and set of conventions, it is important to tackle each one separately. We will first describe the various standard formats and conventions and then give you an opportunity to prepare a business document yourself using those formats and conventions. All businesses have their own 'house rules' about the layout of their documents. You will learn what these particular rules are and will have to make sure you use the correct layout each time.

Business letters

Normally a business letter is sent to an individual outside the organisation. Letters may be written for a number of different purposes, including:

- contacting customers (or potential customers) – people who are either buying or may buy the organisation's products or services
- communicating with suppliers – other businesses that provide products, or services to the organisation
- answering customer complaints
- telling lots of existing customers about a new product the business might be about to make available
- contacting someone who has applied for a job with the organisation.

Build-up Exercise

We've given you five reasons why a business might write a business letter. Can you think of any others? Write down your other reasons for an organisation writing a business letter. Remember that a business letter goes out of the organisation.

Business letters need to be neat, accurate and well presented; businesses see their letters as a reflection of their professionalism in everything they do. Most businesses use headed paper, which means many of the details in the following list are printed onto the paper and appear on every letter that leaves the organisation. This also means that the person preparing the letter does not have to type these details onto each letter. Headed paper usually contains the following information:

- name and address of the business
- telephone and fax number of the business
- e-mail address of the business
- website address of the business
- registered address of the business (this could be a different address from the normal postal address of the business)

- the business's registration number (this is a number given to the business by Companies House when it is created and registered there, as required by law for most businesses)
- the names of the owners or directors of the business
- the names of other organisations associated with the business, such as professional organisations.

Figure 1.2

A business letter is ordered in a certain way to make sure it contains all the necessary information. As well as the details printed on the headed paper, it will contain:

- **The name and address of the recipient** (the person to whom the letter is being sent).
- **The date** the letter is being prepared or sent.
- **A reference**, sometimes – this can be the initials of the writer or a set of numbers. It helps the writer of the letter to know where to file it and also to keep all the paperwork together if there are many letters relating to the same subject.
- **URGENT or CONFIDENTIAL**, words which tell the recipient how important the letter is and whether or not it is private.
- **A salutation** – this is the start of the letter and could be, for example, 'Dear Mr Smith' or 'Dear Sir'. If the name of the recipient is known, it is usual to use it and start with their name. If the name

of the recipient is not known, it is more appropriate to use 'Dear Sir' or 'Dear Madam'.

- **A subject heading** which will help the recipient see immediately what the letter is about.
- **The paragraphs** contained in the letter itself come next.
- **The complimentary close** – this is the way the letter ends. If 'Dear Sir' or 'Madam' has been used in the salutation, then the letter is ended with 'Yours faithfully'. If the name has been used (for example 'Dear Mr Smith'), then 'Yours sincerely' is used in the complimentary close.
- **The printed name** of the person sending the letter (and their job title) will come after the complimentary close, leaving enough room for their signature.
- If any additional items are included with the letter, this is indicated at the end of the letter by the word 'Enc', which is short for 'enclosure' ('Encs' for more than one enclosure).

The most common way of displaying a business letter is the fully blocked method of display shown in Figure 1.3. This means that each part of the letter starts at the left-hand margin.

COMPANY HEADED PAPER

Ref: DES/JDS/291003

29 October 200-

CONFIDENTIAL

Laura Buchan
The Old Post Office
Loddon
Norfolk
NR31 6BJ

Dear Ms Buchan

Your application for the post of administrator

XXXXXXXXXXXXXXXXXXXXXXXXXXXXXXXXXXXXXXXXXXXXXXXXXXXXX
XXXXXXXXXXXXXXXXXXXXXXXXXXXXXXXXXXXXXXXXX

XXXXXXXXXXXXXXXXXXXXXXXXXXXXXXXXXXXXXXXXXXXXXXXXXXXXXXX
XXXXXXXXXXXXXXXXXXXXXXXXXXXXXXXXXXXXXXXXXXXXXXXXXXXXXXXX
XXXXXXXXXXXXXXXXXXXXXXXXXXXXXXXXXXXXXXXXXXXXXX
XXXXXXXXXX

Yours sincerely

Jonathan Sutherland
Recruitment Officer

Enc

Figure 1.3

Different businesses have different ways in which their business letters are displayed. Some prefer to 'indent' at the beginning of each paragraph (this means spacing in so that the first line is a few spaces away from the left-hand margin).

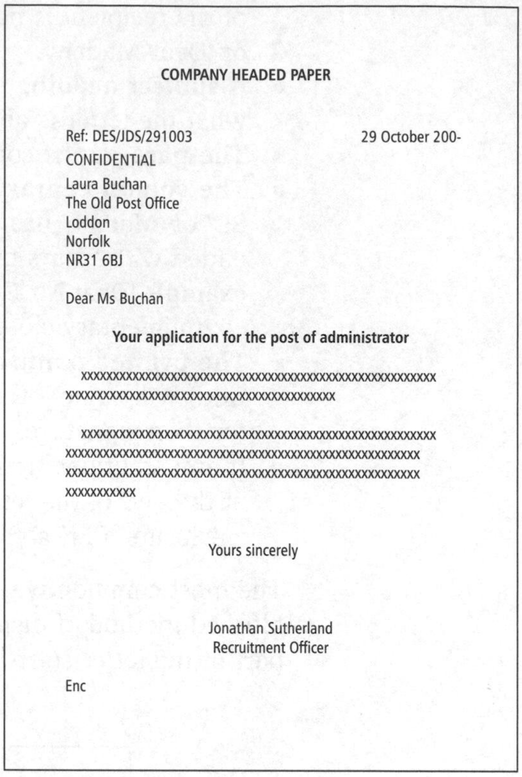

COMPANY HEADED PAPER

Ref: DES/JDS/291003   29 October 200-
CONFIDENTIAL
Laura Buchan
The Old Post Office
Loddon
Norfolk
NR31 6BJ

Dear Ms Buchan

Your application for the post of administrator

xxxxxxxxxxxxxxxxxxxxxxxxxxxxxxxxxxxxxxxxxxxxxxxxxxxxxxxxx
xxxxxxxxxxxxxxxxxxxxxxxxxxxxxxxxxxxxxxxxxxxx

xxxxxxxxxxxxxxxxxxxxxxxxxxxxxxxxxxxxxxxxxxxxxxxxxxxxxxxxx
xxxxxxxxxxxxxxxxxxxxxxxxxxxxxxxxxxxxxxxxxxxxxxxxxxxxxxxxx
xxxxxxxxxxxxxxxxxxxxxxxxxxxxxxxxxxxxxxxxxxxxxxxxxxxxxxxxx
xxxxxxxxxxx

Yours sincerely

Jonathan Sutherland
Recruitment Officer

Enc

Figure 1.4

Routine and non-routine letters

Businesses will disagree as to what they consider routine and non-routine letters. Usually the term 'routine' applies to letters whose content follows a standard format; they may be little more than a simple covering letter, sent out to customers who have requested a catalogue or brochure. Such routine letters can be stored on the computer and simply need to have the name, address and date changed as the same letter is sent out to different customers. Routine letters can also be used to deal with regular or repeated communications which have a standard content.

Non-routine letters are usually letters sent in response to either a rare or unusual request, or a particularneed to communicate with a customer or other individual. Rather than sending out a letter with standard contents, non-routine letters have to be specifically written to answer particular questions, or deal with particular issues raised by the enquiry. A non-routine letter requires much more thought and careful consideration before being sent out by the business.

Although most businesses use a word processor to prepare their business letter, it should be remembered that some are still hand-written. Whether hand-writing or word processing a business letter, remember that it needs to have a beginning, a middle and an end. For most letters:

- **The beginning** should contain the reason for writing and might refer to a previous letter, telephone call or document.
- **The middle** provides the recipient with details of the information you wish to give them. This may involve giving instructions, or asking for information. The middle could consist of several

paragraphs, and numbered or bulleted points could be used to break down detailed information.

■ **The end** should be used to review what has already been stated. It could also include any action you have promised to take or anything you wish the recipient to do. The final sentence usually takes the form of a simple, closing statement, such as 'Please let me know if you require any further information'.

Correct address

It is surprisingly easy to type an incorrect address on a letter. Many mistakes are made, particularly in typing postcodes.

It is a standard convention for each part of the address to appear on a separate line. This raises problems when an address is particularly long and will not fit a standard 'window' envelope. In these cases the address may have to be written or typed onto the envelope, or an address label typed for the envelope. Bear in mind that the clearer the address, the less problem the Royal Mail will have ensuring the letter reaches the right place and is read by the right person.

It is always worth checking unlikely words that appear in an address, even if they have been typed onto a letter to which you are replying. Do not necessarily rely on the person who has sent you the letter to get their own address right, unless of course it is part of a company's headed paper, which will have been checked thoroughly. Odd or confusing addresses should be double-checked before the letter is sent out, particularly if there is an incomplete postcode. Important points to check are:

■ the spelling of the recipient's name
■ that the spelling in of the recipient's name the address line matches that in the salutation
■ that each part of the address begins on a new line
■ that you have included the postcode.

Build-up Exercise

Here are the addresses of four customers who have asked for a catalogue to be sent to them. The addresses have been taken down from telephone messages and now need to be written onto envelopes.

Mr Richard Sutherland, 7 Old School Villas, Stradbroke, near Eye, Suffolk, IP49 3BN

Ms Frances Hathaway, 42 Station Road, Huntingfield, Suffolk, IP14 2PS

Dr L James Franklin, The Manse, The Street, Metfield, near Harleston, Suffolk, IP12 4BP

The Reverend Kenneth Smith, The Maltus Vicarage, Mulbarton, near Norwich, Norfolk, NR31 2EE

▶▶

Which of the following addresses have been copied out correctly and which are incorrect? Put right any errors that you find by writing out the addresses as they should appear on the envelopes. Then get someone to check that you have done the job accurately!

The Reverend Kenneth Smith,
The Maltings Vicarage,
Mulbarten,
near Norwich, Norfolk,
NR31 2E

Dr L James Franklin
The Manse
The Street
Metfield
Near Harleston
Suffolk
IP12 4BP

Ms Frances Hathaway,
44 Station Road,
Huntingfield,
Norfolk,
IP1 42PS

Mr Richard Sutherland
7 School Villas
Stradbrooke
Near Eye
Suffolk, IP49 3BN

Appropriate language, tone and vocabulary

There is no right or wrong way of writing a business letter. However, you cannot go far wrong by following these 10 key tips:

- **Start at the end** – you need to decide what the outcome of your letter should be. First list in rough the things you want to say and read through them. Good letters have a sense of purpose.
- **Don't mess about; get to the point** – the most important point of your letter should appear in the first paragraph.
- **Think about the reader** – how would you respond to the letter which you have just written? Is it pleasant? Is it polite? Is it too negative? How could it be improved?
- **Plain speaking** – try to write as you talk and avoid sentences which are longer than two typed lines.
- **Cut out unnecessary detail** – if you can cut out words, sentences (or even paragraphs) which do not add to what you are saying, do so. It will make your letter more understandable and the reader's job much simpler.
- **Be active, not passive** – it is much better to say 'We have reached a decision', than 'After discussion a decision has been reached'. Avoid weak and confusing sentences.
- **Be human** – try to make your letter read like a conversation; begin by addressing the reader by name and, if possible, fit the reader's name into the letter itself. Use words such as 'I', 'we' and 'you' to make it more personal.
- **Don't be angry** – if you write a letter in anger, there is every chance that it will say the wrong thing. There is always some way to handle problems other than by resorting to anger.

- **End by suggesting an action** – your letter should suggest what the reader should do next, such as 'Please do not hesitate to call' or 'If you have any problems please get in touch' and close with a simple ending and your signature.
- **Be professional** – use a clean, logical format for the letter. Paragraphs that are too long, poorly punctuated or contain mistakes give the wrong impression to the reader.

Table 1.1 *Summary of conventions for a business letter*

Standard conventions	Description
Headings	Subject heading – so the reader can see what the letter is about as soon as they open it.
Standard formats	Include your own and the reader's address.
	Include a salutation (Dear Mr, Ms, Mrs, Miss, Dr, etc.) or Dear Sir or Madam.
	Use blocked layout (unless your organisation does it differently).
	Use the appropriate complimentary close – Yours faithfully or Yours sincerely.
	Remember to sign the letter.
	If an enclosure is to go into the envelope with the letter, indicate this with Enc or Encs.
Methods of addressing recipient	Use full name if known in the address but the salutation will be simply their title (Mrs, Mr) and surname.
Methods of closing	Yours faithfully is used when you start with Dear Sir or Madam.
	Yours sincerely is used when you have started the letter with the recipient's name.

Table 1.2 *Advantages and disadvantages of business letters*

Advantages	Disadvantages
- Can be personalised. - Can use a standard format. - Can deal with a single problem - or a wider issue. - Has a professional look if correctly formatted. - Can be used as a simple covering letter when sending other information.	- Can be rather formal. - May not convince the reader to respond. - Can take too long if a separate letter has to be written each time. - May be delayed in the post. - Can give a bad impression if content is not accurate and is not well presented.

Try it out

You will need plenty of practice in writing business letters. Try the following two to start with.

1 You work in the human resource department of a business and you received a letter from someone who has applied for a job and has been invited to come in for interview. They cannot make the time set for the interview as they have to go to hospital for a small operation, but have told you they could make the same day and time the following week. Your business is very keen that the interview should take place. Write a letter to Mrs Susan Dodd, 75 Chancery Lane, West Bromwich, WB41 5DT, dated today, informing her that you would still like to interview her, but can only make next Friday at 11.30 in your office. Imagine you are using your company's headed paper.

2 Imagine that your first job of the day, at a busy supplier of garden furniture, sheds and fences, is to listen to the answerphone tape and jot down the names and addresses of people who have requested brochures. You have noted down the following names and addresses and the brochures which they have requested:

Mr Richard Sutherland, 7 Old School Villas, Stradbroke, near Eye, Suffolk, IP49 3BN – he wants the garden sheds brochure and the wheelbarrows brochure

Ms Frances Hathaway, 42 Station Road, Huntingfield, Suffolk, IP14 2PS – he wants the gates and fence panels brochure.

Dr L James Franklin, The Manse, The Street, Metfield, near Harleston, Suffolk, IP12 4BP – he wants the compost bins brochure and the wheelbarrows brochure

The Reverend Kenneth Smith, The Maltus Vicarage, Mulbarton, near Norwich, Norfolk, NR31 2EE – he wants the fence panels and the sheds brochure.

a Design a standard letter that could be sent to any customer requesting a brochure. You will need to leave blank the name and address, the salutation and details of any brochures enclosed.

b Now complete a standard letter, with the correct details, for each of the four customers who have requested brochures.

E-mail

Electronic mail, or e-mail, enables people to send text messages, pictures and files to other people via the Internet. To send and receive e-mail both the sender and the receiver need to have e-mail software, such as Microsoft's Outlook Express. Most e-mail software packages allow you to write, send, receive, store and manage e-mails. The sender

Figure 1.5

and the receiver each need to have an e-mail address. Many e-mail addresses are available free through websites such as Yahoo.

Businesses that have their own websites will have a number of e-mail addresses, such as bert.smith@thisismybusiness.com. Customers can use this to contact the business.

Electronic mail allows the same e-mail to be sent to several different people at the same time, providing the sender has the correct e-mail addresses. E-mail is a fast and convenient way of getting into contact with people, as messages can be sent and received almost instantly (or at least in a few minutes), unlike normal posted mail which can take several days to arrive. E-mail allows businesses to exchange messages with people anywhere in the world equally quickly.

Using electronic mail businesses and individuals can communicate with one another without having to use a telephone, or having to write, print and post a formal business letter. Because e-mails can be sent and received at any time of the day or night, any day of the week, messages can be sent and received without worrying whether the post will be collected or delivered.

E-mails are not only ideal for sending simple messages, but they can also contain complex messages, and various other documents can be attached to them. E-mails can be printed and stored. (See Figure 1.6.)

Many people are discouraged from using e-mail because they don't understand all the jargon associated with it, but sending and receiving

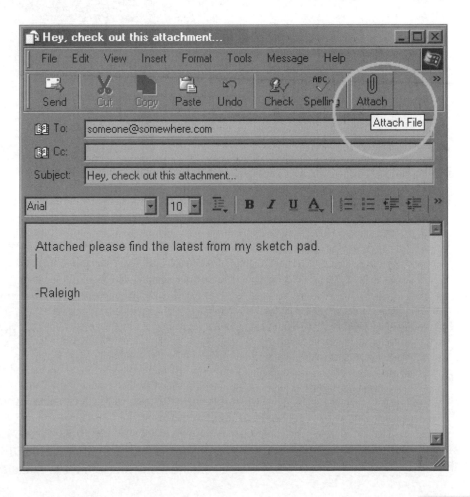

Figure 1.6

e-mails could not be simpler, provided of course that you have an e-mail account.

Unlike a real address (an actual location to which post is sent) e-mails have what could be described as a 'virtual address'. This means that wherever you are and whichever computer you are using, as long as you can remember how to access your e-mail account, you can send and receive e-mail.

Many of the bigger Internet Service Providers (ISPs) provide you with a CD which you use to set up your computer for the Internet. It allows you to load onto your computer all of the software needed to access the Internet. It also allows you to set up an e-mail account. If you are using an Internet-connected computer at school, college, an Internet café, or a library, you will be able to set up your own e-mail account by simply going to one of the main Internet search pages, such as Yahoo.co.uk.

On these pages you will find the word 'mail'. Simply click on this button (or word) and follow the instructions to set up your own e-mail account. The process will give you an e-mail account name and you will need to note down and remember your own password to access your account. Once you have done this, wherever you are, you simply need to return to this page to send and receive e-mails whenever you like.

Figure 1.7

Figure 1.8

There are many ways of making your e-mails more effective, including:

- choosing an informative and appropriate subject line
- changing the subject line when you reply to a message that someone else has sent you
- letting the reader know what the purpose of the e-mail is in the opening line of the message
- if you want the reader to do something, making it clear what it is you want them to do
- using short paragraphs; long ones are difficult to follow on a computer screen
- using headings, or bullet points, to make it easier to follow a series of points
- making sure your e-mail is not too long as this causes reading problems on the screen and difficulties in printing it out
- spell-checking your e-mail to make sure there are no mistakes

- avoiding unnecessary capital letters; an e-mail message written in capitals can give the reader the impression of 'anger'
- avoiding using 'emoticons' such as :-), :-o) or  because they are not professional
- remembering to include a greeting or opening and a suitable complimentary close for longer e-mails.

Figure 1.9

Try it out

Go to Yahoo.co.uk and follow the instructions for setting up your own e-mail account if you do not already have one. You will need an e-mail address, or permission to use one, in order to carry out some of the other activities in this unit of the book.

E-mail addresses

E-mail addresses are as important, as far as accuracy is concerned, as normal postal addresses. Perhaps it is even more so. Unlike some forms of post, which allow you to confirm whether the person to whom you have sent the letter has received it, there is no such double-check for e-mails. If you type in the wrong e-mail address, the e-mail message may disappear forever, although some e-mail systems do tell you if the e-mail message could not be delivered because the address could not be found. Also if you type an incorrect e-mail address that is in fact the e-mail address of another person, your message will be delivered to them. It is therefore very important to make sure that e-mail address is completely accurate and it is often safer to reply to an e-mail rather than to create a new one and have to retype the e-mail address yourself. This ensures that the message is sent to precisely the e-mail address from which it was received in the first place.

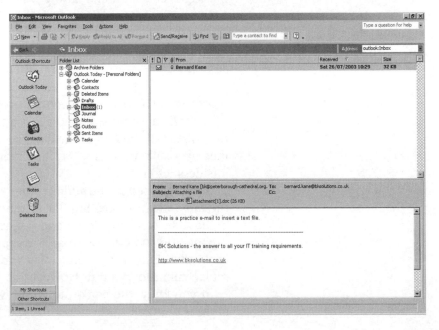

Figure 1.10

Many e-mail account systems have address books, which save e-mail addresses that you have already used. This is especially useful if you are constantly sending e-mails to the same people.

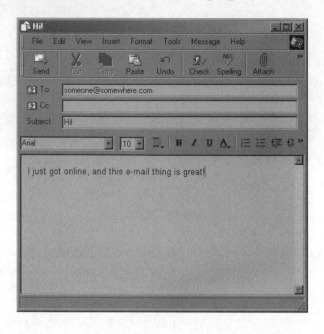

Figure 1.11

E-mail addresses often have a person's name, then an @ sign (pronounced 'at') and then the name of the e-mail account provider. For example:

Bernadette.smith@busby.com, or

bernadettesmith@busby.com, or

b.smith@busby.com

E-mails are very popular with businesses, because not only can messages be sent immediately, but also the same message can be sent to hundreds (or thousands) of people at the same time, anywhere in the world. Many e-mail systems have a box which either says 'copy to' or 'c.c.'. By typing additional e-mail addresses into this box you can send the same e-mail to many different people.

Appropriate opening and complimentary close

All e-mails have what is known as a subject line. This is where you type the subject of the e-mail message so that the recipient knows what the message is about. It is rather like typing the subject heading on a business letter.

Having typed in the subject line, you now type your message into the large area, or box. Similar formats and conventions can apply to e-mails as to business letters and you should address individuals by their proper title and close with an appropriate 'Yours sincerely' or 'Yours faithfully'. E-mails written in this way are simply an electronic replacement for a letter. However, most e-mails are not so formal.

If you know the person to whom you are sending the e-mail, little more is required than simply to type 'Hello' or 'Hi' at the beginning of

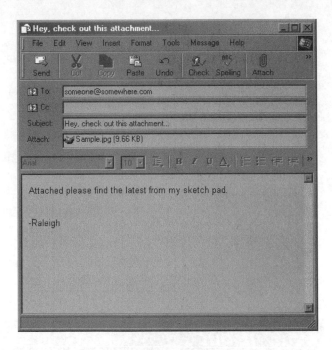

Figure 1.12

the e-mail and 'Regards' or 'Best wishes' at the end. You should remember, however, that if you are sending an e-mail to a more senior member of the business you should use their correct title. You should also never use this approach if you are dealing with customers. The more informal approach is only suitable for other people you work with or friends.

Although the person receiving your e-mail may infer correctly who you are from your e-mail address, you should type your name at the bottom just to confirm who has written the message.

Table 1.3 *Summary of conventions for an e-mail*

Standard conventions	Description
Headings	Use a subject header to state what the e-mail is about.
Standard formats	If formal follow the normal business letter format.
	If informal there is no need to follow any particular format.
Methods of addressing recipient	Use 'Dear Mr, Mrs, Ms' etc. if formal.
	You can use 'hello' or 'hi' if you know the person and the e-mail is informal.
Methods of closing	Use the appropriate complimentary close if the e-mail is formal.
	Use 'Regards' or 'Best Wishes' if the e-mail is informal.

Table 1.4 *Advantages and disadvantages of e-mail*

Advantages	Disadvantages
■ Can be sent instantly. ■ Saves on telephone costs, stationery and postal charges. ■ Can be sent or received anywhere. ■ E-mail systems store all sent and received messages for later reference. ■ E-mail addresses can be stored and accessed without having to retype them each time. ■ Hard copies can be printed out if needed for records.	■ There is no way of knowing whether the e-mail has been opened by the recipient. ■ There is no way of knowing whether the e-mail has been opened yet by the person it was addressed to. ■ The sender and the recipient both need to have Internet access and e-mail accounts. ■ Computer faults may lead to the loss of all e-mail records if they have not been printed.

Try it out

Ask at least six of your friends of colleagues for their e-mail addresses. You are going to send each of them the same message. Ask them to e-mail you back when they have received your message so that you know you typed in their address accurately and used the computer correctly to send them. Here is the message you should send:

Dear ....

I am studying for the OCR Level 2 Certificate in Administration. For Unit 1 I need to be sure I know how to send e-mail messages accurately. Can you let me know please that you have received this message?

Thank you for your help.

Yours ....
[Your name should be printed here]

Fax

The fax (short for facsimile), is fast becoming outdated and is used less and less in business as e-mail takes its place. The fax machine sends an exact copy of a letter, photograph or series of images via the telephone line so that a second fax machine can print out something like a photograph of the original at the recipient's end.

Fax messages are sent following a particular procedure, depending upon the type of machine used to send the message. Faxes can be sent directly from a computer, without having to print out the original, provided that the computer is attached to a telephone line. More commonly, however, paper copies of the original documents are fed to

Figure 1.13

the fax machine, rather in the way one uses a photocopier. The usual procedure is:

- An original document is prepared, which may be typed, handwritten and contain graphs, charts or diagrams.
- The recipient's fax number needs to be readily to hand.
- It is common practice to prepare a fax cover sheet, which normally contains a short message, the name of the recipient of the document, the name of the sender, the fax numbers of the sender and the recipient and, importantly, the number of pages in the fax message, including the cover sheet (see Figure 1.14).

Figure 1.14

FAX TRANSMISSION FORM	
To:	From:
Fax number:	Fax number:
Date:	Number of pages:
Message	

- The first document (the cover sheet) is placed face down on the fax machine, or fed into the fax machine.
- The recipient's fax number is next entered into the fax machine.
- A connection will then be made and the first page will be sent. The fax machine will prompt the sender to confirm whether this is a single page, or whether there are more pages to be sent as part of the fax message.
- Once a connection has been made, each page will be sent in the same order as they are inserted into the sender's fax machine. If the recipient's fax line is engaged, then the fax machine will try again after a minute or so.
- Once the transmission of the fax is complete some machines issue the sender with a transmission report. This gives the date, time and length of the call, along with the recipient's number, the sender's number and the number of pages sent.
- At the recipient's end each of the pages sent as part of the fax message will show the sender's fax number, name, the date and page number. On some fax machines the recipient can also ask for a transmission report to be printed once the fax message has been received.

One of the major advantages of a fax message is that it can be a handwritten cover note and a number of other pages, perhaps photocopies, copies of invoices, or even a standard business letter or a document with, or without, pictures or diagrams. Many businesses still prefer to receive faxes rather than e-mails, as they feel that a paper copy, with a proper signature, is far more valuable than just an e-mail message.

Build-up Exercise

You have been asked to prepare the covering sheet for a fax which has to be sent. Complete the covering sheet with the following details:

The fax is going to be 10 pages long and needs to be sent today to Brian O'Donnell at ABC Displays Ltd. Your boss, Sonia Gilroy, is sending the fax and her number is 01477 289400. ABC's fax number is 01894 700711. Sonia wants to tell Brian that the pages she is sending are the artwork he requires for the project they are working on together.

Table 1.5 *Summary of conventions for a fax*

Standard conventions	Description
Headings	Use a fax cover sheet, which should include: subject, recipient, sender, date, recipient's fax number, sender's fax number, number of pages.
Standard formats	None, but all faxes should have a fax cover sheet.
Methods of addressing recipient	Can be formal or informal, but addressing the recipient should be restricted to the fax cover sheet.
Methods of closing	Can be formal or informal, but the method of closing should appear on the fax cover sheet.

Table 1.6 *Advantages and disadvantages of fax*

Advantages	Disadvantages
■ Provides a hard copy which is an exact replica of the original. ■ Has date and time sent on the copy received by the recipient. ■ A fax transmission report can be printed to confirm the message has been sent and received. ■ Allows the recipient to have a conversation with the sender after the fax has been sent, ensuring that they are both looking at the same documents. ■ Can be sent anywhere in the world that has a fax machine.	■ Requires both the recipient and the sender to have fax machines, or fax software on their computers. ■ Paper-based hard copies will require filing for future reference. ■ Only the most modern fax machines allow you to send colour images or colour pages. ■ Fax machines can break down during transmission, making it difficult to know how many pages have actually been sent or received.

- A fax machine can be left switched on to receive faxes, even when no one is present.

- Fax machines need to have a ready supply of paper in order to print received faxes.
- Faxes are not accepted by many businesses as legal documents; they prefer originals via the postal system.

Memorandum (memo)

An inter-office memorandum is used within a business to communicate between different departments. Such memoranda are often called memos and are usually shorter than a business letter. They usually deal with only one subject, but when more than one point is being made it is normal to number each one.

Memos are not signed in the same way as business letters, although the sender will often initial a memo at the end.

A memo compares with a business letter in the following ways:

- Both letters and memos should always be dated.
- Both often have a reference, which helps to identify where the document should be filed and can be quoted in future communications.
- URGENT, CONFIDENTIAL, PRIVATE or PRIVATE AND CONFIDENTIAL can be used on both business letters and memos.
- Enclosures are indicated on business letters, but memos are sometimes not placed in an envelope. Any additional paperwork accompanying the memo is identified as an attachment and the letters 'ATT' are placed at the bottom of the document.

Many businesses use pre-printed memo forms, as in Figure 1.15.

Figure 1.15

MEMORANDUM	
To:	From:
Ref:	Date:

The clear format of the pre-printed memo encourages information to be passed on quickly from one person to another in a business, but in a more formal way than a note. However, if the memo is to a more senior member of the business, then the correct title should always be used.

Like a business letter, a memo should be structured. The beginning of the memo should provide any background information required (this may be the reason why the memo is being written), followed by a series of paragraphs. The memo should end with a short review of what has been proposed or requested. A memo, although less formal than a business letter, should always be checked for accuracy, and should only include relevant information.

Table 1.7 *Summary of conventions for a memo*

Standard conventions	Description
Headings	Headings are often pre-printed; relevant information should be inserted.
Standard formats	Usually a more informal way of communicating, and can often be handwritten.
Methods of addressing recipient	There is no salutation, as in a business letter, but often the recipient's name is included at the beginning of the memo.
Methods of closing	There is no complimentary close and a signature is not always required, but the sender will sometimes initial at the end of the memo.

Table 1.8 *Advantages and disadvantages of memos*

Advantages	Disadvantages
■ Pre-printed headings remove the need to write the same thing several times. ■ Can be handwritten or typed. ■ The pre-printed headings can be saved on computer as a template. ■ Memos are a much less formal method of communication. ■ They can be used as reminders. ■ They can be used as a notice to a large number of members of the business. ■ They can be sent to a number of different individuals.	■ Because they are paper-based memos often have to be filed. ■ They are more formal than just handwritten notes and often require the recipient to act on them.

Try it out

Imagine that you have been asked by your employer to write a memo to all your colleagues who use the car park at the back of the business's buildings. In two weeks' time the car park is going to be closed for four days because of some work that needs to be carried out on the fencing that surrounds the area. You and your colleagues will have to park in the public car park opposite and the owners of your business have agreed that they will pay the parking fees, provided all those involved produce appropriate receipts. Write one memo, addressed to 'All staff', and tell them of the arrangements, which will be in effect from Monday to Thursday inclusive the week after next.

Completing forms

Businesses use forms for a variety of different reasons, including the following:

- **Application forms** – for people wishing to apply for a job in the business.
- **Employee record forms** – for people working in the business to complete. These might include forms that log details of medical conditions, overtime worked, expenses claimed or travel undertaken on behalf of the business.
- **Visitor record forms** – to identify who has visited the business, who they called to see, at what time and when they left the building.
- **Customer record forms** – used to record details of customers so that the business can contact them when, for example, they decide to test a new product or when they want to sell a product they think the customer might want to buy.

Build-up Exercise

Can you think of any other types of form that might have to be completed for a business's records? Write down any you can think of and give a brief reason why each form would be needed.

Anyone working in administration will need to complete forms quite regularly. Here are some useful guidelines for completing forms of any kind:

- Always use the colour of pen requested – it sometimes stipulates at the top of the form that only a black pen should be used.
- Concentrate while you are completing the form and make sure you understand what is being asked of you.
- Make sure you have answered all questions honestly and to the best of your ability.
- Make sure your writing is legible.
- Make sure you have used the correct spelling, particularly of names.
- If the form has to be signed, make sure this has been done.
- If the form has to be dated, make sure this has been done.
- Make sure all questions on the form have been answered appropriately.
- Make sure the form goes to the right person or the right department once it has been completed.

Try it out

Figure 1.16 is an application form for a job. Take a photocopy of the form and fill it in to the best of your ability. Make sure you answer each question as fully as possible and that you sign and date the form. Get someone to check the form to make sure they can read what you have written.

APPLICATION FOR EMPLOYMENT - **CONFIDENTIAL**

1. PERSONAL DETAILS

Surname	Forenames	Title
Address	Telephone No. (Evening)	
	Telephone No. (Day)	
	Date of Birth	
Post Code	National Insurance No.	

2. DISABILITY AND ARRANGEMENTS FOR INTERVIEW

Do you consider yourself disabled?   Yes /No

If so, do you require any arrangements

to assist you if called for interview?   Yes/No

If yes, please state the arrangements which would be needed for you to attend

3. HEALTH

How many days have you been absent

from work due to illness in the past two years?

Is there any additional information you wish to provide?

4. EDUCATION AND QUALIFICATIONS

Secondary

Education   Please list below any qualifications obtained while in secondary education

Date	Type of examination eg GCE, GCSE etc.	Subject	Result/Grades

Further and

Higher Education   Please list below any qualifications obtained whilst in further or higher education

Date	Educational Establishment	Title of Qualification eg BTEC, BSc Econ,etc	Main Subjects	Result/Grades

Figure 1.16 *(cont'd)*

5. PROFESSIONAL QUALIFICATIONS AND MEMBERSHIP

Please list below any professional qualifications obtained and/or membership of professional bodies

Organisation	Title of Examination, Date and Result	Type of Membership and Joining Date

6. EMPLOYMENT HISTORY

Please give details of the posts you have held starting with your present or more recent employer
(continue on a separate page if necessary).

Employer Name, Address, and Nature of Business	Date(s)		Job Title, Duties, Responsibilities and Reason for Leaving
	From	To	If your job was part-time, please indicate

7. RELEVANT TRAINING

Please give below any relevant training which you have received.

8. ADDITIONAL INFORMATION

Please give below any particular skills which you would bring to the post
and any other information relevant to your application (continue on a separate page if necessary).

9. REFEREES

Please give details of two referees, not related to you, one of which should be your current
(or most recent) employer. Referees will not be contacted until the interview process is complete.

Name: Name:
Address: Address:

Phone No: Phone No:
Relationship: Relationship:

10. DRIVING LICENCE

Do you have a full current driving licence?   Yes /No
Do you have access to a car?   Yes/No

11. DECLARATION

The information given by me on this application is,
to the best of my knowledge and belief, true and correct

Signed: Date:

Figure 1.16

Designing forms for use by others

One of an administrator's jobs may be to design forms for the business to use in order to gather and record information. There are several key considerations when thinking about designing forms, which are:

- Make a rough copy first – you can then check the form for layout and whether or not it is well presented.
- Make sure you have included all the necessary headings and questions.
- Make sure the headings and questions make sense and are clearly worded.
- Leave enough space under each heading for an appropriate response.
- Get someone to check the form – others can often see mistakes which you have missed.
- Make sure the form looks attractive, is easy to use and that its layout is consistent. Headings should all look the same and fonts and type sizes should be used consistently.
- Make sure you are completely happy with the form before you decide on the final version – it is better to change something slightly now than to settle for something that's not quite right.

A business will want to control the way their forms are used. This means they will want their employees to use each form at the right time, and that the right procedures are in place to ensure that they are completed and ends up in the right place. The business will want to be sure that:

- each form is really needed
- they are simple to understand and simple to complete
- each form is the right size, in terms of both the number of questions asked and storing it for future reference
- the questions are logical and are asked in the correct order
- the questions are up to date (will they need to be amended in some way from time to time?)
- the form is appropriate – in other words, does it serve the purpose for which it was produced in the first place?

Try it out

Thinking back to the memo you sent regarding the use of the public car park for four days. You are now asked to design a form which allows all those involved to reclaim their car parking fees from the business. Think about the questions you need to ask each of those involved and remember that not all those involved parked on each of the four days. Get someone to check your form to make sure you haven't made any mistakes or missed out something vital. If possible your form should be wordprocessed.

Agendas

Meetings are held in all businesses; they can be formal or informal, depending on the type of business and the purpose of the meeting. All meetings, however, tend to generate some documentation. Meetings may be held for one or more of the following reasons:

- to share information
- to discuss new ideas or proposals
- to maintain interest
- to ask for assistance
- to report back on an activity
- to report on progress
- to discuss problems.

Figure 1.17

The document used to inform individuals about a forthcoming meeting and what is to be discussed at that meeting is called an agenda. The following basic information is given at the top of an agenda as shown in Figure 1.18:

- the date of the meeting
- the time of the meeting
- the venue (place) of the meeting.

Safety Representatives' Meeting

A meeting of Safety Representatives will be held in the business suite on

Friday 25 January 2004 at 11.00.

Agenda

Figure 1.18

As can be seen in Figure 1.19, there are a number of other items that often appear on an agenda, which are:

- **Apologies for absence** – this will always be the first item on the agenda and will be the apologies received from members not able to attend. Apologies are sent to the meeting via the secretary.
- **Minutes of the last meeting** – this will be the second item on the agenda and involves checking for accuracy of the minutes (i.e. the written record) of the previous meeting held (if any). Once this

checking has been done, the Chairperson will sign them as being a true and accurate record of what took place at the previous meeting.

■ **Matters arising** – this, the third item on the agenda, relates to the matters arising from the minutes of the last meeting.

Safety Representatives' Meeting

A meeting of Safety Representatives will be held in the business suite on

Friday 25 January 2004 at 11.00.

Agenda

1. Apologies for absence
2. Minutes of the last meeting
3. Matters arising from the minutes

Figure 1.19

Following these three common agenda items, the chairperson will list those issues that are to be discussed specifically at the meeting. There could be any number of these items, and certain individual employees could be given the task of presenting information to the meeting on particular agenda items.

The agenda usually concludes with:

■ **AOB** – this is short for 'any other business' and is an agenda item which gives the members of the meeting the opportunity to introduce any matters they wish to discuss which have not been included on the agenda.
■ **Date of next meeting** – the final item on the agenda allows the members of the meeting to decide when and where they will next meet.

The whole agenda may look something like Figure 1.20.

Safety Representatives' Meeting

A meeting of Safety Representatives will be held in the business suite on

Friday 25 January 2004 at 11.00.

Agenda

1. Apologies for absence
2. Minutes of the last meeting
3. Matters arising from the minutes
4. Report on research into safety issues on the factory production line
5. Report on financial cost implications of the proposed extension to the production line
6. Any other business
7. Date of next meeting

Figure 1.20

The chairperson calls the meeting. Once the meeting gets underway the chairperson will control the order of the discussion, making sure everyone has a chance to speak. The chairperson will ensure that every item on the agenda is fully discussed in the correct order.

The minutes of the meeting are an accurate, written record of the meeting and they are provided to all those who attended, as well as those who offered their apologies and could not attend. The minutes are distributed after the meeting and are organised in the same order as the items on the agenda. Minutes include the following information:

- a list of those present at the meeting
- an account of the discussions which took place during the meeting
- any specific jobs given to individuals during the meeting
- any reports received from individuals during the meeting
- any specific actions that have to be taken before the next meeting
- any specific decisions made or votes taken during the meeting.

Minutes do not have to be a word-for-word account of what was said. They should be brief and to the point, but they must be accurate.

Try it out

Get together with your fellow students and decide on what you would like to discuss at a meeting of your group. Make it something that needs a bit of research – your tutor may be able to come up with some ideas.

Now create an agenda for the meeting and print enough copies for all those you wish to invite. Include all the common agenda items, as well as the specific items you propose to discuss. In this, your first meeting, you nothing to discuss for items 2 and 3, but at the next meeting you will report on the results of this first meeting.

Before you hold actually hold the meeting it is important that you have covered the next section in this unit – Business notes.

Business notes

Business notes are taken in a variety of situations at work. They not only allow you to remember what has been said, and to recall instructions you have been given, but also can be referred back to much later if needed. You might take business notes while you are having a telephone conversation. You might also take them during a meeting.

Note taking is very important. It is not always possible to remember exactly what people have said and what decisions have been made; your notes provide you with your own record of these which can be referred to later if necessary.

There is no wrong or right way to take notes, but to be efficient and make sure that you understand and remember what has been said, there are a number of skills which you should try to develop. These are:

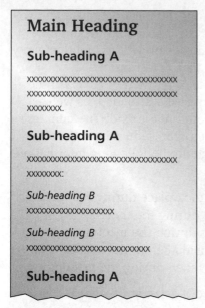

Figure 1.21

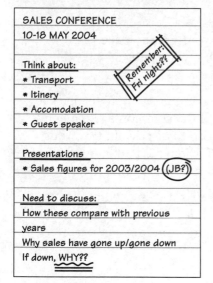

Figure 1.22

- Think before you write – remember that the notes you write down may not be referred to for several days and you will need to recall what the sentences mean.
- Raise any questions at the time if there is something you do not understand.
- You should try to develop your own way of standard note taking – you may prefer to use plenty of sub-headings (see Figure 1.21), or choose to underline particularly important parts of your notes see Figure 1.22).
- Try to keep your notes in a notebook so that you always know where they are; separate scraps of paper can easily get lost.
- Leave gaps underneath each part of your notes; you may wish to add more information later if the subject crops up again during the conversation or meeting.
- Remember to take thorough, helpful notes; the objective is not to save paper!
- Do not try to write down everything that is being said – it is impossible and not everything which is said is important. Listen carefully and take down only the main points – if you are too busy writing fast you cannot possibly listen properly at the same time.
- Listen carefully for important points and leave a gap in your notes when a point is raised – this will help you later when you refer to your notes and the main points are spaced out neatly on the page.
- Concentrate on the main points and do not get lost in the detail – a lot of the details may not be very relevant.
- Make sure that you can actually read what you have written – the faster you write the less chance you have of being able to read your own handwriting later. If you abbreviate (shorten) words or use people's initials, you will need to remember what these mean.
- If you are in a meeting, try to find a seat which gives you an uninterrupted view of the person who is speaking – they may show diagrams or visual aids which you will also need to look at, but may not have to copy into your notes; such material may be handed out later.

In a meeting, an average person will speak between 125 and 140 words a minute, but the average note taker can only write around 25 words a minute. This means that you cannot possibly write down every word. Instead you will need to listen carefully and translate what is being said into your own notes. As long as you are writing legibly, in a clear and logical way, you need not worry about spelling, grammar or punctuation. Notes are for your own benefit, not for anyone else.

Build-up Exercise

Use the following checklist to assess your note taking skills whilst you attended the meeting you prepared the agenda for in the previous activity. Answer 'yes' or 'no' to the questions:

▶▶

1 Have I prepared myself for note taking by reading information given to me before the meeting?

2 Did I sit near the front so I could see and hear better and be less distracted?

3 Did I focus on the main points of the meeting?

4 Was I really listening all the time and did I bring my mind back to the meeting when my attention started to wander?

5 Do my notes make sense?

6 Did I revise and review my notes after the meeting?

7 Is my handwriting clear?

8 Did my notes cover the main ideas and the important information discussed?

9 Is my note taking system right for me?

10 Have my notes helped me to remember what was said?

11 Did I write any examples under my main points?

12 Did I ask any questions if I did not understand what was being said?

13 Did I need to ask someone else who attended the meeting about any point that I did not understand afterwards?

14 Did I exchange and compare my notes with someone else who attended the meeting?

15 Did I make any links between what was being said and what I am expected to do?

If you answered 'yes' to at least 12 of these questions, then your notes should be effective, but you should still practise in order to improve your score.

Reports

Most people find report writing quite difficult. However, with all reports you should follow a particular pattern, regardless of what kind of report it is. These are the basic steps:

- Make a plan.
- Discuss what should be in the report.
- Draft the report and show it to someone else.
- Leave the report for at least a couple of days.
- Revise and edit the report and make sure someone else checks it.

There are a number of different types of report, but in general they begin with an introduction. This usually describes the problem to be solved and the significance of that problem. The conclusion suggests the answer to the problem and the rest of the report is a series of statements, evidence or arguments which allow the reader of the report to understand how and why you have reached your conclusions.

To be effective your report should be written in a clear and direct style. You do not have to use complicated words and as long as the report is logical and you have mentioned all of the main points related to the problem before you arrive at the conclusion, then your suggestions will be as valid as those of anyone else.

Reports are used to examine particular problems and the responsibility of writing a report is usually given to either an individual or a team. They are expected to investigate the problem and receive assistance from anyone who has experience of the problem. Although the writing of the report is left to the report writers, the collection of information to help them is a joint effort.

There are several different types of reports which you may be expected, at some point in your career, to write. We will begin with the simplest, which we will call a 'memo-style short, informal report'.

The memo-style report is very flexible and can include tables, charts and diagrams, but like all other reports it should be wordprocessed. If you are asked to prepare a short, informal report in a memo-style, you should remember the following:

- Always include a heading which states the subject of the report.
- Always include an introduction which states why you have prepared the report.
- Under the heading 'Information' provide any information which you have researched for the report.
- Under the heading 'Conclusions' summarise the findings from your research and, above all, note down your recommendations.

Figure 1.23

> **MEMORANDUM**
>
> To: From:
>
> Ref: Date:
>
> **Subject heading**
>
> **Introduction**
>
> **Information**
>
> **Conclusions**

It is normal practice to use what is known as a 'decimal point referencing system'. For example, if we consider the information section of the memo-style report, then using the decimal point referencing system, it would look like Figure 1.24.

Figure 1.24

> **2 Information**
>
> 2.1   Paper used for printing and photocopying
>
> 2.2   Paper storage
>
> 2.3   Paper recycling

Each of the main sections of the memo-style report is given a number (1 to 3) and each sub-point under each of these sections is then given a decimal point reference and a sub-heading; as shown in Figure 1.25.

> **MEMORANDUM**
>
> **To:**   **From:**
>
> **Ref:**   **Date:**
>
> **Subject heading**
>
> **1 Introduction**
>
> **2 Information**
>
> 2.1   Paper used for printing and photocopying
>
> 2.2   Paper storage
>
> 2.3   Paper recycling
>
> **3 Conclusions**

Figure 1.25

A full memo-style report using a decimal point referencing system would, therefore, look like Figure 1.26.

> **MEMORANDUM**
>
> **To:**   Jane Cotter   **From:** Diane Sutherland
>
> **Ref:** JC/DS/2910   **Date:** 2 February 2004
>
> **Report on the Investigation into Paper Wastage**
>
> **1 Introduction**
>
> At the departmental meeting last month you requested that I investigate and carry out some research on the paper wastage in the department, following the increased costs in paper over the last three months.
>
> **2 Information**
>
> The use of paper within the department was investigated and the following sub-sections show how paper is currently being used.
>
> 2.1   Paper used for printing and photocopying
>
> All staff with access to a printer or a photocopier were asked to complete a questionnaire. The results of the questionnaires were analysed and it was discovered that around 25 per cent of all

Figure 1.26 *(cont'd on next page)*

paper used was actually wasted. This figure includes company headed paper, memorandum paper and blank sheets. Those who completed the questionnaire felt that they could cut down on this paper wastage but that they often missed errors on the screen and only saw the errors in their typing when a hard copy had been printed out.

2.2 Paper storage

Each person who has their own printer has at least a box of each type of paper in a cupboard near their workstation. Some have several boxes and there seems to be no clear procedure regarding re-ordering boxes of pre-printed paper. It is therefore difficult, without manually checking the stock levels at each workstation, to state how much paper there is in the department. Photocopy paper is stored in a large cupboard near the photocopy machine and at any one time several packs of paper have been opened. Spot checks revealed that several sheets of photocopying paper are thrown away with the wrapper when the pack is almost empty.

2.3 Paper recycling

There is no facility to recycle paper. All paper is thrown into waste paper baskets. This includes drafts of documents, documents with errors, additional copies of documents printed in error. At the photocopier there are piles of photocopies of documents which have been discarded for various reasons.

3 Conclusions

The research which has been carried out has proved that there is unnecessary wastage of paper in the department. The wastage is not restricted to one area and therefore it is unlikely the situation will improve unless action is taken. It is therefore recommended that the following steps are taken:

3.1 Headed paper and memorandum paper should be stored centrally and additional supplies should be signed for on production of an empty box.

3.2 Regular maintenance of the photocopier needs to be put in place, as many of the wasted copies are a result of the photocopier not functioning correctly (for example, jammed paper and the toner cartridge running out). An individual from the department should be given the responsibility of checking the toner cartridge and ensuring that a monthly maintenance check is carried out.

3.3 Photocopy paper should be kept in a locked cupboard and brought out on a daily basis.

3.4 At least four recycling boxes should be positioned around the department for the disposal of wasted paper.

3.5 Any documents with errors or photocopies taken and not used should be shredded and this paper should be deposited in the recycling boxes.

Figure 1.26

Try it out

At a recent meeting you were asked to investigate the car parking problems in and around your business. Over the past few days you have spoken to various people and made checks on the parking situation at various times of the day. All of this information you have written down in note form in your notebook. Here are the notes you made:

Car parking problems
There are 40 people working at the business
26 people drive to work
There are 12 car parking spaces
4 other spaces are reserved for managers and visitors
Local residents have complained that their drives are blocked by cars
The area behind the main building, if cleared and tarmac was laid, would take a further 10 cars
Parking is on a first-come, first-served basis

Possible solutions?
Remove visitor parking spaces?
Tarmac area at the rear of the building?
Rent unused building plot 3 minutes walk down the road?
Start a car share scheme?
Ban employees from parking on road?
Start charging employees to park at work?
Issue car parking badges to senior employees only?

You must now translate your notes into a memo-style short, informal report and mark it for the attention of Marjorie Groves, Personnel and Administration Manager.

Report writing is vital to a business; it is carried out in order to achieve goals or objectives. Businesses can commission reports for many different reasons, including the following:

- to identify problems and find solutions to these problems
- to provide progress reports on particular projects
- to investigate particular areas of the business's activities
- to identify the need to change policies.

Although memo-style reports are useful for faster responses to problems, a more formal and longer form of report also has its place. There are many different ways in which these reports can be written, but generally they have the following features:

- **Title page** – gives the subject of the report.
- **Terms of reference** – replaces the introduction of a memo-style report and states what you have been asked to do or research.

1 Title page
2 Terms of reference
3 Procedures
4 Findings
4.1
4.2
4.3
5 Conclusions
6 Recommendations
7 Appendices

Figure 1.27

- **Procedure** – details how you have gone about gathering the information which you have included in the report.
- **Findings** – in effect this replaces the information section of a memo-style report and states what you have found out.
- **Conclusion** – this is the general statement of your findings and is similar to the first part of the conclusions in a memo-style report. Here you conclude and sum up your findings.
- **Recommendations** – this is like the second part of the memo-style conclusion. On the basis of your findings and conclusion you make your recommendations.
- **Appendices** – in the last Try it out exercise this would be a summary of the questionnaire which was used to collect information. This is the place to put documents, charts, diagrams, tables and other information which is referred to in the rest of the report. This is where the more detailed information is placed.
- You should also sign and date your report.

Sub-sections can be used in a formal report, as shown in Figure 1.27.

Build-up Exercise

Now convert your memo-style report in the last exercise into a formal report. You don't have to type it all out again; copy and paste from your original document.

Articles

Many businesses have their own company newsletter. Company newsletters are used as a way of passing on information to employees, so they are designed to be read only by people working for the company. You may become involved in preparing, writing, printing and distributing a company newsletter. It will probably contain a number of short articles, with perhaps photographs or illustrations, telling people various pieces of news, updates, changes in policy and procedures or simply news about other employees.

One of the most useful tools in preparing company newsletters is a desktop publishing program, such as Microsoft Publisher. Such software offers a number of different formats, or templates, to choose from. You can replace the text, pictures, logos and headings on the templates with your business's own images and text.

Preparing an article for a publication such as a company newsletter obviously involves some research and, of course, note taking. Articles vary in length, but usually they are fairly short and to the point. Articles are always improved by a picture, diagram or illustration. These help draw the reader's attention to the article and give them something to remember the article by, other than plain text.

Figure 1.28 shows an example of a short article and the notes which were taken to prepare it.

Frederick (Fred) Keeble is 66 next month.

He is retiring at the end of this month from the distribution centre.

He has worked for the company for 23 years.

He is going to live in Spain with his wife Glynis.

His son, Brian and his two children and wife will visit frequently.

Fred started out in the warehouse and has worked in virtually every department.

Fred's current job is head of the distribution centre.

Next Tuesday Fred will be presented with an engraved watch and some new luggage from a collection made.

Figure 1.28

GOODBYE FRED

Fred Keeble, our Head of Distribution, will be retiring after over 20 years of service. Fred has worked for us in virtually every area of the business and at 66 has finally decided to retire to a home in the sun. As grandparents, Fred and Glynis are looking forward to a peaceful retirement and frequent visits from their grandchildren to their new home in Spain.

Although Fred will be leaving us this coming Friday, a special presentation will take place at 17.00 on Tuesday to present him with an engraved gold watch and gifts purchased from the collection made by his friends and colleagues.

Build-up Exercise

Now it is your turn to write an article from notes. The following notes relate to two new employees joining the business.

Sarah Murphy
27 years old
Recently completed an OCR Level 2 Certificate in Administration at the local college.
Has two children, Paul and Rosie
Will be our new receptionist

Luke Northover
Taking over Fred Keeble's old job.
Degree in Business Administration
Single
24 years old
Born in Ipswich, Suffolk
Very keen on football

The newsletter needs an article covering these two people, no more than 100 words, with headings and photos.

Although a newsletter article remains inside the business, one version of an article, known as a press release, is designed to be sent out to the media (newspapers, local radio) or even, in some cases, customers. Businesses are very keen on having stories (good ones) about them in the local press and press releases are an ideal way of informing local newspapers and encouraging them to write about the business. Press releases are an important way of maintaining good relationships with the media. They are useful and easy to produce; and they can be sent to appropriate people in the media before a new product or service is launched, or before embarking an activity that's new to the business.

There is no magic formula for producing a press release which is guaranteed to have positive results every time, but a press release usually has a much better chance of appearing in a newspaper or magazine if you follow these guidelines:

- **Embargo date** – this is the date which is printed at the top of a press release. It tells the media that the information contained in the press release should not be published before this date. Press releases are usually sent out ahead of something happening to allow the media time to read the press release and decide whether to use it.
- **Headlines** – a headline or subject heading should say what the press release is about. This is all part of making the job of the media as easy as possible and a good headline may well be used in the newspaper or magazine itself.
- **Factual opening statement** – rather than having to read all of the press release before desiding whether or not to use it, it is useful to have a short paragraph at the beginning which summarises exactly what it is about.
- **Facts** – the media likes press releases which contain interesting facts and figures. Any information given must be true and supportable.
- **Quotations** – the media is always interested in having a 'human angle' to a story. Direct quotes from someone in the business are always useful because they give the impression that the newspaper or magazine has actually interviewed someone. Adding quotations to a press release increases its chances of being published.

- **Closing paragraph** – this is really a summary of the press release. It provides the media with a series of short, concise sentences which they could use if they did not have much space for the whole article.
- You should try to attach a photograph to the press release, saving the newspaper the trouble of having to contact you for one.

Press releases, like many other forms of business communication, have particular conventions or styles. These include the following:

- If the press release goes over onto another page, the phrase 'more follows' is typed at the bottom of the first page.
- If the press release does go over onto another page, then the last two or three words of the first page are repeated on the second page (this is to ensure that the sentence follows on from one page to the next).
- At the end of the press release the word 'ends' is used to show that the press release is complete.
- The business's name, address, telephone number, fax number, e-mail address and website should be placed at the end of the press release.
- The name of an individual from the business should be given so that the media knows who to contact for further information, such as photographs.

To make press releases as effective as possible:

- always be factual
- don't be emotional
- be truthful
- be newsworthy and don't exaggerate
- include a human interest angle
- don't cram in too many facts or figures
- be as up-to-date as possible
- make sure there are no spelling mistakes and that it looks professional
- include all relevant information and contacts.

Try it out

Look back at Figure 1.28 on Fred's retirement and add the information to the extra information that follows. Design a short press release of no more than 200 words, following the above format and style suggestions.

Extra notes:

'Working here for 23 years has given me some of the happiest days of my life' – Fred at his presentation.

'I'll not only miss you as a friend, but also as a valued colleague' – Managing Director at the presentation.

Fred is moving to Spain in two months, but first he will take a holiday in Mauritius with his wife and promises to use the luggage.

Job descriptions

A job description explains what a job involves. Job descriptions are used by businesses to match the right people to the right jobs. If your job is in the human resource department of a business, it is likely that it will involve writing job descriptions for any vacancies that occur. A job description usually includes the following items:

- The job title – the title of 'manager' or 'supervisor' is included if the job involves having responsibility for, and authority over, other employees.
- Where the new employee fits in within the business. In other words, their position within the structure of the business.
- The tasks and activities that the new employee is required to carry out.
- The roles and responsibilities that are required of the new employee.

The amount of detail included in a job description will depend on the type of job that is being described. A job with management responsibility will probably require more details than a job for a junior person with fewer responsibilities. Figure 1.29 shows the typical headings on a job description.

Figure 1.29

> **JOB DESCRIPTION**
>
> **Job title:**
>
> **Department/function/section**
>
> **Wage/salary range**
>
> **Main purpose of the job**
>
> **Duties and responsibilities**
>
> **Responsible to:**
>
> **Responsible for:**

Build-up Exercise

Look through the job advertisements in your local paper. Choose an advertisement for a job you think you would like to do at some time. From the advertisement see if you can write a brief job description for the job advertised. Choose an advertisement that includes a lot of detail, although you might be able to think of some duties that are not included in the newspaper advert.

If you can't find any suitable job advertisements, choose one of the following occupations and write your job description around that role:

- an office junior
- assistant to office manager
- receptionist
- accounts clerk
- mail room assistant.

You may find that talking to family, friends and colleagues will help you to complete the duties and responsibilities section.

As well as a job description, a business may sometimes draw up a person specification. This is a description of the kinds of qualities a person should have to satisfactorily carry out a job. A person specification is the business's checklist of the ideal person for a particular job and will include a description of:

- the previous experience the person should have
- the skills the person should have
- the physical characteristics the person needs to have, including things like their height, weight, hearing or eyesight; which could affect their ability to do the job
- the qualifications required
- the personality and temperament required – this is important if the job involves working closely with other employees or customers
- the level of motivation required – this is the ability, for example to work alone and not be supervised, to want to do a good job.

Build-up Exercise

Go back to the job description activity and now, for the same job role, draw up a person specification. What qualities or attributes would the person need to do that particular job?

Try it out

Using a clerical assistant job as an example, prepare a list of criteria which you would consider 'essential', 'desirable' or just 'required'. These criteria may fall into some or all of the categories we have given you already, as well as some of the following:

- current achievements (qualifications, driving licence, etc.)
- aptitudes (social skills, listening, communication skills, handwriting)

- interests (relevant sports or leisure activities)
- personal circumstances (whether they are willing to work overtime or weekends etc.)
- physical attributes (appearance and ability to speak clearly).

Notices

When a businesses wishes to send information to a large number of their employees, they may choose to do so by placing a notice on the staff noticeboard. The notice can be formal or informal and could tell the employees about a change to usual procedures or perhaps inform them of a forthcoming social event. Notices have the advantage of being quick and easy to produce and transmit information to a large number of individuals.

Staff can also use a noticeboard to inform other employees, for example about items they may have for sale or events they have planned or are involved in.

Figure 1.30

Whatever type of notice you need to prepare, the following guidelines should help.

- Remember that most noticeboards are fairly small, so don't use large paper which will take up all the space and hide other notices.
- Make the notice bold enough to get noticed.
- Don't use too much text, but state clearly and concisely what it is you want to say.
- Make sure the reader of the notice knows what they have to do – if they have to contact someone, then make sure that person's name and contact address or number is clear.

- Put a date on the notice so that the reader can tell when it was first placed on the noticeboard; and also so that the reader will know if the notice is still current or if it is out of date.

Notices need to be well designed. You want the notice to have impact and attract attention. You could use any of the following features:

- bullet points (● ▲ ◆ ■ ❑)
- different fonts to make words **more** or *less* obvious
- different type sizes to make important words stand out
- CAPITAL letters, **bold,** underline and *italics* to make text stand out
- sub-headings to break up the text
- pictures or graphics to add emphasis and make the notice more eye-catching.

Try it out

Prepare a notice for the staff noticeboard which informs all employees of the get-together for Fred Keeble's retirement presentation. Make sure you follow the guidelines given above.

Leaflets and advertisements

Although notices are often only seen within a business, leaflets and advertisements are aimed at customers, actual or potential.

Leaflets are often produced in large quantities and can be delivered by a variety of means, including being hand-delivered through letterboxes, inserted into newspapers and magazines, or distributed in the street by representatives of the business. Leaflets can be a form of

Figure 1.31

advertisement, but usually when we refer to advertisements we think of those that are printed in newspapers and magazines, or appear on TV and radio.

As a guideline to producing leaflets and advertisements let us consider a technique known as 'AIDA', which stands for:

- **Attention** – do something in the leaflet or advertisement that grabs the attention of the reader.
- **Interest** – to gain the reader's interest in the leaflet or advertisement, you need to tell them something that appeals to them.
- **Desire** – try to make the reader either want to buy what you are offering, or contact you because they are interested in what you are saying.
- **Action** – try to make the reader do what you want them to do, for example ask for more information, contact you or buy your product or service.

If you think of the number of different leaflets or advertisements you see each week, you will realise how important it is to make your own ones special.

Build-up Exercise

Collect some leaflets and advertisements – these could have come through your letterbox at home, or could be from your local newspaper or a magazine you take. Make sure you collect at least five different advertisements. Have a good look at all of them and compare them with each other. Decide which one you like the best and consider why it appeals to you. Why does it stand out from the others you collected?

Now think about the one you liked the least. What made you dislike it? What would you do to improve this leaflet or advertisement?

It is very important to get the reader's attention. The following list can help you do this:

- **Use a headline** – this is where you promise the reader something, or make them feel they need something; this will make them want to read on.
- **Offer a benefit** – you should try to promise the reader something, for example a solution to a problem or another kind of benefit that they would receive by reading further.
- **Appeal** – try to appeal to the reader personally and encourage them to keep reading.
- **Say it with pictures** – use images; these help to reduce the amount of text (words) you need to use, and make the leaflet more eye-catching.

- **Use sub-headings** wherever possible to reduce the amount of words needed.
- **Explain** – be careful what you say and how you say it so that the reader does not misunderstand your message.
- **Help the reader** – by giving them all the information they need to do whatever it is you want them to do, for example include any contact names, addresses and telephone/fax numbers, e-mail and website addresses.

As can be seen in Figures 1.32 and 1.33, the styles can be very different. The first advertisement is for a job in a large organisation and the style is formal. However, the advertisement has captured the readers' interest; it has given all the facts and also given the reader the details they require to contact the business if they are interested.

JOB ADVERTISEMENT

We invite you to exercise your talents and qualifications by joining us.

Full-time Administrative Assistant Required

Duties: reporting to the Assistant Manager, this position will be responsible for providing a variety of administrative/clerical and reception support duties.

Qualifications: OCR Level 2 in Administration. Proficiency in the use of wordprocessing and spreadsheet applications is also required.

Salary: Pay Level 6

Closing date: 16.00, April 10, 2004

Interested persons should submit their CV and details of their experience to: Assistant Manager, Walpole Marine, PO Box 1838, Walpole, Suffolk. Telephone/fax: 0207 425 0045. E-mail: Walpolemarine@bt.com

Please quote: 102 WM 07

Your covering letter and CV should clearly demonstrate related qualifications and experience since selection will be based on the information provided.

Figure 1.32

Cleaner Wanted

Cleaner needed for 12 hours a week
Flexible start – finish times

£6.50ph

Call Rachel on 01884 4437821

Figure 1.33

Try it out

Imagine you work for a local college of further education. The college wants a simple advertisement to appear in a newspaper which should be no bigger than a quarter of an A4 sheet of paper. You need to ensure the following information is in the advertisement:

Open days – September 6, 7 and 8
Opening hours – 08.30 to 21.00 daily
College address, phone and fax number (you can make these up)
Refreshments available free
Crèche available free
Expert guidance available
Wide variety of courses on offer
Practical demonstrations taking place on each of the days

Analyse, extract and adapt information to meet a given purpose

All businesses are awash with information. On a daily basis data, including facts and figures, come into the business or are generated by the business. One of the most important tasks of employees and managers is to be able to understand the relevance of what arrives on their desks. It would be impossible for everyone to read every piece of information. It is therefore vitally important that someone takes responsibility for analysing the data and identifying what is relevant and what is not.

Figure 1.34

Also, many facts and figures are presented in ways which are not immediately useful, either to the business or to a particular department. Again, someone has to look through the data, find what is relevant and then present it in a useable format. There are various ways in which this can be achieved. We will examine some of the most important techniques which you will need if you are to analyse data, extract what is relevant and adapt it to a format suited to a particular purpose.

Importance of relevance and context

Not all facts and figures that are generated by a business, or arrive at a business, have obvious relevance to the work of the business. This does not mean that facts and figures should be ignored or discarded if they do not immediately appear relevant. There may be something hidden within the data which is important and does need to be considered.

In many businesses the same data can be adapted for different purposes. Here is an example of how one set of figures, in this case sales figures, are relevant in several different ways:

- A sales department would be interested in the sales figures because it would tell them exactly what has been sold, when and where.
- Purchasing would be interested in the sales figures because they need to make sure that products which have been sold are re-ordered.
- Finance and accounts would be interested in the sales figures because they are concerned with the total amount of money received by the business. They will also analyse individual product sales figures so that they can see which of the products is providing the business with most of its profit.
- The owners of the business will be interested in the sales figures because they will show them how well the business is performing and how much profit the business is making.
- The human resources department will be interested in the sales figures because if sales are increasing they may need to employ more sales staff. If sales are falling, however, they may have to consider reducing the salesforce.

Build-up Exercise

Think about how much detail each of the above departments or sections of a business would need regarding the sales figures. Who do you think would need the most information? Who would need the least information? Give reasons for your decisions.

As you have probably realised, different parts of a business often need the same information, but in more or less detail. Some will need very detailed facts and figures in order to make decisions. Others will only need general outlines to help them make decisions.

Whenever you are required to analyse, extract or adapt information, think about what is, and what is not, relevant to the person or group of individuals for whom you are preparing the information. The better you target the information and the shorter the summary of that information, the more likely the reader is able to understand the relevance of what they are being shown.

Identification of information that is not appropriate for inclusion in business documents or for specified context

Let us accept that it is not possible for every employee to read everything on the basis that only a small part of it may be relevant to their work. If information is not adapted properly, individuals will be swamped with facts and figures. They would be spending all of their time trying to read lots of information which does not help them do their job.

If you were asked to look through a long document and find specific information it is likely you would be given guidelines as to what to summarise and what to leave out. You should also be told the purpose for which the information is needed. It is very time consuming and often impossible for people attending a meeting to either read through long, complicated documents beforehand or to have to refer to them several times during the meeting.

The skill is to identify the information which is, or is not, appropriate to include in a business document and summarise or present in a different way the information that is retained.

Build-up Exercise

Imagine you are working as an administrative assistant for a shop. One of your responsibilities is to keep a record of overtime worked. It is now the middle of January and the shop manager wants to know how much overtime has been worked over the Christmas and January sales period. Your information is based on a timesheet of overtime which you send monthly to the personnel department at the business's head office. You will need to find the relevant overtime figures for the period December 15 – January 7 inclusive. The shop manager is only interested in the total number of overtime hours worked, not who worked them.

Table 1.9 *Monthly overtime timesheets for December and January*

December overtime worked (hours)

December	1–7	8–14	15–21	22–28	29–31
Sharon	0	2	3	5	4
Clive	2	2	2	2	2
Robin	3	4	4	4	4
Petra	2	2	0	2	4
Alex	5	0	0	5	2

January overtime worked (hours)

January	1–7	8–14	15–21	22–28	29–31
Sharon	5	2	2	2	2
Clive	9	4	3	2	1
Robin	11	2	3	2	1
Petra	2	5	2	2	0
Alex	5	0	0	2	2
Clare	5	4	4	4	1

You should present your total overtime figures in the form of a memo to the shop manager, Katie Walsh.

Identification and extraction of relevant information from one or more given documents/sources

Sometimes you will be asked to extract information from more than one document or source and to collate it into a new format. You will need to be careful, as the information in one document may not exactly match the information in another document. In such cases you need to make sure that you are using the right information and it is probably a good idea to check which set or figures or facts the person who has asked you to look at the document would like you to use.

When you are combining two different documents you may need to create new information. This may mean you need to make calculations. You may also need to collect some information from one document and add it to information from another document, creating a third document which is a summary of the other two.

Build-up Exercise

Refer back to the last Build-up Exercise. The shop manager has now asked you to calculate the total cost of the overtime over the same Christmas and January sales period. Katie has given you a confidential summary of the hourly pay rates and grades of the staff. You must now calculate how much the overtime cost the business. You will need to add up the total hours worked by each member of staff and multiply that by their hourly pay rate. Then find the total for all staff.

Table 1.10 *Pay rates and grades for staff working overtime*

	Pay rate (per hour)	Grade
Sharon	£7.54	Assistant manager
Clive	£6.42	Senior sales staff I
Robin	£5.94	Sales II
Petra	£5.68	Sales I
Alex	£6.42	Senior sales staff I
Clare	£4.98	Casual worker

Again, you should give Katie your answer in the form of a memo.

The importance of checking all sources of information carefully, including instructions

Many of the documents that you will be working from you will not have created yourself. It is therefore difficult to know whether the information contained in these documents is correct. Nor is it always possible to find the same figures in two sets of documents in order to double-check. It is very easy for figures in particular to be incorrectly typed onto a document and simple things, such as a decimal point being in the wrong place, can make a huge difference. Dates, people's names and many other important facts can also be easily typed in or written incorrectly.

Sometimes the instructions which you receive to carry out a particular task may not be very clear and it is always best to ask before you begin working if you are unsure as to what you are supposed to do. Whoever has asked you to carry out the task will be more pleased that you have made sure you are doing it right than to do something incorrectly.

Build-up Exercise

Following the last activity, you have just received a memo from Katie.

MEMORANDUM

TO: **FROM:** Katie Walsh

REF: KW/Overtime   **DATE:** February 2 2004

Total overtime figures

I am afraid that the figures which you have supplied me are incorrect. You have forgotten that overtime payments are 50 per cent more than the hourly pay rate. You have also forgotten that Petra has now been promoted to Sales II.

Please amend the figures immediately – I require this information by 3.00 pm at the very latest.

Figure 1.35

Now carry out her instructions as requested.

Adaptation of information to reflect specified purpose, document format and context

Your adaptation of the information provided will not always be required in the same format as the original documents. Facts and figures which are hidden in paragraphs of text may need to be converted into tables, charts or diagrams. Equally, charts and diagrams may have to be converted into text, with explanations as to what the figures actually mean.

When you are given instructions to analyse, extract and adapt information, you will also be told how the information you are working on needs to be presented. For the most part adapted information needs to be put in a format which is easy to understand and can be used for quick reference.

Build-up Exercise

You have received yet another memo from Katie, who needs to present the information which you have given her at a shop managers' meeting. She doesn't want to stand and read out the figures – she wants to pass around a chart to the other managers. Here are your revised figures:

▶▶

Table 1.11 *Overtime hours and earnings for December and January, combined*

	Overtime rate per hour	Hours of overtime worked	Total overtime earnings
Sharon	11.28	15	169.20
Clive	9.63	15	144.45
Robin	8.91	23	204.93
Petra	8.91	8	71.28
Alex	10.13	12	121.56
Clare	7.97	5	39.85

Copy the figures onto a spreadsheet and produce a chart of your choice for Katie to use. Katie wants each employee's name and the total overtime earnings for each person shown on the chart.

Adaptation and presentation of relevant information for use in business documents/formats

You will need to learn how to adapt information for a number of different kinds of business documents. You will either be requested to present information in a particular way, or it will be left to you to decide which is the most appropriate format. This means that once you have analysed and extracted information from a variety of different sources, you will then have to choose the most appropriate document or format in which to present that information. As you already know, different types of business documents and formats are applicable to different circumstances.

Sometimes it will be obvious which type of document or format you should choose. In other cases you may well have to think carefully about how you are going to present the information at the outset, as this will affect how you adapt the information.

Each of the major types of document or formats are now considered. In each of the activities you will be required to create an appropriate document, or use an appropriate format.

Forms

Remember that forms are used to allow individuals to enter information into a document using a standard format.

Build-up Exercise

You have received the following memo:

MEMORANDUM

TO: **FROM:** Katie Walsh

REF: KW/Overtime   **DATE:**   February 10 2004

This is just a quick note to say thank you for the very useful diagram which I used at my recent meeting. The other shop managers were very impressed and have asked me to ask you to design a new overtime form which brings in the features of our original form for noting overtime, but also has boxes where we can insert the overtime pay rate. We would also need a total box at the end of each line so that the total amount earned as overtime can be put into this box at the end of each monthly period.

I am sure that this new form would speed up our overtime payment calculations and make it far easier to convert it into a diagram should we need to do so.

You might want to put the new form into a landscape A4 format rather than portrait.

Figure 1.36

Carry out the task as suggested by Ms Walsh.

Letters

Remember that letters are usually used to communicate with people outside the business or other organisations. Letters need to be professional, both in language used and their format.

Build-up Exercise

You have just had a conversation with Jane Cotter, for whom you prepared the memorandum report regarding the use of paper and recycling. She has asked you to write to at least two local paper recycling businesses, asking them to arrange to pick up paper for recycling on a monthly basis. Jane has suggested that you check the local *Yellow Pages* for suitable recycling businesses. You should use your own version of the following company headed paper for your business letter:

142 The High Street

Framlingham, Suffolk, IP22 4NN

00 22 3344 7158

E-mails

E-mails can be used for either internal or external communication. Remember that in order to use e-mail both the sender and the receiver need to have an e-mail address.

Build-up Exercise

You have received a letter from a local recycling company who have confirmed that they will pick up paper on a monthly basis. They will collect the paper on the last Friday of each month. Jane Cotter has asked you to send an e-mail message to all members of staff, telling them about the new arrangements and reminding them to make sure that waste paper is in the recycling bins by the last Friday of each month. She does not want waste paper to be left piled up around the office unnecessarily. The recycling bins are green and the recycling company will come and collect these bins shortly before lunchtime. They will not collect any paper that is not placed in the bins.

You will need to design a suitable e-mail message which can be sent to all members of staff, giving them the above information.

Faxes

Faxes are useful in allowing a business to send or receive an exact copy of an original document. They can also be used instead of the telephone as a more formal way of confirming arrangements. Many businesses fax their business letters, rather than posting them, because it is quicker.

Build-up Exercise

You have received a telephone call from the recycling company your business is going to use. They want to know by 5.00 pm today how many recycling bins there are in the department. They need to know this so they can allocate a suitable van and the right number of staff. Jane thinks there are six, but you can only find five.

Prepare a business letter confirming the number of bins, and any other appropriate documents (the information must be in a form that is suitable for faxing).

Memos

Remember that a memo is used for internal communication. A memo can be sent either to individuals or to all members of staff.

Build-up Exercise

You have just attended a departmental meeting and Jane is rather angry that members of staff have not taken a great deal of notice of the new recycling procedures. It seems that people are not putting waste paper into the recycling bins, and neither are they shredding confidential documents which have errors on them. For the first collection by the recycling business, only four of the bins were full, one was empty and the other one had gone missing. When Jane walked around the department the following Monday, she collected up enough waste paper to fill two bins.

Jane has asked you to send a memo to remind all concerned to make sure that recycled paper is dealt with in an appropriate manner and that she does not expect to see waste paper littering the department from now on.

Summaries

As part of your work you may be given long articles or reports to read and then be presented in a more concise way. (Original documents may be long and complicated; make sure you understand the information you read before you begin any form of summary.)

Summaries, or précis, require you to take out unnecessary information and detail. Here are some guidelines which will help you to summarise information:

- Read through the whole document first without trying to understand everything.
- Re-read the document more thoroughly. You could now highlight the important areas at this stage, or cross out any unnecessary information.
- Make a list of the items you have to include and compare your list with the original document to make sure that you have not forgotten anything.
- Write a draft summary. You may want someone to read this to check that you have covered the main points. If you are happy with this attempt you may move on to writing a final draft of the summary.
- Once the final draft has been agreed you can write the final summary.

To create an effective summary you need various skills and abilities. You will need to be able to:

- **Understand the initial information**. You need to understand what the original text is about before you can make any real attempt to summarise it. Read through it at least twice; once to get the main idea and a second time, stopping to look at words or sentences you don't understand and highlight areas where you may need help.
- **Order the information**. To do this you first need to identify related points or topics in the original document. These can then be put together in a suitable orderas key points in your summary. Underline or highlight these key points and phrases.
- **Analyse the information**. Is there an argument or point of view which is being developed in the original document? Try to summarise the key points of the argument in just a few sentences.
- **Make a judgement about the information**. Which points are important? Which are less important? Try listing the points in order of their importance.
- **Select the appropriate information**. Think about the most important points which are being made in the original document. From this choose the ones you wish to include.
- **Present the information in an appropriate format**. This may mean choosing either a series of bulleted or numbered points, a series of short paragraphs with headings, or changing the information into a totally new format, such as a table, a chart or a flow diagram.

Try it out

Read the following passage 'Examination Procedures'. Your tutor wants this text summarised. Try to reduce the length of the text but ensure that you include all the facts. You can remove the headings so that it is continuous text and the numbered paragraphs could be indicated using bullet points.

Examination procedures

As part of the selection procedure to help us to decide whether you are a suitable candidate, we will ask you to sit a series of examinations. This information sheet gives you an indication of the kinds of questions included in these examinations.

Part one

The questions in the first examination require you to spot relationships between combinations of words, letters and numbers. It is a reasoning test and requires no specialist knowledge.

Part two

The second examination is composed of illustrations representing elementary scientific principles. You will be asked questions orally and you will indicate your answers on your printed question sheet.

Part three

The third section is straightforward arithmetic, intended to test your speed and accuracy in handling figures.

Part four

In this examination you are given mathematical problems to solve. These are of a varied nature.

Part five

This section is designed to test your graphic skills. You will be given random shapes and asked to refit them from two sections.

General hints

1. Pay careful attention to the invigilator who will give you precise instructions at the start of the examination. He/she will explain what is expected of you, and you may ask questions before you begin if you are not sure of anything.

2. Read carefully the directions given at the head of each part of the examination and be sure to follow them correctly. Failure to do this can lose you valuable time and marks.

3. You may find that you are unable to finish the questions in any one part of the examination. Do as many as you can and do not spend too long on any question you find difficult.

4. If you make a mistake in one of your answers, cross it out and write the correct answer clearly beside it. DO NOT LEAVE MORE THAN ONE ANSWER FOR ANY ONE QUESTION.

Tables

Converting a mass of facts and figures into a table makes them far easier to understand and helps the reader appreciate their importance. It is not always possible to obtain information in an easy-to-read and understandable format. In many cases you will be asked to extract and adapt information which may be hidden amongst lots of other, irrelevant information.

Designing a table requires you to think carefully about how you need to present the information and, indeed, whether the information is suitable for conversion into a table. Provided all the information you have is all in the same form, then converting it into a table should not prove too difficult.

Try it out

Prepare a table for the six months sales figures using the information in the paragraph below:

Last month's sales figures proved to be better than expected. Overall our sales figures for last month were 25 per cent up on the previous month. The £40,000 for last month was twice that of three months ago. Four months ago the sales figures were just £10,000, but that was twice the month before. Our first month, the month before, saw just £2,000 in sales, so last month's £40,000 total is a great result.

Create your table with the following headings:
Month; Sales figures.

Messages

When colleagues or outside callers wish to talk to someone, that person may not always be available. One of the many tasks in business administration is to note down messages accurately which you can leave on the relevant person's desk for them to see when they return. You will often need to summarise the important information that needs to be passed on, which may include telephone numbers, names, dates or other details about orders. Unlike written material, telephone calls do not allow you to look back at the information and make a judgement as to what is important and what is not; you have to summarise as you listen to the message. However, you can ask the caller to repeat certain things, such as telephone numbers.

Try it out

Imagine you have just picked up the telephone and the caller wants to speak to Katie Walsh, who is at lunch. Note down as a message the most important parts of the following conversation:

▶▶

'Hello, my name is Suzannah Burman. I'd like to leave a message for Katie Walsh please. I should have phoned earlier, but I've been a bit busy doing my shopping and when I got to the car to drive home I found I had a flat tyre, so it took me longer than expected. Would you tell Katie that Alex has called me and his cold is a lot better now. He phoned to say that he will be back in work tomorrow. He can't remember what shift he is on tomorrow, perhaps she would be good enough to find that out for me. He tells me that he must visit the doctor tomorrow at 9.15 so in any case he won't be able to get into work until at least 10.30 and he hopes that is all right. Thanks very much and will you tell Katie that Alex would like to thank her for sending the get well card, bye for now.'

It is important to pass on messages quickly and accurately. You cannot and should not pass on a word-for-word message, so when taking a message for someone else the following points should be remembered:

- Listen very carefully to the message.
- Make notes as you listen.
- Your notes should contain key words and important information, including the date and time of the call and the name and details of the caller.
- Once you have taken the message, before you pass it on, write it out in a form that can be easily understood.
- Do not include any unnecessary information.
- Make sure you mention names, addresses, telephone and fax numbers, order numbers, etc. and any deadlines which need to be met.
- Pass on the message by telephone, by writing it on paper or a form, or face-to-face.
- You should ensure that your tone and style is correct when both receiving and passing on the message.

Build-up Exercise

Before you try the two messages in the next Try it out Exercise, design a simple telephone message form. It should include the following:

- who the message is for
- who the message is from
- who they represent or what business or department they belong to
- their telephone and fax numbers and/or e-mail address
- the message itself
- any action that needs to be taken
- who the message was taken by
- the date and time of the message.

Telephone message pads are often printed on brightly coloured paper and vary in format, but they all have spaces in which to note down important details of the message. Remember that accuracy and efficiency are essential.

Try it out

Using your own telephone message form, accurately and efficiently note down the most important information from the following two messages.

1 *'I'd like to speak to Miss Doyle please. Oh, she isn't there, well can I leave a message then? Can you tell her I was supposed to be coming in to see her next Friday. I think that's the 12th, no it's the 13th. Well I can't come I'm afraid because I've got a dental appointment at 11 and then I have to go down to London. Could you tell her I can put it back a week and make it 11 o'clock if that's OK with her? Perhaps she could ring me to confirm? My name's Sally Scadding and I'm with Associated Electronics on 01244 505050. Oh and my extension is 279. Thanks very much.'*

2 *'Hello, can you put me through to Miss Smith please? Oh, she's not there. Is she likely to be back later on? It doesn't matter. My name is Ken Smith, no relation. I'd better leave a message hadn't I? I need to speak to her urgently. We received your delivery this morning and I'm afraid I am very unhappy. One of the boxes has burst in transit and they are quite unusable. I ordered the three boxes two weeks ago. The order number is 12479 and they cost £555.39. I need you to send me out a replacement batch immediately. I've got customers waiting for these. I'm also very cross and I want to make a complaint as this is the second time this has happened. She really must ring me as soon as she gets back. If she's not at her desk by 3 then she will have missed me so she had better speak to Brian. His extension is 271 and mine is 248. I should have said we're Smith Communications and our number's 01256 0000.'*

Leaflets and advertisements

Leaflets and advertisements should be simple and draw the reader's eye to the most important information. Whilst leaflets can carry more information than an advertisement in a newspaper or magazine, you should not be tempted to overload the reader with unnecessary detail. Leaflets really need to look eye-catching and should put across information in a direct, concise way.

Advertisements work best with the minimum of words, so you need to think very carefully about what you say and how you say it. Advertisements also benefit from illustrations and different fonts in different sizes.

Try it out

Following a meeting with other shop managers, Katie Walsh has just announced to all of the employees that the shop will now be open Monday to Saturday between 10 in the morning and 10 at night. The shop, Arnolds, will also be opening between 11 and 4 on a Sunday. In the past the shop used to close at lunchtime on a Thursday and was only open late on a Wednesday and Friday night. It was closed on a Sunday. Some of the staff are unhappy but others are pleased that there will be more overtime.

Katie has asked you to design a leaflet which can be handed to customers who come into the shop and also to people passing the shop. She also wants you to design an advertisement for the local newspaper to tell the readers about the new opening hours.

Agendas

An agenda is used to tell people who are to attend a meeting what will be discussed at the meeting. An agenda will give the date, time and venue of the meeting and also sets out the programme of business. Remember that all agendas will have the same first three items, namely apologies for absence, minutes of the last meeting and matters arising from the minutes of the last meeting. The last two items on the agenda are also common: any other business and the date of the next meeting.

Try it out

Katie has called a meeting of all members of staff to discuss the new opening hours and she has asked you to draw up the agenda. She wants everyone to attend at 08.00 on Tuesday of next week in the staff canteen and Mr Paul Trigg from head office will be attending. Katie wants to include in the meeting a discussion about the implications of Sunday working, as well as the need to improve stock-taking checks on the shop's goods. Two other members of staff have also asked you to add an item to the agenda. Alex wants to discuss the increasing problem of shoplifting and Clare would like to have a discussion about staff uniforms.

Create your agenda and decide how many copies will have to be produced.

Reports

Remember that reports can be short and informal (memo-style) or they can be more formal, like a business report. Reports are usually written after some kind of research has taken place and are wordprocessed. Reports can incorporate headings, sub-headings, numbered points and decimal-pointed headings or items.

Try it out

At the meeting you had last week, you were asked to do some research and prepare a report about the increased amount of shoplifting at your branch of Arnolds, which is in Worcester, for Paul Trigg at head office in London. You have found the following information, which was compiled from a crime, disorder and community safety order in 2001. Compile a short, memo-style report addressed to Paul Trigg, using the information given and summarising its findings. Any diagrams, charts or graphs should be redrawn using a computer, printed on separate sheets of paper and attached to the report as appendices. Each appendix page should be numbered.

Shoplifting

Shoplifting accounted for almost 11 per cent of all crimes in Worcester in 2000/2001.

How have shoplifting rates changed?

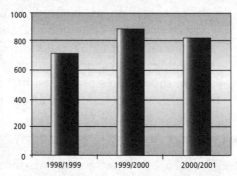

A total of 819 shoplifting offences were recorded in Worcester in 2000/2001. This compares with 891 in 1999/2000 and 712 in 1998/1999. The 2000/2001 figure represents an 8.1 per cent fall on the previous year but an increase of 15 per cent over two years.

The Safer Worcester Partnership Strategy (1999–2002) set a target to reduce shoplifting in Worcester by 5 per cent per year over three years (10 per cent by the year 2000/2001). The figures show that we have failed to meet this target – witnessing a 15 per cent increase instead.

How does shoplifting vary by neighbourhood area?

The highest levels of shoplifting in Worcester are found in the city centre which accounts for 73 per cent of all offences. There are, however, differences among the neighbourhood areas. The highest shoplifting figures occurred in the same three residential neighbourhood areas each year of the audit period – St John's North, Brickfields and Old Warndon.

Shoplifting in Worcester: total number of offences in top four areas

Neighbourhood area	1998/1999	1999/2000	2000/2001
City centre	469	615	597
St John's North	95	73	41
Old Warndon	35	38	54
Brickfields	31	48	34
All other areas	1–17	0–15 (one 27*)	0–16 (one 26*)

* The area recording 27 offences in 1999/2000 was North Worcester, while the 26 offences in 2000/2001 were recorded in St Peters.

How have shoplifting rates changed in the city centre?

Shoplifting accounted for just over a quarter of all recorded crime in the city centre in 2000/2001. A total of 597 shoplifting offences were recorded in the city centre in 2000/2001. This compares with 615 in 1999/2000 and 469 in 1998/1999. The 2000/2001 figure represents a 2.9 per cent fall on the previous year but an increase of 27.3 per cent over two years.

When do people shoplift?

The vast majority of shoplifting offences occur in the daytime during normal shopping hours. It is, however, interesting to look at how shoplifting varies during the week and over the year.

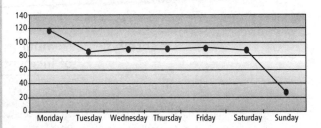

The graph above shows there is a peak in shoplifting offences on Monday – 40 per cent above the average per day. Again, it must be remembered that this is just the level of *recorded* crimes.

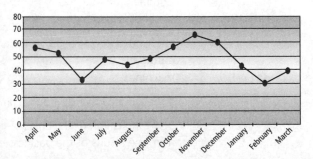

In 2000/2001 there was a peak in the frequency of shoplifting offences in November when 67 of the 597 offences were recorded. Although it is not possible to identify trends using one year's data, the above graph does seem to suggest that shoplifting increases in the pre-Christmas period.

When considering the times when business crime occurs, it is, however, worth noting that the pattern is different for different business crimes. The business crime survey found that several companies perceived the risk of crime to be higher during the night and for the summer months.

Who steals from shops?

Of the offenders caught for shoplifting in 2000/2001, 59% were male and 41% were female. It is interesting that this is the only offence committed by almost as many females as males. Of the known offenders 95% were white (as would be anticipated given the ethnic composition of the City's population). Of known offenders in 2000/2001 82% were under the age of 30 and, again, the highest number of offenders (26%) were aged between 15 and 19.

How much does crime cost businesses?

The Home Office research study looking into the costs of crime can be used to give an estimate of the cost of commercial crimes in Worcester (see table below). There are, however, limitations to this exercise as business crimes can be coded in a number of different ways and are not always easy to identify within individual crime codes.

The cost of recorded business crimes in Worcester

Offence type	Number of incidents	Average cost per incident	Total cost 2000/2001
Other thefts (not vehicle)*	835	£340	£283,000
Shoplifting	819	£100	£81,900
Commercial burglary	169	£2,700	£456,300
Criminal damage to other buildings*	270	£510	£137,700
Theft from automatic machines	33	£340	£11,220

* These categories may include crimes that are not against businesses.

Some indication of the costs of crime to businesses is also available from the results of the business crime survey conducted in July 2001.

Job descriptions

Job descriptions provide details of the exact role and responsibilities, along with tasks and duties, which an individual doing the job must undertake. Legally a job description is part of a person's contract of employment and therefore must be accurate. That said, most people tend to do more than is written in their job description.

Build-up Exercise

Clare is very pleased to have been informed that her job as a casual worker has now been made a full-time, permanent post. She is to become a permanent member of staff from next Monday. Look back at the section on job descriptions earlier in this unit and wordprocess a copy of Clare's job description. Her job title was given in a previous activity as a casual worker, but now she will be a Sales I assistant. You should decide what Clare's duties and responsibilities would be as a sales assistant. You should already know where Clare fits into the business, i.e. to whom she is responsible.

Articles

Articles can be included in company newsletters or they can be sent as press releases to the media. Articles need to be informative and, in the case of press releases, interesting and eye-catching enough to grab the attention of the newspaper's editor.

Try it out

Paul Trigg is very happy about the increased sales that have been enjoyed as a result of the new opening times. Katie is pleased too. She has asked you to encourage people to continue to use the shop by writing an article for the local newspaper. The article needs to be interesting, and somehow encourages people to visit the shop. Base your article on what you think is important from the following information:

- Sales figures are up 30 per cent.
- More than 1,000 customers visit the store on an average Sunday.
- Evening sales now account for 20 per cent of the total sales.
- Sunday sales account for 20 per cent of the total weekly sales.
- Staff are very happy; some take overtime or days off.
- Arnolds will be offering a special 10 per cent discount to customers who visit the store after 7 pm and the same discount on a Sunday.
- Customers spending more than £100 will be entered into a special raffle to win a meal for two at one of the leading restaurants in the city.

Presentation of documents for ease of use and to reflect purpose

Now we have investigated the different types of business document and their formats, and considered their different uses, it is important to remember that the way in which they are presented and laid out makes a big difference to the impression they give to the reader. All documents in whatever format need to be easy to use, which means they have to be easy to read and to extract information from. Wherever possible you should try to use headings or sub-headings. These help break up blocks of text and tell the reader that you are making a new point.

Do not be tempted to try to say everything about a particular point in a single paragraph. Break the text up into a number of paragraphs which are easier to read.

Above all, whatever business document or format you are using, your ideas need to be presented in a logical sequence. Pretend you are telling a story which has a beginning, a middle and an end.

- The beginning can be an introduction, because it tells the reader what you are about to say and why you are saying it.
- The middle is often the largest part of a business document, because here you put all of the necessary information which supports what you have stated in the introduction.
- The end may be a conclusion (or conclusions), a series of recommendations, or simply a request for the reader to now do something.

Always ensure that whatever document you are producing is easy to use and fits the purpose for which you are writing it. This can be achieved by simply adding headings and sub-headings, breaking up paragraphs and making sure the text follows a logical sequence.

Build-up Exercise

Go back to the article you wrote for the local newspaper. Evaluate the work you have done by asking yourself if you could have made the presentation more effective, perhaps by using bulleted points, headings or sub-headings. If you think you could improve the presentation, then go back to your computer-saved file and amend the document.

Use appropriate tone and style for different purposes

Think of all of the ways in which you talk or write to different people in your life. Do you speak the same way to your friends as you do to your parents, elders or teachers? Would you use the same language to your employer as you would to your closest friend? Probably not, and there are ways in which you are expected to use your tone and style of speaking and writing in different situations at work.

The ways in which you talk to someone you work with will differ enormously from the way you might be expected to talk to customers. This is what is meant by using the appropriate tone and style for different purposes.

Selection and use of vocabulary to suit the specified context

Vocabulary is your choice of words, and this choice has to change in different circumstances. You cannot always expect to be understood if you use jargon or complicated words; do you understand what others are saying when they use lots of words that you find difficult to grasp? Use of vocabulary is not about intelligence, showing off by using complicated words, or even trying to impress someone. The most important thing about your use of vocabulary is that whoever you are talking to or writing to understands what you mean. Talking and writing are both about communication, and for successful two-way communication, both sides need to understand what is being said or written.

Try it out

Choose a friend in your group and try out the following sentences on them. The sentences all say the same thing, but each time they are simplified to make understanding easier. Say each sentence then ask your friend to tell you whether they understood what you were saying. If they did not, try the next sentence and keep going until they do understand.

1 'In formulating any concept of interaction one must primarily focus upon the inherent content and delivery of the said interaction.'
2 'Interaction and its success is dependent upon the information contained therein and the format in which it is delivered.'
3 'Successful communication is the sum of the content of that communication and how it is delivered.'
4 'Communication depends upon the complexity of the information and how it is said.'
5 'Clear communication needs to take account of the content and the way it is said.'

Use of a style that reflects business context

We have looked at the various ways in which information can be passed on to others and the ways in which complicated information can be 'translated' into different formats to suit particular readers. People have their own style, or way of passing on information to others, but businesses will sometimes have preferred ways of doing this of their own. Style can actually mean several different things:

- Style can mean the way a business prefers to format documents, such as letters, and of opening and closing letters.
- Style can include preferred spellings, such as using 'z' instead of 's' in words such as organisation (organization).
- Style can also be set out in the use of particular forms, which the business expects everyone to use.
- Style can be described as conversational (write like you speak), technical (which assumes the reader will understand technical jargon) or formal (which will require you to be polite, tactful and clear about what you say or write).

You need to know how to speak or write in particular circumstances. The business may have codes or rules about this and expect you to follow them at all times.

Normally, the style of writing or speech you adopt is different in each of the following situations:

- Dealing with colleagues at work who are on the same level as you are (and probably know you quite well).
- Dealing with someone who is senior to you.
- Dealing with customers or suppliers.
- A particular type or format of business document may demand you use another style.
- You will have yet another style if you are preparing a document which will be read by others who you do not normally work with.

Try it out

Have a look at the following styles of communication. One could be used in an e-mail, another in a formal business letter to a customer and another in a telephone message for your manager. Can you identify which one is suitable in each case?

1 'I regret, therefore, that under current company policies we cannot refund your payment at this time.'
2 'Toni, get me the figures for last month when you've got a chance, cheers, Mike.'
3 'When you were at lunch, Mr. Sinclair called. He is keen to talk to you about an order, but wouldn't confirm his order until you have spoken to him. Can you call him back please between 3 and 4 this afternoon? His number is 07924443333.'

Use of a tone that reflects needs of the recipient(s)

We've already seen that style is important, but tone also should be taken into account. Some of the examples in the previous activity not only showed differences in style, but also in tone. Tone is about the approach you adopt in what you say or write. Tone means putting something across in the right kind of way to get the right kind of reaction from the person you are communicating with. You should adopt a different tone in different situations to match the needs of the person you are communicating with, otherwise they may not understand or appreciate what it is you are saying or writing. Tone also depends on the type of individual you are addressing, either in speech or in writing. Table 1.12 gives some examples of appropriate tone.

Table 1.12 *Examples of appropriate tone in various circumstances*

Type of person spoken/written to	Tone to be used
Person working with you, not senior to you	Friendly, familiar tone, not too formal; can use jargon if you both understand it.
Person working with you, senior to you	Friendly, but not too familiar. You may need to be formal; you can use jargon.
Customer	Friendly, polite and respectful. The customer may always be right, but sometimes they are not. You must be clear, forceful, but not rude.
Supplier	Friendly, polite, quite formal. Depends on how well you know the supplier. They will expect you to be rather formal, but need you to be clear.

Try it out

Choose a partner in your group and try out different ways of using tone to say the same thing. Your partner will take the role of each of the following:

- a person working with you
- your manager
- a customer
- a supplier.

Convey the following facts using the appropriate tone in each case:

'The business will be closed next Tuesday for stock-taking.'

Adaptation of tone to meet non-standard circumstances, e.g. complaints, personal problems

Customer dissatisfaction may lead to complaints and requests for help. Reasons for dissatisfaction can include the following:

- The product or service purchased was either faulty or not suitable.
- The customer requires a product which the business does not stock or which is out of stock.
- The customer feels they have received poor service.
- The customer has a problem they feel no one seems able to help them with.

Most businesses have a formal complaints procedure for customers who are dissatisfied. It is usual practice for complaints to be referred to a manager who has the power to act on them and make on-the-spot decision to help deal with the situation. Here are some key stages which you should follow in the event of a complaint:

- If listening to the complaint, do not interrupt; give the customer the opportunity to explain the situation.
- Always appear to be sympathetic to the customer.
- In particularly complicated cases, make sure that you write down all of the details.
- Once you have listened and written down the details, check with the customer that you have got the main points right.
- Even if the customer is rude or abusive, stay calm and polite.
- If you feel that you cannot solve the situation yourself, refer the matter to a more senior member of staff.
- Never give the customer a vague answer or an unbelievable excuse.
- Do not directly blame another member of staff.
- Even if the customer provokes you, do not lose your temper.
- Never give the customer the impression that you are not taking the complaint seriously. Remember it is an important problem as far as the customer is concerned.
- Always tell the customer exactly what you are going to do, particularly if this involves referring it to another member of staff.
- Never make promises which you cannot personally fulfil or ensure that someone else will fulfil.

Try it out

Choose a partner and try out the following problem. One of you is an employee at a business and the other is a customer who has a complaint. The idea of the exercise is for the employee to calm down the customer and the customer must try to make the employee lose their temper!

The complaint is that the kettle purchased yesterday was faulty and caused a minor fire in the customer's kitchen.

Dealing with personal problems at work requires a different approach in terms of tone. Personal problems require very careful handling and a degree of sympathy. Here are some facts and figures which may surprise you:

- Nearly 10 per cent of the population suffers from depression.
- Depression is the leading cause of death or disability at work.
- Stress is more dangerous to employees than either cancer or heart disease. Stress accounts for roughly half of all working days lost.
- Managers can spend, on average, up to 20 per cent of their time dealing with employees' personal problems.

This means that more and more businesses are starting 'employee assistance programmes' to help support their staff in terms of their mental health and well-being, to create a healthier and more productive workplace.

Employees face a variety of personal and family concerns that may affect their ability to do their jobs. Some may suffer depression; others may be alcoholic or dependent upon drugs. Many staff have problems with the people they work with or, even more likely, problems at home, illnesses, anxieties or stresses.

Most employees do not want to discuss their personal problems at work, especially with their manager or supervisor. The only visible symptoms are often lower work output, lateness, sick days taken or absences from work.

Dealing with others' personal problems may not be your role at work, but a friendly ear can help in many cases. To deal with situations such as these you will need to:

- improve the way you listen
- apply what you know to other people's situations
- identify the limits of how much and what type of help you can give
- suggest where help can be found (both inside and outside the business)
- know when it is appropriate to tell a manager or supervisor about what you have been told, particularly if you are worried about the welfare of the person concerned.

Try it out

Type up this simple questionnaire and ask 20 people you know to fill it in.

Are you currently employed?	Yes No
If yes, in what kind of position and how many hours a week?	
At your current job, how often do you discuss personal problems at work?	Every day Frequently Sometimes Never
How comfortable are you discussing personal problems at work?	Very comfortable Somewhat comfortable Not comfortable at all
Away from work, with your closest friends, how often do you discuss personal issues?	Every day Frequently Sometimes Never
How comfortable are you discussing personal problems with your closest friends?	Very comfortable Somewhat comfortable Not comfortable at all
In your everyday interactions do you find that you communicate differently at work than with friends?	Yes Sometimes Never

▶▶

In your everyday interactions do you find that others communicate differently at work than with friends?	Yes Sometimes Never

Figure 1.37 *Work and personal problems questionnaire*

What do your results tell you about discussing personal problems at work?

Write a 150-word article outlining your findings and conclusions.

Use of tact, diplomacy, persuasion and technical style to meet circumstances

It has been said that a diplomatic person can tell you to go to hell in such a way that you actually look forward to the trip! At work everyone needs to work together to achieve the tasks and duties they have been set. If you have a reputation for being rude or short-tempered, or if you make cutting remarks about people, it is unlikely that others will be happy either to work with you, or to listen to what you say.

A huge part of how successful you are at work depends upon how you relate to your manager, supervisor, co-workers, customers and suppliers. If you can maintain a strong and healthy working relationship it is more likely that you will succeed.

What is diplomacy? It is the art of staying on good terms with people, most of the time. Diplomacy and tact (being sensitive and aware of what annoys or angers others) are key success factors in getting on at work. They allow you to keep your cool, get on well with other workers, work well with them and help them to help you turn out quality work which will be recognised by supervisors and managers.

To be tactful and diplomatic at work you need to understand, be aware of and sensitive to those with whom you have contact. Here are some key things to remember:

- Always speak quietly and clearly.
- Do not get over-emotional.
- Do not be arrogant or rude.
- Always keep the bigger picture in mind.

You should also:

- Use 'we' and not 'I' when reporting that a task you've been working on with other people is completed successfully.
- Never criticise someone you work with in public – solve problems with them behind closed doors.
- Think about what the other person wants to get out of working with you and try to help them achieve that.

- Resist talking to, or sending mail (or notes) to, people with whom you are angry – wait until you have calmed down and then speak to them in private.
- Be aware of how things are expected to be done – don't go directly to supervisors or managers if you have a problem you could sort out yourself with your co-workers.

Build-up Exercise

Here is a list of things to do at work which all involve diplomacy and tact. Type up your own version of this list with illustrations you think would help get the points across. Print off enough for several people to have copies, then tactfully and diplomatically discuss which is the best version.

1 Learn how to voice your opinion with authority and tact.
2 Learn to be a good listener.
3 Learn to give others the chance to express their opinions.
4 Learn to leave no room for misunderstandings.
5 Learn to be polite and courteous and don't get involved in gossip; it's not professional.
6 Learn to not say things that might be hurtful or offensive and to speak wisely.
7 Learn to realise that there is nothing wrong with having fun at work, but make sure your sense of humour does not offend others.

Persuasiveness is *not* about convincing others that you are always right and that they should follow your lead. Being persuasive means that if you think you are right then you should say so carefully, calmly and with confidence.

In order to be persuasive you need to be able to argue your case. Persuasion means that you are trying to change the listener's (or reader's) mind. Effective persuasion does need some preparation, whether you are speaking or writing:

- Create a list of ideas to support your point of view.
- Now list a series of points *against* what you believe (i.e. the other side of the argument).
- Now look at the points in favour of your point of view. Are they enough to persuade the person you are going to talk to or write to?
- Select the best four or five points in favour and two against your point of view (this will show you how to appreciate and give thought to the argument against your point of view).
- Now think of a good reason why someone should listen to your views.
- Select a couple of examples (of real-life situations) which back up your point of view.
- Try to find some common ground between your point of view and the opposite view. There may be areas which both sides could agree on.

Think about the way in which you are studying this course. How would you reorganise the course if you could? What could improve the way in which you are being taught? What could improve your success? Write down at least five suggestions to improve the course and think about the reasons why these suggestions might not be taken up.

Whenever you are trying to be persuasive, you need to maintain the listener's or the reader's attention. Here are some key guidelines to help you do this:

- Try to be interesting. If you can 'sell' yourself to the other person, you are part way to 'selling' them your ideas.
- Show that you are a reasonable and trustworthy person who has thought about the advantages and disadvantages of your point of view.
- Show the person that you do have a real interest in and knowledge of the situation, and are not just talking so as to gain attention or make an impression.
- Use each of the points you have developed as a separate part of the argument.
- If you are writing, each of the points should be separated, either as bullet points, paragraphs, separate headings or numbered points, depending on the format you are using.
- Never be critical of the opposing view; say you understand it but you feel there is better approach.
- Emphasise your strongest point as the main point which makes your view the best approach.
- When you can, support your ideas with reasonable and realistic examples (particularly if you have facts and figures to back up what you are saying).
- Conclude what you are saying in an interesting way.
- Restate your suggestion and summarise your main points at the end of your presentation.

Build-up Exercise

Now you have read this second set of guidelines, rewrite your suggestions from the previous activity. How do you feel about the strength of your argument now? Are your points more persuasive?

Technical style applies to written work which includes numbers, units, equations or technical jargon. There are a number of things to bear in mind regarding technical style:

- **Clarity** – you need to be clear so that there is no room for confusion. A reader or listener should not have to work out what you mean – it should be obvious.
- **Clear purpose** – there should be no misunderstanding about what you are saying or writing. Remember that the readers may be busy people who do not have the time to work their way through muddled or confused documents.
- **Say it briefly** – state your ideas as concisely as possible; your important ideas should have sub-headings and form the basis of your document.
- **Use words appropriately** – you should always try to use the right words, and to back up what you are saying with charts, tables, graphs, icons, illustrations or drawings.
- **Be concise** – a skilled writer replaces phrases which we commonly use in speech with much shorter ones (for example, 'along the lines of' becomes 'like' and 'for the purpose of' becomes 'for').
- **Jargon** – use only words that everyone you are communicating with will understand. In many cases, documents may be read by people who do not understand jargon terms, so it is best to either avoid them or provide a glossary of terms.

Try it out

You probably know by now exactly what is involved in this unit. Have another look at the content for Unit 1. It is quite jargon-based. Translate the first assessment objectives into common language so that someone who does not know about the course would understand what they mean.

Importance of appropriate tone and style to reflect the business context and specified purpose

Each time you are asked to produce a document you will need to use the right tone and style to suit the type of document and its intended readership. This may take a little practice and it is probably best to look at similar documents which have been completed in the past to get an idea about the required tone and style.

Build-up Exercise

Here is some basic information. You need to vary the tone and style to meet two different purposes. You must get across the same ideas and main points, but to different audiences.

First, prepare a letter to be sent out to customers, outlining the main points, and secondly provide a brief summary for internal use.

'Serious design problems have been found in the new washing machine sent out over the past three months. We have sold around 500 of these machines. One of our customers was badly injured when the washing machine burned out and set fire to their kitchen. We need to warn all customers not to use the machine until it has been checked by one of our repair workers. We will not take responsibility for damage after we have sent out the letter should the same thing happen. Customers must call our helpline immediately to arrange an appointment. We will complete the repairs and changes at no cost.'

Importance of tone and style as a reflection on the writer and the writer's employer

Finally, let us consider how the tone and style of what is said or written is viewed by those outside the business. Rudeness or poorly chosen words are clearly likely to give a bad impression of both the writer and the business. All written material intended for other people needs to:

- be tactful
- be polite
- be clear
- be helpful
- be informative
- offer a solution to a problem.

Table 1.13 shows different ways of dealing with people and the impressions they give about the writer and the business.

Table 1.13 *The effect of tone and style on customers' perceptions*

Discourteous	Indifferent	Courteous	Attentive
Confrontational	Uncaring	Polite	Very courteous
Rude	Bored	Friendly	Problem solving
Impolite	Disinterested	Positive	Adaptable
Aggressive	Evasive	Approachable	Caring

Think about the different impressions given and how they reflect on you as an employee and the business as a whole. If people are handled correctly it can lead to:

- fewer customer complaints
- more time to spend on things other than dealing with problems
- a more positive working environment
- greater job satisfaction
- more business for the employer.

Try it out

Which of the following sentences if they were part of a letter to a customer, would not give a good impression of yourself or the business? Why are they not appropriate? When you have identified the inappropriate sentences, reword them to make them more acceptable.

1 We have considered your request for a refund and will not be giving you one.
2 We have decided to withdraw this product as we have designed a better one and therefore cannot repair your old one.
3 We have taken legal advice on this issues and will therefore not compensate you for your losses.
4 We have despatched the goods you have ordered, our apologies for the delay.
5 Rest assured we will not be supplying such poor quality goods on subsequent occasions; the replacement of them is a big hassle.

Use English correctly

We have discussed throughout this unit the importance of using the correct format for business communications and making sure that they are well presented. However, none of these considerations will make any difference to the overall impression you give if your use of English is poor.

Although we often feel we rely on wordprocessors which have a spell-check facility, it is very important that all documents are proof-read to make sure there are no errors. A wordprocessor cannot identify words that are spelt correctly, but wrongly used. All types of documents need careful checking. Mistakes can creep in and, together with poor use of punctuation, grammar, spelling and English, can end up making the document confusing and hard to understand. Careful checking of all finished work is therefore essential.

Build-up Exercise

Proof-read the following text and identify the spelling and use of English errors that appear:

A verb is a word what describes a action. It is sometimes known therefore as a doing' word. For e.g. 'The manager open the door'. A sentence is not compleat withough a verb. For example 'The new ofice layout a big success'. This does not make a compleat sentence without the missing varb – is. The doing or action words in a sentence is usually the verbs.

Accurate spelling of common words

Poor or inaccurate spelling in a business document can be very annoying for the person receiving the document. This is the last thing a business wants – to upset its customers or suppliers because of a simple thing like a spelling mistake. Nevertheless, these errors do occur and unfortunately the only way that an individual can improve their spelling and general use of English is to keep on thinking about it.

If you are not very good at spelling, you need to make sure that youdo the following:

- **Pay attention to the spell-checker on your computer** – if the machine identifies a spelling error it will underline the word in red. If it identifies a grammatical error it will identify the words in green.
- **Get used to using a dictionary** – it's no good saying 'how can I use a dictionary if I don't know how to spell the word'. You can nearly always guess the first few letters. Get into the habit of having a dictionary on your desk and double-checking each time you are not sure. You will soon be able to spell correctly several of the words you were unsure of before.
- **Get used to asking someone else** – most people prefer to see a correctly spelt word because the individual writing it has asked for help, rather than constantly having to tell them to go away and do the typing again. If you are unsure how to spell a word and can't find it in the dictionary, then ask for assistance from a colleague.

Lots of people have problems with the plural of words (for example, the plural of 'dog' is 'dogs'). A plural is usually formed by adding an 's', as in the example of dogs. However, some words can be both singular and plural, such as 'sheep'. Other words need more than just 's' to transform them into a plural. For example, words ending in 'y', such as 'library' or 'facility', require the 'y' to be removed and 'ies' added to the end to make the plural ('libraries' and 'facilities'). Words ending in 'ss', for example 'mass', usually require an 'es' to be added to give the plural (e.g. 'masses').

Some nouns ending in 'f' or 'fe' need to drop the 'f' to make a plural and replace it with a 'ves', for example 'calf' ('calves') and 'knife' ('knives').

Try it out

See if you can write the plurals of the following words:

donkey	record
family	jacket
ability	paper
gateau	people
architecture	knife
leaf	life

If you know you have a problem with spelling, then every time you come across a word you need help with, write it down correctly. This may sound a bit like getting ready for a spelling test at school, but it is the only way you will get to grips with the problem. The more you practise spelling, the better you will become.

Build-up Exercise

The following words are those that people often have problems with spelling correctly. Use these words to start off your own list of words to practise your spelling.

acceptable	accommodation	assessment
behaviour	budgeted	colleague
committee	convenient	criteria
definite	environment	hygienic
initial	initiative	liaise
necessary	receive	receipt
recommended	separate	transferred
undoubtedly		

Another area of spelling confusing to some people are the words 'their', 'there' and 'they're'. These three words sound the same but have different meanings. They are likely to occur whatever you are writing and it is easy to confuse them and use the wrong word; it can make nonsense of your sentence. You should try to remember the following:

- **Their** – this word means 'belonging to them' and could be used to describe 'their' work, or 'their' children, or 'their' home. Their is the plural form of words like his, her or its.
- **They're** – this word means 'they are' and is like 'I'm' or 'we're' in that a letter is missed out and replaced with an apostrophe.
- **There** – this word is used to show a place or to indicate something, for example 'there is' or 'go over there' or 'I'll meet you there'.

Build-up Exercise

Correct the deliberate mistakes in the following sentences:

1 The girl went their because she was the only one.
2 There happy to be doing that kind of work.
3 The children have always enjoyed there time at the beach.
4 We told her we would be happy to meet her their.
5 We met them after they had collected they're belongings.

Punctuation is accurate and consistent

Punctuation refers to full stops (.), commas (,), question marks (?), dashes (–), semi-colons (;), colons (:), apostrophes (') and capital letters.

Here are some golden rules to help you remember:

- A full stop should be used at the end of a sentence.
- A capital letter should be used at the beginning of a sentence and for the first letter of the names of people and places (proper nouns).
- A question mark is used to replace a full stop at the end of a sentence which asks a question.
- A comma is a way of showing a pause in the middle of a sentence and can sometimes be replaced with a dash (–), e.g.

'We will all be happy when he is back, and safe again with us.'
'We will all be happy when he is back – and safe again with us.'

Commas are used to separate a list of words or to separate linking words, such as 'therefore' and 'however', from the rest of the words in the sentence.

- A semi-colon is a little like a full stop but weaker. It breaks a sentence into two halves, but not quite into two short ones, e.g.

'We were thinking of going on holiday again in September; June seems such a long way off now.'

- Colons are used when a list is included in a sentence, e.g.

'We will have to take lots of items with us: the beach ball, the umbrella and something to wear if it turns cold.'

The apostrophe causes confusion and many people use it incorrectly. There are two different uses for an apostrophe:

- To show that a letter (or letters) have been missed out of a word, e.g. 'I'm' for 'I am' or 'won't' for 'will not'.
- To show that something belongs to someone or something, e.g. 'the manager's car' or 'the dog's tail'. This is known as the possessive apostrophe.

The only two common exceptions to the use of the possessive apostrophe are the words 'its' and 'hers', which take no apostrophe. So when you see the word 'it's' it always means 'it is', e.g.

'It's a better car than hers, but its paintwork is in a poor state of repair.'

Build-up Exercise

Try to place the apostrophe in the correct place in the following words:

1 Claires desk
2 the directors office
3 Jons dog
4 the girls coat
5 The girls couldnt find their pens and pencils.
6 Its a nice day isnt it?

If you were unsure how to do this last activity, turn around the words to read:

1 The desk **of** Claire
2 The office **of** the director
3 The dog **of** Jon
4 The coat **of** the girl

In order to show who owns the items.

When there are several owners of something, the apostrophe goes after the 's', for example 'the companies' shareholders' or 'the bees' hive'.

Build-up Exercise

The following sentences contain no punctuation at all. Rewrite or retype them, inserting the correct punctuation marks throughout:

1 The naughty boy was told therefore to report to the headmistresss office the next morning bringing with him his latest school report his outstanding homework and his packed lunch
2 maurices car was always giving him problems so he decided he would sell it soon and buy himself something brighter quieter and more reliable
3 When we all go to greece this year we have made a decision that we will travel by boat it is so much more relaxing than the airport
4 She expects to depart the station at 4 oclock and to arrive at birmingham just before it gets dark
5 if theyre late then we will have to find somewhere to sit and wait for them to arrive that should not be to difficult

Complex sentences are structured correctly

We have already looked at how punctuation and spelling affect the impression given by a business document, but there are several other issues relating to the use of English that we need to address. These are the ways to help ensure a sentence is structured correctly:

'I' and 'me'
This is a question lots of people ask frequently, but there are some golden rules to help you remember. One way to remember is that it is always polite to mention yourself last and the other person first.
If you are saying '*Jon and I will meet you there*'
But you are not sure if it should be '*Jon and me ...*'
Then in your mind remove the words '*Jon and*'.
This leaves you with either '*... me will meet you there*' or the correct version, which is '*... I will meet you there*'.
You will then realise that the correct sentence should read
'*Jon and I will meet you there*'.

'Who' or 'whom'

This is best explained in the following two sentences:

- *'Jon, who is training to be a teacher, will be qualified next June.'*
  In this example, Jon is the subject of the sentence (the person that 'does' something).
- *'When you tried to call Jon and he was out, to whom did you give the message?'*
  In this example, Jon is still the subject but the unknown person is the object of the sentence (not the 'doer' in the sentence).

You always use 'who' or 'whom' when you are referring to people.

'Which', 'that' or 'what'

You never use 'which' or 'that' when you are referring to people:
*'This is the colour **that** I like the best.'*
not *'This is the colour **what** I like the best.'*

'Is' or 'are'

If there is only one subject in the sentence you use 'is'.
If there is more than one subject in the sentence (plural) you use 'are':
*'Jon **is** going to be delayed'.*
*'Jon and his family **are** going to be delayed'.*

'Nothing' or 'something'

Confusing the words above can result in what is known as a double-negative. This means that if you say:
'I didn't get to do nothing'
what you have actually said is that you did get to do something.

Try it out

The 10 sentences given below are all incorrect in some way. Find the mistakes in each and write or type them out correctly:

1. Me and Rosie enjoyed our day at the seaside but we didn't see nobody we knew.
2. Brian is the one what said it in the first place and we all blamed him.
3. The secretary told us that one of the letters what were sent out was full of mistakes.
4. My teacher is good at learning me the different ways of spelling words.
5. Chris and Laura said they would of come to the party but they was away for the weekend.
6. Pamela and me will be able to attend the meeting but Susie Charlotte and Tim will be away on holiday.
7. There friends sent them fewer cards than there family did send.
8. The sun shined all day it was only when it begun getting dark that it turned coolest.
9. If you will make sure the letter gets posted by Monday I would have been very relieved.
10. At Easter all of them what like to go to church to celebrate the resurrection of Christ do so.

Organising of information into paragraphs

There are a number of reasons why text becomes more interesting and easier to read if paragraphs are used to break up the text. You should start a new paragraph when:

- you are beginning a new topic within a section
- you are including quotations, in which case each quotation would appear as a separate paragraph
- you are changing slightly from one viewpoint to another within the text, for example if you are giving someone else's opinion
- the text is sequenced, for example if you are moving from discussing what occurred one year to something that occurred a different year.

Paragraphs in business documents are important because:

- if structured correctly they allow the reader to work through the document in a logical and clear way
- paragraph headings can be used so that the reader can skim through the document and pick out the paragraphs that are of particular interest to them
- they break up the text and make the document look less complicated and dense.

Try it out

The following text looks very heavy-going. Read through it and decide where you think the paragraph breaks should go. Add paragraph headings, numbered or bulleted points if you think this helps either the presentation or the comprehensibility of the document.

The Women's Land Army consisted of girls from every walk of life; they were attracted by the posters of smiling girls bathing in glorious sunshine working in open fields. The truth was that many of the girls who volunteered for work knew little about the countryside or agricultural work and many of them said they would never understand country folk. Many of the girls were homesick, particularly those who stayed in private billets; those who lived in the hostels told a very different story and were far more settled. In 1939 the total number of agricultural workers was 607,000. By 1944 it had increased to 741,000, an increase of 134,000 or 22 per cent. Three-quarters of this increase took place between 1940 and 1942. The increased numbers were made up largely by women and girls (an increase of 108,000 or 148 per cent), both regular and casual workers, including a substantial proportion provided by the Women's Land Army. There was also an increase in the number of male casual workers. However, due to call up to the Forces, the number of regular male workers declined by 24,000 (5 per cent). From 1944, occupiers were required to furnish details of the

▶▶

numbers of members of the Women's Land Army and prisoners-of-war employed on the farm or holding. It is not known how these forms of labour were returned in previous years so comparisons year on year are not possible. However it appears that returns from occupiers have understated the numbers of these two categories. The Women's Land Army, often referred to as 'The Forgotten Army', was actually formed in 1917 by Roland Prothero, who was then the Minister for Agriculture. The Great War had seen food supplies dwindle prompting the creation of the Women's Land Army (WLA). Girls had to adjust to Land Army life very quickly and erratic love lives, resentments and bad behaviour all had to be contained. To this end representatives for each County had to be elected. Each County had its organising secretary and local representative. The rep had to ensure that all the girls within their area were content but disciplined. The rep in turn reported to the organising secretary directly who saw that all conditions of employment were being met. It is important to remember that the WLA was not a military organisation in any way, which was often forgotten by government.

Maintaining effective working relationships

Working with colleagues (Element 1)

Eight key assessment objectives

- Contribute to the work of a team
- Confirm own responsibilities including work arrangements
- Carry out tasks allocated
- Work with others to complete tasks
- Communicate effectively with others
- Maintain effective working relationships
- Review your contribution to the team activity
- Review the overall performance of the team

Contribute to the work of a team

In many work situations you will be expected to work as part of a team and contribute to the activities and success of that team. Teams are created for a variety of reasons, but they often have the following objectives:

- to help solve problems and make improvements
- to help team members learn and develop
- to try to create a true team spirit
- to encourage creativity and exchange of ideas
- to work together in a constructive way
- to develop both the team's overall skills and the abilities of the team members
- to break down complex tasks into a series of simpler tasks.

Businesses may create teams to undertake a variety of tasks. Teams can also be set up for a specific series of jobs or, indeed, long-term jobs to make the team responsible for certain work (such as a customer service team).

Importance of teamwork and its contribution to the work of the organisation

Working as part of a team is a fact of life in most businesses. Sometimes, teamwork can be frustrating as your individual goals and talents have to be put aside for the team to meet its goals. Teamwork requires patience and understanding. However, it can be very enjoyable to work within a team that works well. Strong friendships can develop and you may learn many things which will help you in the future. Most people do enjoy working as a member of a team. It is important to remember that a business creates teams because teams can often produce far better results and work far better than several individuals working on their own.

Businesses try to get their teams working as well as possible, as quickly as possible and team leaders have a major role in making sure this happens.

Try it out

Complete this questionnaire with the answers:

Always, Sometimes, Occasionally or Never.

1 Are you able to work long hours?
2 Do you find problems a challenge?
3 Can you come up with good ideas to solve problems?
4 If you started an activity and were struggling would you be prepared to keep going?
5 Are you able to keep going with an activity or problem until it is completed, regardless of how you feel about it?
6 Would you always put your own duties before anything else, including your leisure activities and your family?
7 Do you consider success to be measured in terms of how much praise you get?
8 Are you able to cope if you are unsure about how to carry out a particular task?
9 Do you consider yourself to be self-confident?
10 Are you able to take criticism?
11 Do you tend to ask for feedback on your performance so that you can do better next time?
12 Do you feel that your success or failure relies on others too much?
13 Do you tend to be a leader in certain situations?
14 Are you good at finding the right person or source of information to help you achieve what you want?
15 Do you have the ability to realise that in certain circumstances you may need help?
16 Do you set high standards for yourself?
17 Do you take risks rather than being cautious?
18 Are you healthy?
19 Do you have the ability to pass jobs on to others?
20 Are you able to identify which decisions are important and which are unimportant?
21 Do others think of you as a survivor?
22 Do you find coping with problems a real difficulty?
23 Do you respect other people's views and opinions?
24 When others express an opinion or offer advice or information, are you able to accept what they say?

If you have answered these questions mainly with ALWAYS or SOMETIMES then you are probably a good teamworker.

Teamwork, as we will see, is vitally important to businesses. You have probably already worked as a team member, either during this course or as part of a team at work. Think back to the last team you worked with and look at the following activity.

Build-up Exercise

Ideally you should complete this activity with at least one member of the team. The purpose of the activity is to try to reach agreement on the following questions. Remember that all teams work differently and that the answers you arrive at may not be the same as those for other teams.

1 What vision does your team share?
2 How do you communicate with each other?
3 How often do you communicate with each other?
4 What support do individuals in the team need to get their work done?
5 How do you manage conflict or disagreements?
6 How would you want team members to behave towards one another?
7 How are you going to make decisions?
8 How do you recognise and celebrate individual or team achievement?

Many of these ideas about teamworking are important to a business. The business, through a manager, supervisor or team leader, may try to control the way in which the team operates so as to enforce particular answers to the above questions. Above all, they will want the team to be capable of carrying out specific tasks and fulfilling a particular role in the business because the team has to be effective and efficient at what it does.

Functions of a team and roles of individual members

What do teams do? What is the purpose of a team? Why do many people prefer working in a team to working on their own? These are key questions to ask ourselves when considering the functions of a team. The simple answers are that teams can do a variety of tasks for a business, their purpose being to make sure that the tasks are carried out and, as far as individuals are concerned, it's about having close social relationships at work.

There have been many attempts to explain the exact nature or role of teams. Before we look at their main functions, here are some research findings about teams that show why businesses are so keen on developing them.

In studies:

- Teams increased productivity (getting things done) by up to 80 per cent.
- With teams the quality of work increased in about 70 per cent of cases.
- Over 50 per cent of teams reduced the amount of waste (in time and materials).
- Over 65 per cent of team members say that teams gave them more job satisfaction.
- Nearly 60 per cent of teams managed to improve customer satisfaction.

Many businesses have now reorganised themselves to take into account the fact that teams work and should be used. The following diagram shows how this can be organised:

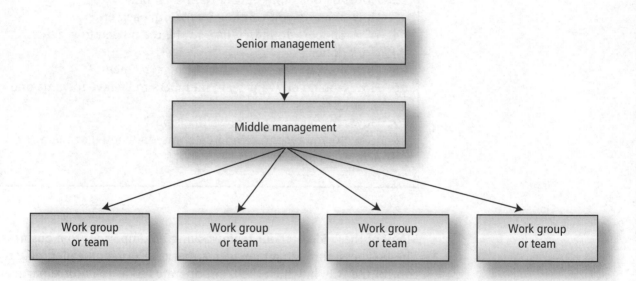

Figure 2.1 *Management structure for teamworking*

Team functions can be broken down into three main areas which take up the team's time and effort:

- **Tasks** – the time and effort which is put into the achievement of the team's objectives or goals. In effect this is the actual 'doing' of things.
- **Interaction** – this is the contact between the members of the team. To begin with the interaction will be all about setting out how things are to be done and sorting out conflict. Once the team is established, interaction between team members (talking to each other etc.) will revolve around asking for support and help when it is needed.
- **Self** – this is about putting time and effort into making sure that you, as an individual, are doing what you need to do to support the team. It is also about being noticed and satisfying your own needs relating to the work which you are carrying out.

Try it out

Which of the three approaches to the function of a team means more to you? See which of the following extremes relate more to the way you think about things:

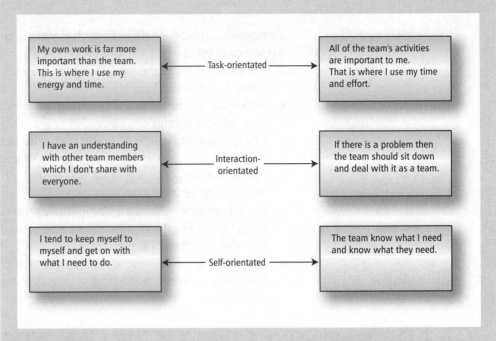

My own work is far more important than the team. This is where I use my energy and time. ←— Task-orientated —→ All of the team's activities are important to me. That is where I use my time and effort.

I have an understanding with other team members which I don't share with everyone. ←— Interaction-orientated —→ If there is a problem then the team should sit down and deal with it as a team.

I tend to keep myself to myself and get on with what I need to do. ←— Self-orientated —→ The team know what I need and know what they need.

Figure 2.2

How does your view of your ideas compare to the way you are viewed by other members of the group? Ask them if they think you are more task-orientated, interaction-orientated or self-orientated.

Individual roles within the group are important and there needs to be a good mix of different types of people, with skills and abilities which support one another. The following are some ideas about the kind of people that could be combined for teams to be efficient and effective.

Task-based (getting the job done) characteristics

- **Initiators** – these are people who set goals and suggest ways in which things can be done and ways of dealing with team problems.
- **Information or opinion givers** – these people provide the team with figures, ideas and suggestions.
- **Information seekers** – these are people who need facts and figures to get their work done.

- **Elaborators** – these people clear up confusion by giving examples and explanations.
- **Summarisers** – these people pull together various facts or ideas and keep the team informed about the progress of the task.
- **Agreement testers** – these people check that all of the team members agree with what and how tasks are being done.

Function-based (enabling the work to be done) characteristics

- **Encouragers** – these people accept others and are responsive and friendly towards them.
- **Expressers** – these people share their feelings with the team and help establish relationships.
- **Compromisers** – these people want the team to work and will give way on things if it helps the team to function.
- **Harmonisers** – these people try to deal with problems in the team and reduce tension.
- **Gate-keepers** – these are the people who encourage some of the team to get involved with a task and freeze out others that they do not want working on it.
- **Standard-setters** – these are people who try to set the minimum standards of work and try to get everyone in the team to stick to them.

Try it out

Look at the task-based and function-based roles outlined above. Which of the statements do you think refer to you? Are you more task-based or function-based in your approach? Think about the others in your team. Are they the same or do they have a different approach?

Important aspects of team working

Now that we have looked at team functions and roles, it is important to consider what a team does. This does not mean the team's task, rather how the members of the team organise themselves to do the task.

Target setting and planning

The classic way to approach target setting is to remember the word SMART. SMART is an acronym (a word made up of initials) and stands for:

- Specific
- Measurable
- Achievable
- Realistic
- Timely

All of the major goals or targets which are set for a team should be broken down into manageable pieces. It is easier for teams and individuals to achieve short-term goals (which are more under their own control) on the road to achieving the major goals. The steps along the way need to be put in order of priority (the most important first). Teams should also write down their goals, so there is no doubt about them. It is also useful to write down the ways in which you achieved those goals as the job proceeds. As each goal is achieved, it can be ticked off before moving onto the next one.

Build-up Exercise

What are the targets over the next month for this course? What are the important priorities? Which tasks and goals are team-based and which have to be tackled on an individual basis?

Planning is a crucial element in every job, but few people are trained in how to plan effectively. Most people can get by with their own personal planning to handle their own responsibilities, but planning as a part of a team can be quite difficult.

A good plan needs to be 'alive'; it needs to be flexible. A good plan can also take a lot of pressure off the team and the team leader. It offers them a 'map' for achieving objectives and targets.

Planning can involve deciding:

- what the objectives of the team are
- what the main objectives of the team are
- which of the team's goals need to be achieved to reach the objectives
- what strategies are needed to achieve the objectives (i.e. how to do it)
- who within the team will do what.

Team planning usually takes place during meetings arranged to decide what the team has to do and how it will be achieved. A meeting may proceed something like this:

- Team members evaluate where they are at the moment (look at their progress).
- The team considers any approaching deadlines by which particular goals must be achieved.
- They then decide how to prioritise the goals or deadlines.
- The team tries to reach an agreement on the above issues once everyone has had a chance to say what they feel.
- The team next allocates individual responsibilities to team members, arising out of the priorities and deadlines they have agreed.
- Finally, the team allocates resources to the team members to help them fulfil responsibilities that they have been given.

Build-up Exercise

We will be referring back to this activity at various points in the first part of this unit. To complete the activity, you will need to be in groups of four or five.

Your assignment is to submit a bid to the Pharaoh of Egypt, who wants you to build him one or more pyramids. You bid will take the form of a five-minute presentation.

Three or four of you will work as the team to produce the bid and another one of your group will act as an observer. The observer notes down how you have agreed certain things during the activity and tells you later which roles s/he thinks each of the team members adopted.

You will need the following items for the activity:

- paper
- card for building your model of the pyramid or pyramids
- scissors, glue, rulers, pens, flip chart and a calculator.

Your team task:
Your team is a business which builds pyramids. You have been approached by the Pharaoh. He is likely to live another 10 years. The Pharaoh wants you to build him an impressive monument. He is not sure whether he wants one big pyramid or two smaller ones. It is your decision as to what to build. He is also not sure where he wants the pyramid(s) to be built. Again, he wants you to give him your recommendations.

The Pharaoh has put aside 10.5 million gold pieces. If you spend more than that he will have you executed.

He also wants to see the completed pyramid(s), so you have 10 years to build. If you do not have the pyramid(s) finished within the 10 years, he will die and leave instructions that you are to join him in the pyramid(s) once they are completed.

For the presentation you will need to use a scale model, or models, and flip-chart paper. Use the flip-chart paper to show your calculations and other information you feel is important. Your presentation needs to include:

- the proposed site
- the size of the pyramid or pyramids
- the time it will take to complete the project
- the total cost
- scale model or models
- a sales slogan promoting your organisation.

The following information has been provided to help you work out your bid:

1   The employees are slaves. They work seven days a week. They do not get paid, but it costs half a gold piece each day to feed each one of them. If you do not feed them they will die.

2   You have a total of 1000 slaves available to you.

3   It takes 20 slaves to move one block of stone.

4   There are four different sized pyramids available to make:
Size one (small)   needs 80,000 blocks of stone
Size two (medium)   needs 120,000 blocks of stone
Size three (large)   needs 170,000 blocks of stone
Size four (massive) needs 240,000 blocks of stone

5   The cost of the blocks of stone are:
from the Odan quarry   50 gold pieces each
from the Mepash quarry   30 gold pieces each

6   Transportation and erection takes the following times:
Mepash quarry to site A   =   3 days
Odan quarry to site A   =   1 day
Mepash quarry to site B   =   2 days
Odan quarry to site B   =   4 days

Further instructions:
You should allow one hour to make all of the necessary calculations and prepare your bid. Your presentation should last no longer than five minutes.

Clarifying objectives

Clear objectives are vitally important to any team activity as they help to determine:

- why the task is being done
- for whom the task is being done
- what will be the outcome of the task
- when the task has to be done.

Clarifying means making clear or dealing with any confusions that might arise about the objectives. The clearer the objectives, the better chance the team will have of achieving them.

The clarification of objectives can come from those who have set the objectives in the first place. This means that the senior manager, middle manager or team leader who has set the objectives explains clearly what the objectives are. Based on this, the team will then set in motion all of the steps needed to fulfil the objectives.

More often than not, however, the original objectives are not clear and this means the team has to ask for clarification. This may happen because the objectives are rather vague, or perhaps contradictory. Figure 2.3 may help to show you where clarifying objectives fits into the overall scheme of work.

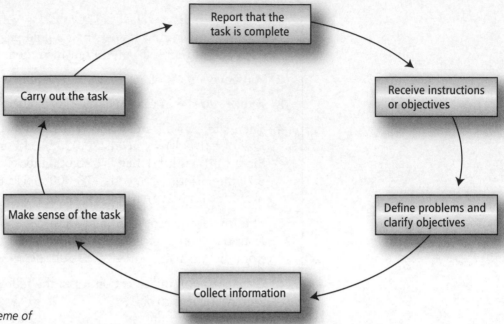

Figure 2.3 *The usual scheme of work*

Clarifying objectives, therefore, involves knowing (or at least deciding) what it is you need to know about the objectives. After all, it would be foolish to assume that you understand them, or pretend you understand them, when you do not, and then go on to carry out a task only to find that this was not what was required.

Generally speaking, objectives should be measurable and concrete. A clear, reasonable and concrete objective may be:

All staff will have an e-mail account by the end of the month.

Compare this to the less concrete and measurable:

Members of staff will be encouraged to open an e-mail account in the near future.

The second objective is by no means clear, and it would be difficult to assess whether it had been achieved.

Try it out

Look at the assessment objectives of this unit, such as 'Contribute to the work of a team'. That is not a very clear, concrete or measurable objective. The additional information under the 'knowledge, understanding and skills' column of the unit does clarify the objectives.

Choose three of the assessment objectives and, without writing out the whole of the knowledge, understanding and skills column to explain it, make the objectives more clear.

Compare your ideas to the attempts made by others in your group.

Identifying resources and timescales

Resources and timescales often mean the difference between success or failure of a team activity. Too few resources or an unreasonable timescale can put enormous pressure on the team without them really having what they need to do the job or the time to do it in.

Resources include:

- **Equipment** – such as computers, photocopiers, telephones, etc.
- **Facilities** – such as space, an office, desks, etc.
- **Finance** – money basically, to spend either on resources needed or wages to pay the team overtime if necessary.
- **Materials** – actually known as consumables, which means things you use up in carrying out a task, such as paper, pens, envelopes, stamps, etc.
- **People** – the team members, their skills, abilities and expertise.

As far as timescales are concerned, it is useful to think about three different sets of timescales which could apply to a task or an objective:

- **Short term** – this really means that the activity has to be done immediately or certainly over the next few days.
- **Medium term** – possibly a couple of weeks or perhaps months, but certainly not immediately or some vague time in the future.
- **Long term** – probably reserved for really major objectives, perhaps as long as a year, but certainly several months.

Working with resources and to a timescale involves a degree of planning and forward-thinking. The more complicated an objective, the more resources might be needed and the longer the timescale might be. It is always valuable to think about complicated tasks or objectives as a series of mini-tasks or mini-objectives; break down the major job into manageable chunks. You need to know what has to be done first before you can get on with the next phase of the work.

In business, breaking down large tasks and objectives (sometimes known as projects) is known as setting up 'milestones' (see Figure 2.4). It suggests you identify key things which have to be completed on your

Figure 2.4 *A team project planning table*

	Collect data	Questionnaires	Telephone interviews	Final report
March				
April		Design		
May		Send out		
June				
July		Receive back		
August		Analysis		
September				
October				
November			Analysis	
December				

route to achieving the main objective. It also means that you can predict when you will need particular resources and when you will reach each of the milestones as a team.

Using this kind of table, the team members would be able to work out when they will need certain resources and when the most work would have to be done.

Build-up Exercise

Look at the milestone diagram in Figure 2.4 and answer the following questions:

1 When would the team need to have a stock of envelopes and stamps ready?
2 When would the team need to be using the telephones for the interviews?
3 What months could be used to analyse the information they have collected?
4 What is the overall length of the task?
5 When must the final report be ready?

Exchanging information

The exchange, or swapping, of information between team members is absolutely vital if tasks, series of tasks or major objectives are to be achieved. Continual communication between the team members means that everyone is kept up to date with the progress of the project and that any problems which occur can be dealt with by the team as a whole. It also means that information collected by one of the team members is available to all of the others; they may need these facts or figures to carry out their part of the task.

Exchanging information can happen during regular meetings, or information can be passed on when it becomes available. However, there needs to be a foolproof way of making sure that information collected or received by one member of the team is not simply missed, or overlooked or not exchanged with the others. If this happens, the whole idea of working as a team begins to break down.

The process of exchanging information can either be formal or informal, as we can see in Table 2.1.

Table 2.1 *Methods of information exchange*

Formal	Informal
Meetings	Conversations
Reports	E-mail messages
Memoranda	Business notes
Circulated documents (with sign-off sheets to show they have been seen)	
Presentations	
Updates or newsletters to all team members	

Build-up Exercise

Think about the following situations when information would need to be exchanged amongst team members. Which method of information exchange would be the most effective?

1 The deadline has been brought forward by two days to complete the task.
2 New figures are available in one week's time.
3 A key team member will be off sick for at least a week.
4 A team member has just received a message for another member to make a telephone call.
5 Some members of the team have finished their part of the task and want the others to see what they have done and discuss it.

Co-operating with others

Teamwork relies on co-operation, as each of the team relies on the others to do their work. Co-operation means being helpful, available and open to suggestions. Here are some guidelines for co-operative working:

- Team members should be more concerned about the needs of the rest of the team than themselves.
- Team members should try to work in a friendly and sociable atmosphere.
- The team should try to avoid conflict (arguments).
- Team members should avoid competing with one another.
- Team members should feel that they are part of a close-knit group.
- Team members need to follow the rules of the group.
- Team members need to trust one another from the start.
- Each of the members' points of view should be respected.
- Members' own expectations of the others should be fulfilled by the group (if possible).

Team members must remember that to achieve tasks, they need one another. This means that the team has what are known as 'mutual goals'. They all should be striving to achieve the same thing, which can only be achieved if they all work together at all times. In addition to this, the team has to share resources and fulfil any role which has been given to them.

Team members can help one another by:

- helping
- sharing
- encouraging
- explaining
- discussing
- teaching.

Build-up Exercise

Think back to the pyramid activity. Write down in your own words, using the headings from the list above, whether the members of the group co-operated in any of these ways. Give examples of the types of co-operation they gave.

Compare your ideas and observations of co-operation with the notes made by the observer in the group. How do they differ? Did the observer spot things you did not notice?

Confirm own responsibilities including working arrangements

Each team member should make sure they know precisely what is expected of them. It is not always clear exactly what ecah person's role or responsibility may be in a team, or what their tasks are and how they relate to the work as a whole. Basic questions to ask are:

- What is my role in the team?
- What am I expected to do?
- When do I need to do this?
- How long do I have to do this?
- To whom do I report?
- Where can I receive help?
- What do I do if I get stuck or do not understand?

Some tasks and responsibilities may be obvious and not require a person to confirm their responsibilities with anyone. But many job roles within a team become confused and such roles will change over a period of time.

The term 'working arrangements' may mean a variety of different things, including:

- start and finish times of the day
- days of the week to be worked
- times of breaks, including lunch
- who is in charge if the team leader, or manager, is not available
- when the work is to be reviewed and progress monitored
- who has the right to instruct the team
- where the team operates (does it have its own area or office?)
- how the team goes about getting additional resources when it needs them.

Build-up Exercise

Allocating time off for members of a team which needs to cover the work at all times can be difficult. Here is a typical problem:

It is the beginning of the summer and three members of the team have already booked off time over June, July and August. Three more want time off, but you need to have a minimum of five people available to cover the work at all times:

Table 2.2 *Summer holiday timetable for the team*

June	Week 1	Justine Off
	Week 2	Justine Off
	Week 3	Pete Off
	Week 4	Pete Off
July	Week 1	Sylvia Off
	Week 2	Sylvia Off
	Week 3	Sylvia Off
	Week 4	Sylvia Off
August	Week 1	
	Week 2	
	Week 3	
	Week 4	

Liz wants to book three weeks, hopefully in July, but part of August would be OK. Seamus wants a week off in June, one in July and two in August. Tariq wants three weeks in August. You also have yourself (you do not want to take a holiday until September) and Mike, who has already taken all of his holiday.

Work out a rota for the summer break, making sure you have no less than five staff available. It may not be possible! If this is the case say what you will do to overcome the problem.

Confirming action and resources required

One of the many ways in which you can confirm what is required of you is to ask other people for information. Asking reasonable questions about what you are expected to do is acceptable. Sometimes you may need to ask a person who is very busy, but it is better to ask them than to carry on with something you might be doing wrong.

It is always sensible to ask for help and advice, as well as making sure you are on the right track. Experienced colleagues may be able to help you, as they may have faced exactly the same problems in the past.

A more formal but clearer way of confirming actions and assessing what you need to do is to design your own task log sheet. Figure 2.5 shows an example of what one could look like, but you may be able to redesign one to suit your own particular needs:

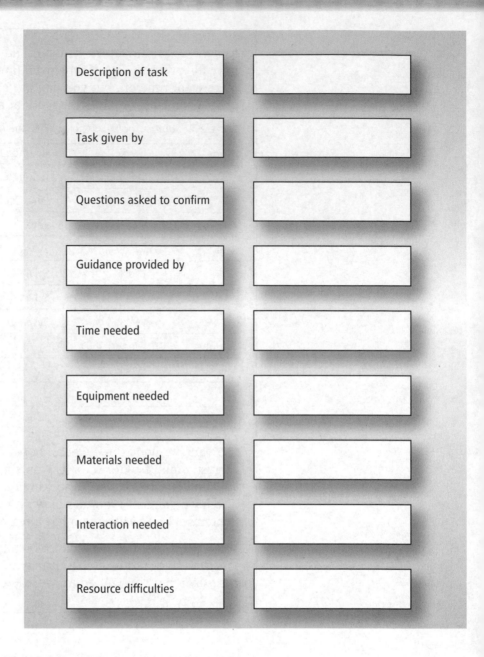

Figure 2.5 *Example of a task log sheet*

You may also wish to include a box at the end of your form in which you note down how you felt the task went.

Try it out

Using your form, investigate the following:

You need to provide a map of the immediate area in which you work, with all desks, doors, equipment, windows and other fixtures. Indicate on your map of the area where the emergency exits are in case of a fire.

Timescales

Timescales refer to both the amount of time that you have been given to complete a task and the deadline by which it must be finished.

This means that any task needs to be prioritised in terms of its importance. Broadly speaking, tasks can be divided up into the following categories as far as priorities are concerned:

- urgent and important tasks
- urgent, but not important tasks
- important, but not urgent tasks
- not urgent, nor important tasks.

It is natural to concentrate on the first two because they are urgent and to put the other two aside. The problem is that non-urgent tasks then sometimes get forgotten.

Try it out

Using the four priority categories in the above list, try to categorise your immediate workload either at college or at work.

Where do most of the tasks or jobs you have to do fall? If there are many tasks in the higher priority categories, how do you prioritise them?

Let us look at timescales and priorities in a little more detail. Within a typical office job:

- First, you will have a series of fairly routine tasks to complete (these include filing, answering the telephone and photocopying, for example).
- Secondly, you will have large tasks to complete (such as checking and ordering the stationery or keeping a track of the petty cash).
- Thirdly, you may have tasks which do not occur that often (such as preparing for the end-of-year accounts, clearing out the stock cupboard or sending out a mail-shot to customers).
- Fourthly, you will have a series of small tasks which tend to crop up when you least expect them (such as carrying out a job for a more senior member of staff or dealing with something because someone else is not available).

Broadly speaking, all of these tasks can still be considered to be either:

- important or not important, or
- urgent or non-urgent.

At the end of the day, only you can decide whether a job is important and urgent enough to drop everything else and get on with it. You probably need to think about the following questions before making your mind up:

- What will happen if you don't manage to meet the deadlines you have been set?

- Who actually gave you the work? How senior are they in the organisation?
- How long would the job really take if you did concentrate on it (assuming that you can)?
- Can the deadline be altered?

Try it out

Have another look at the list of tasks which you prioritised in the last activity. Which of the tasks could be set aside for now? Which of the tasks could have their deadlines renegotiated? Have you prioritised your tasks because some of them have been demanded by senior or important people?

Procedures if work falls behind deadlines or unexpected problems are encountered

A deadline is the latest date by which a particular task must be achieved. Some people actually respond well to a series of deadlines as they are challenged by the prospect of having to complete jobs by a particular date.

At the earliest stage possible, it is important that you begin to take account of deadlines and work towards the completion of tasks by the required time. This becomes all the more difficult if you have to rely on others in the team to contribute towards completion of the task.

What happens when it becomes obvious that the deadline is not going to be met, for whatever reason? Rarely when working for a business will you enjoy the opportunity to work on one task, finish it and then start another. Work is never quite that simple. Therefore, as we have seen, prioritising jobs is the only real way forward.

Each deadline and task needs to be looked at separately. The best policy, however, when it becomes obvious to you and the team that a deadline will not be met, is to inform your team leader or the individual who has set you the task as soon as possible. There may well be room for renegotiation of the deadline (pushing the deadline back) or for work that is not a priority to be put aside so that you can concentrate on the most urgent task.

Unexpected problems which could lead to a deadline becoming difficult or impossible to meet include the following:

- staff shortages (either not enough staff or staff off on sick or holiday leave)
- other work piling up which has the same degree of priority
- difficulty in collecting information to do the task
- difficulty in contacting individuals who you need to communicate with to complete the task.

In many cases, difficult deadlines and unexpected problems arise out of not having thought about the task and its implications in enough detail at the very beginning. We will be looking at planning in the next assessment objective.

Try it out

Managing your day and the work load is a difficult task in itself. You will always have several people and several tasks making demands on your time. Here is a typical day's work, with the times (deadlines) needed for each of the tasks. Order the work so that you can attempt to get all of the tasks completed as close to the deadlines as possible.

1 You work flexi-time, so you could start at 08.00 or 09.00 and finish at either 16.00 or 17.00.
2 Call Mr Peters by 10.00 (duration 10 minutes).
3 Call Mrs Jones (duration 10 minutes).
4 Photocopy 100 copies of the sales price list by 12.00 (duration 45 minutes, needs collating).
5 Type up minutes of yesterday's meeting (45 minutes).
6 Distribute copies of yesterday's meeting (20 copies) (duration 30 minutes) by 12.00.
7 Attend sales meeting at 14.00 (duration 1 hour).
8 Check and re-order stationery (30 minutes) – order needs to be with the supplier by 16.00 to ensure next day delivery (call duration 10 minutes).
9 Call Ms Smith at 15.30 (duration 10 minutes).

Need to identify colleagues and resources required

With all teamwork, the idea is to use the skills and abilities of those you work with. Some of your colleagues will be more experienced at doing certain things and will have access to information you need. Teamwork, as we have seen, needs co-operation. This means that you should turn to those who have more experience or knowledge and are, perhaps, specialists in certain areas of work.

Correctly identifying who can help you when you need it requires experience and getting to know the strengths and weaknesses of those with whom you work.

Build-up Exercise

Take a typical team, with a variety of skills, and you will find that some of the team members are good at particular things and not so good at others. You will face situations in which you will need help. Look at the list of people and their skills and then match them to the various tasks outlined.

Team member Skills
Lucy   Excellent communications, good with customers.
Tansy   Thorough; knows about all the business's policies and procedures.

▶▶

Colin	A bit disorganised, but great for ideas.
Simon	Reliable, doesn't mind boring work.
Anne	Great at English; always knows how to say things.

Tasks

1 You need to check back on old invoices for the past two years and find all invoices for customers in Northern England.
2 You need to write a letter to a customer who has complained about poor delivery. The customer is an important one and you need to be tactful.
3 You have been asked to complete some forms for the accounts department and you are not sure what to do with them.
4 You have been asked to suggest ideas for a new business logo to be painted on the delivery van.
5 A Mrs Patel has called several times. She has called from France and wants to know how to set up an account with your business. Her English is not that good and the line is very poor. She needs to be called back.

Resources which are needed for particular tasks are often directly to hand, such as telephones, photocopiers, computers and information in the form of records (letters, invoices, etc.).

One of the best ways of identifying the resources you would need to do a task is to think about a similar task you have done in the past and use that as an indication of what you might need this time. If you have not had experience of something similar, there is always another person who has and who may therefore be able to guide you.

Build-up Exercise

Look at the following tasks and assess the resources you would need to carry them out. You could use the task log sheet you designed earlier to do this.

1 Hamish Macmillan, the sales manager, has asked for copies of the past four price lists. Only one copy of the old price lists exists in the records. Each of the price lists is six pages long. He needs this by 14.00 today to prepare for a meeting in the morning.
2 You have been asked by Guiseppe Rava, your team leader, to design a short questionnaire about customer service and to call, at random, 50 customers and ask them the questions. You are then to compile the results and offer recommendations arising out of the information.

> **3** The estates manager, Frances Bodley-Smith, has asked you to assist her in designing a form which can be used to identify all of the fixtures and fittings (including equipment etc.) in the offices.

Need to identify limits of own role

On the face of it, you would expect to know what is and what is not your duty or role from your job description. Experience will show you, however, that the job description is just a guide, nothing more, as to what might be involved in your work. You do need to be prepared to carry out reasonable requests to do work that you might not normally expect to be part of your job. The tricky part comes in knowing when to make your own decisions about what you do, and when to refer a decision to a senior member of staff to find out what is acceptable.

Generally, if you think that a particular decision is too big to be made on your own, or should really involve a more senior member of staff (such as your team leader or manager), you should stop and seek advice. Taking on work that is not really your responsibility is one thing, but making decisions you should not make is quite another. You may not know the proper procedures for dealing with tasks you do not normally handle.

It is always useful to have an idea about what you and your team are expected to do. The following list may help you:

- What areas of work is each person responsible for?
- What are the current tasks to do and who is involved?
- Who does the team deal with on a regular basis, both inside and outside the business?
- Who is expecting to receive a call or a visit in your team?
- If they are not available, when will they be back?
- If they are not available, but something urgent may need to be dealt with, what action should be taken?

This list is fine to begin with, but what happens when you are expected to take on new duties and responsibilities? You should at least consider these points:

- Which aspects of your job involve you being asked to take on more responsibility?
- What will the new responsibilities mean in real terms?
- Are you any good at these aspects of your job?
- Will you need any additional skills or training?
- How long do you have to gain these skills?
- Will you be receiving help and assistance, at least at first?
- Who will support you, initially, to gain the skills and experience?

> ### Build-up Exercise
>
> Sarah has been working as a receptionist at a busy insurance company for the past three years. She is quite bored and has asked for extra responsibilities to keep her busy during the quieter periods, particularly in the afternoons.
>
> Her supervisor, the team leader of customer services, Mrs Dixon, is pleased with Sarah's attitude and wants her to deal with the incoming and outgoing mail.
>
> Briefly outline the kinds of skills and training Sarah might need to be able to deal with this new area of work.

Carry out tasks allocated

Once you have been assigned a task, or a series of tasks and, hopefully, understood what is required of you, the next job is to actually get started. There are many different ways in which you can do this, but it is always the best policy to give yourself a few minutes to think about what needs to be done before you pitch into the task. In this part of the unit, we will be looking at the realities of getting work done.

Planning and prioritising

Generally speaking, planning will help you to work efficiently and effectively. This means that you will need to deal carefully with all of the aspects of your job and the tasks which have been given to you. Getting a task completed begins with planning, so it is appropriate to begin there. (See Table 2.3.)

Table 2.3 *Elements of the planning and prioritising stage*

Planning and prioritising stage	Description
Get the facts about the task	What do you need to do, when does it need to be done, how does it have to be done, who do you need to contact (or refer to) and who can help you do it?
Clarify what has to be done	Ask questions now before you get on with the task. If you need help or assistance in deciding what has to be done, ask now.
Is the task part of your normal job?	It may not be clear to you whether the task fits what you are normally supposed to do. If you are not trained to do the task, you could say this, but you do need to be flexible at times.
Identify the resources you will need	Resources fall into three categories: ■ equipment ■ materials ■ information. Identify what you need and whether it is available.
Prioritise	Routine tasks may have to be set aside if the task is important or urgent.
Be flexible	Priorities can change. What is important or urgent to some is not to others. You may also experience changes in the deadlines. Be prepared to re-plan or to scrap what you have already started!

Build-up Exercise

Here are your day's tasks. Each person needs an answer today. The tasks are detailed in Table 2.4 as well as the initial information you have collected. What would you do next in each of the following situations?

Table 2.4

Task	First information collected
Your team leader has asked you to make 10 photocopies of the minutes of the last meeting for the next meeting which starts in 10 minutes.	The photocopier is broken down and will be out of action for an hour.
You need to fax over a copy of an invoice to the accounts department.	Their fax machine is turned off.
A manager has asked you to book a table at a particular restaurant for tomorrow night to entertain an important customer.	The restaurant is fully booked.
One of the team's laptop computers was dropped on the floor yesterday afternoon and will not work. You need to arrange to have it repaired.	The supplier has asked you if it is under warranty or insured.
A manager has asked you to insert diagrams from a document on a disk he has given you into a new version of the document.	The disk has a virus.

Following instructions and agreed working practices

As long as a task's instructions are clear at the beginning, or at least you can obtain confirmation about how to carry out the task, then following instructions should be fairly straightforward. Once you have been given clear instructions, the responsibility is yours to follow them through and complete the task to the best of your ability.

The larger the business, the more likely there is to be set procedures, or working practices, related to your work. As we will see, health and safety and accident reporting may be just part of a whole set of working practices.

Other working practices, or organisational procedures as they are sometimes known, could be in place to govern:

- procedures for dealing with visitors to the business
- allocation of car parking spaces

- how photocopying, for both small and large amounts, is managed
- where information is stored and how it is filed
- forms which require completion to order items via the purchasing department.

Build-up Exercise

If you are in work, ask your employer for the following information, otherwise use the college at which you are studying this course as your example.

1 What are the procedures for dealing with official visitors?
2 What paperwork has to be completed to order a box of photocopy paper and a set of highlighter pens?
3 Are there parking permits? If so, where are these obtained? What forms are necessary?

Working safely

In any situation, place of work or role at work, there are safe and unsafe ways of doing things. Table 2.5 shows some examples of what could be considered safe working practices and others which are definitely unsafe.

Table 2.5 *Safe and unsafe working practices*

Safe working	Unsafe working
• Complying with instructions	• Not switching off equipment at the end of the day
• Walking, rather than running	
• Lifting heavy objects which you can manage	• Not using the correct equipment for a job
• Making sure that when you are carrying things you can see where you are going	• Not reading the instructions
	• Balancing a drink near to electrical equipment
• Closing desk drawers and filing cabinets when you have finished with them	• Using equipment you know to be faulty
	• Using equipment you have not been trained to use
• Tidying up your desk or work area and putting away your personal things	• Being messy and leaving rubbish lying around the place
• Putting rubbish away in the correct containers	• Not using protective clothing when required to do so
• Stacking items but not so high as to cause toppling	• Not taking a break when you are clearly tired
• Only using the right equipment for the job	• Ignoring instructions
• Doing what you have been trained to do and asking for help when you need it	

Try it out

Think of five other safe working practices and five unsafe working practices from your own experience of work.

Respecting confidentiality and security issues

You may be asked to deal with information as part of a task which involves you having to respect confidentiality. Information may not only be confidential, but it may also be sensitive and therefore security needs to be paramount. It is not acceptable to leave confidential or secure information lying around your desk. Neither may it be appropriate for you to ask others their opinion of it, or what to do with it. Here are some examples of confidential information:

- personal details about other employees (their addresses, bank account details and telephone numbers)
- appraisal information or confidential notes, letters or memos about employees
- payroll details (salaries and pay scales)
- business information (such as product details, suppliers, costs and prices)
- plans (ideas and plans to be undertaken by the business in the future).

You will not always find that confidential or sensitive information is labelled as such and you should use your own judgement before letting anyone else see it. The following list suggests some basic steps to take:

- Be careful about photocopying; you might leave a copy in the copier or someone could be looking over your shoulder.
- Make sure you lock the documents away and do not leave them lying unattended on your desk.
- Make sure you seal envelopes if the documents have to be sent to other people.
- Make sure you use the shredder to destroy unwanted documents or copies.
- Check with your team leader or supervisor to make sure whether particular documents are confidential.
- If you have a confidential document on your computer, switch off the screen or close the document before leaving the computer.

Try it out

Think of some examples of confidential information you may have access to. What might be the implications if the documents were seen by the wrong people?

Meeting deadlines

As we have seen, meeting deadlines can often be difficult, particularly if there are a number of priority tasks to be completed. Everyone will want specific tasks completed as soon as possible, but you will always have to remember the routine work that still needs to be done.

Build-up Exercise

Meeting deadlines is all about prioritising your work. Categorise the following tasks into the categories:

> Urgent and important
> Important and not urgent
> Not urgent and not important.

Here are your tasks:

1 yesterday's filing of invoices
2 answering a customer who has called twice and left messages
3 preparing information for this afternoon's meeting
4 photocopying the business newsletter for distribution the day after tomorrow
5 stock-checking the first-aid box
6 writing a memorandum to the human resource department to complain about the mould on the carpet near the window
7 sorting out the printer, as it keeps jamming.

Using initiative to identify and solve problems

There will be occasions when there is no one to ask for assistance or guidance and it will be left to you to decide whether to carry on with a task or to wait.

Unfortunately, putting off doing work just because you cannot gain help is not always an option. Therefore you need to make a judgement as to whether you can proceed with the work or not. You must use what is known as your own initiative (or judgement) in these situations – there may well be an answer to your probem without having to ask someone.

In most jobs you will be expected to show your initiative and not ask for assistance every time there is a problem which you cannot immediately solve yourself. As you become more experienced you will be able to make these judgements more quickly and easily and more often than not be able to solve problems without having to ask for help.

Build-up Exercise

Which of the following situations would you need to work through yourself, using your own initiative, and which should you postpone until you have help? Give reasons why in each case.

1 The photocopier is jammed. You open it up and see the paper trapped and torn inside.
2 The stapler will not work; it keeps jamming inside.
3 A customer wants a price on a product now. No one else is around and you will need 10 minutes to look up the price.
4 There are three wasps in the office and they keep coming near you.
5 You left a £5 note on the top of your computer and now it is gone.

Work with others to complete tasks

As we have seen, working with others, either on a one-off basis or as part of an established team, is commonplace in many organisations and you should now know how such teams actually work. In this part of the unit we will be carrying out a practice exercise to look at the steps involved in working with others.

Build-up Exercise

In groups of at least three, complete the following task:

If you are at college: On three different days count the number of people entering or leaving through one of the entrances. You must identify and total the following:

1 males and females
2 students, staff and visitors
3 whether the students are full- or part-time
4 the number of bags or cases in and out of the entrance.

You must count the traffic in and out of the entrance over three separate periods of half an hour.

Required information:

1 Report the team's progress in choosing appropriate times for counting purposes.
2 Report the completion of an appropriate questionnaire or tally form, which you will use to keep a log of numbers.
3 At the end of each of the half-hour periods, report on the number of individuals counted.

4 Co-operate and allocate team members' time according to the amount of work involved in each half-hour period.

5 Note any difficulties encountered during each half-hour period.

If you are at work: Identify and report a suitable team activity you are undertaking at work. Your tutor or assessor will advise on its suitability.

1 Where appropriate, you must report on progress to your tutor in the form of brief memoranda at agreed intervals throughout the duration of the task.

2 Note the information you have been asked to collect as part of the task and include in a memorandum how you have passed that information on to those who required it.

3 Also note in your memoranda any help received or given during the task.

4 Identify in a memorandum any difficulties you encountered during the task and how these were dealt with at the time.

You should provide your tutor or assessor with at least three updated memos during the course of the task.

Communicate effectively with others

Effective communication in business is absolutely essential, particularly as part of the normal activities of a team. Even organisations which are not concerned with profit-making activities need to respond effectively to all the pressures they find themselves under. This can place enormous strains on the staff. They have to work fast, accurately and try to make the right decisions at all times. At the heart of this is effective communication.

Day after day information will flow in and out of the business. This needs to be checked, read, understood and, above all, those who need the information have to be told about it. Communications can take the form of:

- telephone calls
- e-mail messages
- business letters
- faxes
- reports
- sales documents (invoices etc.)

Businesses are likely to have routine contact with the government, their bank, insurance companies, customers, suppliers, shareholders and a host of other groups and individuals.

For the business to make the right decisions or take the right courses of action, information needs to be communicated as quickly as possible, and accurately too. No matter what your role in the business, effective communication extends to your role.

Communication can be be made effective by:

- ensuring the information is accurate
- making sure that your communication has been understood
- preparing or presenting information in such a way that the receiver understands it
- choosing the most appropriate form of communication (e-mail, fax, letter, etc.)
- making sure that the information reaches the right person when they need it.

Build-up Exercise

In many cases, communication is ineffective. Here are some examples of ineffective communication. In each case you should:

- identify what has gone wrong
- suggest what could happen as a result
- suggest what could be done to deal with the situation
- suggest how you would have dealt with the situation.

1 You arrive back at your desk after lunch to find a scribbled note which says 'Call Mr Smith urgently'. You do not recognise the handwriting and there are nine Mr Smiths on the customer database.

2 Last night you were asked to send a fax to a customer, but with other work to do you forgot about it. You have faxed it this morning, but have just received a call to say that the fax has arrived too late to stop the delivery of an unwanted order.

3 Two days ago you called a hotel in Blackpool to book a room. The hotel confirmed the booking on the telephone. Today, after the sales representative has already left for Blackpool, the hotel has faxed you with a confirmation of the booking, but the date of the booked room is for tomorrow night, not tonight as required by the sales representative.

4 Last week you were asked to re-order some stationery. Instead of using the supplier's catalogue, you used the code numbers on the side of the stationery boxes. The order has arrived today and they have sent you the wrong stationery.

5 An hour ago a customer called, gave you his telephone number and asked you to call back with some information. He is a new customer. The telephone line was poor and you wrote down the wrong number.

Verbal and written communication

Before we look at the specific types of verbal and written communication, let us consider the general advantages and disadvantages of these two forms of communication; see Tables 2.6 and 2.7.

Table 2.6 *Advantages and disadvantages of verbal communication*

Advantages	Disadvantages
• Communication is quick. • Communication is cheap. • You can use your voice to emphasise points. • You can receive immediate feedback from the receiver of the communication. • You can confirm straightaway that the receiver has understood what you have told them. • In some cases you can use your body language and facial expressions to help explain things.	• You need to speak clearly. • You need to be clear about what you are saying. • It is not ideal for communicating long or complicated iteams of information. • Other things going on at the same time may distract the receiver of the information (e.g. a noisy office). • If there is disagreement or anger, then this can be difficult to handle. • You do not have a written record of what has been said.

Table 2.7 *Advantages and disadvantages of written communication*

Advantages	Disadvantages
• Written communication is more formal than verbal. • A record of the communication is created (which can be kept and filed). • The communication can be re-read and referred to later. • The communication can be copied for others to read. • It is ideal for communications that might invoke anger as there is a distance between the sender and the receiver. • Written communication can use photos, diagrams and instructions to support it.	• Can take a long time to produce the communication • Needs to be accurate and error free • Must not have spelling mistakes and look untidy because this gives a bad impression of the business • Needs to legible (the receiver must be able to read what the sender has written) • Consumes resources (paper, computer time, etc.)

Face-to-face communication is the most important way in which we all communicate every day. In any organisation there are many different kinds of face-to-face communication, including:

- conversations which take place in the office or at a person's desk
- brief chats in the corridors or at lunch breaks in the canteen
- informal meetings, when one or two members of staff meet to talk about something
- formal meetings, when a group of employees are called together to make decisions or sort out problems.
- speaking with customers or suppliers in person, say at a reception desk

- discussions in which a customer or supplier asks an employee for some advice, guidance or information.

There are a number of important things to consider when having a face-to-face conversation, or when you are talking on the telephone (another method of verbal communication). Bear in mind:

- the way you speak, for example whether or not you are making yourself clear, or whether you are using slang during your conversation
- the pitch and tone of your voice
- how carefully you are listening and pay attention to what is being said
- when not to speak or interrupt
- what questions to ask
- your body language – are you putting across the right messages? Body language is very important in face-to-face communication, unlike on the telephone where the two people having the conversation cannot see one another.

When talking face-to-face a mixture of verbal (spoken) and non-verbal (body language) is used. For effective verbal communication, you need to:

- read other people's body language
- be aware that your body language can be read by the other person.

Build-up Exercise

How good are you at reading body language? Sit opposite a friend and see if you can express different feelings just by the expression on your face. Try showing each other the following expressions, but don't use any words:

anger	happiness
annoyance	polite smiling
shock	disapproval
boredom	fear
irritation	

Let us look at body language in a little more detail.

Facial expressions

These are the most common form of body language and we should always be aware of what our face is telling someone else. For example:

- A smile can make a big difference when you meet someone.
- Our eyes widen when we are surprised and narrow when angry.
- Our eyebrows move upwards when we don't believe something and lower when we are angry or confused about something.
- We can look bored if our mouth is pouting.

Gestures

We use our head and hands a lot when we agree or disagree with something. We can use various gestures.

- We agree with someone by nodding our heads.
- We disagree with someone by shaking our heads from side to side.
- We wave our hands to greet someone from a distance.
- By pointing with our finger we give someone directions.
- The 'thumbs up' sign lets someone know everything is OK.

Posture (the way we sit or stand)

Posture can also tell us a lot about what we are thinking or how we are reacting to someone else.

- Sitting well back in a chair with ankles crossed gives the impression of being relaxed or confident.
- Sitting on the edge of a seat gives the impression of being nervous.
- Standing straight with head high gives the impression of confidence.
- Standing slumped with shoulders down gives the impression of being depressed or lacking confidence.

How close one gets to other people

Apart from shaking hands, we do not often get close to people we meet at work. Most people have an 'invisible circle' around them that they prefer others not to enter. This means that they may feel uncomfortable if others get too close to them. Getting too close to someone else's face can be a sign of aggression.

Whether one is sitting or standing is also important. Someone who is seated and having a conversation with a person who is standing up can often feel 'lower' in importance.

Eye contact

Eye contact should always be made with the person one is talking to. Eye contact shows the other person that you are giving them your full attention and often helps them to understand what is being said. Sometimes it is possible to get a better idea of how someone is going to react by looking into their eyes. Be careful though not to stare into someone's eyes as this can be a sign of aggression.

When using face-to-face communication it is important to:

- be polite
- be helpful
- make the other person feel valued – try to use the person's name during the conversation so they feel valued
- try not to be distracting by losing eye contact and looking elsewhere, or by fiddling with your clothes or pulling at your hair
- let the other person finish the conversation, especially if they are a customer.
- always leave with a smile and say 'goodbye'.

Telephone calls are different from face-to-face communication because you cannot use body language to help reinforce what you are saying. You can express your attitude, but only through your voice. This means that the way you speak and phrase things gives the other person an impression of how you are feeling.

Voices always sound different on the telephone. People answering the telephone on behalf of the organisation should have a good telephone technique, which includes the following:

- Answer the telephone as quickly as possible; don't let it ring for ages before picking it up. If the person who normally answers is busy, someone else should answer the call and assist the caller..
- Answer with 'Good Morning' or 'Good Afternoon'. This is not just to be polite, but to give the caller the opportunity to realise that the phone call has started.
- Give the name of the person answering the call, or the name of the organisation or department in which they work. This tells the caller if they have not got through to the right section or are not talking to the person they intended to talk to.
- Get into the habit of answering the telephone with the hand you do NOT use for writing. This leaves your writing hand free for jotting down any notes.
- Always have a pen and paper next to the telephone. Some organisations give their employees telephone message forms to use. These have a series of different headings to remind the employee what questions they need to ask the caller.
- If the telephone call involves you finding out more information for the caller, it may mean that they can't be helped straightaway. If this is the case take their name and telephone number and call them back immediately you have the information they need.
- If the telephone call is not for you, give the caller these options:
  Can someone else help?
  Can you take a message?
  Can someone else call them back when they are free to do so?

Listening is important in both face-to-face communication and telephone calls. We all listen to a great number of different people during a single day. But not many of us could remember exactly what has been said to us in each one of those conversations. That is why, especially when you are at work, it is a good idea to take notes during an important conversation. This helps you to remember what has been said.

Build-up Exercise

How good a listener are you? In pairs, get your partner to tell you about a recent holiday or outing they have had. They should talk to you for at least three minutes about this visit. Now you have to recount everything that you have remembered about their visit. Did you remember most of it or did they have to remind you about some things?

Now it is your turn to talk and your partner's turn to listen and recount the details.

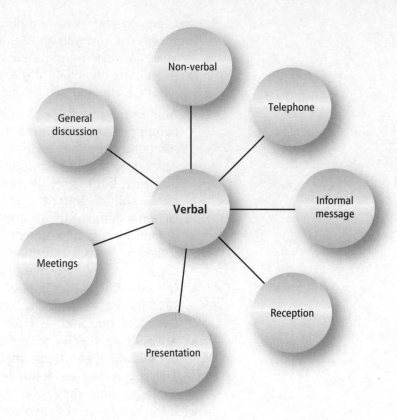

Figure 2.6 *Forms of verbal communication*

Written communication

Written communication is vitally important to any business. We will look in detail at the ways in which organisations contact those outside the business, for example their customers, a little later in this unit. But those inside the organisation, there are various ways of presenting written communications to each other, including:

- memos
- reports
- newsletters
- notices
- agendas
- minutes of meetings
- newsletters
- company newspapers
- notes and messages
- e-mail messages.

Build-up Exercise

What method of written, internal communication do you think the managers of a business would use to:

1 invite a manager from another branch of the business to join them for lunch after a meeting

2 provide the results of some research to all the managers of the business
3 inform all employees about a change to the car parking arrangements
4 tell someone they have a pay rise
5 tell all employees the details of the forthcoming Christmas party?

Figure 2.7 *Forms of written communication*

Styles and manner of address, using language and tone appropriate to the situation and the use of diplomacy and tact as needed

Now we have looked at the various forms of communication, it is time to look at the other aspects of communication, namely:

- the style and manner of address (how you address people in verbal and written communication)
- the use of correct language and tone in a variety of situations
- the need to learn diplomacy and tact where appropriate.

Maintain effective working relationships

Most businesses attempt to strike a balance between making sure that all of the work which needs to be done is completed effectively and efficiently and trying to maintain good working relationships between staff.

Build-up Exercise

Here are four different situations where either verbal or written communication is necessary. You must identify the right way in which to address the receiver in each case. You should produce a document in the case of written communication and a written account of what you would say in cases of verbal communication.

Remember to use the right styles in each situation. You will also have to use the correct language and you may have to be diplomatic and tactful.

1 You have a note on your desk which reads:

```
Call Mrs Cornish. She is very disappointed that
her order has been cancelled. She has explained
why the outstanding invoices have not been
paid. She blames us for her business
difficulties.
```

You check the customer records for Mrs Cornish and discover the following:

> Mrs P. Cornish, Wavegear Sports Ltd., 17 The High Street, Poole, Dorset, PO4 4NB
> Outstanding balance of account   £763.42
> Amount overdue   £541.83
> Reminder sent to customer   3 November 2004
> Account stopped – no further orders to be taken until overdue amount settled.
> Credit limit of account   22/10/200–   £1000
> Credit limit of account   03/11/200–   £750

2 You are a team leader. Yesterday afternoon one of your team colleagues, Frank Spencer, returned back to work after lunch. You could see that he had been drinking alcohol over the lunch break and was not drunk, but nearly so. Despite drinking several cups of coffee, he fell asleep at his desk later in the afternoon. When he woke up he was abusive to other members of the team and managed to break the photocopier. You have been called to see the human resources manager in half an hour. What will you say that you have seen?

3 You work in a large, open-plan office (there are no doors and everyone has their desk in the same area). There is a continual movement of employees, customers and visitors through the office all day. Over the past three weeks, two purses and a wallet have been stolen from the office. You are to suggest, in the form of a memorandum, how to improve the office security and offer advice to employees to keep their personal possessions safe.

▶▶

4 At the next team meeting you have been asked to present your ideas about covering work over the lunch break. The management of your business is concerned that there appears to be no rota in place to ensure that no more than half of the staff are absent at any one time. Over the last week you have checked each day and discovered the following:

Total number in team – 12

	Number of people at lunch	
	12.30–1.30	1.30–2.30
Monday	6	6
Tuesday	8	4
Wednesday	7	5
Thursday	5	7
Friday	9	3

Two of the people who take their lunch from 12.30 to 1.30 must do so to pick up young children from nursery.

Three people must take the 1.30 to 2.30 break as they start at 10.00 and finish at 18.00 each day.

Despite some very bad examples of employers who bully and harass their staff, the vast majority of businesses would prefer that their employees are happy. Happy and co-operative staff tend to work together far more efficiently. They are not distracted by problems, so they can concentrate on producing good quality work.

Nature of business relationships

The exact nature of business relationships very much depends on the size, nature and structure of the business in which you work. You will have contact with a variety of people within the organisation, either on a routine, daily basis, or occasionally where you need to work with them. Above all you should be attempting to establish what could be called a 'productive working relationship' with people. Productive working relationships can mean some or all of the following:

- people involved are co-operative
- others' feelings are considered
- people are courteous to each other
- people are respected and supported
- people are loyal to one another
- managers, team leaders and supervisors thank and praise people for doing a good job when appropriate
- the decisions made are reasonable
- the reasons behind decisions are explained to those involved
- people listen to one another and try to understand the views of others.

There are many cases, of course, when circumstances create an unproductive working atmosphere. Such circumstances could include:

- people are blaming and distrusting one another
- a manager, supervisor or team leader is a bad leader and has favourites
- some people are refusing to listen to others
- there is fighting between team members
- some team members are not working as hard as the others.

Try it out

What would you do in the following situations?

1 You want a long weekend away to visit some friends. It is very busy at work and several people are off sick. You could rearrange your plans, or pretend you are ill and take the Friday off anyway.

2 One of your fellow team members is very moody and is always criticising you. Should you ignore her, talk to your team leader or confront her?

3 You overhear a telephone conversation and one of the team is obviously having marital problems. Do you say nothing at all, tell other members of the team when he is not around or just confide in one person but swear them to secrecy?

Rights and responsibilities in the workplace

Employers have a duty to ensure that reasonable care is taken to provide their employees with:

- a safe place of work
- safe working methods
- appropriate training
- safe equipment.

Just as the employer has these responsibilities, employees too have responsibilities in relation to safety. Employees, for example, should not block exits, or leave cables trailing across the ground. Employees should make sure that they follow the correct instructions when using equipment, even simple pieces of equipment such as staplers. Employees should not try to do things or use equipment for which they have not been trained. If a piece of equipment is known to be faulty or unsafe, an employee should not be tempted to use it.

Rights and responsibilities go even further. These include:

- Making sure that both the employee and the employer comply with the terms of the employee's employment contract. This means that the employee is entitled to pay, holiday pay and sick pay, and there is a clear disciplinary procedure.
- Both the employer and the employee have to comply with health and safety regulations. This includes not only a safe working

environment, but also that equipment and systems are safe and serviced regularly and that accidents are investigated.

- Both employers and employees also have to comply with anti-discrimination laws. This means that people cannot be treated differently on the grounds of their gender, ethnic background, age, disability, religion or sexual orientation.

All of these rights and responsibilities help to create an effective, safe and fair working environment. If the employer is taking these responsibilities seriously, then it is easier for the employees to maintain effective and productive working relationships.

Build-up Exercise

1   What do you think the term 'reasonable care' means?
2   Find out the proper name of at least two health and safety laws.
3   Find out the name of the organisation which deals with equal opportunity issues.
4   Find out the name of the organisation which deals with race discrimination.

Personal qualities of an effective team member

Individuals require many different qualities to be an effective team member. Very few people will have all the necessary personal qualities to be an ideal team member, but many will hope to acquire some of these qualities over time. Typical personal qualities include the following:

- **Judgement** – being able to weigh things up and make a logical decision about what needs to be done.
- **Initiative** – being able to make decisions on your own and work on your own.
- **Integrity** – being trustworthy and dependable.
- **Foresight** – being able to see what problems may be about to occur and alert the team to these possibilities.
- **Energy** – being continually committed to completing a task, even if you are tired or bored.
- **Drive** – being enthusiastic and encouraging to others who work with you.
- **Decisiveness** – being able to make a decision and stick with it to get a task completed.
- **Dependability** – being the sort of person that the rest of the team knows they can rely on, come what may.
- **Emotional stability** – not being moody, rude or argumentative.
- **Fairness** – being able to see things from the point of view of others.
- **Dedication** – being loyal to the team and to the business.
- **Co-operation** – being prepared to help others when requested.
- **Understanding** – appreciating that it is not always possible for others to do things as you would do them.

Try it out

Choose a person that you work with on a regular basis. How many of the personal qualities listed above does that person possess? Can you list five of the qualities in which they do not excel? Now do the same for yourself.

Importance of negotiation and democratic agreement

When you work as a member of a team, various decisions will always have to be made and people will have different views about how to approach things. Most teams, although they are organised and controlled by a team leader, supervisor or manager, will try to make decisions together. If decisions or ways or doing things are imposed on the team, there is no guarantee its members will accept or understand them. It is therefore important to discuss decisions before they are made and to try to reach agreement on the way forward.

Negotiations and agreements about how to do things may occur formally at a meeting, or may develop through a series of informal conversations as work progresses. The important thing is that everyone feels their view has been listened to, even if the rest of the team have not necessarily agreed with them. Decisions and agreements need to bring in the views of as many of the team as possible. Doing this should ensure that all of the team members, or at least most of them, will feel that they have made a contribution.

Normally it is advisable for each team member to be given the opportunity to contribute to the decision-making process and outline their approach to the problem. Once all of the team have had a chance to put across their point of view, the way forward should be decided democratically; that is by majority decision.

It is not always possible, however, to set aside time for negotiations and democratic agreements and sometimes decisions have to be made quickly by the team leader, or by the team members who are directly involved in the work. On other occasions the team may have no choice in how a task is to be approached, as this will already have been determined by more senior management.

Importance of co-operation with others

If you are only interested in yourself and what the job can provide you with, then you are probably not going to be a very good team member. Effective teams rely on co-operation, and to co-operate with others you need to have a number of qualities. As a successful team member you should:

- be loyal and supportive to the team
- communicate and listen to what others say
- be happy to drop what you are doing to help another team member if they are in difficulties

- adopt a flexible approach to your work and realise that the day's plans may be changed at any minute
- be prepared to learn new skills which will help you and the team
- stick to your promises and if you have said that you will do something make sure that it is done
- not expect other team members to be co-operative, communicative or helpful at all times
- think before you speak and be tactful
- above all, be as happy with the team's successes as you are with your own successes.

Dealing with different personalities within a team

Not all people are the same; it would be a boring world if everyone was. Personality represents the way in which people think, feel, behave and relate to others. Some people are what is known as extroverts; lively and sociable people. Others are introverts who tend to be rather shy and may find it difficult to communicate with others.

The problem with having a mixture of people with different personalities is that you will have to deal with them in different ways. Extroverts, on one hand, whilst they are loud, lively and sociable, can be quite excitable and highly strung. You will find that most extroverts are quite friendly and confident. Introverts, on the other hand, can also be highly strung, but are often confident, calm, shy and somewhat trusting.

Try it out

Although the results of this short questionnaire are never totally accurate, answer 'yes' or 'no' to the following questions to see whether you are more extrovert or introvert.

1 For no apparent reason do you sometimes feel happy and sometimes depressed?
2 Do you sometimes have mood swings without apparent reason?
3 Do you tend to be moody?
4 Does your mind often wander?
5 Do you start thinking about other things, even when you are involved in a conversation?
6 Do you sometimes have plenty of energy and at other times feel very tired?
7 Do you prefer doing things rather than planning to do things?
8 Are you at your best when you are involved in something that needs to be done immediately?
9 Are you usually the one who introduces themselves first to new people?
10 Do you tend to be fairly certain of what you are doing?
11 Would you consider yourself to be lively?
12 Would you be unhappy if you were not working as a member of a team?

▶▶

Scoring

For questions 1–6, if you said yes give yourself 1 point.

A score of 6 shows that you are rather emotionally unstable.

A score of 0 shows that you are emotionally stable.

For questions 7–12, 1 point for each time you have said yes and 0 points for each no.

A score of 6 indicates that you are an extreme extrovert.

A score of 0 indicates that you are an extreme introvert.

Strategies for handling conflict

Working as a member of a team means that you will inevitably at some point be in conflict with other people. There are two common reasons for this. The first is that you will not always agree on how a task should be carried out. This is usually the easier kind of conflict to sort out. People tend to have different ways of doing the same thing, and some ways work better for some people than others. When it comes to important issues like how information is filed away or the order in which tasks are carried out, then there may be major problems if someone is doing the job differently from the rest of the team. Some people may become very angry and not be prepared to compromise, even over the most trivial of matters. In all cases, conflicts such as these should be dealt with calmly and logically. The argument should be about the facts and not about the personalities involved.

The other common source of conflict is when personalities clash or people object to the way in which someone is behaving towards them, or when people bring their problems with them to work. Some of the most frequent sources of conflict include:

- criticising a team member in front of an outsider
- leaving a team member out of the decision-making process
- allowing one team member to develop a strong dislike for another
- saying hurtful or tactless things to one another
- being intentionally awkward or unpleasant.

There are many ways in which conflict can be resolved. You may consider being more assertive and saying what you feel. In some cases you may reconsider and realise that you have over-reacted. It is a good idea to watch how other people deal with an awkward individual, and it can be helpful to talk over the problem with a friend from whom you may get a different perspective on the situation. If all of this fails, then you may have to make the situation official and speak to your team leader, supervisor or manager. In many cases, however, referring it to one of these people may make the situation worse to begin with, before it is finally resolved.

Build-up Exercise

Imagine you work in a busy office. Unfortunately, towards the end of each afternoon the sales representatives, who have been visiting customers all day, drop their customer order forms into a tray in your office. This normally happens between 16.00 and 17.00 each day. By that time, because of flexitime, there are just three of you left in the office. You need to input all of the information onto the computer so that it can be transferred to the warehouse so deliveries can be sorted out for the following morning.

One of the other team members, Francine, has to leave promptly at 17.30 to pick up her children from a childminder. You like to leave no later than 17.30 to make sure that you catch your bus home. This leaves only one team member, Stuart, to finish off the work. You have noticed over the past few days that he has become very moody and unco-operative with the pair of you after everyone else has left.

Now answer the following questions.

1 Should you and Francine report Stuart's moodiness to your team leader?
2 Should you tackle Stuart yourself?
3 Should you decide to stay until the work has been completed?
4 Should you offer to take it in turns with Stuart to stay late?
5 Should you ask Francine to make other plans?

Review your contribution to the team activity

One of the best ways of improving your longer-term efficiency and effectiveness in relation to team activities is to look at your own performance and contribution to activities which you have already undertaken. Part of your assessment for this unit will be a report in which you assess your performance and that of your team. So that you don't always have to rely on your memory to produce the report, you could use the following to help you recall what happened:

- notes of meetings
- a diary which details jobs done and deadlines met
- a tracking sheey that identifies what jobs had to be done by whom and when.

In this part of the unit we will be referring back to the pyramid game activity which you tackled earlier.

Reviewing whether own tasks have been successfully completed and objectives met

A good way to get started is to divide your experiences and ideas into good and bad. It might be useful to list them under headings, such as:

- I was good at...
- I was bad at...
- I felt this went well
- I felt this went badly.

You should try to keep to the point, and obtain a copy of the observer's notes for the activity to help you record things that may not have occurred to you at the time.

To review your contribution properly, you must be honest; you will learn more this way. You should write exactly what you want to say and not be concerned about the comments you might get back as a result. As with the next part of this unit, you should try to be positive, productive and useful. After all, how else will you or the team be able to progress or improve?

When you are involved in a team activity, it is often a good idea to create your own log sheet, or tracking document. The form does not need to be complicated, simply use the following columns:

- time and/or date (when something happened)
- my tasks (what you did at the time)
- team tasks (what the team did at the time)
- problems (what difficulties you had).

Using a tracking sheet you should be able to look at the whole team activity and see exactly when things have happened, whether the team is on course to complete the activity and the reasons behind any problems that may prevent the task being competed by the deadline.

In the review that you will be expected to undertake for successful completion of the unit, you will have to look back over the two team activities. Points to make sure you have covered are:

- that you understood what you had to do and the purpose of the tasks
- that you have described the tasks you performed
- that you have made comments about how well you felt you contributed to the team. Was it as good as you had hoped, or maybe it was better than you had hoped?
- that you have commented on how you got on with the other team members
- that you have mentioned how you and the team dealt with any difficulties you came across.

Own performance and contribution to the work of the team

Reviewing your own performance means thinking objectively about what you did or did not do and how you managed to cope with your part of the activity. You need to be honest with yourself about what you have managed to achieve and what you felt went right or wrong in terms of your contribution.

Nature of relationship with rest of the team

This may not have been the first time you were engaged in a team activity with these individuals. If this was the first time you'd worked with the other team members, you will have been learning about them whilst you were doing the activity. This means that there will have been more to take account of and perhaps far more to say about how you got on with the rest of the team than if you worked with them before. If you did already know the team members and had worked with them before, then this activity may have shown you different aspects of their personalities. Key things to consider are:

- How did you decide to approach the activity in the way you did?
- What could you have done to have made the activity easier?
- Did you take account of everyone else's opinion when you planned the activity?
- Were you and other members of the team happy with the workload which was allocated to you?
- Were you and the other team members happy with the outcome of the activity?
- How could you and your team's performance be improved if you were asked to do this activity again?

Try it out

Assuming that you have followed our advice from the beginning of this assessment objective, you will now be able to write your review of the pyramid activity under the following three headings:

- own performance
- your contribution to the work of the team
- your relationship with the rest of the team.

Review the overall performance of the team

Reviewing the performance of a team is usually the responsibility of the team leader, supervisor or manager. But to improve your own performance and that of the team you should also think about it yourself. For this last assessment objective you need to think about how the team managed to complete the pyramid activity and look at whether the objectives which were set at the beginning of the activity were met.

Remember that teams are made up of a number of individuals. If the team is to work effectively, then each individual within that team has to make a contribution. Certainly, the team as a whole has to:

- be honest with each other
- listen to each other
- learn from any mistakes they have made in the past
- have a good relationship with one another, so that they are able to make comments or criticisms freely
- work together for the good of the team.

In addition to keeping a log (or tracking sheet) of your activities and the work of the group, it is also useful to keep a note of all of the meetings held by your team. Part of the assessment of this element in this unit requires you to review the overall team performance. There are various ways in which you could collect information to help you to do this:

- You could note down the specific tasks that each person in your team has to complete. You could then note whether it was done, and if so when it was done (early, on time or late, for example).
- From your list of individual responsibilities, you could then note whether other team members (or yourself) had to help another individual to complete their tasks (this shows cooperation).
- You could also prepare a simple form, one for each team member. During the course of the activities you could then note down, under two columns (strengths and weaknesses), what the individual team members proved to be good at and those things they were not so good at.
- Once you have a list of strengths and weaknesses for each of the team members, you can then see whether any of the strengths and weaknesses were shared by the whole team. Don't forget to note down your own strengths and weaknesses.
- If everyone in the team writes down their own strengths and weaknesses, then individuals can compare what they consider to be true about themselves with what others have noticed about them.

The review itself requires you to note the following:

- whether you understood exactly what the team was required to do in the activities (the objectives of the activities)
- whether you recognised that the objectives of the team had been met, or not met, at the end of the activities
- a statement about the individual performances of each of the other team members – for instance, what were individuals good at doing, what were they not so good at doing, did they contribute well or not so well to the team?
- a summary of the overall strengths and weaknesses of the team – for instance, was the mix of people in the team good? Did you all work in a professional and business-like manner? Did you help one another when needed?

Reviewing whether the team task has been successfully completed and objectives met

Passing judgement on the performance of other individuals, particularly if you are not in a position of authority, is not recommended. What you should do, however, is review how the team performed as a whole. The view of other members on how the team performed may differ from yours, based on what you observed. It is useful in this instance to look at what the observer wrote, as they were part of your team, yet outside the activity itself, and will therefore have a more objective view.

Performance of other members of the team

You may wish to use a version of the headings which we suggested when you reviewed your own performance during the last activity. You should not be frightened to say what you mean and, once again, you should be honest, as this is an exercise in recognising the strengths and weaknesses of different team members.

Strengths and weaknesses of the team

Strengths and weaknesses can be looked at either individually or for the team as a whole. As we have seen, some people are particularly good at doing certain things. Some are more communicative than others; some are extroverts, others introverts. It is the mix of people in a team which makes the team as a whole effective or ineffective.

Consider the overall strengths and weaknesses of the team. Were you all too alike? Did one person take the lead and the others follow? Did you fail to agree on anything? Was the activity actually completed? Did you encounter any conflict whilst you were doing the activity?

The simplest way of judging the strengths and weaknesses of a team is to look at whether the team completed the activity successfully. But this does not tell you how the team interacted while the activity was being carried out.

Factors contributing to success or failure of the team

You should now have a clear picture of what, if anything, went wrong and why. It is always difficult to carry out a complex series of tasks if you do not have any prior knowledge of the other team members. You may not know their strengths and their weaknesses. If you are working with people you already know, you are aware of their strengths and weaknesses, but unless the team makes use of each individual's strengths, the activity may still end in failure.

Each team should try to make use of the best qualities of each of the individuals, and assign them to tasks which best suit their abilities. It would be inappropriate, for example, to assign the calculations to someone who is weak at maths.

Another factor which may have been outside the control of the team is the time allocated for the activity. The team may fail if there was simply insufficient time to complete the task properly. The time allocated for the task would have been deliberately set to put pressure on the team, because in work you will rarely have as much time as you feel you need to do what is required.

Were there other external factors, such as resources not being available, that caused the team problems? This is an important part of planning, and in many tasks the first thing you need to do is to gather together all the resources you will need to complete it successfully so that you are not hunting for them while the task is actually in progress.

Try it out

You should try to be as honest as possible. Remember that you are not passing judgement on other people, you are simply reporting your experiences of how the team performed during the pyramid activity. You need to write briefly under the following three headings:

- **Performance of other members of the team** – what did they do and how did they do it? Were they effective?
- **Strengths and weaknesses of the team** – you should tackle this individually and then from the viewpoint of the team as a whole. What were you good and bad at as team?
- **Factors contributing to the success or failure of the team** – what factors which the team created themselves caused success or failure? What external factors contributed to that success or failure?

Working with customers (Element 2)

Eight key assessment objectives

- Present a positive image to customers
- Follow company procedures for communicating with customers
- Interact effectively with customers
- Use appropriate tone and manner
- Convey information clearly and accurately
- Resolve difficulties using organisational procedures
- Record information accurately
- Ensure customers' requirements have been met

Present a positive image to customers

The image the general public has of the business is very important to an organisation. Many businesses spend a great deal of money on advertising to put across a good image to the public. They want the public to think their organisation is reliable, and that their products or services are good value for money, and they want people to recommend the business and its products or services to their friends and family.

Providing an effective customer service is one way of projecting a good image to those who might be considering using the organisation. If potential customers hear about the organisation by recommendation they are more likely to use it themselves. If they hear lots of positive comments about the way the organisation provides advice, assistance and looks after its customers, they are even more likely to be prepared to spend their money on the business's products or services.

Most of us work hard for our money and because of this consider our purchases carefully. Not many people would choose to spend their money with an organisation that has a poor public image. If they come away as happy customers, they will probably return. Remember also that customers need to feel confident about what a business provides before they are likely to either use it or recommend it to others.

Build-up Exercise

Think about four different organisations you either know about or have had some dealings with. They don't have to be ones you have worked in. If you are a college student, one of your organisations could be the college in which you are studying this course.

For each organisation you should answer the following questions:

1 Can you describe the image that the business is trying to give to the general public?
2 How do you think the business manages to portray this particular image?
3 How do the employees help the business maintain this image?
4 Would you, as a customer of the business, recommend it to your family and friends? Whether you say yes or no to this question, you should give your reasons why.

Possible range of customers internal and external to the organisation

Many organisations have a wide variety of customers. External customers, that is those who do not work inside the organisation, might be:

- individuals
- groups
- customers from different age groups
- customers from different cultures – this means people from different backgrounds or from different countries
- non-English speaking customers
- customers with specific needs, for examples those who are sight or hearing impaired, those in wheelchairs, or young children
- other businesses, for example suppliers of the business's raw materials.

Internal customers, on the other hand, are those who work for the business. These are individuals or departments within the organisation itself. For example, the personnel section makes sure enough trained staff are available, but the accounts or finance section pays them.

People work to provide themselves with an income, and in many cases they rely on the business they work for to provide them with opportunities to gain new skills and to develop and progress in their jobs.

In a smaller business there may only be a few employees, or internal customers, and they may all answer the telephone and take messages for one another. This makes communication and the passing on of information very straightforward and there is not too much likelihood that problems will arise.

In a larger business, communication can be more complicated. The organisation may well be divided into different departments and these may be situated on different floors, or even in different buildings. Members of one department or section are the internal customers of another department or section. This means that should one department require information from another, it is important that the correct, accurate information is passed on. After all, employees are all working for the same organisation, even if they are working in different departments.

Build-up Exercise

Think about the different departments of an organisation (you may want to refer to Unit 3). List the different departments, and beside each write the name(s) of the other departments they would need to communicate with. In other words, who are the department's internal customers?

Importance of one's impact on others and factors that affect this

If it is important to a business to project the right image to its customers and the general public, then the employees of that business should be aware of the way we dress, the image they give, the way they write to or speak to customers, and what they say and how they say it, as all these affect the impression they give of the business as a whole.

Personal presentation

In organisations whose employees have direct contact with their customers, it is important that the staff look presentable. To present an image of a company in the best way possible, an employee should think about the following:

- the way they dress for work
- their personal hygiene

- the way they behave when they are at work
- their personality – whether or not they are often bad tempered or sometimes a bit too loud
- their general attitude at work – whether or not they are approachable and how they treat other people.

Sometimes staff receive a uniform that they have to wear for work. Uniforms are issued by some organisations for a number of reasons, including:

- they form part of the company image in that the uniforms may have the company logo printed on them
- employees are easy for the customer to find because they are all wearing the same clothes
- they avoid having to pay their employees an allowance for their work clothing
- all their employees will turn up for work in the appropriate clothes and, hopefully, they will all look smart and well presented.

If an individual doesn't work for an organisation that issues a uniform, they will be expected to dress in clothes appropriate to the job. This usually means as smartly and as tidily as possible. Very often organisations insist on certain dress codes. These are rules about what can or cannot be worn for work. Some of them are based on health and safety requirements such as:

- long hair needs to be tied back if the job involves working with food
- no nail varnish can be worn when food is being handled or prepared
- dangling jewellery should not be worn in case it gets tangled in equipment or machinery.

As well as health and safety considerations, sometimes organisations insist that their employees wear name tags or passes for security reasons. This is to ensure that only authorised people get into certain areas of the organisation.

What you choose to wear for work very much depends on the job being done. For instance:

- some organisations insist that male employees wear a collar and tie to work
- some organisations do not allow their female employees to wear trousers.

Importance of providing effective customer service

An organisation will often have set ways in which they want their employees to deal with customers. These are known as 'procedures' and employees are made aware of these when they first start their job. Sometimes organisations issue booklets to all employees containing details of the procedures for dealing with customers. Procedures cover all aspects of customer care.

If all the employees are working with a good knowledge of these procedures, they should all be doing the same thing, hence ensuring that customers are treated in the same way by all staff. This helps the organisation to project a more professional and efficient image to their existing and potential customers.

If a business is to provide an efficient and effective customer service, trained and experienced staff must carry out a variety of tasks to a high standard. For example, they will regularly:

- provide information, assistance and advice to customers
- receive and pass on messages from customers
- keep accurate and up to date customer records
- deal with customer complaints.

Customer service is all about effectiveness, efficiency and reliability. Often an organisation will make a commitment to its customers by producing a charter. This makes promises about the standard of service a customer can expect from the organisation.

Many businesses have customer service departments that routinely contact customers who have made purchases and ask them how the product has performed and whether they are happy with it. Sometimes businesses do this by telephone. Alternatively they may e-mail the customer or send them a questionnaire by post. By finding out customers' views and whether or not they are satisfied, a business may be able to avoid mistakes or problems in the future.

Follow company procedures for communicating with customers

For this part of the course you will need to provide evidence that you understand and are capable of following an organisation's procedures for dealing with customers. You already know how important it is to deal with customers in the correct way, whether on a face-to-face basis or via the telephone.

Build-up Exercise

Obtain a copy of either your employer's or your college's charter (if they have one). This is the way the organisation tells its customers what it promises to do for them. If you are a student, remember that you are one of the college's customers and it could be that a charter is included in your student handbook or the college prospectus.

Does the charter give specific promises to the customers of the organisation? If so, make a list of the things it promises.

If the organisation does not have a charter, perhaps you could consider what promises it should make to its customers.

Procedures for dealing with customers face to face and by telephone

Whatever the type or size of an organisation, it will have its own systems in place with which its members of staff must comply. The business will want all employees to be aware of the image it is trying to convey to customers and to follow its procedures in order to ensure this image is put across.

Build-up Exercise

Does your organisation or college have a set of procedures that state the way employees should carry out verbal communication with its customers? If it does, it is important that employees understand completely how they should behave, and the image they should give to customers. If the procedures are available, make a summary of them in the form of numbered points.

Providing prompt attention

How many times have you been kept waiting by a receptionist? How did that make you feel? Did it affect your opinion of the organisation you were visiting?

Prompt attention and a quick response to customers is important in an organisation. Greeting visitors politely, promptly and courteously helps give the right impression, and the same applies when dealing with people by telephone. Some organisations have a policy of answering the telephone after only three rings and guaranteeing the customer that their request will be dealt with in a certain amount of time. Organisations have realised that prompt response is often an important factor in a customer's decision to purchase something from them. This reputation for efficiency may well then be passed on to business contacts, friends and relatives.

Build-up Exercise

You should refer again to your organisation or college's procedures. Do they state how quickly employees should answer the telephone? Do they state how quickly each request for information or advice should be dealt with?

Styles of address

Regular customers are vitally important to any organisation. A great deal of hard work, not to mention advertising and other costs, have been incurred in making someone a regular customer. It is, therefore, essential to build and maintain good relationships. Try to remember the following when you are greeting a visitor to your organisation, or talking to them on the telephone:

- introduce yourself
- try to use the customer's name during the conversation
- try to remember something about the customer, their business or their family
- tell customers the truth
- inform regular customers about special offers
- inform regular customers about any changes to products or services (for example, if an item they regularly buy is about to go out of stock).

Build-up Exercise

These are just some of the styles of address an organisation may choose. Does your organisation or college have other styles in their procedures? If so, add them to the list above. If some of those in the list above are not part of the organisation's procedures, state whether or not they would be a suitable procedure for the business to adopt. Give your reasons.

Dealing with complaints

An organisation that is concerned with improving its customer service will carefully check all the complaints it receives. It will want to know how often different customers complain about the same thing. If it finds that similar complaints are occurring regularly, then an attempt should be made to improve the situation. Often the company will have a special form that customers have to complete. Reading these forms helps the organisation's managers to decide if the service can be improved or if extra services can be added to help the customer remain satisfied.

If part of your job involves handling complaints from customers, you should remember to:

- listen carefully to what the customer is saying
- apologise for the inconvenience they have been caused
- let them know that the matter will be investigated
- let them know that the organisation wants the matter to be put right
- let them know that you understand and can see the problem from their point of view
- keep calm and never argue with the customer
- try to find a solution to their problem while they are there with you; if this is not possible, promise them that you will come back to them with a solution

- ask the right questions to make sure you have got all the information you need
- agree the solution with the customer
- make sure that what you promised to do for the customer actually gets done!

Confidentiality of company information

You may occasionally be asked by customers to provide either sensitive or confidential information regarding the business. If you are unsure whether or not you should do so, you should arrange to get back to the customer or individual and then check with your team leader or supervisor. You should never disclose information such as:

- personal information about other employees
- information about other customers
- information about the business's future plans
- information about the business's financial situation.

Sometimes different parts of a business are very competitive with one another and a manager may consider his or her future plans for their department to be confidential; they may not wish other managers to know what is being planned.

Try it out

Read the following telephone conversation and then answer the questions:

'Good morning, Devon Holiday Cottages.'

'Hello this is Clive, is that Sarah?'

'Yes it is.'

'I don't know if you remember me Sarah, but I work for Framlingham Stationery and I visited you with the sales rep last month.'

'Yes I do Clive, hello, what can I do for you?'

'I was wondering if you could sort me out a cottage for August to fit six people?'

'Yes, I don't think that will be a problem. Do you want me to send you a brochure?'

'Yes that would be useful but I wanted to talk to you about prices. I talked to Simon, the sales rep, on the way back from your office and he told me that you had sorted him out a 20 per cent discount for a holiday next July.'

'Did he really?'

'Yes and I wondered if you could do me the same deal?'

'I'll have to check on that, Clive.'

'Thanks. Oh and one other thing, you know Florrie in your office? She's not got a boyfriend has she? I want to send her a bunch of flowers. Could you give me her home address?'

'I can't really say and I can't give you the address, it's against company policy.'

'Go on, I only want to send her a bunch of flowers.'

'Alright then, she is single and she lives at 42 Nelson Drive, Taunton. But don't tell her it was me that told you.'

'Thanks that's lovely. I'll look forward to getting the brochure and hearing from you about the discount.'

Questions
1 What information should Sarah have had to hand to tell Clive?
2 What information should she have not told Clive?
3 How could she have withheld the information about Florrie without offending Clive?
4 What might be the likely result of Sarah having given Clive confidential information?

Interact effectively with customers

To achieve this element of the course you will have to show that you can interact effectively with customers. In this next set of assessment objectives we will look at the various ways in which you can make best use of your communication skills in dealing with customers.

Importance of communication

Communicating effectively with customers relies on many things:

- how promptly you deal with customers
- the tone or manner in which you deal with customers
- the messages which you give to customers
- your non-verbal (body language) signals
- your listening skills
- your ability to understand the customers' body language
- your ability to deal with problems as they arise.

Build-up Exercise

Your communication skills can very much depend on how comfortable you feel dealing with people. The following list gives some examples of strengths or weaknesses that you may, or may not, have. Which are your strengths and which are your weaknesses? What can you do to improve on any of these strengths or deal with any of the weaknesses?

Table 2.8 *Strengths and weaknesses in dealing with customers*

Strengths	Weaknesses
• You like dealing with people	• You are moody
• You are patient	• You don't like being interrupted
• You can always find the right words	• You are impatient
• You are tactful	• You are quite tactless
• You are aware of others' feelings	• You are rather shy
• You are a good listener	• You think customers are a nuisance and are often stupid
• You like to help people	• You think dealing with is simply hard workcustomers
• You realise people have different views	• You have never met a customer who is right

Use of appropriate verbal and non-verbal communication skills

Just as each employee is different, so is each customer and while there is no foolproof way of dealing with every customer, the following list suggests some of the more usual ways of using your verbal and non-verbal communication skills to best affect:

- Always approach the customer with either a smile or a greeting, depending on whether it is face to face or on the telephone.
- Try and build a good relationship with the customer from the beginning, by looking at their body language or listening to them.
- Make sure you have listened to and remembered what the customer has said.
- When giving a customer information, be confident and accurate.
- Do not make promises which you cannot keep.
- Be aware that the customer is getting a mental image of you from your voice and body language.
- Find out what the customer actually wants rather than assuming you already know what they want.
- If you need to take more time than usual in dealing with a customer, this is acceptable.

Body language can send various messages to the customer. You should always remember the following:

- Turn your whole body towards the customer and not just your head when you are speaking to them. This shows you are interested in what they are saying.
- Do not stand too close to a customer as they may feel intimidated.
- Make eye contact with the customer. It shows that you are genuinely in what they are saying interested and are being honest with them.
- Do not show signs that you are frustrated or bored,for example by fiddling with a pen or tapping your feet.

- Stand, or sit up straight – it shows that you are confident.
- Nod your head at appropriate points while the customer is talking to show that you are concentrating on what they are saying.

Importance of effective questioning and listening to clarify issues

Sometimes we have to ask a number of questions to make sure we understand exactly what is being said or what is required of us. Before we can ask these questions we have to be sure of a few things, for example:

- Are we are supposed to be asking questions? If we are not one of the important people in the conversation, it may be better to sit quietly and wait for the right time to ask an appropriate question.
- Are the people in the conversation interested and listening to what is being said? In a one-to-one conversation, it is important to feel confident that the other person is listening.
- Will the people in the conversation be able to answer the question? The person asking the question has to be aware of the listener's own knowledge of the subject being discussed. It would be pointless to ask them a question they are obviously unable to answer.
- Is the question appropriate? It is important that questions are related to the conversation. In the same way, the question has to have a purpose, otherwise it is pointless and confusing for the other people in the conversation.

Remember that a silence or pause in the conversation doesn't always mean that the other person has finished. It could be that they are thinking about what to say next, or considering what they should do next.

There are many different types of questions a person can ask to get more information. These can be grouped as either closed questions or open questions.

Closed questions

These are where the person answering the question might only need to say yes or no in reply.

Examples of closed questions are:

- Did you purchase this product from us?
- Will you be available to take a call tomorrow?
- Have you got the receipt for the product?

Open questions

These are questions which require the other person to give more than a simple yes or no answer.

Examples of open questions are:

- Which products have you bought from us in the past?
- What appears to be the problem?
- How long ago did you purchase the product?

Open questions usually start with the words: how, which, what, why, when, where or who.

Build-up Exercise

Turn the following closed questions into open questions, for example by starting with a different word.

1 Did you enjoy work today?
2 Did you go out at lunch time?
3 Was the bus on time?
4 Did you see many people that you knew at the cinema?
5 Have you eaten much today?

Obviously, an employee who is trying to find out information about what a customer really needs would probably need a longer reply than just yes or no. They would want to encourage the customer to give them full answers. You can do this by not responding immediately after the customer has given a short answer, allowing them the opportunity to expand on what they've just said.

You can also get more information by using follow-up questions. But to get the most information it is not a good idea to ask question after question. Stick to one subject and ask a few questions about that before moving onto something else.

Whatever type of question is asked, it should be:

■ clearly understood by the other person
■ not repeated
■ asked using the right tone of voice.

The way you ask a question is very important. Be careful not to sound sarcastic or give the impression that you are making fun of the person when asking a question. Don't try to be funny either – people's senses of humour differ and one person's idea of 'funny' might not be the same as someone else's. Questions should be asked at the right time – never interrupt when someone else is speaking.

It is also important to make full use of your listening skills. To become a good listener you need to:

■ concentrate on what is being said
■ avoid becoming distracted, either by other people or by simply letting your attention wander
■ if your concentration lapses, repeat the important words or phrases in the conversation in your head
■ look at the person speaking and respond to them by nodding or smiling so they are aware you are paying attention to them
■ be ready for when the other person stops speaking – this is when it is most noticeable if you are not concentrating and a sudden silence can be embarrassing for both people
■ when the other person stops speaking respond to them by commenting on what they have said or by asking them a question.

When we are listening to someone else during a face-to-face conversation, it is easy to respond by using gestures such as nodding or smiling to show we agree or understand, or by frowning to show we don't really understand. This is not so easy to do when you are on the telephone.

Potential communication problems and how to address them

There are a number of reasons why communication fails to be effective. Some of them will not be obvious until a problem occurs. Some problems are avoidable if the communication methods are thought through properly. In other cases the problem will remain until something dramatic is done to improve things. 'Barriers to communication' are problems that exist between the sender and the receiver of the information that stop the message getting through or in the intended way. Here are some common barriers to communication.

- **Lack of training** – if employees are not trained to use the different ways of communicating they will either make mistakes or not be able to use that form of communication at all. Training in the use of equipment and the ways in which communications should be written or spoken are essential. Such training will often be part of organisational procedures.
- **Lack of information** – one of the most common barriers to communication is not having all the information you need to make a decision or to help someone else make a decision. If, for example, a customer contacting a business to ask for the price and availability of a product is told that it is out of stock, a sale is lost. If the employee taking the call had known that the warehouse had just received a delivery of that product, the sale could have been made.
- **Personal relationships** – one of the commonest reasons why communications are ineffective within an organisation is that individuals either do not like or do not understand one another. Personal likes or dislikes may mean that employees avoid one another, even if as a result information is not passed between them, and this has a bad affect on both their own work and the business itself. This is a very difficult barrier to deal with but can be solved by either resolving differences between the two individuals or changing the job role of one of them so that they do not have such direct contact with one another. An alternative is for the business to help them get along better by giving them some team-building training.
- **Faulty systems** – there may be a problem with organisational procedures, where something in the process has been forgotten which causes a breakdown in communications. Perhaps, for example, one part of the whole process of dealing with an order has not been considered.

Barriers to good communication with customers might include:

- writing something down incorrectly
- not hearing the customer's request correctly
- losing important notes or documents
- not telling the right person about a problem
- having too many other things to do
- not realising the importance of the query.

Figure 2.8 *Barriers to effective communication*

Try it out

Read the following text and then answer the questions.

It had been a long, hard week for Hamish and there was only half an hour before he could leave and forget work for the weekend. Hamish was sorting out his desk when he looked up and saw Miss Brandish. His heart sank. Miss Brandish was a regular customer, but always arrived unannounced and took up hours of staff time. Hamish decided to ignore her, but Miss Brandish spotted him and walked straight up to his desk.

'Young man, I require some bonded envelopes, some sticky labels and some blue paperclips. I'm organising Long Norton's dog show and I will need to take these away with me today.'

Hamish grunted and reached for the customer order pad, scribbled down Miss Brandish's requirements, tore the top sheet off and thrust the piece of paper towards her without looking at her. Still without looking at her he said:

'You know where to go.'

'Well!', she replied, turning on her heel and heading off towards the warehouse.

'They can deal with her at this time of the day,' Hamish thought to himself.

Twenty minutes later, as Hamish was putting on his coat, an irate warehouse manager, being nagged by Miss Brandish, appeared. Hamish did not leave the office until quarter to six.

Questions

1 How should Hamish have greeted Miss Brandish?

2 What was wrong with Hamish's body language and attitude towards her?

3 How might simple questioning have speeded things up?

4 What impression did Hamish give Miss Brandish of his attitude and her value as a customer?

5 What might the warehouse manager have said about Hamish's attitude?

Use appropriate tone and manner

As we have seen, you will often be asked to provide information, take messages or provide support to customers. This begins with an assessment of the customer's requirements, and you will need to adopt the right tone and manner from the outset.

Being helpful at all times

To be helpful to a customer you need to begin by finding out what the customer actually needs. You should either write down or remember their requests. This will allow you to give them accurate information. Be careful not to offer to do something for them which is not part of your job or under your control. For the customer to be satisfied, you need to ensure that whatever they have ordered is delivered within the timescale they require. You should also check to see if there is anything else the customer might need at the same time.

Dealing with customers politely, calmly and with confidence and the use of appropriate language and tone

In some cases you may encounter a customer who is either angry or annoyed. You should always try to make sure that you:

- do not argue with the customer
- do not get angry with the customer
- do not shout at the customer
- do not blame someone else
- do not make excuses
- do not interrupt
- apologise if you need to
- get help if you need it
- see it through and make sure the customer leaves satisfied.

How well you deal with a customer often depends upon how reasonable the customer is. But in all cases your tone and manner can help.

Try it out

Thinking back to Hamish's manner of dealing with Miss Brandish, you must now rewrite the conversation the way it should have gone. Write what you think Hamish should have said to have dealt effectively with Miss Brandish.

Convey information clearly and accurately

All information which you pass to a customer should be accurate and complete. It is not always possible to give a customer all the information they require, as you may not have that information to hand, or you may not be confident in how you should convey it. It is always a good idea to check with another person to make sure you have got the facts right. You can always offer to call a customer later with the information, or ask them to wait while you check it.

Some information can be obtained easily, but the more complex the customer's query, the more difficult it may be to put your hands on the correct information immediately, and to be confident that it is correct.

Importance of conveying appropriate and sufficient information accurately, clearly and concisely

If a customer is asking a specific question there is little point telling them about other things which they might be interested in, or giving them more information than they really need. It is often a question of deciding what to say and what not to say, what to put in and what to leave out. The more complex the information you give them the more chance there is they will not fully understand it or will be confused by what you have said. You therefore need to be selective in what you tell customers and give them only enough information to answer their question. Whatever you tell them must be accurate, clear and as concise as possible. This saves both your time and theirs.

Need for confidentiality and recognising the limits of information that can be provided

As we have already mentioned, it is important for you to be aware of what you should and should not tell customers or visitors to your business. Confidential information is difficult to define, but it largely covers information which under normal circumstances a person would not need to know. Some information circulating in your business will be marked as 'confidential' but this does not mean that other, unmarked information is not confidential. If in doubt you should always ensure that you check with a more senior member of staff before passing it on to someone else.

These points need to be considered when you are giving out any form of information. If you work for a computer manufacturer, for example, you should not tell anyone the sources of the components unless you are authorised to do so. If you work in a hospital you are not permitted to give out any information about patients. Similarly, a bank employee cannot tell anyone the details of a customer's bank account.

Try it out

You work as an administrative assistant on Ward 4 of your local hospital. During one morning you have received the following requests for information from patients' relatives. How would you respond to each of these questions? Say whether or not you would feel confident giving out the information and if not, why not.

1 Can you tell me what my brother is allowed to eat please? He is hungry and wants us to bring him some extra food.
2 What time can I visit this afternoon please?

3 Can you give me Dr Patel's mobile number please? I have been trying to get him or his secretary for a week now and I really need to speak to him.

4 Can you tell me which staff nurse will be on duty on Thursday please?

5 I'm not a relative; I'm a reporter on the local newspaper. Can you confirm the name of the man that was brought in by the police last night and is now in intensive care? We want to come in and interview him.

Resolve difficulties using organisational procedures

It is difficult to give specific advice regarding the use of organisational procedures to resolve difficulties, as organisational procedures differ from business to business. If you are currently in work you will be able to learn what your company's organisational procedures are. If you are studying this course at college then you may have to research the college's organisational procedures to provide evidence for this assessment objective.

Recognising customers' special requirements and communicating appropriately

Customers may have a number of special requirements. For instance, they may:

- have special needs as a result of their own personal circumstances
- have a physical or mental impairment (they might be in a wheelchair, be hard of hearing or have an eyesight problem)
- not be able to speak or read English very well
- have special needs that are dictated by their culture or religion
- have an unusual request
- want to complain
- want some advice, information or guidance.

Complaints

Staff should always be able to deal with complaints and respond positively to the customer. As you already know, employees should:

- listen carefully to what is being said
- ask questions to make sure they understand exactly what the complaint is about
- explain to the customer what they can do to help them with their problem
- get help from someone else if it is a problem they can't deal with themselves
- keep the customer informed of what is being done at all times.

Sometimes customers get angry. If this happens, you should make sure you remain calm and do not argue back. There is a saying 'the customer is always right' but this is not always the case. Sometimes customers get angry because they know they are wrong. But this doesn't mean an employee has the right to be rude, even if they suffer abuse.

Anyone dealing with an abusive customer should:

- apologise for the fact that they are getting upset about something to do with the organisation
- show sympathy, for example, tell the customer they understand why they are so upset
- ask the right questions to get to the bottom of what they are complaining about
- let the customer see they are trying to do something about their problem
- get someone to deal with the situation as quickly as possible
- try to explain what is being done at every stage to the customer
- try to explain why the problem might have arisen in the first place
- do not put the blame on someone else
- try to agree with the customer what would be best for them
- promise the customer that they will do all they can to make sure that the solution actually happens
- keep their promise.

Queries and problems

Sometimes customers may need help and assistance. Sometimes wheelchair users or others with a disability of some kind may require assistance to gain access to a particular part of the organisation. Whatever the nature of the request, employees should always be polite and show the customer that they are happy to help. It is important that however small the request for assistance might be, the customer feels valued and that the staff actually care about them.

A customer might have a query about one of the organisation's products or services. You should make sure they are clear about what they need to know. It may be that they need information or advice about the price of the product or it could be that you have to give them additional information to convince them to buy the product. They might also need information about the different methods of payment for the products and services on offer.

Build-up Exercise

We mentioned the term 'methods of payment' above. Can you list the different ways a customer might be able to pay for products and services? After you have written your list, say when they are likely to use each one.

Procedures for dealing with difficulties, including identifying people to whom appropriate difficulties should be referred

In either your business or the college there will be situations when it will be impossible for the regular staff who deal with the customers to cope with certain people who have complex problems. While most staff are trained to deal with routine problems, your business or your college will also have specialists who know far more than other employees about the area in which the customer is having difficulties. In these cases, you should take down the basic information about the customer's problem, promise to pass the information on and ensure that the appropriate member of staff to whom the difficulty is referred follows it up. Remember, even when you have referred a problem, the customer will remember *you* as being the person they approached in the first place and if the difficulty is not resolved there is every likelihood that they will ask for you again to enquire about progress.

Importance of expressing regret on behalf of the organisation without admitting liability

As we have said before, if it is appropriate for you to apologise to the customer on behalf of the business, then you should do so. However, there are some situations where making an apology infers that the business accepts responsibility for the error. This may cause problems for the business as the customer may want to claim compensation (money) from the business as a result of any losses or damages they have suffered.

Under most circumstances, however, a simply apology in relation to a late delivery, or not calling a customer when promised, is reasonable. In more complicated situations, for example delivering faulty goods that a customer needs urgently, it would be best simply to give a basic apology and promise to refer it to a more senior member of staff.

Try it out

Here are some statements from customers. Write down what you would say in response to them:

1 I paid express delivery and you promised me that it would be delivered this morning. It is now two o'clock. Where is it?
2 So, you are out of stock. I've got five customers waiting for these. Now that's your problem. What are you going to do about it?
3 Not faxing that information through to me in time has cost me a lot of money. I have a good mind to take your business to court.
4 When I got the box home it was supposed to have batteries and it didn't. My son was really disappointed.
5 What do you mean she is off sick? She arranged for me to call her this morning.

Record information accurately

Another important way that any organisation can provide effective customer service is to keep accurate and up-to-date information about its customers. They will want to know as much as possible about their customers so that they can provide them with exactly what they need.

Importance of keeping accurate records of customer information/enquiries/feedback for information and/or evaluation

Different types of organisations keep customer records for different reasons. All businesses need details of their customers' names, addresses, telephone numbers and e-mail addresses. But they may also try to get other customer information so that they can:

- find out how often customers spend their money (their spending habits)
- find out what customers like to spend their money on (their tastes)
- record how often they visit the organisation and what they spend their money on when they do so
- find out what customers intend to spend their money on in the future.

If organisations have enough information about their customers (or potential customers) they can make sure the products and services they offer meet their requirements. This helps the organisation to keep their existing customers and attract new ones. It may also help them get an 'edge' over their competitors.

Procedures for recording and following up complaints

In carrying out their business activities, most organisations will at some time receive a written complaint from a customer. As we already know, receiving complaints is something organisations should act on, using them to find ways of improving their customer service provision.

In response to a letter of complaint, the organisation should write back to the customer. Depending on the type of complaint, this could be a simple letter of apology, or it could involve in addition to the letter of apology:

- an offer of a refund of some or all of the money spent by the customer
- an offer to replace faulty products or services bought by the customer
- an offer of a cash payment to compensate the customer for any problems or inconvenience they have been caused.

Obviously, an investigation into the complaint would also have to be undertaken by the organisation. They will be interested in finding out whether the complaint was a result of some action by an employee or group of employees. If this were the case, they will want to reassure the customer that those responsible would be suitably disciplined.

If, after investigation, the organisation discovered that the customer had no real cause for complaint, they will still want to respond to the customer. Often they will:

- apologise to the customer for the fact that they have found cause to complain
- make a 'token offer' to the customer – this could be a voucher to be spent at the organisation in the future

They will do this so that the customer feels satisfied with the way the organisation had handled their complaint. The organisation acts to maintain the customer's 'goodwill'.

All letters of complaint should be handled as quickly as possible. Even when an enquiry or investigation has to be undertaken before a solution is found, the customer should be kept informed as to what the organisation intends to do and when they intend to do it.

Ensure customers' requirements have been met

It is rare to receive thanks from customers, but sometimes you may be surprised and they will express their satisfaction about the service they have received by writing to you or phoning. To make sure that customers are satisfied with the service they have received, you should do the following:

- Make sure that you agree on what you have offered to provide in the first place.
- Ensure that whatever you have offered meets with customer approval and satisfies their needs. If possible, you should even try to improve on it.
- If you have agreed to sort out a problem or deliver something by a particular date, then ensure that this is done and that they are not disappointed.
- Ensure that the quality of what you give the customer is acceptable – at the very least, it should be acceptable to you.

Summarising the situation and confirming any decisions taken

It is very important to ensure that any dealings with customers, particularly complaints or problems, are recorded and reported. Many businesses have forms which are specifically designed to allow employees to summarise the situation and, where appropriate, describe what they have done to deal with the customer's requirement. This form therefore not only summarises the situation, but also confirms that the requirements have been met and notes any decisions which have been made relating to the meeting of those requirements.

Keeping a written record

Many businesses consider customer complaints and problems to be useful, as they alert the business to potential difficulties which they may not have considered. In dealing with particular complaints or difficulties the business is able to change or amend its policies or procedures and, hopefully, improve its products or services. It helps the business and ensures that customers do not encounter the same difficulties in the future.

Written records are stored by staff who deal specifically with customer service issues. These staff may require the various departments that have contact with customers to forward written records of problems and complaints to them for analysis.

Checking that all details are correct

As with any record, it is important that all of the details of the customer complaint or problem are recorded accurately. In many businesses, although it is you who may receive the customer complaint, face to face or on the telephone, you may not be the individual dealing with it. To give the person who is dealing with the complaint the best opportunity to be efficient and effective, they need to have all the correct information. It would not project a very good image of either yourself or the business as a whole if vital customer information about the nature of the complaint was incorrect. It is therefore important that you check with the customer that you have recorded the correct information, particularly telephone numbers, which are easily written down incorrectly.

Need to ensure that customer is aware of any further action required and knows what happens next

Unless you can deal with a customer difficulty immediately, you will need to contact the customer at a later date. You should promise to keep the customer informed and you may be able to obtain some guidance on your company's procedures for contacting customers.

You should always ensure that if you have promised to contact the customer that you do so. The customer should not have to continually contact you for information.

Many businesses now use computer software to enter customer queries and complaints. The system alerts the user that update contact should be made at specific times, in line with the organisation's procedures.

Try it out

1 The first part of this activity is to design a simple customer complaint form. It should include the following sections:

Name of customer
Telephone/contact details of customer
Nature of complaint
Action taken
Customer informed and kept up to date
Customer satisfied and situation solved

2 The second part of the activity is to give your customer complaint form to another member of your group. You must then quickly read out loud the following information:

Telephone number 00224 43333. Delivery value £407.98, including £20.53 postage. Express delivery – arrived two days late. Wants his £20.53 back. Mr Cowley, Wenhaston Stationery Supplies.

3 Now compare what your partner has written on your form with the information you gave them. The information was deliberately given in a different order from the way it is displayed on the form to assess the usefulness of your form in different situations. If necessary, now amend your customer complaint form to make it easier to fill in. Did you leave enough space for certain sections? Is there anything that you should have put on your form that is missing?

4 Now give the form back to your partner and tell them the following, which was written on a post-it note left on your desk:

3/11

Pamela Gilbert has credited Wenhaston Stationery Supplies for half the postage. You need to contact Mr Cowley and tell him.

Your partner should update your customer complaints form as appropriate.

5 Assume that you have called Mr Cowley and left a message on his answerphone. He leaves a message on your phone the following morning, so you will now need to update your complaints form again:

'Cowley here. I'm not at all happy with your attitude. I'm just writing the cheque for your invoice and I will be deducting the remaining half of the postage from the full amount. I have hand amended your invoice to match.'

6 You now have to refer the matter to the accounts department. Take a photocopy of your form and write a covering memo which explains what steps you have taken.

7 A member of accounts calls you after receiving your memo and says that they have received the cheque from Mr Cowley and it is £10.26 short. She wants you to write him a letter and inform him that on this occasion the business will accept responsibility and cover the cost of the postage.

8 Update your customer complaint form and write the letter to Mr Cowley (you can make up the address).

3 Working in business organisations

Four key assessment objectives

- Describe and compare business organisations
- Explain how business organisations are structured
- Identify and explain effective working practices
- Identify and explain issues affecting working conditions

Each of these broad objectives covers a number of specific skills relating to working in business organisations.

In this unit you will learn how to:

- identify and compare the main types of business organisation
- explain how business organisations develop
- describe why an organisation must have clear aims and objectives
- identify the broad functional areas of business organisations and describe the main activities carried out in each
- describe how activities are organised to meet the organisation's objectives
- outline the roles of people at different levels of the organisation
- identify and evaluate the importance of effective administration
- explain the importance of planning work effectively
- explain the importance of organising the work area effectively
- explain the importance of working flexibly
- identify the factors that impact on efficiency
- identify ways of improving performance in the workplace
- explain how the environment can affect efficiency
- identify and explain health and safety issues in an administration environment
- describe employers' responsibilities under the health and safety legislation
- outline the rights and responsibilities of both employers and employees as set out in the contract of employment
- describe other protection offered to employees by employment and equal opportunities legislation.

Describe and compare business organisations

Different types of organisation differ a great deal, but they all have some common features, including:

- they all use resources (such as people, money and materials)
- they all provide something (usually a product or a service)
- they usually compete with other business organisations.

Each business, or business organisation, undertakes a variety of tasks or functions to operate effectively within their area of business. Some of these tasks are:

- **Managing employees** – usually through a human resource department.
- **Selling products or services** – providing customers with the required product or service.
- **Distributing products or services** – making sure the customer can get what the business provides.
- **Purchasing products or services** – ordering stock with which to manufacture their own products or provide services.
- **Marketing products or services** – carrying out research to find out what customers need and making sure they know what the business is offering for sale.
- **Keeping financial records** – monitoring the money coming into and leaving the business.

Organisations have to make sure that when they make a choice it is the right one. Businesses may not always have the same aims, but all organisations have considerations and choices to make. These often involve the most effective way to use their resources to meet the business's objectives, or to make a profit.

Identify and compare the main types of business organisation

Generally speaking, business organisations fit into two different sectors:

- **Private sector organisations** – these include sole traders, partnerships, private limited companies, public limited companies and charities.

Figure 3.1

- **Public sector organisations** – these include public corporations and local authorities.

You will need to be able to distinguish between private and public sector organisations and compare the different ways in which each works. Let us look at the private sector organisations first.

Distinguishing features of private sector organisations

Private sector organisations are independent of the government and include:

- **Sole traders** – organisations that are usually owned and run by one person, for example a newsagents.
- **Partnerships** – organisations owned by groups of people, for example a group of solicitors.

Figure 3.2

- **Limited companies (private and public)** – organisations owned by shareholders; they have either Ltd (Limited) or plc (Public Limited Company) in their name.
- **Charities** – organisations which do not function to make a profit; they may make money, but it is for the cause they are representing. An example is Oxfam.

Sole traders

The sole trader is, perhaps, the most common type of business organisation, although in recent years the numbers of this type of organisation have been declining. The sole trader is responsible for everything the organisation does. He or she is responsible for supplying or borrowing all the money required by the business and for actually running the business on a day-to-day basis. Perhaps the most common sorts of sole trader are plumbers, decorators, electricians, mobile hairdressers, window cleaners, garden handymen, etc.

Sole trader organisations cover a wide variety of activities, but they share some common features, including the way in which they start up. The person running the business has to be very flexible and usually willing to work long hours.

Figure 3.3

Figure 3.4

Table 3.1 *Advantages and disadvantages of sole trader organisations*

Advantages	Disadvantages
■ There are no particular legal formalities to complete before starting trading.	■ The amount of capital the owner can use is limited to their savings, their profits or money they can borrow.
■ There are no particular legal formalities about the way in which the business's accounts are produced. to raise the money to meet the business's debts.	■ The owner has sole responsibility for debts. If they do get into financial difficulties they could have to sell their own personal possessions.
■ The accounts of the organisation do not have to be audited.	■ All the responsibilities of running the business, such as dealing with the paperwork, with customers, completing legal documents and contacting suppliers, falls upon the shoulders of one person.
■ The owner has the freedom to run the business as they wish, without consulting anyone else.	■ To achieve success for the business the owner usually has to work very hard and put in long hours.
	■ If the owner has an accident or is ill, this could affect the proper functioning of the business.

Build-up Exercise

Using a copy of the *Yellow Pages* for your local area, first of all identify at least 10 sole traders. The *Yellow Pages* will not necessarily indicate the type of business, but you should be able to tell which ones are sole traders. How have you identified these organisations as being owned by a sole trader? What did you look for when deciding whether or not they were sole traders?

You will need to use the *Yellow Pages* again for the next few activities in this Unit.

Partnerships

A partnership may be formed as a way of overcoming the problems a sole trader can face in raising enough capital to operate. A partnership consists of between two and 20 people, who set up in business together and share the responsibility for that business. Partnerships of accountants, solicitors and Stock Exchange members can have more than 20 partners.

Each partner is required to contribute some capital and they share out the profits (or the losses) between all of the partners. Control of the business is the responsibility of all partners and decisions made by one partner are always binding on the others.

In most partnerships, all partners have what is known as unlimited liability. This means that any debts incurred by the partnership have to be met by all the partners.

Individuals who enter into a partnership can do so without any formal, written agreement, but newly formed partnerships usually draw up what is known as a partnership agreement. This agreement is a set of rules to follow in the case of any disagreements and usually includes the following items:

- the amount of money (capital) each of the partners is putting into the business
- the percentage of profits (or losses) to which each of the partners is entitled. Usually the more money the partner has put into the business, the bigger the share of profits they will be entitled to
- the wages or salary each partner will receive
- the rules for allowing new partners to join the business
- the rules for allowing partners to leave the business
- the rights of each of the partners in terms of voting or making decisions about the running of the business
- the rules for ending the partnership.

Table 3.2 *Advantages and disadvantages of partnership organisations*

Advantages	Disadvantages
■ It is easier for partners to raise capital than it is for sole traders. All the partners can put in as much capital as they can afford, which will be more than just what one individual could offer.	■ A partner is personally liable for the business's debts.
	■ If one or more partners are not contributing to the business, then disagreements can occur.
■ Partners can share their experience.	■ The amount of capital a partnership can raise is still limited.
■ Partners can share the workload.	
■ Partners can cover for one another during times of holiday or illness.	■ Decision-making can be slow because more than one partner has to be consulted each time a decision has to be taken.
■ Accounts do not have to be published or audited.	
■ More capital can be raised by introducing more partners into the business.	■ The death or retirement of one partner can bring a partnership to an end.
	■ All profits have to be shared.

There is another type of partnership, known as a limited liability partnership. In such partnerships, certain partners are known as 'sleeping partners' and they have no input into the decision-making process. If the business fails, sleeping partners are guaranteed not to lose any more money than the original capital they invested in the business. The rest of the partners, known as general partners, still have unlimited liability (they have to meet the remaining debts of the business). By law there must be at least one partner who has unlimited liability.

The most common type of partnership is the ordinary or general partnership, in which all of the partners play an active role in the running of the business and each has unlimited liability. It is important in this case that all partners are trustworthy, honest and hard-working, because the mistakes made by one can affect all of the others.

Partnerships are frequently found in the accounting and law professions, as well as amongst doctors, dentists and veterinary surgeons.

Build-up Exercise

Using the *Yellow Pages*, see if you can find at least 10 partnerships. Answer the same questions as you did in the previous activity on sole traders. This time decide how you identified them as being partnerships.

Limited companies (public and private)

The limited company is one of the most common forms of business organisation and is formed when individuals put capital into the business. They then become known as the business's 'shareholders' and each own part of the business. Shareholders share a percentage of any profits that are earned and they elect a number of directors who run the business on their behalf.

Figure 3.5

The law requires that shareholders meet once a year, but they do not usually have any input into the day-to-day running of the business, unless they are also directors, or workers who have bought shares. A number of Companies Acts and other laws have been passed which protect the shareholders' interests.

Setting up a limited company is quite simple and cheap to do, although the following two documents have to be drawn up:

- **The Memorandum of Association** – this is the equivalent of the business's rule book and includes the name and address of the company's registered office, the types of activities the business will be carrying out and the type and amount of capital which has been invested to set up the business.
- **The Articles of Association** – this document deals with the inside working of the company and must contain:
  - the procedures that have to be followed at the annual meeting of the shareholders (known as the AGM or Annual General Meeting)
  - the duties of the directors of the company
  - the voting rights of the shareholders
  - how the profits (or losses) of the business are to be shared between the shareholders
  - how the officers of the business will be appointed
  - how the accounts of the business will be kept and recorded
  - the rules for issuing new shares in the business
  - the rules regarding how shares can be transferred from one person to another.

The Memorandum of Association and the Articles of Association have to be registered with the Registrar of Companies at Companies House before the business can begin trading. The Registrar issues the business with a Certificate of Operation or a Trading Certificate.

There are two different types of limited company, both of which have to have a minimum of two shareholders:

1 **The private limited company** – you can always tell that a company is a private limited company when the word 'Limited' or 'Ltd' appears after the company name. The shares in a private limited company are not freely available to the general public and the transfer of shares is agreed only by the directors of the business. Private limited companies are often family businesses, or were so originally. This is the type of organisation that a sole trader would choose if they wished to expand but still wanted to keep overall control of the business.

2 **The public limited company** – tends to be a large organisation and often has the initials 'plc' after the business's name. These types of organisation raise their capital through selling their shares to the general public on the Stock Exchange. By doing this they get more flexibility in the amount of capital they can raise. There is no maximum number of shareholders, but a public limited company needs at least two. Once the public limited company has received its Certificate of Operation it prepares what is known as a prospectus. This is a way of inviting members of the general public to buy shares and the business will have to decide how the shares are to be sold and how many shares each member of the general public is allowed to buy.

Public limited companies have to file an Annual Report with Companies House. This gives the details of the directors and the shareholders of the business. This information is required by law and can be inspected by members of the public at Companies House.

Private limited companies and public limited companies have to send a copy of their audited accounts to the Registrar of Companies, including:

- a directors' report, which contains information about the business's activities
- an auditor's report, which is a report by an independent auditor on the business's accounts
- a balance sheet, which shows the business's income and expenses for the financial year
- the source and application of funds, which shows where the business has obtained its money and what the business has used the money on
- an explanation of the accounts, which also breaks down the way the business has obtained money and what it has spent money on.

Table 3.3 *Advantages and disadvantages of limited companies*

Advantages	Disadvantages
■ The shareholders have limited liability.	■ The running costs of a limited company can be high.
■ It is easier to raise capital through the selling of shares.	■ Decision-making can be slow because of the number of individuals involved.
■ Because the business is larger, it is often easier to raise money through banks.	■ The employees of the business might not even know who the shareholders of the business are.
■ The business can operate on a larger scale because it can obtain money easier.	■ The general public knows all the information about the business's affairs and activities.
■ Because the business is larger and can obtain money easier it is often possible to employ specialists (such as legal advisors or management consultants).	■ The Companies Acts are very strict and a limited company breaking these rules has to pay heavy penalties.
■ Suppliers often feel more confident dealing with larger organisations.	■ Because the business is large, the employees, customers and suppliers might feel management is too big to approach.
■ The directors are not liable for the debts of the business, provided they follow the rules of the organisation.	■ Limited companies often have to pay higher tax on the profits they make than sole traders and partnerships.
■ It is easy to pass the shares in the business down from one generation to another, so the control of the business can be kept in the family.	
■ The business's name is protected by law.	
■ The business could pay less tax if it gives shares to the employees.	

- Because the business is a large organisation it can offer employees extra benefits, such as a company pension scheme.
- Illness or the death of the shareholders of the business does not affect the running of the business's activities.

Build-up Exercise

You need the *Yellow Pages* again. This time, answer the same questions as you did for sole traders and for partnerships but identify at least five limited companies and five public limited companies in your area.

Charities

Charities approach their business activities differently from other organisations. Charities can be described in either of the following ways because some operate to make a profit and others do not consider making a profit to be their main aim:

- **Non-profit making charities** – not all charities operate to make a profit. If they do make a profit then this is usually put back into the business. The charity is not owned by anyone and there are no shareholders, so they do not have to make a profit for owners or shareholders.
- **Profit-making** – many charities do aim to make a profit from selling their goods and by fundraising, but the money is not given to shareholders or owners – it is used to support new activities or to purchase equipment.

A charity is not subject to many of the legal considerations that other types of organisation have to comply with. Obviously they have to consider the legal aspects of health and safety and contracts of employment for their employees, but any profits they make are not taxed. Good examples of charities are Oxfam, Help the Aged and Scope. Many schools have now decided to adopt this form of organisation.

Distinguishing features of public sector organisations

The public sector consists of organisations that are either owned or controlled by the government. The most common forms of public sector organisation are:

- **government departments** (the Civil Service) – these are departments which are responsible for running central government activities in a specific area, such as the Department of Trade and Industry (DTI) which assists businesses of all types

Figure 3.6

- **local government** – such as county, metropolitan, district or borough councils that provide services, assist businesses and promote their area
- **public corporations or enterprises** – these are also known as nationalised industries and provide services in a particular part of the economy. The Bank of England is an example of a public corporation.

Public corporations

When we consider the government, places like the Houses of Parliament, Downing Street and Whitehall are known to many people. But the government works in other areas that we do not readily think about. Many organisations are controlled by the government in some way, for a variety of reasons, including:

- to avoid duplication – there may be no need for many identical services offered by different companies
- to enlarge a business – the larger the business, the cheaper it can obtain materials and labour. If a business can carry out its activities more cheaply because it is bigger, then the public pays less for its products or services.
- to help control unemployment – by employing people in a public corporation, such as a Tax Office or a Job Centre Plus, the government can employ many people in areas of high unemployment.

One way that the government can safeguard the running of its public corporations is to set up organisations to keep an eye on them.

Although public corporations operate independently, they are controlled to some extent by government. It is the government's responsibility to make decisions about the closing down of parts of a business, or the investment of money to improve another. But on a daily basis the chairperson of the corporation and the other managers make decisions about wages, prices, industrial relations, etc. The government may intervene, however, where these decisions affect the general public.

Like a limited company, a public corporation has to prepare an annual report, but in this case it goes to the government minister responsible for monitoring the corporation's activities. The minister gives a report to the Members of Parliament, who will then make criticisms or support the corporation and how it is being run. At the same time a committee made up of Members of Parliament meets on a regular basis to keep an eye on the day-to-day running of the corporation and reports back to Parliament on how it is being operated. This is known as a Select Committee.

Figure 3.7 *The Minister reports to the House of Commons on the performance of a public corporation*

In addition to public corporations, there are two other areas where the government gets involved in the business world.

1 The first is when an activity is actually run by a government department. A good example is the Customs and Excise Department, which deals with the supervision and collection of taxes due on products entering and leaving the country.
2 The second is when the government is a shareholder in a public corporation.

Local authorities

Perhaps the most common form of government organisation is one with which you are probably more familiar; local government, or the local authority. In the UK certain services are run by local councils supervised by locally elected councillors. These councils usually run local services, such as swimming pools, sports centres, bus services, car parks, shopping centres and public toilets.

Local councils have their own staff for some functions but also employ private businesses to do work for them. They use a process known as tendering to find the most suitable business to do the work. It works in the following way:

Figure 3.8 *Local authorities run many local, public services*

- The local council gives a detailed description of the service it wishes to offer.
- Companies that are interested in running the service put sealed bids into the council. These bids explain what it would cost to run the service and what they would be providing.
- The council then chooses which company should run the service (not necessarily the one that put in the lowest tender) and offers them a contract to do the work.

- The council is then responsible for monitoring how well the business operates the service.
- If the business fails to reach certain standards the contract is taken away from them.

To pay for private businesses to carry out services, the local council gets money from:

- grants, directly from the government
- local taxes, such as business taxes and the community charge that people in the area pay.

Local authorities also help businesses that provide benefits to the community, such as parks, which by their nature are unlikely to make a profit.

Try it out

Find the website of your local government offices. Research where they get their money from and what they spend it on. From your findings write a memo-style report for you tutor. Your report should identify where are the sources of local government money and how it is spent. Use headings, sub-headings and bullets or numbered points to break up the discussion in your memo.

Compare ownership, control, objectives, liability

Probably the best way of comparing the different types of business organisation we have discussed is to refer to Table 3.4. The table summarises what we have covered so far and you can use it to revise this aspect of the unit.

Reasons why different forms of ownership may be appropriate to different situations

Different forms of organisational ownership suit different situations. The preferred type of ownership will depend on:

- the age of the business
- the desire of the owner(s) to keep the business under their own control.

The owners may wish the business to grow and make a bigger profit, but that does not mean they are willing to change the way it carries out its activities, or to give up their ownership of the business.

Remember, when a business moves from being a sole trader organisation into a partnership, the original owner loses some control of the business to the new partner or partners. Similarly, when a partnership or a sole trader offers the general public the chance to buy shares, the owners will lose some control as the directors and managers of the business will become involved in the decision-making process.

Table 3.4 *Characteristics of different types of business*

Type of organisation	Ownership	Control	Objectives	Liability
Sole trader	One owner	The owner	To make profit to reinvest in the business and pay the owner or any employees	Unlimited
Partnership	2–20 partners	The partners	To make profit to reinvest in the business and to pay the partners	Unlimited (except in limited partnerships)
Private limited companies	The owners	Owner, directors and managers	To make a profit to reinvest in the business and to pay the shareholders	Limited
Public limited companies	The owners	Owner, directors and managers	To make a profit to reinvest in the business and to pay the shareholders	Limited
Charities	None	The trustees of the charity	To promote the cause in question. Any profits are reinvested in the cause	Depends on the structure and charitable status – can be limited or unlimited
Public corporations	Central government	The Prime Minister, cabinet ministers, civil servants	Any profits are reinvested in the Treasury	Not applicable
Local authorities	Central government via the local authority	Local councillors and officials	Any profit made is reinvested (usually in local community benefits)	Not applicable

Try it out

Pelican Training was founded in 1966 in Nottingham. For the first 10 years Frances and John Thompson ran the business as a partnership, as there was little need for additional money. By the 1980s the business had grown and the Thompsons had taken on several new members of staff. They also wanted to set up branches in other cities around the UK. So they decided to float Pelican Training on the Stock Exchange. Pelican Training became a plc, meaning it had access to large amounts of money (capital) to help it expand.

Like many businesses, Pelican Training plc was hit very hard by problems in the country in the 1980s and its share price fell. Income also fell as many of its customers cut back, or went out of business.

By the end of the 1980s Pelican Training plc was £5m in debt. The financial position had got so bad that the Thompsons failed to submit their accounts and their shares were suspended on the Stock Exchange.

The Thompsons had worked with Nigel Baker for some years and he came to the business's aid, investing £10m in the business. But this meant that Pelican Training plc became a limited company and was no longer quoted on the Stock Exchange. Nigel had become the biggest shareholder.

Pelican Training Limited, now run by Sarah, the Thompson's daughter, and Frank, Nigel Baker's son, remains a limited company and now looks forward to a far more stable future.

Questions
1 Why might setting up a partnership mean that the business cannot gain access to additional money?
2 Give three reasons why a business may become a plc.
3 Why might a business stop being a plc and become a limited company?
4 What does it mean to be 'the largest shareholder in a business'?
5 Why might the Stock Exchange suspend a business's shares?
6 If Sarah and Frank wish to expand the business, what would you suggest they do to raise money?

Explain how business organisations develop

Business organisations can develop in many different ways and some may choose not to develop or change at all. Generally speaking, businesses can develop either by reinvesting money which they have made themselves or by finding an alternative source of money (finance). The problem with the second option is that borrowing money or encouraging others to invest money in the business means that the investors will want some control over the business itself. This is quite reasonable, as they will wish to protect the money which they have invested.

Businesses can turn to banks, building societies, private investors, or even the government for the finance to expand or develop. The majority of these cash loans have to be paid back over an agreed period of time. Before a business borrows money it needs to be sure that it can increase its profits enough to pay back the loan, and the money it cost to take out the loan (interest). Otherwise it will find itself in debt.

The other main way for a business to raise finance is to offer a share of the business to someone else. In the case of a sole trader, for example, a partner may be sought to bring money (and skills) into the business. Whereas before the sole trader would have controlled all of the business, now the partner would control part of it.

This situation becomes trickier when shareholders become involved. Large plcs may have literally thousands of shareholders and even private limited companies may have hundreds of shareholders. All of these shareholders are looking to the business to provide them with a profit from their investment and this places an extra strain on the business itself.

Although there is no one way in which businesses always develop, Figure 3.9 shows how an organisation which is concerned with making a profit may develop over a period of time. Bear in mind that this process is not fast; it may take several decades, if indeed it happens at all.

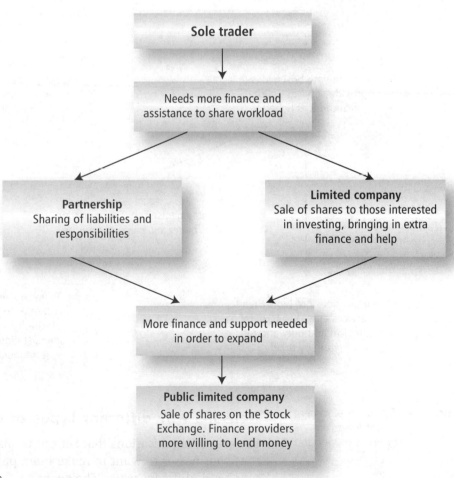

Figure 3.9 *Typical development of a profit-related business organisation*

Not all organisations, of course, are interested in making a profit. There are many organisations that still develop, but are not primarily concerned with making money. Within this group are all local authorities, charities, support groups, housing associations and a variety of other organisations which provide services to the community or to particular groups. There is again no single way in which all of these organisations develop, but many become larger and get involved in more issues the longer they exist. Charities raise funds by various means (donations, grants, subscriptions, etc.) to provide services or support for their client groups. Ways in which these types of organisations could develop are outlined in Figure 3.10.

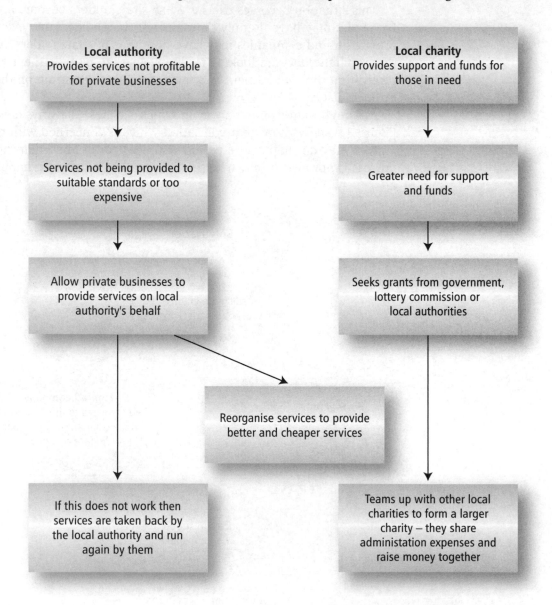

Figure 3.10 *Typical development of not-for-profit business organisations*

Reasons why different types of organisation develop

Looking at organisations that set out to make a profit, it is natural for these businesses to want to make more profit. They can do this in a number of different ways. They can:

- **become more efficient** – which may not mean becoming bigger, but just becoming better at what they do
- **become bigger** – which may have its own problems, such as additional employees and higher costs, but can place the business in a position to take advantage of situations as they arise
- **join forces** – small and medium-sized businesses may decide to join together to become both bigger and more efficient
- **do other things** – the business may decide that there are other activities which would provide it with additional opportunities to make profits.

Need for capital

All businesses need capital to survive. This capital can come from a variety of different sources; it can be:

- created by the business from the profits of its operations
- borrowed as a loan from banks, building societies or other finance providers
- acquired by the sale of shares in the business.

Businesses need capital for a number of uses which ensure that they continue to operate. These include:

- the purchase of products and services from other businesses
- the payment of wages and salaries to the employees of the business
- the payment of rent, rates, electricity, gas, water and other services
- the payment of running costs and equipment, such as paper, office equipment and machinery to make products.

Above all, a business needs to manage its funds so that it has sufficient money to pay its immediate bills, which take money out of the business.

Liability

Sole traders and partnerships have what is known as unlimited liability. This means that if the business fails whilst owing money to other businesses or individuals, the owners of the business must find the money from their own resources to pay it back. This could mean that the owners of the business lose their homes, cars and other possessions to pay what is owed by the business.

Shareholders, on the other hand, whether they own shares in private limited companies or public limited companies, only stand to lose the amount of money which they invested in the shares in the first place. Their own private possessions are protected. So shareholders have what is known as 'limited liability'.

Specialisation

Some businesses may begin by offering a wide variety of different products and services. Over time they may discover that it is easier, or more profitable, to offer only a limited range of products and services.

The business may become expert at providing particular products and services. This is known as specialisation and because the business is so good at providing these particular products and services, it is more efficient and effective and makes higher profits, even though it is offering a more limited range than it did in the past.

An example of this may be a sole trader who begins trading as an odd-job man. To begin with, this individual does gardening, painting, decorating, repairs, some plumbing and some bricklaying. The sole trader may discover that there is not much demand for painting and decorating and, in any case, he or she is not very good at it. They may therefore decide to concentrate on gardening and becomes a specialist gardener, thereby developing the business by specialising in one area.

Diversification

Diversification is another way in which a business can develop. It is, in some ways, the opposite of specialisation. A business which chooses to develop through diversification becomes involved in a wider range of business activities. An example would be a small electrical retailer who sells vacuum cleaners, fridges, kettles and other small electrical appliances. They decide to diversify and sell CDs and music systems in their retail shop. They have diversified into an area of business which complements their existing one and which will hopefully bring new customers into the shop. They may later decide to employ a repair person who can undertake repairs for their customers, rather than sending faulty appliances back to the manufacturer. This is another form of diversification since it relates to the type of work they are already involved in.

The larger the business, the more opportunities there are for diversification. Diversification does not necessarily mean becoming involved in areas of business which the company is already involved in. A good example would be easyJet; this is part of a related group that includes car hire, insurance, finance, hotels and Internet cafés.

Try it out

Have a look at the easyJet website on www.easyjet.com and find out what other businesses are in the 'family'. Now compare the types of businesses in this family with the Virgin family of businesses at www.virgin.com. How many of the businesses are related to one another? Why do you think the major owners of these businesses have chosen to diversify so widely?

Mergers, de-mergers and takeovers

Mergers take place when two or more businesses join together to create a new business, using the resources of both businesses. There are different ways in which businesses can merge:

- One business may buy the majority of the shares of another business. This is known as a takeover. If the business which is being bought is happy to be purchased by the other business, it is a 'friendly takeover'. If the business being purchased does not want to be bought, but is purchased all the same, it is known as a 'hostile takeover'.

■ Two or more businesses may combine some of their resources to create a completely separate business. This is known as a 'joint venture'. A joint venture is usually involved in an area of business which the two or more original businesses were not involved in before. The businesses combine their expertise, perhaps transferring staff as well as resources to the new business.

It is worth remembering that any merger between two or more businesses not only means the joining together of resources, but also the joining together of liabilities. Any money or debts which were owed by either of the businesses now become the responsibility of the newly merged business.

Mergers have implications for employees and shareholders. It is often the case that when businesses merge, employees who are carrying out similar jobs find that both sets of staff are no longer needed. The newly merged business will only require one accounts department, and probably one set of customer service employees; other duplicated jobs will also disappear.

As far as shareholders are concerned, their shares in one of the original businesses now become shares in the newly merged business. There are various complicated rules about changing the names and the values of shares, but it is usual for the shareholders to receive a number of shares in the newly merged business that is related to the number of shares which they held before the businesses were merged. It is usually the case that the shares in the merged business are worth more than the original shares.

Try it out

Go to www.competition-commission.org.uk. Find out what the Competition Commission does and what its role is in the case of businesses that merge.

Review the impact of development on organisations

To provide evidence that you have understood the impacts of development on organisations, you should carry out the following activity.

Try it out

Go back to the activity relating to Pelican Training's development over the years. You now need to review the impact of these changes on the business. Write a report to your tutor, making sure that you take each event separately. You should not just write another ▶▶

account of what happened to Pelican Training; look at this activity as a review process. Consider the implications to the organisation at each stage of its development. When considering the implications for the organisation also include the implications for the employees, owners and subsequently the shareholders.

Describe why an organisation must have clear aims and objectives

All business organisations, whether they are small, medium or large, have a set of aims or objectives which they wish to achieve. However, there are some things that can affect whether or not a business is able to meet its objectives, some of which may be out of the control of the organisation itself. Such factors include:

- **changes to the law** – such legal changes might affect, for example, the manufacture of its products, or the way in which it advertises them to the customer.
- **internal problems** – such as financial difficulties, can affect the way an organisation works towards meeting its objectives.
- **change in ownership** – for example if a sole trader becomes a partnership this can affect the original business's objectives and require the new partnership to draw up a new set of aims or objectives.

A good starting point for anyone starting a business is to write down its main aims, purposes and objectives in what is known as a business plan. Having written a business plan, however, the business owners must be aware that they need to be flexible. The environment in which the business is operating can be constantly changing and the objectives will change along with it.

The business objectives that could be included in a business plan differ for each organisation, but could include any of the following:

- to be successful
- to make a profit
- to break even – this means that the business makes enough money to pay its bills, but not to make a profit
- to sell products
- to sell services
- to survive.

Obviously, it is in everyone's interests to identify the exact business objectives of the organisation, but it must be remembered that business objectives may change with time. Objectives are the medium- to long-term targets which help the business to achieve its 'mission statement' (see below).

There are a number of different methods of ensuring that the employees know about the business's objectives. The employees must have a clear picture of the organisation's objectives. Organisations use some of the following ways to keep their employees up to date with changing objectives:

- staff meetings
- newsletters
- company newspapers
- bulletin boards
- notice boards
- e-mail messages
- press statements or press releases
- organisational videos
- letters or memos sent directly to all employees.

Mission statements (corporate objectives)

An organisation's mission statement is different from its business plan because it describes what the organisation as a whole stands for rather than its aims and objectives. It is an agreement between the managers and the employees of the organisation regarding a number of goals. Everyone involved in the business will have an opinion about the way goals should be achieved, but the mission statement should ensure that they share at least some ideas about how they will be achieved.

A business's fundamental policy will be contained within the mission statement. It describes the organisation's business vision, including its values and purpose. A business may choose to include within its mission statement a vision of how it wishes its employees to respond, react and fulfill the needs of its customers.

Businesses try to ensure that whatever is contained within their mission statement will be achieved. They often put in place employee development programmes and training to achieve the goals described in the mission statement.

Strategic plans

Once an organisation has set its objectives it has to find ways of achieving them. The organisation employs strategies and tactics:

- **Strategies** – the long-term ways the business hopes to achieve its objectives, for example to increase the sales of products by 10% over the next 2 years
- **Tactics** – the short-term ways the business hopes to achieve its strategies, for example to increase the sales of products by 10% over the next 2 years, the company may decide it needs to find cheaper suppliers and increase the money it spends on advertising.

A strategic plan is a series of activities which aims to establish the ways in which the business's objectives can be met. Strategic planning should be a continuous process, with the ways in which the business is aiming to achieve the objectives being carefully monitored and controlled.

How objectives affect company policy and the culture of an organisation

A business's objectives will have an effect on the way in which the organisation decides to carry out its work. Equally, the way in which the organisation decides to carry out its work will affect how the employees work on a daily basis.

A business's policies and culture are created to allow the business to achieve its goals and objectives. The process begins with deciding what the corporate objectives should be. These may be quite broad and simply, say, to double in size over the next five years, or to open a branch in every major city in the UK in the next 10 years. Other objectives could relate to activities within the business itself. The objective may be to cut waste, to improve efficiency or to always provide excellent customer service. As far as organisations and customers outside the business are concerned, all they will probably ever see is the business's mission statement (if it has one). This will be an even simpler version of its corporate objectives.

Once those running the business have decided on the corporate or company objectives, they will seek to create policies, rules, regulations and procedures to help the company reach those objectives. When people refer to a business culture, in some respects it is referring to these policies and procedures. But it is more than that; it includes training and developing employees and managers to recognise and work towards the business's objectives in the most effective and efficient way.

Organisational culture can mean many things. It can include some or all of the following. Note that some may seem odd and somewhat petty, but they are all part of an organisation's culture:

- the style and colour of its fixtures and fittings
- how meetings are conducted
- how appraisals and staff development are undertaken
- dress codes (the way employees are expected to dress for work)
- the appearance of the organisation's buildings
- steps taken to ensure quality
- the use of and access to IT facilities
- car parking rules.

A business's culture develops over a period of time. The business will begin to push to create particular patterns of work or codes of behaviour aimed at achieving the organisation's objectives.

When new employees start work they are gradually introduced to the business's culture. Often they will have a short induction programme which introduces them to the company's policies and procedures and the ways of doing things at work. They will not necessarily understand why things are done the way they are, but as they gain experience and meet and work with existing employees, they will gradually adopt the same culture as the other people working in the business.

A business's culture should help everyone to understand how to do things, why they are doing it that way and, above all, that in doing it this way others in the business will receive the information and assistance they need in the way they need it.

Try and find out about different organisations' cultures. If you are at work you could ask a few of your colleagues to describe your business's culture. If you are at college, ask two or three of your tutors to describe the college's culture. You could also try to obtain a copy of either the college or your business's mission statement which should identify the organisation's main purpose. Ask family and friends who work in different organisations what they consider to be the organisational culture of their business. See if they know what the business's objectives are.

When you have gathered this information, compare the cultures of different businesses. You could try to categorise them as task-based (the culture revolves around people's ability to do things), rule-based (the culture is controlled by rules), power-based (the culture relies on trust and personal communication), or person-based (based around people co-operating with each other).

Present your findings in the form of a table, using the four different types of organisational culture as your column headings.

Explain how business organisations are structured

The easiest way to visualise an organisation's structure is to think about a pyramid. At the top of the pyramid there are a few people making the most important and the biggest decisions about the business. As you go down the pyramid there are various layers of managers. After the managers are team leaders or supervisors. At the broadest part of the pyramid, the base, are the rest of the employees.

Now imagine an arrow running from the top to the bottom of the pyramid. This represents instructions or orders being passed down the various layers of the organisation, until they reach the employees at the bottom. Now put another arrow pointing in the opposite direction; this represents the information provided by employees to their team leaders or supervisors, who then check that information and pass it up the various layers of management. The management then passes this information on to the owners of the organisation. Armed with this information the business's owners can now make their decisions and create orders and instructions that are passed back down to ensure the business continues to run successfully. Figure 3.11 illustrates this process.

The way in which an organisation chooses its structure depends on a number of issues, including:

- the size and nature of the market in which it operates
- the type of business in which it is involved
- the need for good communication throughout the organisation

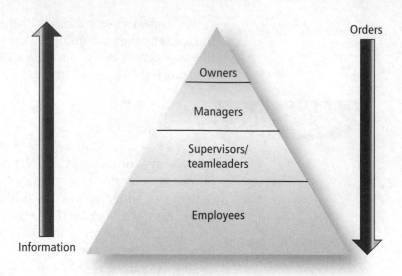

Figure 3.11 *Representation of a business as a pyramid*

- the size of the organisation
- the number of different branches or sites owned by the organisation
- the type and number of customers the organisation has
- how much the organisation is affected by government laws
- how much the organisation is affected by new technologies
- the organisation's responsibilities and obligations
- the way the organisation was structured in the past
- the way the organisation is currently structured
- what the organisation's plans are for the future
- how complex the organisation's activities are.

There are a number of different organisational structures that a business might choose. In this part of the unit we will consider what is known as a functional structure. Other types of organisational structure will be considered later in this unit.

The functionally-based structure

A functionally-based organisational structure is usually designed around the different parts of the organisation that produce, market and sell the product or service. The different departments or functions are controlled by a board of directors, who elect or appoint a managing director. The managing director is supported by a range of senior managers, each of whom has responsibility for one particular function (department) of the organisation. Figure 3.12 shows a functional structure.

Build-up Exercise

Consider either the college in which you are studying this course, or your place of work. You might also have a part-time Saturday job with an organisation on which you could base this activity. See if you can draw up an organisation chart (like Figure 3.12) for your business or college. Instead of worrying about people's job titles, put in their names if it makes the task easier.

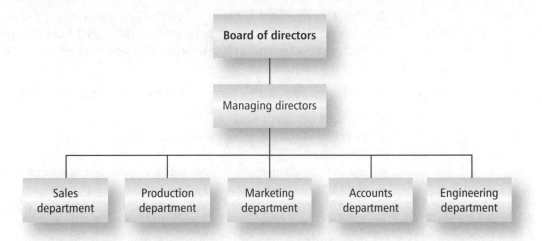

Figure 3.12

Identify the broad functional areas of business organisations and describe the main activities carried out in each

Many organisations, particularly large ones, use a functional organisational structure. The functions form, in fact, the different areas or departments of the business. The business needs to be organised in the best possible way to meet its objectives. Its structure helps to define what individuals do and the responsibilities of each department.

With a functional organisational structure a business can group similar functions that it carries out under the supervision of a single manager. There are four ways of grouping the different functions of a business:

- by what is produced (the product)
- by employee function, or what they do for the organisation
- by process, which means how they do it, for example by having various regional offices
- by type of customer served, for example whether the business deals with other business organisations or with retail outlets.

Functional areas of organisations

The functional areas of an organisation (often these are the same as the departments within the organisation) are all concerned with specific jobs. To understand fully what this means, we need to look at each of the departments or functions separately.

Finance/accounting

The finance or accounts department of an organisation supervises all matters involving money. Computers and calculators are used extensively. Sometimes the finance department is split into two sections:

1 The day-to-day accounting procedures are handled by the '*f* accounting section'. This section keeps track of all money (into and going out of the business.

2 The 'management accounting section' concentrates on analysing the financial figures and trying to predict (forecast) how much the business will earn, and how much the business will have to pay out, in the future.

The finance department records and monitors the following:

- **sales** of the business's products or services
- **purchases** the business has made to make its products or provide its services
- **manufacturing costs** – how much it costs the business to make its products
- **running costs** – how much it costs the business to keep running, for example, the lighting and heating bills
- **dividends** to shareholders – the money the business pays those people who own shares (only in private limited companies and public limited companies)
- **wages and salaries** – the money the business pays its employees
- **departmental and organisational budgets** – how much each department is spending and how much the organisation as a whole is spending. A budget is often worked out for each separate department. In order to stick to their budget, each department has to provide the finance department with details of what it has earned, what it has spent and on what it has been spent.

The finance department uses this information to find out whether or not the business is making a profit. It checks to make sure that the business's revenue (the money coming into the business) is greater than its costs (the money being spent by the business).

The information the finance department calculates is needed by the directors, shareholders and senior managers of the business. The finance department gives this information to them in written documents, including those called balance sheets and profit and loss

Build-up Exercise

We have mentioned that the finance department deals with wages and salaries. From your business or from your college, see if you can find out the following:

1 What information does the finance department need to keep about each of the employees?
2 Does the finance department of your business or college do all the tasks discussed here, or does it employ another business to do some of them?
3 What information does the finance department have to provide by law about employees for the Inland Revenue, the government department that collects tax?
4 What information does the finance department keep about each of the employees regarding their pensions?

accounts. By law the finance department has to keep written records of all financial decisions taken by the business, including all sales made and items purchased.

Human resources

The main function of the human resources department is to recruit new employees and organise them so that they provide the type of work the organisation needs to meet its objectives. The human resources department is also sometimes known as the 'personnel department'.

It closely monitors the selection of new employees, but this is not where the function of the human resources department ends. It also tries to ensure that employees are adequately trained and developed, and that suitable employees are given higher and often better paid jobs (promotion) within the business.

The human resources department stays in close contact with all other departments to make sure that the employees are receiving the right kind of training. It will organise:

- **the induction of new employees** – telling them about the organisation when they first start
- **training** – perhaps to cover how to use new technology
- **retraining** – perhaps when an employee's job has been moved from one department to another, or has changed in nature for some other reason.

The human resources department is also responsible for keeping all employee records, including details of:

- holiday entitlements – days of holiday already taken and the number of days the employee has left to take
- sickness records – the number of days the employee has taken off due to illness
- qualifications of each employee
- experience of each employee, both before and whilst working for the business
- wage or salary of each employee
- pension details for each employee
- confidential reports from the employees' line managers or supervisors
- details of the training each employee has undertaken.

By law all confidential information of this kind has to be carefully stored. The Data Protection Act lays down rules that tell human resources departments who can see such information and how it is to be kept by the business.

The human resources department is also the main negotiator on behalf of the business in matters relating to trade unions and employee associations. They negotiate about general problems, for example regarding pay and the working conditions of employees.

When an employee leaves an organisation this is known as 'termination of employment'. The human resources department oversees this procedure and ensures that the person leaving receives all relevant documents.

Employees leave organisations for a number of different reasons, including:

- **retirement** – when they have reached the age where they are entitled to receive a pension and wish to give up working
- **redundancy** – when the business has decided that the employee's job is no longer required and they are not required in another department of the organisation
- **resignation** – when an employee simply decides to move on, to another business perhaps
- **dismissal** – when the employee has behaved in a way that is not acceptable to the business and is asked to leave.

Build-up Exercise

Human resources department employees often have the pleasant task of informing the most suitable candidate that they have got the job they applied for. However, they also have to tell the unsuccessful candidates that they have not been successful. This needs to be done as tactfully as possible and involves using the right tone and style in the letter of refusal.

Imagine that you work in the human resources department and have the task of writing to three unsuccessful candidates. Compose a standard letter that could be sent to all of them.

Production

The production department is the principal department in actually producing the products or services for the customer. The production department monitors levels of wastage to ensure the most efficient use of resources and checks the cost of raw materials and parts purchased to make sure that profit margins are maintained.

As new products are developed, and technology changes, the production department is responsible for purchasing all the new machinery or equipment required. But the main function of the production department is to organise the production process.

In collaboration with the sales department, the production department must make sure that it can manufacture or supply customers with the quantity they require, when required. Tight monitoring of production levels should allow the production department to know the time needed to produce enough to meet any particular order. Advance planning and close contact with the sales department are vital, as deadlines must be met.

The production department is also responsible for the quality of the business's products. Each product must meet a number of strict quality standards. Products are selected from the production line and tested by either the research and development department or, if the business has one, the quality assurance department.

A good production department will also monitor the methods of production used by the business's competitors and take steps to adopt any useful methods they identify.

The production department is responsible for the following activities:

- manufacture of the business's products
- monitoring of wastage and the relevant costs of the production process
- design of machinery
- writing or buying-in computer software to help the production process
- control of the rate of production
- monitoring and control of the quality of the products
- monitoring of competitors' production processes.

The production department communicates and works closely with most of the organisation's other departments. It also communicates with the business's suppliers. The production department does not necessarily communicate directly with the business's customers.

Build-up Exercise

Look at the following list of other departments the production department might work closely with:

Sales   Finance
Marketing   Human resources
Purchasing   Administration
Research and development

Use each of these departments as a heading in a table. Under each heading give the reasons why you think the production department might need to communicate with that department. What information would the production department need to give each of these other departments? What information would the production department need to obtain from each of these other departments?

Research and development (R&D)

Working closely with the marketing department (which keeps a close eye on the business's competitors), the research and development department attempts to come up with new product ideas for the business.

But the main function of the research and development department is not just to come up with new products or services; it also has to devise the most efficient and effective method of production. It will, after carrying out a number of tests, pass on to the production department its designs and proposed production methods. The production department then takes over the responsibility of putting the new methods into practice, or of making the new product.

On a routine basis the research and development department tests samples of the products being manufactured to determine whether they are of a high enough quality to meet the standards set by the business and those set down by the government.

The research and development department may also test the products of the business's competitors. They do this to find out how they have been manufactured and how they compare with the business's own products. The R&D department keeps a close eye on any new technologies that become available to see if these could improve the business's products or production processes.

Build-up Exercise

The research and development department is often known as just 'R&D'. Using a dictionary, see if you can find out what these other initials or acronyms represent:

ABTA	LAN	PABX
E&OE	WAN	CAD
COHSE	CAM	

Purchasing

The purchasing department is responsible for assisting other departments of the business in ordering and buying the goods and services they require. This is an important function. The purchasing department ensures the supply of the following:

- **Raw materials** – these are the unfinished or basic materials which some manufacturing businesses require. Raw materials include things like coal, metals, wood, building materials (sand or gravel) and many other items which had not had a great deal done to them (processed) before they are delivered to a customer. Raw materials are the base materials which are used to make other things, or allow other things to be made. Coal, for example, may simply be used to heat a building, but it may also be used to provide fuel for machinery. Tree trunks can be turned into planks of wood or, through a series of processes, into paper.
- **Components** – these are parts which make up finished goods. A computer has hundreds of components, which include various pieces of wire, switches, circuit boards and memory chips. Many businesses take delivery of components and are involved in putting these components together to make a new product.
- **Consumable items** – for example paper, envelopes, company-headed stationery, pens and pencils.

Whatever the purchasing department orders from its suppliers, it needs to ensure that the company is receiving the best possible price, as well as ensuring that the goods are received when they are required. The purchasing department keeps a stock of catalogues and price lists from suppliers. When the purchasing department's employees receive a purchase requisition (a request to purchase) from elsewhere in the organisation, they research the various suppliers until they find the right product, at the right price, with the right delivery time.

Build-up Exercise

See if you can obtain a copy of a catalogue from an office equipment business and one from an office stationery business. You work in the purchasing department of a business and have received a purchase requisition for the following:

- two reams of A4 white photocopy paper
- two pine desks
- one typist's chair.

Have a look through the catalogue and see if you can find out:

- the cost of each of these items
- the total cost of the order
- details of how long it will take to receive the order.

Now write a memo to your tutor, informing him/her what you have discovered.

Sales

The sales department's main responsibility is to sell the business's products or services. Many organisations employ a large salesforce. Sales staff may be employed at a local level in the case of retail outlets (shops), or in the case of organisations which supply other organisations, on a regional basis.

The greater the emphasis on selling to individual customers, the larger the salesforce needed. But businesses that rely on large amounts of advertising to gain customers' interest can have a relatively smaller salesforce.

The sales department draws up a sales plan, which includes target figures to be met by each of the areas or regions of their salesforce. It also includes the level of profit that is expected from each product sold.

The sales department works closely with the marketing department, supplying sales information that includes:

- the current level of sales
- the activities of the business's competitors
- requests from customers for new products
- requests from customers for improvements to particular products or their design.

The information supplied by the sales department is analysed by the marketing department. Often the sales department also develops what is known as 'point-of-sale' materials. These include posters, leaflets, brochures, pamphlets and catalogues.

Build-up Exercise

Salesforce employees often have to work out their own schedule or timetable for the week. Imagine that you are a sales representative for your business and you have the following constraints and commitments lined up for next week:

1 You only have to be present at head office for two hours during the week.
2 You have a total of over 200 customers on your customer list.
3 Your sales area covers one-tenth of the UK.
4 You usually spend at least 20 hours per week in the car, travelling to visit customers.
5 You spend on average 20 minutes with each of your customers.
6 Keeping your paperwork up to date takes at least one and a half hours each day.
7 Telephone calls (including those made on your car phone or mobile) take up at least one hour each day.

See if you can draw up a timetable that would allow you to include all these items in a normal Monday–Friday, eight-hour day, working week.

Marketing

The main function of the marketing department is to try to meet the current needs of the business's customers and to predict what they may need in the future. Working closely with the sales department, the marketing department carries out a great deal of research to discover what customers want, where they want to be able to buy what they want and how much they are prepared to pay. It also tries to design the best way to inform customers about what the business is offering.

The marketing department also works closely with research and development. Together they develop attractive and saleable products, update existing products and try out new ideas on customers in an attempt to meet any changes they have found in customer taste and demand.

The marketing department is responsible for advertising the business's products and ideas through marketing campaigns. The design and development of these campaigns is a co-operative effort with the sales department and other interested areas within the business.

The marketing department communicates persuasively the business's message to its customers, and those they hope will become new customers. Persuasive communication tries to:

- convince the customer about something
- motivate the customer into doing something
- influence the customer to do something

- advertise a new, updated or amended product
- sell a new, updated or amended product
- promote a new, updated or amended product and the business itself.

It uses descriptive words like new; improved; delicious; healthy; exciting; special to attempt to persuade customers to buy. It does this to:

- launch a new product or service
- try to keep existing customers
- try to increase the current number of customers
- inform the public about an updated product or service
- try to make more people aware of the company's products.

Build-up Exercise

You have been asked by your business to contact several hundred possible new customers about a new service it is offering. The business does not wish to spend too much on postage, so it wants you to design something which can be delivered with the free local newspaper that everyone in the local area receives through their letterbox. Here is the information you have been given:

We are planning to expand the services we currently offer by now offering delivery. The sandwich take-away shop is doing very well, but we think we can increase our customer numbers by offering a delivery service too. All the local office blocks might want to have sandwiches delivered at lunch times and we think there may be some people who would like us to prepare sandwiches for them if they have guests or are holding parties.

Distribution

The effective and efficient distribution of the business's products is the responsibility of the distribution department. Very often this department is split into two sections:

- **The stores or warehouse** – this is where the products are stored safely. These may be the products that are ready to be sold on to customers. It could also be where all packaging, raw materials or part-finished products are stored until they are required by the production department. This section of the department keeps a careful check on the stock levels of all items for which it has overall responsibility and informs the relevant department should stocks begin to approach their 'minimum levels', as they then need to be re-ordered from the supplier.
- **Distribution or transportation** – the main function of this section is to co-ordinate the business's transport needs. This includes the purchasing, or hiring, of company cars, lorries and trucks, as well as ensuring they are serviced and maintained. The department has to

maintain records such as insurance, vehicle registration, road tax, service records and hiring or purchasing agreements for each of the business's delivery vehicles.

In situations when an organisation provides a delivery service to the customer, it is essential that the most efficient and cost-effective (cheapest) routes are used. This is often a task carried out using computer software.

Build-up Exercise

Think back to the last activity when you worked for a sandwich take-away business. If the business decided to go ahead with the proposed delivery service, can you think of particular considerations it would need to think about regarding its delivery vans? How could it advertise the business using the delivery vans? What would be important considerations regarding the freshness (quality) of the sandwiches once they reached the customers?

Administration

Some organisations have what is known as a central administration department. The main function of this department is to control the paperwork and support all the other departments by providing them with secretarial or administrative work, for example:

- wordprocessing or data input
- filing paperwork
- making telephone calls
- dealing with the mail, both incoming and outgoing
- gathering information or collecting data for another department to use
- sending fax and e-mail messages.

The administration department of a business deals with a variety of data and information from a range of different places. The information received is often processed by administration staff to make it useful to others. Such processing may involve the department in any of the following tasks:

- **Researching and obtaining information** – this may involve searching for information on the Internet, or from libraries, catalogues or reference books.
- **Summarising the information** – this could take the form of reading something and then presenting it in a more concise, shortened form.
- **Presenting the information** – administration employees have to be knowledgeable about the ways in which the business prefers to present information. Information can be presented in a number of different ways, including memos, letters, reports, articles or notices.

Build-up Exercise

You work in the administration department of a primary school. The headmistress is expecting four visitors on Tuesday of next week at 11.00 am. They are inspectors who will be touring the school before they come back to spend three days inspecting the school's staff and students. The headmistress has left this note on your desk:

Can you do two things please:

Write to the inspectors (do a standard letter first and I'll check it through before you send it). I want them to know that I will expect them at 11.00 and I have reserved car parking spaces for each of them. We'll have coffee at 11.00 and then I've arranged lunch in the staff restaurant at 1.00. I don't know what else they want me to do, but I assume they will get in touch again if they want anything special.

I also need you to let all the teachers know about the date and the time of the visits. Can you do a memo to all staff giving them the details?

Customer services

Without customers a business is unable to survive. Whatever size a business may be, it must always make sure that its customers are satisfied. Because customers' needs, wants and requirements change all the time, the business must think ahead of its customers' evolving needs.

Increasingly, organisations have recognised the value of responding to customer needs by changing their products or expanding their range of products. There are often particular employees in the customer services department whose job it is to talk to the public and to existing customers.

The customer services department is the main point of contact that customers have with a business. A customer may have a complaint to make, or require more detailed information about a particular product or service. Many organisations have now given customers a bigger opportunity to talk to their employees, understanding that:

- if customers are treated well they will return to the organisation
- customers who have received good service from a organisation will recommend it to their family and friends
- if customers tell their friends and family about a good organisation, this helps to spread a good image of the organisation.

An organisation that is concerned with improving its customer service will carefully check all the complaints it receives. Staff will want to know how often different customers complain about the same thing. If they find that similar complaints are being made regularly, they will attempt to improve the situation. There is often a special complaints form that customers have to complete. Reading these forms helps the organisation's managers to decide if the service can be improved or if extra services can be added to help the customers remain satisfied.

Build-up Exercise

If you worked in the customer services department of a business and were asked to design a special form to log customer complaints, what headings would you include? First of all draft out a form that you think would be suitable for this purpose and once you are happy that you have included all that is needed, wordprocess and print out a copy of the form. You will need this form for an activity later in the course.

IT services

The information technology (IT), or computer services, department is responsible for the hardware and the software that a business uses. It is also responsible for maintaining the business's databases, telecommunication systems and other office technology. As most organisations now utilise computers in many of their routine activities, this department needs to be up to date on any developments in the wide range of technologies used and know how to use new software. Once IT staff have mastered the use of new software, they assist in training the employees from other departments who will be using it regularly.

IT staff also carry out what is known as troubleshooting. This means that when someone from another department, or one of the business's other branches, has a problem with their computer or a piece of software, IT staff will either give them advice over the telephone or visit the department or branch and do what they can to assist and support the employee who is having difficulty.

Sometimes an organisation will employ the services of another business or an individual (consultant) to carry out the work done by an IT department.

Build-up Exercise

Why do you think some businesses prefer to use a computer services consultant rather than have their own computer services department? Have a look on the Internet and see if you can find a computer services consultant or business. What services do they offer?

Describe how activities are organised to meet the organisation's objectives

We already know that the functional, or departmental, way of organising a business means that the different departments all have their own 'areas of work'. They are all striving to make sure that the business meets its main aims or objectives. In a way, each of the departments is specialising in one particular aspect of the business. The employees who work in that department could be regarded as specialists in that particular function of business activity.

Sometimes, however, a business decides that the functional way of organising is not the best one for it to adopt. There are other ways of structuring the business so that it can meet its objectives and we will discuss each one of these in turn.

Product- or service-based organisation

One way to organise a business is by departments which are responsible for each particular product or service offered by the business. These are known as product divisions. Imagine a miniature version of the organisation as a whole, with managers, supervisors and other employees all concerned with just one particular product, product range or service. Figure 3.13 helps explain this.

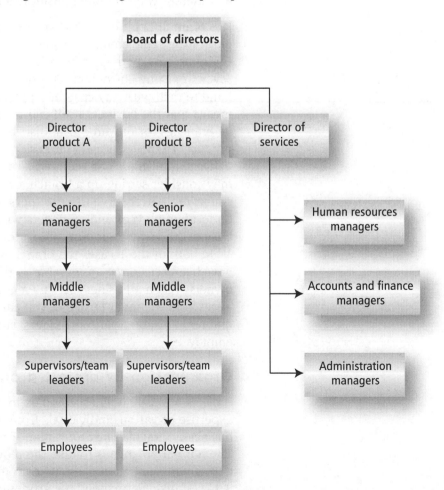

Figure 3.13 *Product- or service-based organisation*

Organisation based on different markets/customers

Some organisations deal with consumers (the end-user of the product or service) and customers who sell their products on to the final consumer. This means that a business may have a retail division, which deals with direct selling to consumers, and also a wholesale division, which deals with customers, such as distributors or other retailers (shops), who then sell to the public on their behalf. As with product divisions, people working in either retail or wholesale divisions may specialise in learning how to deal with these particular types of customer.

Organisation to cope with dispersed geographical locations

It is not always possible to serve customers, whoever they may be, from a single location. Imagine the difficulties in dealing with overseas customers if all of the business's operations are based in one country. There are:

- transport difficulties
- language problems
- time differences between the different countries
- different ways of doing business abroad.

It is often difficult enough to deal with customers who are in a different part of the same country. Businesses sometimes decide to locate part of their business, perhaps a branch, in an area where there are already several existing customers. This means that the employees are closer to hand to deal with any customer problems and to handle orders. It also means that the business itself can transport its products and services to its branches for onward, local distribution, making the delivery of those products to the customers far easier.

Once a business has acquired a number of customers overseas, it may consider setting up a branch, or opening another business, in that country to better serve its customers there. The business can then take on local employees and managers who can speak the language and do business the way their customers are used to.

In both of these cases the branches, or separate businesses, which have been set up are answerable to the main business and to its owners. When a business sets up a company or branch in a location away from the main business, you can imagine a smaller version of the main organisation, with managers, supervisors, team leaders and employees.

Organisation by project groups/matrix structure

Projects are usually fairly complex tasks which require the services and expertise of various individuals from different departments within a business. They may last for a matter of weeks, months or even years. The normal practice is to take the required staff from different departments and create a new team to deal with the project (see Figure 3.14). Unlike 'permanent' departments or branches, or indeed product divisions, project teams tend not to have support staff of their own. They rely on the main business to deal with personnel, accounts, purchasing and other routine matters. The project team concentrates on the project itself and can call upon different parts of the business for additional support as and when it is needed.

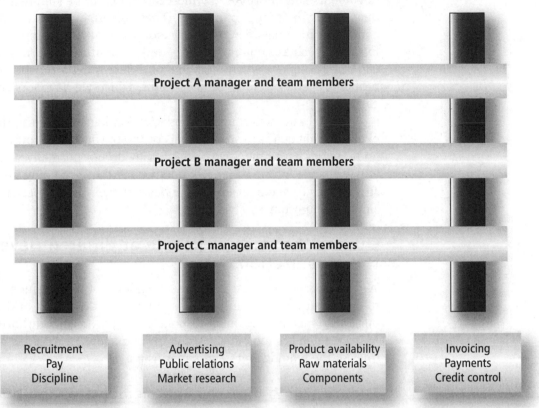

Project A manager and team members

Project B manager and team members

Project C manager and team members

| Recruitment Pay Discipline | Advertising Public relations Market research | Product availability Raw materials Components | Invoicing Payments Credit control |

Figure 3.14 *Project groups within the organisational structure*

Centralised or decentralised services?

When we consider services which are support functions, including personnel, purchasing, marketing and finance, a business has two main options:

- **Centralised services** – to create a single department that specialises in one of the support functions. It can serve all other parts of the organisation centrally and ensure that policies and procedures are the same throughout the business.
- **Decentralised services** – to create support services in each department (such as retail or wholesale) or in each product division. This arrangement means that support services can concentrate on servicing the part of the business to which they belong.

In recent years many businesses have tried to cut back on costs by identifying areas of their business that could be brought together. This has meant that many decentralised services, such as personnel, which had employees working in various parts of the business, have now been closed and brought together into one, overall department which serves the whole of the business and employs fewer staff than the old, decentralised arrangement.

Interaction between departments/groups

Interaction, or communication, between different parts of a business can be either formal or informal.

Formal interaction takes place at meetings and in the exchange of documents and information which is required to be supplied by one department to other departments. There is formal contact and communication between the service departments and other areas of the business, such as human resources and accounts. Formal interaction can also take place when members of different departments are brought together to form project teams, which we have looked at earlier.

Informal interaction and communication happens all the time. It is expected that staff at various levels of the business will routinely talk to and interact with others with whom they do not normally work. They will exchange information, talk about what they are doing and make suggestions to one another on the basis of their own experience under similar circumstances.

Outline the roles of people at different levels of the organisation

Whatever organisational structure, each level of management has a role. The term role means what the managers do as part of their job, but it also means how much responsibility, power and authority they have. We need to look at the different management roles, as well as the roles of the team leaders and supervisors.

The managing director and members of the board

The managing director is the most senior member of the board of directors. In some cases the managing director is also the chairperson of the organisation. It is the role and responsibility of the chairperson to preside over the meetings of the board of directors. The main role of the managing director is to:

- exercise all the normal powers and duties of a director
- exercise power and responsibility in the name of the rest of the board on a day-to-day basis.

The board of directors will have agreed certain guidelines of conduct and policy which it will expect the managing director to follow. The managing director is chosen by other members of the board. They may have chosen the particular individual because they have certain qualities, such as:

- a wide business experience
- a successful business record
- the ability to make good decisions, particularly when under pressure
- a willingness to take responsibility for making decisions
- a willingness to be accountable to the board of directors (and the shareholders of the business)
- a clear idea about the policies and objectives of the business

- the ability to work towards the fulfilment of the objectives of the business
- good communication skills
- the ability to represent the business well in a variety of different situations.

The managing director is responsible for ensuring that the policies drawn up by the board of directors are adopted by the rest of the business. He or she has to interpret the wishes of the board and develop a way to put their policies into practice to meet the business's objectives.

The managing director will need to know which of the business's managers or employees to turn to when assistance is required or instructions need to be given. The managing director will also have to keep the board informed of any problems or crises that may occur.

A private limited company has to have at least one director, but a public limited company needs at least two. The main responsibilities of a director are to:

- exercise power and authority in good faith and for the benefit of the organisation
- put aside personal interests and always consider the organisation first
- try not to be casual or off-hand when dealing with the affairs of the organisation.

Build-up Exercise

If you were a member of a board of directors and had to write a list of the qualities you would expect in a managing director, what would you write down? Think about it and then write your own list.

Managers and department heads

Below the directors are a number of levels of management. It is the duty of a manager to undertake the tasks and duties delegated (passed on) to them by a director. It is the manager who takes responsibility for the day-to-day decision-making and making sure the organisation's policies are put into place. A manager is accountable to a director, the board of directors and shareholders.

A good manager will have a sound working knowledge of the organisation, so directors do not have to interfere with the actual decision-making. A manager's duties depend on their level of responsibility, the department in which they work and the type of organisation they work in. Managers give instructions to supervisors and team leaders.

Supervisors

Supervisors tend to be the level below managers in the organisational structure. They are team leaders in a way, or organisers of specific projects or functions within the organisation. It is often the supervisor who deals with day-to-day tasks, but he or she will receive instructions from managers.

Supervisors are often found in production departments and in administration departments too. They are responsible for making sure that all the employees that work under them:

- have enough work to keep them busy
- are producing work of an acceptable standard
- have duties that support the work of the other areas of the business.

Team leaders

The role of team leader might be temporary. Teams are often created for a specific project, which may last for a week, a month or longer; the team leader's role will only last as long as the team operates. They are not managers or supervisors, but take the role of simply leading the team whilst it is in operation. They have responsibility for making sure that all team members understand what is expected of them. They also have to ensure that the team works effectively and meets deadlines.

Identify levels of hierarchy

The word 'hierarchy' refers to the levels of responsibility, authority and power within an organisation. Most businesses, as described, have various levels of management. The levels of hierarchy usually follow the same steps as the levels of management because decisions are made at the top of the pyramid and instructions are passed down. Information goes in the opposite direction and filters up through the levels to the owners or directors of the business. The bulk of employees are at the bottom of the pyramid and the fewest individuals at the top.

The greatest amount of power and authority sits at the top of the pyramid with the directors and the members of the board, because they have ultimate control over the company's decision making and for putting the company's policies into place. As the pyramid widens there are fewer levels below and individuals have progressively less power and authority.

- Directors have the most power and authority.
- Directly below the directors are the senior managers. In consultation with the directors they set any necessary policies or procedures to achieve the organisation's objectives.
- The task of putting in place the organisation's plan to meet its objectives is the role of the middle managers. They liaise with the senior managers and with the supervisors for whom they are responsible.
- Supervisors work directly with the workforce. They are responsible for ensuring that the tasks set by the middle management are carried out promptly and efficiently.

■ Individuals who make up the bulk of the workforce deal with the work in hand.

Try it out

Using the organisational chart you made earlier in this unit, decide where the power and authority lie in the business. Draw arrows on your chart to show the direction in which instructions and information move through the business. Who has the most power and authority and who has the least?

Identify and evaluate the importance of effective administration

Organisations work in different ways and have different systems and procedures with which their employees are expected to comply in the course of their duties. The running of an organisation requires an organised approach if it is to be efficient and effective. Administration plays a vital role in this approach. Administration is the means by which the organisation is able to operate as a whole.

The administrative systems which the organisation has in place should establish a means by which the operations it carries out can be assessed and amended if necessary. Administrative systems require monitoring to ensure they remain efficient and effective. Systems should also be flexible enough to respond to changes that take place within the organisation.

Outline and evaluate the range of administrative tasks throughout the company and at departmental level

Administrative systems are systems set up to:

■ gather information
■ store information
■ co-ordinate information
■ retrieve information
■ disseminate (pass on) information
■ process information.

These administrative tasks are carried out at all levels of the organisation. In larger organisations there may be an administration department designed specifically for this task. Administrative systems are in place to:

■ allow managers to determine the aims and policies of the organisation
■ control the day-to-day running of the business
■ provide support systems for all resources used by the organisation (human, physical and financial)
■ keep records relating to the activities of the organisation
■ monitor the performance of the business's activities.

At departmental level there are administration considerations too, including:

- receiving and distributing internal mail (mail from inside the business)
- receiving and distributing external mail (mail from outside the business)
- sending mail out of the department
- sending faxes
- sending e-mail messages
- filing paperwork
- storing computer files
- answering the telephone and taking messages
- preparing paperwork for meetings
- preparing and responding to memos
- writing business letters
- preparing articles, notices, leaflets and newsletters
- preparing advertisements.

Try it out

Prepare a table on your wordprocessor. The column headings should be each of the different departments discussed earlier in this unit. Now look at the list of administration duties given above. Under each department key in the duties you think they are likely to carry out on a regular basis. How does your table look now?

Identify and explain effective working practices

One of the most frustrating aspects of work, no matter what your role, is the feeling that you are constantly working hard just to cope with the flow of work passing across your desk. Being effective in any role requires a degree of planning. You also need to prioritise the work which is presented to you.

There are many ways of achieving effective planning, but it is only part of being effective in your job. You will be required to provide information and carry out work according to other people's timetables; they will need what you are doing by a particular date. You will also need to be careful with the information which you receive, as it may be confidential.

Most senior members of staff who ask you to carry out work on their behalf will also wish to be kept informed of your progress. There are many things to remember and many different demands on your time to balance, and in this part of the unit we examine methods of dealing with this.

Explain the importance of planning work effectively

'Action planning' is an important part of setting objectives, targets and goals and of problem solving. Action planning can assist a business to plan for the future, ensuring that changing situations can be controlled. Action planning converts the goals or objectives into a series of steps, to decide what has to be done, by whom and by when. It involves the following steps:

1 Decide a goal or objective.
2 Identify the actions required to achieve this objective or goal.
3 Identify where the plan may go wrong.
4 Having identified what may go wrong; make another plan or decide on more actions to deal with these problems.

The action plan should describe in detail how the business proposes to get from where it is now to where it wishes to be.

Effective action planning requires all those involved to be aware of their role in the process and involves the following stages:

1 Development of a rough action plan – this combines the work of all the individuals involved. It lists all possible activities to reach the goal. Once this has been completed the activities are discussed and the most appropriate ones chosen. These are then arranged in the correct order to make sure tasks are completed by the times needed.
2 Each step in the action plan is now clarified, specifying it in terms of what needs to be done, by when and by whom.
3 The action plan needs careful checking to make sure the skills, time, finance and materials involved will all be available at the right time. Those involved also need to consider how unexpected problems will be dealt with.

Importance of planning to ensure successful outcomes and to make best use of your time and that of others

The importance of planning your own work and how to do so were covered in Unit 2. Good planning skills will mean you:

- waste less time
- make fewer mistakes
- meet deadlines
- avoid starting tasks again
- get more job satisfaction from your work
- are offered the opportunity to take on more challenging work
- will be valued by others for your abilities.

Importance of clarifying the purpose

A task or project is given to you (or your team) on the assumption that it will be completed. You therefore need to make the best use of your time and resources to achieve a successful outcome, by the date required.

At the outset you should have a clear idea as to how, when and why you are doing a particular job. You also need to know precisely what the person who has allocated the work expects. If you are unclear about any of these issues you should clarify this before you start.

In Unit 2 we suggested you create a task log sheet on which to write the necessary task information. You may wish to use a log sheet such as this, or perhaps amend it so that it covers the following:

- What is the required outcome – what does the person who set you the task expect of you?
- What tasks are needed to achieve the required outcome? – break down complex tasks into manageable chunks; tackling the whole project as a single task may prove too complicated.
- Which methods are appropriate? – how exactly are you going to set about the task? What will it involve you having to find out and where is that information? Do you have access to, or knowledge of, the most appropriate methods?
- What is the timescale? – the first real question is whether it is possible for you to meet the deadline. If you have any doubts you should say so as soon as possible.
- What resources are required? – note down the people, equipment or materials which you will need to complete the task.

Prioritising tasks – the difference between urgency and importance

Unit 2 described how jobs will be presented to you which are both urgent and important, as well as routine.

You will need to learn to juggle the various demands placed upon your time. Experience gradually tells you what is truly urgent and what is really important. Remember that your priorities may not be shared by those who give you the tasks. Neither will your priorities be the same as those with whom you may have to work to complete the tasks.

Prioritising is therefore a matter of not only personal judgement, but also negotiation with the task setter and other staff on whom you will need to rely to get the job done.

Need to take account of the requirements and commitments of others

Colleagues and supervisors will have their own priorities, workloads and commitments. Work often relies upon negotiating suitable times to work together and co-operating with others to fit around one another's busy schedules. In the case of requirements or demands by more senior members of staff, you may find that you do not have a choice as to when you carry out work on their behalf. They may decide the priorities; they may also decide how you will organise your workload. You need to be guided by them as they have the responsibility of ensuring that all work is done.

Level of confidentiality

Your access to confidential information will depend upon which part of a business you work in. If you are working for human resources, for example, you may have access to confidential information about other employees. If you work in sales you may know where your business receives its supplies from and how much it pays for them. Some information must not be divulged to people outside the organisation. There should be clear organisational policies and procedures which determine confidentiality.

Equally, some information must not be passed on to those outside your department. Individuals' rates of pay and plans for the department are amongst a number of things that would cause problems if widely known in the organisation. Usually the more junior members of staff do not have access to confidential information, but they will occasionally see confidential information and must assume that they are not to pass anything on, in words or otherwise, unless told to do so.

Arrangements for reporting back

Reporting back to those who have set you work can be either formal or informal. Normally teams and departments have regular meetings in which the progress of work is discussed. However, reporting back also happens informally and you may be asked at any time by your team leader or supervisor to tell them how far you have proceeded with a task and whether you have had any difficulties.

Reporting back means giving a clear, concise and honest update on progress and is also an opportunity to alert others that you may need assistance, or that the task may not be completed on time.

Use of diaries and planners

Organisational skills are very important to anybody who works in administration. They are also important to anybody who is undertaking a programme of study, as you will know from your experiences at school and college. In the business world, disorganisation can lead to time wastage and mistakes, some of which might potentially damage the business. Organisational skills include:

- Keeping your desk area neat and tidy.
- Keeping a diary of dates and times for meetings and a record of any visitors expected.
- Having an efficient way of storing and retrieving documents, whether this is paper-based or on a computer system.
- Having a follow-up procedure in place so that documents are always available at the correct date and time.
- Managing time efficiently – time management does not just apply to those in authority and have many responsibilities at work. It is important for everyone to monitor how they use their time at work.
- Having a 'to do' list. This list can be weekly and/or daily and should list the duties that have to be carried out. Prioritising tasks and ticking off those completed is very satisfying and a finished list is a nice way to end the day.

Planning does not just involve daily or weekly routines. Sometimes you may have to plan months in advance. The simplest way of achieving this is to use a wall chart or planner. You can either write deadlines onto this chart or use a variety of stick-on symbols to alert you to particularly important dates.

Increasingly, people use personal digital assistants (PDAs). These are mini-computers which allow you to enter information, including deadlines, and then alert you to the deadlines as they approach. They can also alert you to the need to be in a particular place at a particular time, so you do not miss meetings or appointments.

As an alternative to the usual diary, some organisations may use an 'electronic diary' for logging appointments and meetings. Information can be stored on a main computer system, a laptop or a personal organiser. The electronic diary enables the user to scroll forwards or backwards by day, month or year. It can store around five years' worth of days and dates. You can therefore store provisional or confirmed appointments, holiday periods and set reminders for particular days, weeks or months in the future. The electronic diary can also be used to detail appointments and cross-reference appointments or tasks.

Try it out

Design a simple questionnaire that allows you to find out how other people you work with keep track of what they have to do. Ask at least 20 of your colleagues what it is that they use. Get them to tell you what else they have tried and, if appropriate, why they have stopped using certain methods and moved on to others.

Explain the importance of organising the work area effectively

Very few people are well organised all the time. People who are, need to be very self-disciplined, keep their work area neat and tidy and have lists of jobs which are waiting to be completed. They also tackle work in a strict order, rather than concentrating on the work which they enjoy.

Without some organisation, a person's work can become chaotic and this puts unnecessary pressure on them. It is therefore important to:

- be able to find what you need
- not keep everything in your head, but on paper
- make the best use of your time
- finish jobs faster
- be more confident
- be less stressed
- be more efficient.

Importance of keeping the work area neat and tidy

Becoming organised begins with your own work area. We have all seen desks piled with papers, reports, memos, letters and scrap paper, all randomly poking out of the heap. Under such circumstances there is always the problem of finding a pen, knowing where you left that ruler or having to move vast piles of things to reach the keyboard.

But it is only natural to say to yourself that you'll tidy your desk once you have a chance. The chance very often never arrives and before long your desk is a mountain of part-finished work.

You need to use the work area which you have been given to best effect. Cleaning up after yourself is not always possible, but by putting things away in the right place you have a much better chance of finding them next time.

Things which you use on a daily basis should be on your desk. Most desks have little trays to put your pens, paperclips and stapler in. Things that you do not use very often should be put away in drawers. Stationery items and files and any other spare paperwork or equipment can also be placed in drawers. This means that what is on your desk should be what you are working on, together with any equipment you need to do that work. It probably takes far less time to actually put something away where it belongs than to hunt for it later.

Many people use a series of trays on their desk. One tray is for information or work which has just arrived – this is known as an 'in tray'. Work that has been completed and needs to be passed on is placed in the 'out tray'. Work that is partly finished is placed in a 'pending tray'. Any information which you have taken from the records, and work which can now be put into the records, is placed in a 'filing tray'.

Build-up Exercise

How well organised are you? Try to answer these questions as honestly as possible.

1 How messy is your bedroom at home?
2 If you have a work area at home, work or college, just how much have you managed to push into your desk drawers?
3 How forgetful are you? Do you rely on trying to remember things rather than writing down what you have to do?
4 If you had to go shopping for various items, would you write down a list or would you try and remember what it is you have gone out to buy?
5 Have you a clear idea about what you have to do each day?
6 How do you prefer to pass on messages to people?
7 When was the last time you lost something important?
8 How often do you have to search for clean clothes or ones that are not crumpled, in the morning when you are getting dressed?
9 When was the last time you failed to get a piece of coursework in on time?
10 Would you know where to find your National Insurance number if you needed it immediately?

How to organise materials and equipment to be used

As we have seen, filing trays and desk tidies are very useful for organising the materials and equipment that you use. They allow you to find equipment straightaway rather than having to search for it.

Paperwork, however, presents a more difficult problem and it is often a good idea to obtain a number of folders. In these folders you can place related documents and write on the folder itself the type of documents inside. You can then put these folders into your filing trays and know that all of the relevant documents are together.

If you photocopy a document, you should staple the pages together immediately so that you know you have the whole document and when you need it there will be no pages missing.

Make sure that you only keep what you absolutely need on your desk. What is on your desk should be easy to reach. If you have a telephone, and you are right-handed, put in on the left of your desk. Your pen holder and notepad should be on the right, so that when the phone rings you can pick up the phone with your left hand and write with your right hand.

Recognising work activities where resources are most frequently wasted

In offices and businesses up and down the country, thousands of tons of paper are thrown into wastepaper baskets every day. Many businesses have begun to encourage their employees to recycle paper. Every sheet which you waste costs the business money. But a fraction of this can be saved by placing waste paper in a recycling bin. Recycling companies collect the paper and pay the business by weight.

You should try to avoid wasting paper as much as you can. Some people have difficulty in noticing mistakes in documents when they are on the computer screen. They therefore print out draft documents to check them. Try to avoid doing this unless it is absolutely necessary, because each draft, if there is a mistake, will simply go in the bin.

Although printers are far more reliable than in the past, there is still the chance that the paper will feed in crooked, or that you will put headed paper in back to front, or upside down. Try to remember how the paper should go in to cut down this type of waste. You could put a note above the printer so you don't have to remember.

Paper, envelopes and other documents which are stacked up by a window will often discolour in the sun. Try to make sure that any stocks of paper are in boxes and put away in a cupboard.

Although your business may have its own policies about waste, the following list gives you some tips as to how you can minimise waste yourself:

- Why not photocopy on both sides of the paper?
- Why not reuse folders by putting sticky labels over old labels?
- Any out-of-date headed paper can be used as scrap paper.
- Store paper away from direct sunlight and heat.
- Check your documents before you print them out.

- Try a single photocopy for quality before you do a long photocopy run.
- Don't make extra copies of documents unless you absolutely need them.
- Try to reuse external envelopes for internal mail.
- Think before you write on anything – you may make a mistake, or not leave enough room and waste the paper or card.
- Use recycled printer refill cartridges if you can.
- Shredded paper can be used for packaging.
- Don't rip open padded envelopes – if you open them carefully they can be reused.

Try it out

This is an activity you should try out at the end of your day at work or college; set aside five minutes of your time before the cleaner arrives. Put a sheet of newspaper on the floor and tip out the contents of your nearest wastepaper basket. How many items in the basket actually had to be destroyed? What kind of waste is in the bin? Should it have been sorted and put in recycling bins? Could any of the paper or envelopes have been used for another purpose?

Explain the importance of working flexibly

One quality that many employers are looking for in their employees is flexibility. This does not necessarily mean doing things for which you are not properly trained, but rather being prepared to help or adapt what you do to make sure that jobs are completed satisfactorily. The more multi-skilled you become through your experience of doing different types of work, the more valuable you will be to your employer.

Flexibility is important; you need to put aside fears of not knowing precisely what to do in a new situation and show you have a desire to learn new things. The need for flexibility applies to nearly all types of work; it is often impossible to set your mind on one task, without either being interrupted or having to change your plans.

Importance of monitoring progress, foreseeing potential difficulties and initiating relevant action

Once you have planned a job and have a clear understanding of what is required, you are in a position to begin work. Team leaders, supervisors and managers may want progress reports, so it is important that you know how much you have done and when you are likely to finish.

Other work and activities going on around you may drag you away from the task at hand. It is vital that you remember where you are so that when you return to the work you can then pick up where you left off. As the work progresses, you may see some difficulties ahead – perhaps a vital piece of information is missing or you discover that there are insufficient envelopes or paper. Rather than waiting until the problem stops you from working, try to deal with it before it reaches that point. For example, if you realise information is missing and that you will need it before the end of the week, take steps to acquire it immediately. In the case of the missing envelopes, a timely order to the stationery supplier would prevent any unnecessary delay to the job.

Responding to contingencies, communicating changes and reporting difficulties with meeting deadlines and targets

It is impossible to work in a business where things do not change. Workloads change, priorities change, the availability of staff changes with sickness and holiday leave. Sometimes work is busier for no apparent reason and there may be pressures on you to carry out other duties which take you away from the tasks you had expected to be doing. As we have seen, if you are aware of where you are with a task and you know where all the information is because it is filed away safely, you can return to it as soon as you have a chance.

If you are working with several other people, or carrying out work for various supervisors or managers, then they will not necessarily know that you have had to abandon the work you were doing for them. Contingencies are situations which arise that could affect your ability to continue working on a particular task. You will have to think about what is necessary to complete the task if you cannot spend the amount of time on it that you expected. If the task is not completed, who will be affected? What will happen if you cannot meet the deadlines? Providing the person who has set you the work knows what your revised plans are, they may be happy for you to reschedule the work and delay its completion.

Some work, however, cannot be rescheduled because it is important and urgent. When the unforeseen interrupts this kind of work you should set aside a little time and think through the implications of not finishing the work before you decide that you must put it aside. At all times you must contact the person who has given you the work, or the person who is relying on you to finish it. They must be aware of the problem so they can put their own contingency plans into action.

Try it out

Suggest whether you could take action yourself to solve the following problems, or whether you should refer the problem to a colleague, a supervisor or a manager.

1 Yesterday you and a colleague were working late to finish a report which needed to be completed for a meeting this afternoon. You both agreed to come in early this morning but on your voicemail you have just taken a message from your colleague. She will not be in today because she is ill. You will not get the work completed alone.

▶▶

2 You have spent the morning calling all of the sales representatives, asking them for their sales figures for the week. You have entered everything into a spreadsheet and have shown a draft to the sales manager. He notices that you have forgotten to put in the figures for the Bristol sales representative. You tell him that you will call the representative now, but you discover that his mobile phone is switched off.

3 You work in the human resources department. It is Friday afternoon and you are just completing a series of induction packs for five new employees who are starting on Monday morning. All of the documents are neatly stacked on your desk and you go to the stationery cupboard to find folders to put the packs in. When you return you discover that the cleaner has put your induction packs into the recycling bin.

Identify the factors that impact on efficiency

In a busy office there are literally dozens of things that could prevent you from concentrating on a job, or from being able to do that job to the best of your ability. Offices are usually busy, noisy places, with frequent comings and goings, phones ringing, people talking across the office to one another and visitors appearing when you least need to see them.

Concentration is not always possible. There is often little opportunity to confirm what it is someone is asking you to do and it is often the case that the person you need to speak to is either busy or unavailable. All of these factors and many more can impact upon the efficiency of everyone in the office.

There are a number of ways in which you can reduce the negative impact of the office on your efficiency:

- Listen carefully to instructions that are being given to you. Ask appropriate questions to confirm what it is you need to do and if necessary, write the instructions down on a task log sheet to serve as a reminder.
- Make sure you follow the instructions given to you. If you have any problems, remember to report them to the right person.
- Try to use your own time as efficiently as possible and not get sidetracked. If you do not use time efficiently you will be putting yourself under unnecessary pressure. If you are co-operating with others you will waste their time if you have not completed the tasks that they are waiting for to get on with their own work.
- Don't allow other people to distract you. Other employees or visitors may have time to chat because their workload is not as heavy as yours, or because they have finished their tasks. Just because they have time to chat doesn't mean you have, at least until all your work is completed.

- If you need to concentrate and the office is particularly noisy or busy, find yourself a quiet area to work if possible. Make sure you tell someone where you have gone and why.
- Since your time and that of others is precious, it is important to make the best use of any chance you have to communicate with them. Effective communication means giving and receiving information in an easy-to-understand and clear way. It also means giving information at the right time.
- Organisations have set procedures for employees to follow because these procedures increase efficiency. Make sure you follow the procedures and that those working with you do the same.

Identify ways of improving performance in the workplace

Senior managers strive to improve their own performance, but they also strive to improve the performance of the whole of their workforce.

You can achieve improvements in your performance by considering everything you do to be a process of continuous development. Every time you carry out a new task you will learn new skills and develop your flexible approach to work. As you work you will also be updating your existing skills, allowing you to progress and become more confident.

How to obtain feedback on achievement at work

Feedback is the response you receive from other people in reaction to your work. Much feedback is informal, which may simply be a 'thank you' for the work which you have done. You should be prepared, however, to receive both positive and negative feedback, as perhaps sometimes your work may not be of adequate quality, or the person may not think you can be relied on in the future – remember, you'll only know this and be able to do something about it if someone tells you.

Many businesses also give formal feedback, usually in the form of an appraisal system. Appraisals are reviews of progress and look at your abilities.

Setting targets and planning to improve performance

Appraisals are opportunities for you and your supervisor to set you targets and discuss plans to improve your performance. Appraisals allow you to talk about your job, what you plan to do in the future and consider whether you would benefit from additional training. Appraisals are confidential and aim to be positive. You should take advantage of these formal feedback sessions as they may be one of the few chances you have to talk, uninterrupted, with your immediate superior about your work.

At an appraisal you are likely to receive both positive and negative feedback. It is rare to receive only positive feedback, as this would be likely to make you feel there is little you can do to improve your performance. Most appraisals contain some criticism of how you work.

It is always a good idea to think about a feedback session before it takes place. Action planning is useful as it helps you identify areas where you are working well, and others where you are not. Action planning suggests ways of dealing with these situations. You should try not to be too defensive about criticism, but if you think the criticisms are unfair ask what you should have done, or what you could do to improve. Overall an appraisal should allow you to avoid making the same mistakes in the future as you may have made in the past.

To improve your performance, targets will be set. It is likely that these are very useful for the following reasons:

- they give you a clear idea of what is required of you
- they identify the key areas that you need to develop
- achieving them will give you satisfaction
- they will improve your confidence in your own abilities
- they will give you a vision of the future.

It is important to make sure that any targets set are reasonable and realistic. To ensure this:

- be specific about what you intend to do
- set realistic targets that are achievable
- don't be too ambitious
- focus on the positive – what you would like to do
- be as precise as possible by setting dates for reviews
- write the targets down so you can remember them
- don't set too many targets, otherwise none may be achieved
- try to set targets that you can achieve yourself, rather than having to rely on others to help you achieve them
- make them your own targets and try not to have targets imposed upon you.

Identifying opportunities for training

This is normally part of the appraisal system, but there may be regular training opportunities that are advertised within your business. If you feel that these training programmes would be of value to you, your team and the business, then there is no reason why you should not enquire about getting involved. You should think about the following when considering training:

- Which additional skills or training do you need?
- How will these new skills or abilities improve your performance?
- Is the training available?
- What will you have to give up in order to do the training?
- Is your employer prepared to support you during the training?
- What will you be able to offer the business after the training has taken place?

Importance of reviewing work with a manager

A good manager will always set aside time to look through the work you are involved in and give you some advice as to your approach. This may be formal or informal and may also take place as a scheduled event, or simply when the manager is checking your progress.

Having an experienced member of staff review your work can be very useful as they will be able to tell you about any mistakes you are making and point you in the right direction to make your job easier and more efficient. These reviews may look at your general work during an appraisal, or just the ongoing work, as and when the opportunity arises.

Importance of self-assessment

Self-assessment does not mean that you have to be harshly critical of yourself. Nor does it mean that you should concentrate only on your strengths. It means trying to step away from yourself and look objectively at what you are doing. Have you met the targets you have been set? Are you able to stick to deadlines? Are you being co-operative, reliable, accurate and following procedures?

Even if you take time only at the end of the working week to reflect on how your week has gone, this is a step in the right direction towards self-assessment.

Try it out

Design your own self-assessment form. You could use this for either your course or your job. Your form should include suitable sections for you to fill in, including:

Your name
Your short-term career goal (within a year)
Your long-term career goal (within 3–5 years)
Your current strengths (including areas of work you would like to develop)
Your current weaknesses (including areas of work which you also need to develop)
Your specific strengths and weaknesses (such as the quality of your work, your knowledge and skills, your personal skills, the quantity of work you produce, your interpersonal skills and your communication skills)
Your training requirements (any programmes of study which would help you reach your career goals)

Identify and explain issues affecting working conditions

Even within an organisation working conditions will depend on an employee's department, where the department is located and its importance within the organisation. The technology used and the surroundings or the number of people with whom an employee works are examples of how working conditions may differ.

The way in which employees are paid and how much they are paid are controlled by an organisation's policy. There are also laws governing working conditions and minimum pay. Working conditions must at least conform to health and safety laws. Beyond this, however, it has long been accepted that employees work much better if the employer ensures that:

- the workplace is well lit
- the workplace is kept at a constant temperature, regardless of the weather
- the workplace is well decorated
- efforts are made to encourage health and fitness and to reduce sickness
- the hours worked can be flexible to take account of employees' personal commitments (for example, child care)
- the employees receive regular training and the opportunity to gain qualifications
- the employees' skills are rewarded – either with money or improved chances of promotion
- experienced employees are encouraged to stay with the business by receiving more money and other benefits
- pay and conditions are attractive and compete with other businesses within the same sector.

Your working conditions, as an administrator, are likely to be very different to those of someone working in a factory. You may work in a carpeted office, with window blinds and comfortable seats. Someone in a factory may have to work in a dirty, noisy environment, standing up all day and doing hard, physical work.

Build-up Exercise

Using the points we have discussed above, consider either the job you do or your college environment. Taking each point in turn, write a statement about the working conditions from your point of view.

Explain how the environment can affect efficiency

Environmental conditions, such as heating and ventilation, lighting, noise and the availability of working space, can impact on efficiency. Businesses organise work areas to try to make the best use of the space they have available.

Importance of office layout for efficiency

Many businesses have tried several forms of office layout and design over the years. Some have decided to make the best use of the space that they have available and reduce the number of individual offices. Others have adopted a more traditional approach and retained individual offices. Many businesses and employees view a separate office as a sign of prestige and consider it a reward.

As the nature of the work being carried out by employees differs, there will always be a need to allow others to access information (for example in filing cabinets or on computers) and equipment which is used on a daily basis (for example the photocopier, fax machine or printers).

Individual offices, also known as 'cellular offices', offer advantages and disadvantages as shown in Table 3.5.

Table 3.5 *The advantages and disadvantages of cellular offices*

Advantages	Disadvantages
■ Offices can be locked. This gives the business the opportunity to restrict access to confidential information and valuable equipment. ■ Each office is private. This means that employees can work with less disruption, hold meetings, meet customers or hold interviews in private. ■ The environment can be individually controlled in each office. Examples include a dust-free office for computers, double-glazing for those near to the factory or extra lighting for those needing it, for example designers.	■ Offices take up more space and it can also mean that the same equipment has to be provided in each of the rooms. ■ Each office has to be decorated, heated and lit, which can be expensive. ■ Junior employees may need to be supervised by more managers if in separate offices.

An open-plan office is a single room shared by several staff, perhaps with dividers separating the work areas. In a very large office there may be the need to put up screens or partitions to divide one department or section from another. It is common in this type of office to find together all grades and levels of employees, from administrators and typists to managers and directors. Table 3.6 shows some advantages and disadvantages of the open-plan arrangement.

Table 3.6 *The advantages and disadvantages of open plan offices*

Advantages	Disadvantages
■ Employees can be supervised more easily. ■ Communication between employees and different departments is improved.	■ Can be noisy because of the amount of 'through traffic' causing interruptions and disruption. ■ More has to be spent on security of equipment and information.

▶▶

- The work can move freely from one desk to another without having to be transferred to another separate office area.
- Resources and equipment can be centralised.
- Managers and supervisors have a better understanding of the nature and the demands of the work carried out by the rest of the employees.
- Open plan is cheaper to maintain and less space is used. Lighting, heating and cleaning are cheaper.
- It is easier to change the look of the space and change the space allocated to each employee.

- There is little privacy for meetings or interviews.
- Employees may be more likely to catch infections, such as colds.
- The levels of heating, lighting and ventilation may not suit all those using the office space.
- It can be an impersonal environment because there are fewer walls to hang pictures, charts, etc..

Effects of poor environmental conditions on performance

Looking at the disadvantages of both types of office it is clear that a poor environment can affect the way in which employees perform their duties. Considerations include:

- **Heating and ventilation** – in a cellular office an employee can control the levels of heating and open windows when they want. This is not possible in an open plan office unless all the other inhabitants agree.
- **Lighting** – the levels of lighting in an open plan office may not suit some employees' work. Someone doing close work, for example a designer or an architect, may need brighter lighting than someone working on a computer.
- **Decor** – in a cellular office employees may choose for themselves what goes on the walls or bookcases. Those in open plan offices have less wall space and there are often rules about what can be put on them in order to avoid disagreements or a 'messy' look to the office.
- **Noise** – open plan offices can be noisy and distracting, whereas someone in a cellular office can close their door.
- **Working space** – open plan offices restrict the amount of useable working space each employee has. Cellular offices, on the other hand, can be used differently. If an employee has to collate several pages of a report, then they can spread out the work on a table and, if necessary, leave it overnight safely by locking the door.

Try it out

Consider either your business or your college. Think about the environment in terms of the points we have mentioned. Now do the following: ▶▶

1 Identify the type of environment in which you work or study.
2 Try to list the specific advantages and disadvantages of its layout.
3 Make some suggestions to improve the office layout.
4 Wordprocess your suggestions and attach them to a covering memo to your tutor or supervisor.

Identify and explain health and safety issues in an administration environment

All organisations have a responsibility to provide their employees and their customers, or visitors, with a healthy and safe environment. This doesn't just mean making sure that slippery floors are dealt with immediately so that nobody falls over. There are mountains of legislation (government-imposed laws) identifying what employers and employees have to do to ensure the environment, both inside and outside the organisation, is safe, hazard-free and healthy.

All employers are legally bound by an important series of Acts of Parliament regarding health and safety. Some of these are general, in that they apply to most businesses, while others are more specific in relating to organisations that deal, for example, with chemicals or toxic substances, or those involved in the manufacture or handling of food. Obviously, if an employer doesn't comply with these laws, the business will be put in jeopardy. If the requirements of the various Acts are found to have been broken, an employer could be faced with court action and be found what is known as 'negligent'.

Importance of being alert to potential hazards

Although you are working in an office, you are still at risk from health and safety hazards. Piles of books, filing cabinets, computers and their

Figure 3.15 *A chaotic office leads to unnecessary risks*

associated cables all add to the chance of an accident occurring in your office. But what, exactly, is the difference between a hazard and a risk?

- A hazard is something that has the potential to cause you, one of your colleagues or a visitor to the business harm. A hazard only becomes a risk if there is a significant chance of an accident occurring.

A good example of a hazard is a trailing cable from a piece of electrical equipment, such as a computer or a photocopier. If the cable is attached to the skirting board, as it should be, or hidden under the flooring, then the risk of an accident is quite low. If, however, the cable trails across a room or across a regularly used route, then there is a risk of someone tripping over it.

Obviously it is in everyone's interests to reduce the risk of injury from hazards to an absolute minimum. To achieve this, an employer should carry out regular risk assessments and rely on the employees of the business to report any new hazards or an increase in the degree of risk involved. Where an employer feels he or she is unable to operate such a policy, the Health and Safety Executive runs an advisory service that businesses can use.

Build-up Exercise

Find the website of the Health and Safety Executive at www.hse.gov.uk. What information does it give businesses to help make sure they are working safely? Print out copies of some of the sheets it provides businesses with.

When considering hazards in an office environment, it is important to remember that a hazard is not necessarily a risk. So, in other words, there are some hazards which, if dealt with correctly, will never become a serious risk to the employees. On the other hand, there are some hazards which, if not dealt with quickly enough or correctly, could easily become a risk. There are a variety of hazards in an office environment, including:

- **Machinery or equipment** – these are run by electricity, which is a hazard in itself. The machinery or equipment could develop a faulty plug, the cable could be inappropriately trailed across a room or there could be a problem with the socket into which it is plugged.

- **Materials or substances** – examples include items with sharp edges, heavy or bulky objects, and poisonous substances such as ink or cleaning fluids. The safe storage of such items is essential, though they should also be accessible to the people who use them. Large or heavy items should never be left in a place where they are likely to cause an obstruction. Toxic or corrosive substances should always be stored in the correct containers and never used if out of date.

■ **Working practices and behaviour** – employees must be aware of the importance of adopting the right approach and attitude to safe working if accidents are to be prevented. This category includes general office safety, fire prevention and regular maintenance of machinery.

■ **Accidental breakages and spills** – all spills should be dealt with immediately to reduce the risk of an accident, either from a fall or from the liquid coming into contact with electrical equipment. Breakages, too, represent a hazard in that an unaware passers-by could either cut themselves, or trip over the debris.

■ **General office environment** – this aspect of health and safety covers the overall level of hygiene within the office environment, for example adequate ventilation, general cleanliness and toilet and hand-washing facilities for employees. It also covers the quality of the physical components of the office, such as the walls, ceilings and flooring. Uneven or worn floors can cause people to trip and fall and should be reported immediately.

Build-up Exercise

What office equipment do you use regularly? Write a list of all pieces of electrical equipment that you use often. You will need this list for the next activity.

It makes sense, then, that a person is unlikely to be able to evaluate risk if they are unaware of the hazards. You have to be aware of the hazards around you when you are at work, and also of what to do if a hazard poses a risk.

If accidents are to be prevented, it is important that people adopt the right approach and attitude at all times, and that precautions are taken whenever possible to avoid accidents. Although responsibility for ensuring safe working practices lies mainly with the employer (via safety committees, officers or representatives), ultimately safety depends on the individual employees. Some common office tasks can cause temporary or longer-term problems, such as repetitive strain injury (RSI). This can be very painful and cause long-term damage to joints and bones. However it is not just incorrect posture or repeated movements whilst using, for example, a mouse or keyboard that need to be considered here.

In most offices a variety of electrical equipment is used on a regular basis. Members of staff may, for example, share a photocopier or fax machine. Something as simple as removing jammed paper from the photocopier could place an untrained person in danger. Equally, using the photocopier in the wrong environment could also cause an accident.

Figure 3.16 *Recommended posture chart for computer/keyboard use*

Build-up Exercise

Select one item from the list of electrical equipment you made in the previous activity. Now imagine a new member of staff has joined the business and is going to use this piece of equipment every day. As part of your responsibility for ensuring a healthy and safe environment, you are to write a list of instructions for the new member of staff. Wordprocess the list; it is going to be given to the new employee the day they start working with you.

Working with a computer everyday can be not only very demanding but also a potentially hazardous job. Someone who is skilled at wordprocessing can spend a lot of time looking at the screen, not only inputting the information, but also proofreading it afterwards. It requires a great deal of concentration if it is to be carried out efficiently and accurately. Similarly, entering accounting or other numerical data requires a high level of concentration. Most people using computers find that they get tired very quickly, particularly if they have been looking at the computer screen for more than an hour. Obviously, tiredness will reduce the effectiveness, efficiency and accuracy of the computer user. The following factors should be considered when using a computer:

- The temperature of the room can affect the performance of the computer as well as the user.
- No food and drink should be allowed in the computing room.
- The posture of the user should be monitored – anyone who is repeatedly in an uncomfortable position for any length of time will inevitably suffer long-term health problems. Adjustable chairs should be provided which incorporate footrests and correct back support.
- The angle and height of the screen should also be checked. If the screen is not positioned correctly, the user can get tired more quickly and make more errors.
- A variety of tasks should be undertaken during the course of the working day to avoid the risk of RSI.

Build-up Exercise

Remember the new member of staff who is joining the business? Part of their daily duties will be to input figures onto a spreadsheet. Write them a list of health and safety points that they will need to follow when they are using the computer.

At work you should be sensible, responsible and display commonsense. You will often be in the company of other staff or be supervised in your day-to-day tasks. Sometimes, however, you will be trusted to carry out tasks unsupervised. The way you behave when not being supervised is just as important as when you are. Any judgements or decisions you make will reflect on other people, on the efficiency of your department and on the business as a whole.

Certainly, from a health and safety point of view, your behaviour at work is vitally important, as is that of the people you work with. You have to know when you can deal with something yourself and when it is more appropriate to report the matter to the relevant colleague.

Although it is difficult to be specific here because every job has its own possible problems and solutions, here are some general guidelines as to when it is appropriate to deal with health and safety issues yourself. You should deal with anything that is related to:

- your own area of work, e.g. your desk and its immediate vicinity. If something goes wrong with, say, your computer, printer or telephone equipment, it is up to you to report this to the appropriate person
- the way in which you work, e.g. switching off electricity supplies at the end of the day or opening windows for ventilation. It is up to you to remember how to do things and when to do them, and to ask for help if you need it
- your own behaviour at work, e.g. eating at your desk or drinking coffee over your keyboard. If you break some of the rules occasionally, then you are not complying with your undertaking to work in compliance with the health and safety at work regulations, and it is up to you to improve your behaviour
- your personal presentation whilst at work, e.g. the clothes or jewellery you wear. Obviously, if your job entails using machinery, it is inadvisable for you to wear long, dangling jewellery which could get caught in the machine. Similarly, if your shoes are broken or your shoelaces undone you might trip or fall on the stairs; such shoes would be in breach of the health and safety regulations.

Health and Safety at Work Act 1974

As already mentioned, organisations have to comply with health and safety legislation and if they are found not to be doing so they stand the risk of court proceedings or closure. It is important for you to appreciate what this legislation actually covers and the number of laws that relate to someone like yourself, working as an administrator.

The legislation was initially brought into force in the early 1970s to try to reduce the number of accidents occurring in the workplace, and it has done this effectively over the past 30 years.

The Health and Safety at Work Act 1974 (HASAW) is probably the most well known and important Act and it applies to all work premises, whatever the size of the business or number of employees. The duties of the employers are based on the principle of 'so far as is reasonably practicable'. This means that each risk needs to be balanced against the costs and other difficulties of reducing that risk. The Act requires employers to use commonsense and take suitable measures to tackle hazards, and employees to take reasonable steps to ensure their own safety and that of others.

The Health and Safety at Work Act (1974)

The requirements of the Health and Safety at Work Act apply to all workplace environments, however large or small. They apply to anyone who is on the premises including employees, customers and even contractors who are involved in maintenance or temporary work.

The act states that:

1 All employers must ensure the health, safety and welfare at work of all their employees 'as far as is reasonably practicable'. Specifically this includes:
   * all entry and exit routes must be safe
   * there must be a safe working environment and adequate facilities for the welfare of staff (somewhere to make a drink, toilet facilities, a quiet area)
   * equipment must be safe and well maintained
   * all articles and substances must be safely transported and stored
   * protective clothing must be provided
   * clear information, instruction and training on health and safety must be given to employees, with adequate supervision of issues to do with health and safety.

2 Where the business has five or more employees there should be a written statement on health and safety policy for the business. The statement should be written by the employer and continually updated to include any changes. This document must be circulated to all employees.

3 The business should allow a trade union to appoint safety representatives who must be allowed to investigate accidents or hazards and follow up employee complaints. Safety representatives should be given time off to carry out their duties.

4 All employees must:
   * take responsibility for their own health and safety
   * take responsibility for the health and safety of others who may be affected by their activities or actions
   * co-operate with their employer to meet health and safety requirements.

Build-up Exercise

Your boss has asked you to summarise the key points of the Health and Safety at Work Act for other employees. Although the key points are displayed on the walls of the business, your boss wants every member of staff to have the summary in their own handbook. Your summary should be 150–200 words long. Sub-headings, numbered or bulleted points should be used to emphasise important points.

Employee rights and responsibilities concerning health and safety

Because employees are representatives of the business they are working for, it is both their responsibility and in their own interests to assist in ensuring that the organisation is providing a healthy and safe environment for:

- all employees, whatever their role within the business
- any visiting workers (such as those repairing, servicing or maintaining machinery or equipment)
- all the customers of the business
- any visitors or representatives from other organisations
- the general public.

It is important to remember that the health and safety regulations do not just apply to the business premises themselves, but also to any work undertaken by the business in other locations. This means that representatives of the business who may be carrying out work in another organisation also have to comply with the legislation. Depending on where the work is being carried out, they may even have to comply with extra regulations. Maintenance workers carrying out repairs on a building site would have to wear hard hats and comply with legislation relating to construction sites.

Just as the employer must heed the requirements of the various Health and Safety Acts, so must the employee. If an employee is negligent and causes injury to him/herself or to another person, the employer may be in a difficult position. The employee may claim that it was not really his or her fault, but as long as the employer provides safe working conditions, it is up to the employee to work in a healthy and safe manner. Should an employee not comply with the legislation, or even worse, do something deliberately to put someone else's life in danger, they could find themselves not only dismissed from their job, but also the subject of criminal or civil proceedings in court.

Build-up Exercise

Have another look at the Health and Safety Executive's website at www.hse.gov.uk. Find the section which gives details of accidents at work. How many of the accidents have been fatal? In other words, how many people have died as a result of an accident at work?

Importance of taking precautions

Think about something as simple as a stapler. You may not have considered it before, but it could be a harmful object, particularly if not used correctly or used without adequate concentration. The photocopier, however, is potentially more hazardous still; think about the fumes it emits, the noise it makes, the light it throws out and the hot, sharp edges contained inside. Certainly use of the photocopier demands thought from a health and safety point of view and the following should always be considered:

- Is the machine a particularly old model?
- Is it located in a room of its own?
- Is the room well ventilated?
- If the room has an extractor fan, is it cleaned regularly?
- Is the photocopier regularly serviced by the manufacturer's representative?
- Have the users of the machine received training on how to deal with minor problems?
- Are the users of the machine aware when to call in the manufacturer's representative?

It is safe to assume, then, that all electrical devices represent a hazard and it is wise to think about the following list before you do any work with them:

- Does the machine look damaged in any way?
- Does the electrical socket look OK?
- Is the wiring intact?
- Are there any water leaks or liquid spillages near the machine?
- Does the machine feel hot or overheated?

Build-up Exercise

Go back to the list that you made for the new employee who is going to be using electrical equipment. Did you consider all the above points when you gave them the instructions? If you didn't you should now amend your list to include checks on these things as well.

Identifying and following safe working practices

When considering safe working practices, it is useful also to consider the term 'unsafe behaviour'. This is a general term that extends from practical jokes through to carrying too many books or heavy objects. It is an important consideration, particularly as the majority of office accidents result from someone using unsafe behaviour or, one might say, not using their commonsense.

The main points to remember about using safe working practices are:

- Don't play practical jokes at work.
- Don't run at work.
- Don't over-stack books and papers.
- Don't place regularly used items on high shelves.
- Don't stand on chairs to reach items.

- Don't leave filing cabinet drawers open.
- Don't block gangways, fire exits or the stairs.
- Don't leave fire doors open.
- Don't allow yourself to become complacent – always be aware of hazards.
- Be vigilant and report any problems you encounter to the correct person.
- Don't ignore safety signs.

Try it out

Imagine you work as an office assistant in a large engineering company. Every day you have to go to the factory to collect paperwork from the supervisors. Every day you see one particular member of staff, Brian, unloading full boxes from a lorry. You always have to squeeze past the boxes he has piled in front of the fire doors and along the main corridor through the factory. Lots of other people have complained to you about this inconvenience, but nobody else seems to realise just how dangerous it is.

Write a memo to Brian's supervisor, Harold Whitman. Your memo should explain what you have seen and why you think Brian is behaving in an unsafe manner.

Dealing with low risk matters

Although the office environment is much safer than, say, a building site, accidents still happen to people when they are at work. Having said that, the majority of hazards are low risk. Consider it from a practical point of view:

- A hazard can pose only a small risk, and can easily be put right without harming anyone.
- There may be set policies to follow that allow you to reduce everyone's risk of injury.
- There may be set policies to follow that protect all those working on the business's premises.
- There could be set policies to follow that eliminate or control the degree of risk involved.

Although employees need to be vigilant, their employer or those working with them do not want to have a continual stream of problems reported to them. Not everything is a hazard, so it is important that only the most important issues are dealt with officially. Each organisation has its own set of procedures in place for employees to report health and safety problems. There will usually be someone within your own department that you can contact initially, for minor issues, or it could be that you just need to speak to your usual supervisor or tutor.

Build-up Exercise

Whether you are at work or at college, there is someone you should be able to turn to if you feel you need to report a health and safety problem. If you haven't already identified that person, or persons, then find out who they are now.

Need to report accidents and potential hazards to the appropriate person

Apart from the minor health and safety issues you may have to report to your supervisor or tutor, you may witness an accident while you are at work. Your organisation will have reporting procedures and you may have to take any of the following actions:

- call a member of the staff trained in first aid
- call the emergency services
- deal with the situation yourself until help arrives
- complete an accident report form and enter the details in the accident book.

Organisations usually keep a record of any accidents that occur on their premises and many are forced by legislation to do so. This means that an accident report form has to be completed for any injury that anyone suffers while they are on the premises. In addition to this, an accident book is usually held in the reception area or, if the company employs more than 10 people, in the first-aid room, and each incident must be recorded here. Businesses use these records of accidents, and also 'near-accidents', to try to improve their levels of health and safety and to make sure their organisation is not having more than the national average for their industry. They also monitor the nature and cause of all accidents or incidents occurring on their premises.

If you are at the scene of an accident it is important to remember not to move anything until either the first-aid member of staff or the safety officer arrives on the scene, as they will need to make a full report on what has happened.

The main reasons for the reporting procedure using individual forms and an accident book are to ensure that:

- insurance claims can be investigated – if a person is hurt at work and makes an insurance claim they will have to prove that the accident actually happened at work; if the incident was logged at the time, this constitutes evidence
- additional precautions can be taken in future – an accident might reveal risks that had not been considered before.

The accident report form and accident book require vital information about the nature of the accident to be recorded, so to be useful it should allow the person completing it to give a full explanation of the situation. Accident reports are likely to require the following information:

- the employee's full name
- the employee's home address
- details of the accident, for example date, time and place it occurred
- the treatment given
- the name of the person giving the treatment
- whether or not the individual required hospital treatment
- the nature of the injury
- the names of any witnesses to the accident
- a description of how the accident occurred
- the nature of the activity being undertaken at the time of the accident.

There are a number of important issues that the organisation will want to establish from the accident report form, including:

- Was the person involved in the activity authorised to do what they were doing? This is an important question and has a bearing on who was to blame for the accident. If the person was not authorised the employer may not be liable for the injuries.
- Was the accident caused by machinery? This is another important question: did a machine actually cause the accident? The employer and safety inspectors will want to know whether the machine was safe, being operated correctly, with the recommended safety guards in place, etc.
- Has an accident of this kind happened before? If so, there should be an investigation into why it is reoccurring.

As a final word on accidents, if you are the only witness to one, then there are a few things you need to remember about reporting:

- Take in as much information about the accident as quickly as you can.
- Identify any dangers to yourself, the injured person or others who may appear on the scene.
- Decide whether you can handle the situation yourself or whether you need to summon help.
- If necessary, get help as quickly as possible.

Build-up Exercise

See if you can look at your business's or your college's accident book. If you can, pick out the five most common reasons for accidents happening at your business or college. Now go back to the www.hse.gov.uk website and find the five most common reasons for accidents occurring in the workplace. Do HSE's reasons match in any way those you have identified at your business or college?

By summoning help swiftly you will be able to do what you can for the injured person. However, the way in which you summon help can cause the loss of several precious minutes if done incorrectly. It is important when dialling 999 to:

- give the emergency services your telephone number
- tell them exactly where the accident has occurred
- tell them the nature and seriousness of the accident
- tell them the names, ages and sexes of the injured people if you know them
- tell them about any hazards that they might encounter when responding to your call
- do not put the telephone down until the control officer clears the line.

Importance of procedures in the case of fire, accident, emergency

Dealing with an emergency and following the organisation's procedures for doing so can differ somewhat from dealing with an accident. By 'emergency situations' we really mean events that require evacuation of the premises. This may happen for many reasons, including:

- fire
- equipment malfunctions
- gas leaks
- contamination risks
- security alerts.

The organisation's set procedures for dealing with emergency situations will determine your actions in such cases. Some industries are more prone to emergency or evacuation situations than others, for example those that have public access (banks, building societies and government buildings) and any buildings attached to a factory that may present a fire or contamination hazard.

The reasons for implementing emergency procedures are the same as for accident monitoring, in that the organisation wants to reduce the risks involved to people and to the workplace. Let us look at the reasons for evacuation in a bit more detail.

Fire

Obviously it is important to keep inflammable items away from any sources of ignition and to keep all fire doors closed. You should make sure that you are aware of your organisation's procedures in the event of a fire. Most procedures will insist that you activate a fire alarm and/or contact the emergency services, but stress that you should not attempt to tackle a fire yourself. Not all fires are accidents; some fires are the result of arson.

Equipment malfunctions

Lots of things can, and do, go wrong with machinery, although regular servicing and maintenance can minimise this. However, a significant malfunction can result in the evacuation of a part of the building to avoid injuries to those employed in the area.

Gas and water leaks

A gas leak is a danger that should not be ignored. If you smell gas act immediately as it could result in an explosion or a health risk to those within the premises who could inhale the gas. Water leaks can be equally dangerous, particularly if the liquid comes into contact with the electric suppy.

Contamination risk

This is particularly relevant in businesses that use chemicals Accidental emissions mean there is a risk that substances hazardous to health have, or may have been, released. Often the premises are evacuated as a precautionary measure to protect employees and to ensure the risk is removed before anyone returns.

Security alerts

These are a little more varied in nature and, unfortunately, more common than they used to be. Security alerts and threats to the premises of an organisation can come from either inside or outside the company. Security threats from inside the company include the theft of goods by one of the employees, and could result in evacuation so that all staff can be searched. Threats from outside the organisation include:

- **robberies or burglaries** – sometimes resulting in some form of violence towards those working within the organisation
- **bomb threats** – often carried out in order to either force the company to do something or to make a political statement
- **activists and spies** – who enter premises in order to do damage to the company or to steal information.

Having clear emergency procedures and regular practice evacuations ensures that in the event of a real emergency, staff think clearly and act quickly; this is the key to safe evacuation. There are a number of things to remember should you find yourself involved in an emergency:

- Move swiftly to get out of the building, or at least out of immediate danger, and try not to panic.
- If you are the last person to leave a room, close the door behind you. This is a way of double-checking that a room has been cleared of personnel and in a fire it will help to stop the fire from spreading.
- Make sure you are aware of notices that show the location of the fire assembly points and fire exits.
- Follow the emergency procedures in operation in your workplace.

Build-up Exercise

How many times in the last year has your organisation or college had to be evacuated because of an emergency situation? Find out this information and include any fire drills or evacuation drills you have been involved in.

Health and Safety at Work (Display Screen Equipment) Regulations 1992

The Health and Safety (Display Screen Equipment) Regulations 1992 deal specifically with visual display units (VDUs) or computer screens in the workplace.

Key aspects of the display screen equipment regulations

All employers must:

- ensure that all workstations, related furniture, computer software and the working environment of VDU users meet the minimum requirements of the Regulations

- ensure that all users have regular breaks or changes in activity – it is illegal to work continuously at a computer all day

- offer eye examinations, on request, to employees who use a VDU for more than one hour a day, and provide special spectacles if the tests show that these are needed

- provide users with relevant health and safety training.

All equipment must conform to the following standards:

- Display screens must have clear characters of adequate size, a stable image, adjustable brightness and contrast, be able to tilt and swivel easily. There must be no reflective glare.

- Keyboards must be tiltable and separate from the screen. There should be 'rest' space in front of the keyboard. The surface should be matt, the keyboard easy to use and the symbols clear on the keys.

- Work surfaces must be large enough for the work being done and must have a low reflective finish. The equipment must be flexible so that it can be arranged to suit the needs of the user.

- Work chairs must be stable and allow easy movement and a comfortable position. The user must be able to adjust the height of the seat and the seat back, which must provide good back support. A footrest must be provided if requested.

- Working environments for VDU users should provide satisfactory lighting to minimise glare. Windows should have blinds or workstations be positioned to avoid reflections. Noise and heat levels should be comfortable. Radiation levels must be negligible and humidity controlled so that it is constantly at a satisfactory level.

- Software and systems must be appropriate for the task, user-friendly and appropriate to the level of knowledge of the user.

Build-up Exercise

Now summarise the above piece of legislation in the same way that you did the Health and Safety at Work Act. Your précis should be 150 to 200 words long and you should emphasise the important information by the use of bullets, numbers or headings.

Describe employers' responsibilities under the health and safety legislation

You will realise by now just how important health and safety legislation is, to both employer and employee. But, you may ask, how does anyone know whether a business is complying with the legislation? The local council or authority has the right to inspect business premises at any time to ensure adequate and appropriate health and safety procedures are in place. In addition, the Health and Safety Executive also has inspectors who visit business premises to examine equipment and machinery. It also has the power to enforce the different Acts of Parliament that concern health and safety.

Your employer will have contacted the local authority when the business was first opened and informed them of the organisation's intention to trade in the premises. There are further steps employers have to take when first starting a business. They must:

- contact either the Environmental Health Department and/or the Health and Safety Executive (depending on the type of business activity)
- take out employer's liability insurance and obtain a certificate of this insurance
- display the insurance certificate within the premises of the business
- draw up a health and safety policy for the business
- display a 'Health and Safety at Work' poster within the business premises
- carry out a risk assessment and keep a record of any potential health and safety risks within the business.

Build-up Exercise

Where is the 'Health and Safety at Work' poster displayed in your business or college? Why do you think this particular location was chosen?

The main requirements of health and safety legislation are that the employer should at least comply with the following:

- to provide a safe working environment (safety)
- to provide adequate welfare facilities for employees (health)
- to ensure all entrances and exits to the business premises are safe (emergencies)
- to ensure all equipment and systems used within the business premises are safe (protection)
- to ensure all equipment and systems used within the business premises are serviced regularly (maintenance)
- to ensure that all items needed for the handling or storage of the business's products are safe (warehousing)
- to ensure that any dangerous or toxic materials used by the business are housed in safe containers (secure storage)
- to provide instruction, training and/or supervision to all employees regarding safe working practices and the use of materials (educational programme)
- to investigate and promptly deal with all accidents by identifying their causes (accident prevention).

Naturally, with the responsibility for health and safety sitting very squarely on the shoulders of the employer, most organisations are very keen to improve their record and to protect their employees. They are also aware that they need their employees to be health and safety conscious and so assist the health and safety process. Many do this by:

- setting their employees practical goals to reach health and safety standards
- encouraging their employees to work together and co-operate in a safe manner
- encouraging their employees to accept responsibility for health and safety matters
- identifying key members of staff to deal with health and safety matters
- regularly addressing health and safety issues and encouraging staff to improve
- ensuring all staff are aware of health and safety issues through an initial induction programme and suitable training courses, and that they are kept up to date with any changes in health and safety legislation.

Accidents within the workplace are often attributed to employees working in an untidy and careless manner. Having said this, the employer also has to take responsibility for ensuring that employees have all the information they need to work safely, minimising risk to themselves, their colleagues and visitors. Such safety information can take several forms, including ensuring that staff are:

- familiar with all equipment being used
- trained in health and safety matters
- provided with manuals or handbooks relating to the equipment or machinery being used
- clear about safe working practices
- familiar with the health and safety policy of the business.

It is not possible to list here all the common risks encountered in an office environment, but the following are probably the most serious:

- risk of injury to part or parts of the body – these risks can include injury to the eyes from chemicals or particles, the ears from loud noise, and the body from falling objects or from slipping
- risk of fire
- risk of contamination
- risk of electric shock.

The main way to minimise these risks is to have a comprehensive safety policy in place designed to reduce them as far as possible, or even to eliminate them.

Having said that, no prevention scheme is completely foolproof and everyone has the responsibility to maintain vigilance.

Safety policy needs to be revised on a regular basis by senior management, and employees should be made aware of changes to the business's codes of practice. The safety policy is a written account of how the business intends to train and instruct its employees on health and safety matters and how it will report and record accidents and emergencies.

Build-up Exercise

Did you receive any training about health and safety when you first joined your business or college? If so, did you receive any written confirmation of what you had to do in the case of fire or emergencies? Perhaps you had some training of this kind during your induction period? Read through anything you might have been given at this time to refresh your memory of what you were told then.

Depending on the size and complexity of the organisation, the codes of practice will include:

- how employees should act in the event of an emergency
- how employees should act in the event of an accident
- a list of trained first-aid personnel within the business
- the location of the first-aid room
- a list of named safety representatives or members of a safety committee.

Larger organisations usually have a safety committee, while smaller businesses may have a safety officer or designated safety representatives. These people keep management informed of any changes in government legislation regarding health and safety and tell them about any problems within the business that could mean they are not complying with the law. They also strive to prevent or reduce risks by ensuring:

- all relevant employees are issued with, and use, personal protective equipment. This includes anyone dealing with dangerous materials or substances.
- all machinery and equipment is being used in accordance with the manufacturer's safety instructions. This is particularly relevant when the use of safety guards is recommended.
- the premises are adequately ventilated. This is particularly important when hazardous fumes or smoke are produced as a result of the business's activities. Extractor fans and machinery to circulate the air can ensure that adequate air quality is maintained at all times.
- suitable fire extinguishers and/or fire blankets are available throughout the business's premises.
- safety warning signs are clearly marked. These need to be displayed prominently so that they can easily be seen by employees, customers and visitors.
- sufficient individuals are trained to give first aid. Under the Health and Safety at Work Act the employer is required by law to make sure that qualified individuals are available when first aid is required.
- employees are adhering to the business's safety policy; it's no good having a safety policy in place if the employees don't follow it!

Very often the business's safety policy will be an integral part of a new employee's contract of employment, issued on starting the job. In addition, the safety policy is sometimes included as a written statement in the business's Charter or promise to its customers. For example, a college might include its safety policy in its communication with new students, who are, in effect, the college's 'customers'.

Any organisation complying with government safety legislation will appoint a number of individuals within the business to have certain safety responsibilities. The purpose of these roles is not only to ensure that management is aware of health and safety issues, but also that employees know who to contact if necessary. It is important to know who to to ask about health and safety, either at work or in your school or college, and to be able to direct someone else if they approach you with a health or safety concern.

Try it out

Imagine that you are the office manager. You have received the following list of complaints from some of the office assistants about general office safety:

1 There are not enough cleaning materials for the computers.
2 The office is not ventilated adequately because the windows are sealed closed.
3 The photocopier is giving out a strange smell.
4 When other members of staff are talking on the telephone it is very noisy.

▶▶

5 You cannot always see the computer screens properly because the sun shines through the windows onto the screens.
6 The rubbish bins are not emptied very regularly and sometimes they don't get emptied at all.

For each of the points, decide what you will do to improve the situation. Now write a memo to all staff, telling them what you have decided.

Outline the rights and responsibilities of both employers and employees as set out in the contract of employment

The relationship between the employer and the employee is a formal one. It is usually governed by and set out in the contract of employment. This states the terms and conditions under which the employee will operate on behalf of the employer, as well as a series of undertakings with regard to how the employer will treat the employee.

The employment contract defining relationship between employer and employee and their obligations to each other

Most of the conditions which determine the nature of a contract of employment between employer and employee (and thus the relationship) are governed by law. A series of laws (or pieces of legislation) have been passed to protect the rights of employees and employers.

An employee who is given the opportunity to develop through varied work and training is of more value to an employer. But this only works if they are both aware of the business's objectives.

An employer has a number of duties towards his or her employee. The contract of employment formalises the relationship and is legally binding on both employer and employee. The contract of employment should include:

- a job description (the nature of the job)
- a job title (the name of the job)
- the requirements of the job (what the employee will be expected to do)
- pay details (how and when the employee is paid)
- any additional payment details (which salary scale the employee is to start on)
- when overtime is allowed
- how bonuses (additional payments) can be earned
- how commission (a percentage of profits, or sales made) can be earned
- working hours (the starting and finishing times of work including lunchtimes and breaks)

- working hours (the total number of hours to be worked per week)
- holiday entitlement (number of days of holiday the employee can take, and any restrictions on when)
- sick pay arrangements (how many days off sick the employee may take and still be paid)
- maternity leave arrangements (how much time off a pregnant employee can take and what the employer will pay her)
- pension scheme details (how much the employer pays into the scheme and how much the employee has to contribute)
- grievance procedures (what the employee has to do in order to deal with any problems they may encounter, with either the employer or other employees)
- disciplinary procedures (under what circumstances an employee can be disciplined, and how the employer will act if discipline becomes necessary)
- training and promotion opportunities
- the period of notice to be worked or given if an employee decides to leave the business, or is sacked by the employer (notice is the amount of time an employee has to work after they or their employer has informed the company they will be leaving)
- details of the business's health and safety rules and procedures.

The contract of employment may also include the following items, although these are often addressed during the new employee's induction period:

- Social and welfare facilities available within the business – for example, employee counselling assistance, clubs which the employees can attend, childcare facilities or social events that take place.
- Company rules and regulations indicating the way employees are expected to, for example, work safely, greet visitors or answer the telephone.
- Codes of behaviour – these set down the ways employees are expected to behave at work and may also include particular dress codes.

Many of these issues are discussed in other parts of the unit. It is important to remember that by law the employer and the employee both have to stick to the contract of employment.

As an employee, you will be expected to comply with your contract of employment and accept responsibility for your actions at work. A contract of employment is like any other legal contract. It gives both parties rights as well as obligations. The contract formalises what was agreed at the job interview and will contain commitments by the employer and employee.

The employer *will*:

- pay wages or salary
- provide work
- pay any reasonable losses or expenses suffered by the employee during the course of doing their job

- provide the employee with a reference if they wish to apply for another job
- provide a safe working environment and safe working practices
- not break the trust and confidence given to them by the employee
- provide the employee with all the necessary information they need regarding their work, pay, conditions and opportunities
- always act in good faith towards the employee.

The employee *has to*:

- work in a loyal, conscientious and honest manner
- accept any reasonable and legal instructions from senior members of staff
- act in good faith towards the employer
- account for any money received from other sources (this is to make sure that the employee does not accept any bribes or fees from other organisations, for example competitors of the business)
- keep confidential information secret
- give faithful service to the employer
- comply with health and safety regulations
- comply with the business's rules and regulations
- comply with the business's codes of behaviour.

Try it out

Imagine that you are about to start a new job. Answer the following questions – you may have to do some further research to answer them all:

1 State at least five things you would expect to find on your contract of employment.
2 How soon after starting your job would you be entitled to receive your contract of employment?
3 If you don't receive a contract of employment, what should you do?

An employee may be disciplined for a number of reasons, including:

- being away from work too often
- constantly arriving late for work
- refusing to carry out instructions
- inability to do the job properly
- deliberately endangering the lives of others
- behaving in an unacceptable manner
- stealing property from the employer or others
- sleeping at work
- being under the influence of alcohol or drugs at work
- fighting at work.

Whatever the eventual reason for disciplinary action, there are recommended guidelines that the employer should follow:

- A written record should be kept at all stages of the disciplinary procedure.
- Copies of the disciplinary procedure should be available to all employees.
- The employees should know who within the business operates the procedure.
- Employees should know who is likely to get involved during the disciplinary procedure.
- The employer should make it clear what kind of disciplinary action will be taken in each circumstance.
- Employees should be made aware that they can appeal against the disciplinary action.
- Employees should know that unless their infringement was very serious, they will not be dismissed from their job the first time it happens.
- Employees should be assured that the disciplinary procedure is fair.
- Employees should be assured that they will not be discriminated against.

The recommended stages of a disciplinary procedure are:

1 **Verbal warning** – if an employee's conduct, behaviour or performance does not meet an acceptable standard he or she will be given a formal verbal warning. If the employee behaves correctly after this warning then the matter will be dropped. If not, disciplinary action will move on to the next stage.

2 **Written warning** – if the employee continues with the same behaviour or if the offence was serious enough, a written warning will be issued. This written warning details the complaint against the employee and states what he or she has to do to sort the situation out. The employee will also be told how much time they have to improve before further action is taken.

3 **Final written warning** – if the employee is still failing to improve his or her behaviour or performance, a final written warning will be issued. In serious cases the employer may issue a final written warning straightaway. The final warning details the complaint and tells the employee that dismissal is the next step if improvement is not made.

Build-up Exercise

See if you can obtain a copy of either your business's or your college's disciplinary procedure. It could be that you were issued with a copy of this when you had your induction. What does the procedure say? Does it follow the same stages that we have looked at in this section? If it is different, how does it differ? Why do you think it is different?

Describe other protection offered to employees by employment and equal opportunities legislation

As well as the health and safety legislation and employment law, there are other pieces of legislation laid down by government which affect both employers and employees. These laws are there to protect the employee from unfair treatment (particularly in cases of dismissal), from being discriminated against at work, and to ensure that everyone has the same opportunities at work.

Grounds for dismissal and protection against unfair dismissal

Dismissal is the ending (termination) of an employee's contract of employment by the employer. The reason for dismissal is often unacceptable behaviour. The employer needs to have a real reason for dismissing an employee and at all times the employer has to show that they are behaving in a fair way to the employee. There are four main reasons why someone might be dismissed. These are:

- **Capability and qualifications** – this is when an employee has shown that they are unable to do the job, even though they have been trained, or retrained, on a number of occasions.
- **Redundancy** – this occurs when the employer closes down the business, or part of the business, and the employee's job no longer exists.
- **Misconduct** – this is when an employee has not complied with an aspect of the contract of employment, for example regular absence, lateness, refusal to carry out instructions or breaking the safety rules.
- **Breaking legal requirements** – this is when, for example, someone who has to drive one of the business's vehicles loses their driving licence because of a drink-driving offence. Losing their licence makes them unable to continue to do the job stated in their contract of employment.

An employer must have a genuine reason for dismissing an employee, otherwise they are guilty of not complying with the government laws which protect employees from unfair dismissal. They cannot single out someone because of their:

- **race** – someone cannot be dismissed because of the colour of their skin or their country origin
- **religion** – someone cannot be dismissed because they have (or indeed, have not) certain religious beliefs
- **gender or sexual orientation** – the employer cannot dismiss an employee because they are male or female, nor because they are homosexual, lesbian or heterosexual
- **pregnancy** – a woman cannot be dismissed because she is pregnant. However, if pregnancy affects her ability to do the job (for example, if the job involves carrying heavy weights) there may be reasonable grounds for terminating the contract of employment

- **criminal record** – if the employer finds out that the employee has a criminal record, but it does not affect the job they are doing, the employee cannot be dismissed as a result. If the criminal record relates to fraud or theft, however, and the employee works in the accounts or finance department, this could be grounds for ending the contract of employment if the employee did not inform the employer about their criminal record before taking up the job
- **trade union membership** – an employee cannot be dismissed because they belong to a trade union.

Try it out

Although it is never easy to know exactly where you stand without referring to an expert, what would your reaction be to the following situations? Discuss these three situations with the rest of your group.

1   Mustapha is a young Muslim who works in customer services. For religious reasons he has not been eating (fasting). On two occasions in the past week he has fallen asleep at his desk. He is complaining of headaches, but his supervisor has just given him a verbal warning for falling asleep at work.

2   You have just been called into your manager's office and told that she has a mind to discipline you for using someone else's photocopier card. You have no idea what she is talking about, but when she checks the records of your card, it has not been used for the past two weeks. Simon, who lost his card two weeks ago, has had his photocopy card used and since you have been the only one to use the photocopier today, it must be you. To be honest you haven't looked at the card so you don't know whether it is yours or Simon's.

3   Claire has been having problems with her marriage and has been quite open about it to the rest of her colleagues. You have noticed she has been a bit unsteady on her legs when she has come back from lunch and she smells of mints and drinks a lot of coffee all afternoon. Yesterday, after having been taken into the manager's office on several occasions for being rude, late, and moody with people, she came back from lunch very drunk and was instantly dismissed.

Equal opportunities legislation

To protect employees from being unfairly dismissed by their employers, there are a number of government laws, or Acts of Parliament. The Acts you need to be aware of are of two types:

- Acts that protect people from being discriminated against
- Acts to ensure people are paid equally.

Discrimination Acts

The Disability Discrimination Act aims to end the discrimination which many disabled people face. This Act gives disabled people rights in the areas of:

- employment
- access to goods, facilities and services
- buying or renting land or property.

The employment rights first came into force on 2 December 1996; they were added to on 1 October 1999; the next amendments to the Act will be released in October 2004.

The Act states that a disabled person is someone with 'a physical or mental impairment which has a substantial and long-term adverse effect on his or her ability to carry out normal day-to-day activities.'

The Act applies to employers with 15 or more employees. According to the Act, there are two ways in which an employer might unlawfully discriminate against a disabled employee or job applicant:

- by treating him or her less favourably (without justification) than other employees or job applicants because of his or her disability
- by not making reasonable adjustments to their working environment (without justification) to allow them to do the job.

The Sex Discrimination Act (1975) protects against obvious discrimination because of someone's gender. It applies equally to both males and females, and includes the following circumstances:

- Victimisation – this occurs where a person is treated less favourably than another person because they have complained. They may have indicated that they intend to bring a case under the law or have given evidence in a case. They might have alleged that something has been done that may be against the law in relation to the Sexual Discrimination, Race Relations or Disability Discrimination Acts.
- Sexual harassment – this is conduct which is unreasonable, unwelcome and offensive, and which creates an intimidating, hostile or humiliating environment. It usually consists of more than one incident of unacceptable behaviour, however one serious instance may be enough to cause an employee to apply to an Employment Tribunal. The Employment Tribunal decides whether the employee has grounds for claiming sexual harassment because of the treatment they have received.

The Race Relations Act (1976) (as amended in 2000) makes it unlawful to discriminate against anyone because of their race, colour, nationality or ethnic or national origin. The Act encourages employers to promote racial equality and applies to taking on new staff, and training existing staff.

Racist incidents, from harassment and abuse to physical violence, are illegal under the law.

Equal Pay Acts

The Equal Pay Act (1970) makes it illegal for employers to discriminate between men and women in terms of their contracts of employment. The Act covers all contractual benefits, not just pay, including holiday entitlement, pension, childcare benefits, sickness benefits and car allowances, and applies to both men and women.

The Equal Pay Act applies to direct and indirect discrimination:

- Direct discrimination – this occurs where the pay a woman receives is less than that of a man with the same skills, qualifications and experience, and the reason for the lower pay is simply because she is a woman.
- Indirect discrimination – this occurs in a pay system where the same rules appear to apply to both men and women, but women are at a disadvantage in practice, maybe because they are only able to work part-time as they have childcare responsibilities.

Under The Employment Relations Act (1999), most employees have the right to:

- up to 13 weeks unpaid holiday when a child is born
- a reasonable period of time off work to deal with an emergency involving a parent, child or other person dependent on them
- maternity leave and maternity pay if they become pregnant.

Try it out

Have a look at the website of an organisation called The Equal Opportunities Commission (EOC) at www.eoc.org.uk. What advice and guidance do they give to UK employers about the Sex Discrimination Act and the Equal Pay Acts? If necessary print out the relevant sections and then summarise their work in your own words. You should restrict your summary on the work of the Commission to 200 words in total.

Following office procedures to complete tasks

Four key assessment objectives

- Identify and describe a range of office-based activities requiring procedures
- Explain the purpose of procedures
- Follow procedures to carry out office tasks
- Review the ways in which procedures are implemented and their effectiveness

Each of these broad objectives covers a number of specific skills relating to following office procedures to complete tasks.

In this unit you will learn how to:

- identify a range of procedures for different activities and list steps within them
- give examples of different types of procedure and their outcome
- list the benefits to an organisation of procedures
- follow good filing practice
- make the best use of photocopier facilities to suit the task in hand
- send and receive information
- control stock and maintain stock records
- process incoming and outgoing post
- identify the ways in which procedures are supported and promoted
- identify possible difficulties in following procedures
- identify possible improvements to procedures
- evaluate the effectiveness of specific procedures when completing tasks.

Identify and describe a range of office-based activities requiring procedures

All organisations work in different ways and have different systems and procedures which they expect their staff to carry out in the course of their day-to-day duties. A procedure is a set of rules, or the business's preferred steps, that employees have to stick to when carrying out their tasks. This section covers briefly the various types of administrative procedure and discusses in more detail the particular skills, duties and tasks required to carry them out.

Administration procedures are important since an organisation's activities must be co-ordinated and planned. If administration procedures are inadequate, the organisation may lack efficiency and effectiveness since staff will not have access to the relevant information they need. Administration procedures inevitably involve some form of filing, be it paper-based or on a computer system.

Administrative systems should also establish a means by which the operations it carries out can be assessed. Most administrative systems can be divided into sub-systems which can in turn be split into smaller sub-systems. Systems should be designed so they can be changed to meet the changing requirements of the organisation.

Administrative procedures obviously play a vital role within an organisation. They are the means by which the organisation is able to operate as a whole. Any organisation can have good ideas and well-motivated employees, but without procedures to ensure that functions are carried out, nothing much will happen. Information received by the organisation has to be processed before it can either be stored (for later retrieval) or disseminated (sent to different people) around the various departments. Alternatively, the information may have to be redirected from the organisation in a different format.

Identify a range of procedures for different activities and list steps within them

Table 4.1 shows us what information may come into a business, what the business might need to do to that information and the type of information that leaves the business.

Table 4.1

Type of information that may enter a business	How information may be processed by the business	Type of information that may leave a business
Fax	Filed on a computer	A reply or response in writing
Telephone message	Sent around the different departments	A reply or response via the telephone
E-mail message		
Business letter	Filed in a filing cabinet	A bill to a customer
Money from a customer	Discussed at a meeting	A payment to a supplier
Bill from a supplier	Followed up by a member of staff	
	Analysed by managers	
	A report produced	

An organisation needs to process incoming information. This is done in a number of different ways, depending on the type of business and the type of information.

It is generally accepted that the term 'administration procedures' describes the following activities:

- Ways of doing things that are set down as rules and regulations by the senior managers.

- Activities carried out by managers to meet the objectives of the organisation.
- Activities carried out to ensure control of the day-to-day running of the business.

Administrative tasks are carried out at all levels within an organisation. In larger organisations, administration will be carried out by an administration department, but in smaller businesses the administration 'department' may be a single individual, responsible for all administration. Whoever is responsible, the basic purpose of the procedures listed above remains the same.

Administration consists of:

- providing support systems for all resources used by the organisation
- keeping records relating to the activities of the organisation
- monitoring the performance of the business's activities.

Specifically, a business will have administrative procedures in place to make sure that:

- information is stored in the right place (either on a computer or in a paper-based filing system)
- information can be found easily once it has been stored (either on a computer or in a paper-based filing system)
- information can be copied or printed (using a photocopier or a printer) and passed on to those employees who need to see it
- information can be received easily by the business (via the fax machine, e-mail and postal system)
- those wishing to send information to the business can do so easily and without problems
- information can be sent out of the business easily (via fax, e-mail and the postal system)
- those who are meant to receive the information sent to the business can do so easily and without problems
- the physical resources (materials, components and items such as stationery, envelopes, etc.) the business's employees need are available when needed; this is known as stock control.

The activities of an organisation may be classified as routine or non-routine. Routine activities are those that are carried out on a regular basis. Some individuals will be responsible for routine administration functions which are unaffected by the organisation's other activities. Examples of such functions are:

- opening the mail each morning
- filing business documents in a filing cabinet.

Build-up Exercise

Write down another five routine activities which staff carry out on a regular basis.

Other employees are required to carry out non-routine administrative activities. Such staff have to be more adaptable as the demands placed on them will change each day and they will not be able to predict their work with any great accuracy. On any one day they may have a series of meetings or tasks to perform without prior notice or instruction.

Routine functions, on the other hand, can be easily controlled throughout the organisation if the correct procedures are in place. Office staff will base these procedures on previous experience and will know with considerable accuracy the demands that will be placed upon them. When an individual or department needs to carry out a non-routine function, they will rely upon a separate set of procedures to support them. If the non-routine task needs to be carried out so frequently that it becomes routine a procedure may need to be created to support the staff carrying out that specific task.

Explain the purpose of procedures

Administrative procedures need to be put in place to track the activities of a business. Organisations have their own procedures, but most will have a way of keeping track of the following:

- the cost of the purchases that the business makes
- the names of those from whom the business has made purchases from
- sales of the business's products or services
- customers who have bought the business's products or services
- enquiries made by customers
- payments made by customers
- outstanding payments from customers
- payments the business has made to suppliers
- outstanding payments to suppliers
- information about the employees of the business (employee records)
- details of training undertaken, or required, by employees
- stock levels (physical resources) held by the business
- records of meetings held within the business.

Build-up Exercise

Think about your own job, or the activities you have to carry out for this course. Do you have your own procedures in place that help you work efficiently and effectively? Do your procedures help you work towards meeting your own objectives? Write down at least five procedures that you use routinely to complete the tasks required of you.

Examples of different types of procedure and their outcomes

Larger organisations tend to have more procedures than smaller ones. The procedures in your organisation or college should help you understand what is required of you and how to carry out the tasks set you. Some procedures are very strict and formal because they are dictated by law (e.g. health and safety procedures); others are dictated by the business's objectives, or what has been found to be the best way to do things. Some procedures are required to ensure the business's confidential information is not leaked, or to make sure the business's buildings are secure. In addition to the procedures we looked at in the last assessment objective, there are the following:

- All visitors to the business must check into reception on arrival at the premises.
- Employees wishing to photocopy have to complete a form to obtain their paper.
- Employees wishing to obtain a file from the filing room (centralised filing) have to complete a form and have it signed by a senior manager.
- All mail delivered to, or sent from, the organisation, has to be dealt with by the mail room (centralised mailing) before distribution to each department by the mail room employees.

Build-up Exercise

Why do you think a business might decide to have all mail handled through a centralised mail room? Write down what you consider the advantages and disadvantages of using this procedure.

Benefits to an organisation of procedures

A business does not create procedures just for the sake of having them. Procedures have to offer some advantage to the business, particularly if setting the procedure up and running it costs the business money. There are a number of reasons why a business benefits from having procedures in place. Under the following sub-headings are reasons why a business might benefit from having administrative procedures in place.

Organisation

Procedures allow a business to carry out all of its activities in an organised way. Decisions about the organisation's objectives are made and the procedures then help the business's staff to achieve those objectives.

If a business's employees approach their activities in an organised way, the impression or image they give their customers and the general public is good. To convey this image staff will try to make sure that, for example:

- all paperwork that leaves the business is giving a good impression because it is neat, accurate and well presented
- all information requested is sent out quickly to the right person, at the right time

- all messages received are dealt with promptly and efficiently
- all customers, or people likely to become customers, receive the same high level of service from the employees
- employees are aware of the need to keep confidential or sensitive information safe
- the business's buildings and employees are kept healthy and safe
- the business is following government laws in the way in which it carries out its activities.

Well-organised businesses gain the following benefits:

- the business's customers are more likely to return and buy again (repeat business)
- the business's customers are more likely to recommend the business to others, which could bring it new customers.

Try it out

You work as an administrative assistant for a double-glazing company called Pressure Glass Limited. The sales office is very chaotic and calls are coming in and going out all the time. The sales manager has called together everyone who works in the sales office, including you, to talk about organisational procedures used in dealing with customers. She wants the business to have a procedure for dealing with customers who ring the business. At the meeting the following ideas were suggested and your sales manager thinks they are all good. She wants you to put them in some kind of order that makes sense. They will be the new organisational procedures.

- We need to say 'Pressure Glass Limited, how can we help you?'.
- Don't forget, we need to tell them about our latest products.
- We need to ask them what they want and who they want to speak to.
- We really should pick up the phone before six rings.
- We should put them straight through to the right person if they are around.
- If we promise to send something out it must go out the same day.
- Tell them we can organise for someone to visit them in 48 hours at the maximum.
- We mustn't forget to tell them we're the best in the area.
- We have got to make sure all letters are checked before they go out – we don't want them to contain any mistakes.
- If someone is not available, tell them we promise to make sure they call them back.
- We should make sure any letters or brochures go out first class.

Clarity of roles and requirements

Knowing what your role is in an organisation begins with your initial interview, where you are told to some extent what will be expected of you. When you receive your contract of employment, a job description may well be included. This will outline your role in the organisation, either as a team member or as an individual who is working to support others in the organisation.

As we have said in other units of this book, the job description only tells part of the story; you should be prepared to be flexible and adaptable, as you may be asked to carry out other duties which are not on the job description. Whether this is the case or not, the term 'clarity of roles' means knowing in a variety of different circumstances exactly what is expected of you and how your work relates to the wider activities of the company.

In both your routine work and in more individual, demanding tasks, organisational procedures can help you understand the processes involved and suggest ideal ways in which the business wants particular things done. The procedures will be a series of steps, supported by checks, to make sure that everything has been covered and completed to the business's (and probably the customers') satisfaction.

Organisational procedures set out the requirements of a particular task. They are usually a series of instructions which alert you to the fact that particular documents must be referred to, other documents and forms completed and certain individuals informed, either to check what has been done or to receive information at a particular stage of the activity. In this way organisational procedures can help you, as an employee, make sure that everything has been done, and also to reassure management that all the necessary steps have been taken in line with their policies.

Build-up Exercise

Think of one particular activity you carry out routinely either in your job, or while studying at college. Can you think of at least three benefits to yourself and three for the business as a whole of having these procedures?

Quality assurance and safe working meeting legal requirements

Organisational procedures are designed to ensure that every activity, whether it involves dealing internally with staff or with customers, is carried out satisfactorily. A business will often develop a preferred method for carrying out a particular task and will always want that task to be carried out in the same way. This approach ensures that a consistent quality of work is applied to all its operations.

Many businesses have formal ways of checking quality of work (quality assurance). These may include spot-checks on tasks and activities to ensure that they are being carried out according to organisational procedure guidelines. Quality assurance should apply to everything that the business does, regardless of time or pressures that mean the task has had to be rushed. The same quality levels should apply to dealings with people inside the business as to customers.

Indeed many businesses encourage staff to think of their dealings with people inside the organisation as customer contact; in either case staff are providing what should be a quality service.

Businesses also apply quality assurance to areas of activity which require them to meet legal requirements, such as health and safety. A business should not expect employees to break health and safety guidelines just to complete a task or activity. The business's procedures should ensure that you meet these legal requirements, as it is the business's responsibility to make sure that health and safety laws are always observed.

Build-up Exercise

Your business (or the college) will have a procedure in place for dealing with the evacuation of a building in the case of an emergency or fire. It will also have a procedure stating who should be contacted if there is a health and safety concern. Obtain a copy of these procedures and make sure you understand what is required of you should these events occur.

Follow procedures to carry out office tasks

You are required in this unit to provide evidence that you can follow organisational procedures to carry out a number of office duties or tasks. Your business or college will have their own set of procedures that you will have to show you can follow when you complete the tasks. However, you will also need to prove that you have the knowledge, understanding and skills required to carry out the following office tasks:

- filing information correctly
- filing information so that it can be found again when required
- copying information
- sending information to another person
- receiving information from another person
- controlling items of stock (for example stationery and envelopes, pens and pencils)
- dealing with incoming mail
- dealing with outgoing mail.

The remainder of this assessment objective gives you the rules and regulations for carrying out each of these office tasks, although you need to be sure that you know exactly what your own business's (or the college's) particular procedures are as well.

Storage and retrieval of information

The words 'storage and retrieval' can often be confusing when one has not worked in an office. In fact, they mean 'filing'. This word can also cause a reaction – often groans and moans! Filing is often thought to be boring and routine, and, in essence, it is. Nowadays, however, storage and retrieval also includes the computerised systems for storing and retrieving information.

The secure storage of information and the easy access or retrieval of that information is imperative if an organisation is to function successfully and efficiently.

Another word for filing is 'indexing'. Obviously this involves a logical and effective way of recording documents and storing them in an efficient system which allows the easy retrieval of information when required.

Filing is the basis of record-keeping and entails the processing, arranging and storing of documents so that they can be found when they are required. The documents are placed in consecutive order and preserved in that system until they are required for reference. Such systems are employed in any number of different ways; a telephone directory is an alphabetical index of names and addresses. Your own address book is also a method of indexing in alphabetical order.

Following good filing practice

So what are the basic techniques required to ensure efficient storage and retrieval of information and documents? Let us look at this in more detail. Here are some pointers to good filing practice:

- Ensure that the papers which have been passed for filing have been marked in some way to indicate that they are ready for storing.
- Sort the papers into order so that they are grouped in the required way.
- Remove any paperclips and staple documents together – this ensures they do not get separated during the filing process.
- Each individual file should be in date order, with the most recent documents at the top or front.
- Handle the documents carefully – curled edges can easily become torn.
- File daily if possible – this makes it less of a chore and also ensures that the files are up to date.
- Follow organisational procedure regarding 'out' or 'absent' cards. These are cards which are inserted into a file when paperwork has been removed from the file by a member of staff. The card indicates who has the file, when they took it and when they should return it to the filing cabinet.
- Follow up regularly all overdue files, that is files that have been borrowed by another member of staff or department and not returned on time.
- Use a cross-reference system whenever a file is known by more than one name. It is often necessary to update files, for example when an organisation changes its name, or when a personnel file changes name because the member of staff marries. This could cause confusion as some people may still refer to the file, or look for it, under its old name. For this reason a system has to be in place which enables the person searching to find it under either of its names. The cross-reference slip is placed either in the old or in the new file, and direct the person seeking the file to the correct place.

- Thin out files when necessary. There will be an organisational procedure regarding the length of time documents are held in the system. When they become obsolete or out of date they may be transferred to the 'archives'. This is an additional storage area where files are stored in boxes in case they are required for reference. The archives could be in another room or even in another building. We look at archiving in more detail a little later in this unit.
- Be aware of health and safety regarding filing cabinets. For example, always close drawers after you have used them and lock drawers and cabinets before leaving the office at night.
- Always ask for help if you are unsure where something should be filed, and do not be afraid to offer ideas if you think the system could be improved.

Using classification methods

Documents can be filed using any of the following systems. Different methods are suitable for different circumstances. The following can be found in any type of organisation and are known as the different classification methods of filing:

Alphabetic

With this method documents are filed according to the first letter of the name. It is the most common filing method used in businesses. The first letter referred to is usually that of the surname of the correspondent, although in a human resources department files could be arranged by the first letter of the surname of the member of staff. There are advantages and disadvantages to using the alphabetical classification method, as can be seen in Table 4.2.

Table 4.2 *Advantages and disadvantages of the alphabetic classification method of filing*

Advantages	Disadvantages
<ul><li>It is a convenient and easy to understand system.</li><li>It requires no index cards.</li><li>It is useful for incorporating miscellaneous documents.</li></ul>	<ul><li>The filing system can become very large and cumbersome.</li><li>Confusion can occur when names are the same or similar.</li><li>Cross referencing is necessary as there is a possibility that files under different names may be requested.</li></ul>

Here are some rules for alphabetic filing:

1 Organise files according to the first letter of the surname and then each letter after that, for example:
   Black, Brian
   Blake, John
   Blakemore, Margaret

2 If the surname is the same, place the first names or initials in alphabetic order, for example:
>   Smith, David
>   Smith, John
>   Smith, William

3 If the surname and the first name are the same, file by second name or initial, e.g.:
>   Jones, Brian A
>   Jones, Brian D
>   Jones, Brian P

4 Treat surname prefixes as part of the name and all names beginning with M', Mc or Mac as if they were spelt with Mac, for example:
>   McBride, Angus
>   McGregor, William
>   MacMasters, Peter

5 File all 'saint' surnames (those beginning with 'St') as if they were spelt Saint, for example:
>   St John, Ian
>   St Luke's Church
>   St Mary's Hospital

6 Ignore titles, for example:
>   Brown, Sir Andrew
>   Grey, Lady Jane
>   Simpson, Major David

7 Ignore words like 'The' and 'A' in the name of an organisation, for example:
>   Card Shop, The
>   Office Equipment Centre, The
>   Tea Shoppe, The

8 Numbers should be filed as if spelt in full, for example
>   55 Club, The (would be filed under 'F' for Five)
>   99 Boutique, The (would be filed under 'N' for Nine)
>   111 Association, The (would be filed under 'O' for One)

Build-up Exercise

Place the following list of names in alphabetical order:

Hutchinson, David	Hurle, Peter
Conway, Malcolm	Aliffe, Burt
Hunt, Peter	Smith, Marie
Woodhouse, John	Smith, Delphine
Jackson, Nick	Wright, Susan
Sutherland, Joshua	Canwell, Rosie
Hewitt, Ernest William	Greene, Susan
Hewitt, Diane Elizabeth	Green, Samantha
Canwell, Stuart	Leggett, Michael
Canwell, Alun	

A quick way of putting a list of terms into alphabetical order is to number them first, according to their position in the alphabetical list, and then write the list out again in numerical order.

Numeric

This classification method of filing is linked by means of index cards to the alphabetic method we have just looked at. Each document or folder is given a number and these are filed in number order. The information contained within the files is sorted into alphabetical order. The numeric classification method also has advantages and disadvantages over other classification methods, as shown in Table 4.3.

Table 4.3 *Advantages and disadvantages of the numeric classification method of filing*

Advantages	Disadvantages
■ The numbered files are more easily found. ■ The numbered files are less likely to be returned to the wrong place. ■ The number reference can be added to any correspondence sent to the customer or supplier. ■ The number of files can be easily increased, thereby expanding the system.	■ An index must be used in addition to the files themselves.

Build-up Exercise

Place the following list of numbers in numerical order:

134	310	180
176	245	76
95	88	21
378	333	209
109	213	

Chronological

Chronological filing means that documents are stored according to the date, with the most recent at the front or top of the file. Travel agents are likely to use this method of filing for their customers' travel documents. The documents would be filed in order of either the customer's departure date or the required payment date. A sales representative might also use the chronological system of filing paperwork according to the dates on which they have arranged meetings with customers. Chronological filing has the advantages and disadvantages shown in Table 4.4.

Table 4.4 *Advantages and disadvantages of the chronological classification method of filing*

Advantages	Disadvantages
■ For some organisations a date is the most significant information available.	■ There are no major disadvantages, it is unlikely that any organisation other than one particularly needing this method would consider using it.

Build-up Exercise

Place the following list of dates in chronological order, putting the most recent at the top:

25 January 1999	20 July 2002
17 September 2001	15 November 2002
1 August 2003	18 November 2003
15 June 2000	21 September 2001
27 June 2000	18 June 2000
11 November 2001	24 August 2003
6 May 1999	21 December 2003

Creating files

The term 'creating files' actually means starting a new file which is to be added to an existing set of files. Your business will have procedures in place that determine who is allowed to create new files. These are there to avoid too many:

■ unnecessary files
■ files with just a small amount of information in them
■ files with the same type of information in them.

Too many files in the filing system can be a waste of paper and valuable space. Some organisations, however, have no option but to create a new file for each new name that is encountered, for examples hospitals, doctors and dentists have to keep all the information about individual patients in one file.

Before creating a new file you should make sure:

■ you have permission to do so
■ there is not already a similar file in existence.

Archiving material in line with procedures

Archiving means storing away old files. There will be procedures in place that have to be followed, mainly because someone in authority must decide when an active file becomes an old file. It could happen because the information in the file:

- relates to a previous customer or business the organisation used to deal with
- relates to an employee who has now left the business
- is now out of date.

Archiving does not mean throwing away. Old files could only be temporarily old (obsolete). There is always a chance that old files may be needed again in the future. They may even become current again. Archiving means storing in another location, for example another room, a cupboard, a storage area or another building belonging to the business.

On a regular basis, the timing of which will be set down in the organisation's procedures, filing cabinets are sorted and those files that need to be archived removed. A note is filed in the cabinet for each file that has been transferred to the archive, just in case someone looks for the file in the future and doesn't know where it is.

Build-up Exercise

Find out the procedures your business or college has for archiving files. How long do files remain current? Where do the files go when they are archived? Who has the authority to determine when the archiving activity is carried out?

Procedures for retrieving information from files

The main purpose of filing paperwork is so that you, or someone else, is able to find it again when it is needed. Finding information in a filing system is known as 'retrieving information'. Information might need to be retrieved in order to:

- add more information to the contents of the file
- obtain some information from the contents of the file.

If someone takes individual documents from a file they may go missing forever. You should never allow just a few pages to be taken from a file unless:

- most of the other information contained in the file is confidential and mustn't be seen by the person requiring the documents
- the whole file is much too large to take away.

The golden rules for making sure that information from a file does not get lost or returned to the wrong place are:

- Record the fact that information has been taken from the filing cabinet by inserting an 'out' or 'absent' card in its place.
- Use a log sheet to record the fact that the file has been borrowed, by whom, when it was taken, where it has gone and the agreed return date.
- Keep information on the log sheet up to date and chase up any files that are not returned as agreed.

Handling confidential information

Many types of confidential information are contained within files, including:

- personal information about employees, filed in the human resources department or the accounts and finance departments
- financial information about the business or department in which you work
- plans for the department in which you work or the business as a whole
- customer information, such as names, addresses, and the amount of money spent with, or owed to, your department or business.

Confidential information must be kept secret and secure. If filing cabinets contain confidential information you must make sure that:

- files are never left unattended on a desk
- files are never taken into any area of the business not concerned with the information contained in the folders
- the contents of the files are never discussed with other employees or those outside the business
- files are never lent to anyone who does not have permission to access them
- filing cabinet drawers are locked and the keys kept safely
- old files remain confidential when they go to the archives
- unwanted files are shredded rather than placed in wastepaper baskets or recycled.

Build-up Exercise

Say whether each of the following files is confidential or not confidential:

1 Details of a proposed merger between your business and another business.
2 The disciplinary procedure of the organisation.
3 Details of customer order forms.
4 Details of products as shown in the business's catalogue.
5 Bank details of a new employee.
6 The business's health and safety procedures.
7 The business's sales figures for the last year.
8 Details of how much the business owes each of its suppliers.

Using filing systems

Filing systems are the actual cabinets in which the files are stored. There are a number of different systems available, but the ones you have to know about for this qualification are the lateral filing systems, vertical filing systems and card indexes. These are the most common systems used.

Lateral filing systems

Lateral filing systems are used for storing papers in files that are suspended laterally with their strips or labels vertically on the front. Suspended pockets, into which the files are placed, hang in rows from one side of the cabinet to the other. Each of the files has a tab attached to it where the file is identified by either its name or its number. Lateral filing cabinets often have a sliding door at the front which can be locked. They are usually made of metal or wood.

Figure 4.1 *Lateral filing cabinet*

Vertical filing systems

Vertical filing cabinets are used for storing papers vertically in files with their strips or labels on the top edge of each file. Each cabinet has a number of large drawers (usually four) and inside each drawer are rods on which suspension folders, in which the files sit, are hung. Cabinet drawers can be locked individually, or the whole cabinet can be locked. Again, they are usually made of metal or wood.

Figure 4.2 *Vertical filing cabinet*

Card indexes

As we already know, numeric filing involves the use of a card index (see Figure 4.3).

Card indexes are very straightforward; they are often small, lockable metal or plastic boxes. The cards filed within the box look like postcards, but are called index cards. Depending on the method of classification, cards are either filed in numerical or alphabetical order.

Maintaining safe filing systems

Whatever the filing system used, it is important to consider the security of the information it contains and the safety of those using it. To maintain safe filing systems you should remember the health and safety points learned in Unit 3 regarding health and safety. The main health and safety considerations regarding filing are:

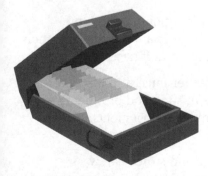

Figure 4.3 *A card index box and contents*

- Be aware of confidential information.
- If filing cabinets should be locked, make sure they are.
- Don't pile lots of boxes, books or paperwork on top of filing cabinets.
- Metal filing cabinets are fireproof, but wooden ones are not.
- Never leave the top drawer of a filing cabinet open as this can cause the cabinet to topple, particularly if the drawers are full.
- Never leave the bottom drawer of a filing cabinet open as someone could trip over it and hurt themselves.
- Never try and move a filing cabinet yourself as they are very heavy.
- Watch your hands on the sharp edges of all metal furniture. The suspension files can also cause injury if handled carelessly.

Build-up Exercise

Imagine that you have a new member of staff starting work next week. She is going to be responsible for filing all the paperwork in your department, which is done using a vertical filing cabinet in which all files are ordered alphabetically.

You have been asked to prepare her a list of instructions to follow. Your instructions should include everything you've learnt about so far, and also any particular organisational procedures you may have come across either in your job or at college. She must be aware of all the health and safety considerations and must also be aware that much of the information is of a confidential nature. Wordprocess her instructions.

Electronic filing

Although Unit 5 covers in detail the way in which electronic files should be handled, it is worth mentioning here some of the ways in which filing can be carried out using a computer.

Microfilm is a method of using film to condense the space occupied by documents. This, to some degree, helps to reduce the amount of paper that so often builds up within an organisation. Additionally, microfilm is used to preserve old or valuable documents by ensuring they do not need to be handled too much. Libraries tend to use this method of storing information as it helps reduce the mountains of documentation that are normally found in a library. The process for using microfilm is as follows:

- The original documents are photographed and processed on the computer.
- The computer is used to access the information required, by 'scrolling' through the film. A specific page of a document can then be viewed on the screen of the computer, and if necessary printed.

Obviously, all information stored on computer must also be protected. Organisations are now more likely to use this method of filing their records because it is easier to store and retrieve documents. If used they must ensure the following:

- back-up copies of documents are made and stored safely.
- staff using the computer use passwords, which should be changed regularly.

In addition to passwords, user codes can be used. These codes are known only to those who are authorised to access the information and relate to specific files or documents stored.

Reproduction of information

Usually the easiest way to copy an electronic document is to print out another copy from the computer. However, there are times when a document has to be reproduced using a photocopier. Photocopiers range widely, from small desktop copiers to large, industrial copiers used for big operations. It is therefore impossible to describe how a typical machine works, or to list the facilities offered.

'Intelligent' copiers are capable of volume copying and can accept information directly from a computer. The original is converted into an image, which in turn is converted into an electrical signal. This signal triggers a laser which reproduces the image and processes it then transmits it to other locations. Such machines are capable of producing up to 150 copies per minute.

Colour photocopiers are also available, and these machines can produce impressive results using colour toners, lasers and heat.

Some photocopiers also have the added facility of sorting, collating, stapling and binding documents, thus making large documents much quicker to copy and reducing the chance of separate pages being lost or forgotten.

To ensure the smooth-running of the photocopier you need to be aware of the following:

- How long does the machine take to 'warm up' at the start of the day?
- Where do I insert the paper when the machine runs out?
- Where do I insert the original document that I am copying?
- How do I tell the photocopier how many copies I need?
- How often does the toner need changing?
- Am I allowed to replace the toner cartridge or does someone else have to do it? If someone else has to do it how do I go about asking them?
- If I am allowed to change the cartridge myself, where is this housed or how do I go about ordering one?
- What do I do if it goes wrong? A small problem like a paper jam can easily be rectified. Most machines display a symbol for each minor problem and list the ways to put each one right. For more serious problems you need to know the location and contact telephone number of the engineer used to repair and maintain the machine.
- What are the health and safety procedures regarding the machine?
- What are my business's organisational procedures regarding the use of the machine?
- How do I close down the machine at the end of the day?

Making best use of photocopier facilities to suit the task in hand

Many modern photocopiers avoid the need for you to spend a long time reproducing documents. To make full use of them, however, it is important that you know exactly what they are capable of doing. You should therefore receive training, unless you simply need to use it to copy odd pages now and then. Most machines let you do some or all of the following:

- reproduce as many copies as you require simply by pressing the number of copies needed into the keypad
- enlarge an image, perhaps from A5 to A4, or A4 to A3
- reduce an image, perhaps from A4 to A5, or A3 to A4
- copy onto both sides of a sheet of paper
- collate a document and staple it together
- diagnose minor problems by means of a series of symbols which flash to identify the particular problem, for example a crossed-out rollers symbol with a letter may tell you that there is a paper jam and show you where it has occurred.

They also tell you when the paper tray needs filling or when the toner cartridge needs replacing.

Build-up Exercise

If you haven't been trained in all the above aspects of using the photocopier, make sure that you know about the ones we have identified.

Checking copying is of an appropriate standard

The quality of the copies obtained from a photocopier is important for a number of reasons, including the following:

- the copies need to be legible
- the presentation of the complete document needs to be of a good standard
- the document may be going to a customer
- the document may be used in an advertisement
- the document may be required by the owners or senior managers of the business
- the document may be going to every single employee in the business
- the document may have to be kept for a long time, as in the case of legal documents.

There are a number of ways you can help to ensure the copies you make are of a good quality, including the following:

- Have a good look at the original – if there are marks on it you can use correcting fluid to remove them so they will not show on the copies.
- Have a look at the glass on the photocopier lid – any dirty marks or smudges will affect copy quality.
- Make sure you use the right paper.
- Make sure your hands are clean when you are handling the original and the copies.

■ Don't leave the original or the copies in a position where they could get damaged by coffee (or other drinks) or by other people.

Logging use of the photocopier

You may need to keep a record of the photocopies you make to comply with the organisation's procedures. It would certainly be a good idea, anyway, to keep your own personal log to help you provide evidence for this unit that you have produced enough copies, of a good enough standard, during the time you are studying for your qualification.

If your college or employer requires you to keep a log of your photocopier use, then make sure that you do. The business will want to know how often the photocopier is used and for what purpose. This isn't necessarily their way of checking up on you; usually it's to account for the money spent on paper, new cartridges and general maintenance of the machine.

Build-up Exercise

If you haven't already got one, design a photocopying log for yourself. Make sure you include the following headings:

■ date photocopies were taken
■ who authorised you to do the copying
■ who agreed that the copying you did was of an acceptable standard
■ whether you met any deadline set you for the task
■ how many copies you had to take
■ whether there were any specific instructions (such as 'enlarge to A3') included in the instructions, or whether you had to collate the document yourself.

Don't print a copy of your log sheet yet – you are going to have to add some more headings in the next two activities.

Following procedures for reporting problems

Just as it may be an organisational procedure to record the photocopies you make, it may also be necessary for you to report any problems you encountered in getting your copying job done on time. There are a number of problems that are likely to occur when using the photocopier, including:

■ no paper available to refill the paper tray
■ cartridge empty
■ paper jammed in the machine
■ a serious fault which requires the maintenance engineer.

Obviously, if you know where to find more paper or how to remove a paper jam, these are not serious problems. However, you may have to contact someone else in the organisation to get the toner cartridge replaced. You would most certainly have to contact someone else to call the service engineer in the case of a serious problem.

If you encounter a problem that you are either unable, or unauthorised, to solve yourself, you should take the following action:

1 Place a notice on the photocopier which explains to others what has occurred and what you have done about it. Doing this saves people time and reduces the likelihood that others will contact the authorised person over the same fault.

2 Report to the authorised person what you have discovered and explain what appears to be the problem. Tell them that you have put a notice on the machine.

Build-up Exercise

Now go back to your log sheet and include a heading which allows you to identify:
1 the type of problem encountered
2 what action you took as a result
each time you use the photocopier.

Minimising waste when photocopying

Minimising the amount of paper wasted within a business is important because it helps reduce the cost of running the business. Because so much paper is wasted, there are a number of easy ways you can contribute to reducing paper wastage when photocopying:

- Make sure the original document is clean.
- Make sure the glass (platen) and the inside of the photocopier lid are clean.
- Make sure you put the original document in the right way up and that it is straight.
- Make sure you key-in the required number of copies correctly.
- Take a draft copy first, before doing multiple copies, to make sure the copy is of an acceptable standard.
- Only print the number of copies you need.
- Photocopy onto both sides of the paper whenever possible.
- Check there is sufficient toner before starting.

Waste paper should be placed in a recycling bin as the business is paid for this by the company that collects it.

Build-up Exercise

The final addition to your photocopying log will be a heading under which you will list any paper you waste while photocopying. Be honest each time you copy. If you have to write down how much you waste it will encourage you to be more careful.

Following safety procedures

Because a photocopier is a piece of electrical equipment, and because it is important that users of all machinery and equipment are health and safety conscious, the following issues should be addressed:

- Is the machine a particularly old model?
- Is it located in a room of its own?
- Is the room well ventilated?
- If the room has an extractor fan, is it cleaned regularly?
- Is the photocopier regularly serviced by the manufacturer's representative?
- Have the users of the machine received training on how to deal with minor problems?
- Are the users of the machine aware when to call in the manufacturer's representative?
- Does the machine look damaged in any way?
- Does the electrical socket look OK?
- Is the wiring intact?
- Are there any water leaks or liquid spillages near the machine?
- Does the machine smell odd or feel too hot?

Try it out

Go to the photocopier you use regularly. Take the above list with you and answer each of the questions about the copier. If you find there is a problem, make sure you know what to do about it. Remember that your employer (or college) has to make sure that he or she is working to the government's laws on health and safety.

Sending and receiving information by fax

If you have already completed Unit 1 you will already know about fax messages as an important form of business communication. However, this section of the book focuses on the fax machine itself and how to use it effectively to send and receive information.

A facsimile machine (fax) is capable of relaying documents and graphics via the telephone network to another location in just a few seconds. These machines have become invaluable to most organisations, particularly if they have a number of sites within the group, or need to contact overseas organisations. The word 'facsimile' means an exact reproduction. The fax machine can be left switched on 24 hours a day, and does not have to be continually monitored throughout the night. This means that the time differences between countries are not a problem.

The procedure for sending a fax message is as follows:

- Prepare the original document.
- Prepare a covering sheet, if one is needed – this, as we discover a little later, shows the name of the recipient, the name of the sender, the fax numbers involved and the number of pages being sent. It may also allow space for a short message.

- Look up the fax number of the recipient in the Fax Directory, or contact fax enquiries. Regularly used numbers are usually kept readily at hand, as with telephone numbers.
- Place the original document into the machine.
- Key in the number of the recipient and follow the instructions given on the machine. Although procedures may vary slightly from machine to machine, the principles for despatching a message are the same.
- Providing a connection has been made, the original document will pass through the machine and you will be informed that transmission is taking place. Should the recipient's line be engaged, the machine will automatically redial the number at intervals until a connection is made.
- Once transmission has taken place, the machine will issue a transmission report. This states the date, time and length of the call, the recipient's number, the sender's number, the number of pages sent and that transmission was successful. Should there be any problems in transmission, the report will indicate this and retransmission may be necessary.

Completing facsimile cover sheets

It is common practice to prepare a fax cover sheet, which will normally contain a short message, the name of the recipient of the document, the name of the sender, the fax numbers of the sender and the recipient and, importantly, the number of pages of the fax message, including the cover sheet. An example of a simple fax cover sheet is shown in the following diagram. Businesses often choose to have their fax cover sheets prepared on their company headed paper, as this is another way that the business can present a good image to all those it deals with.

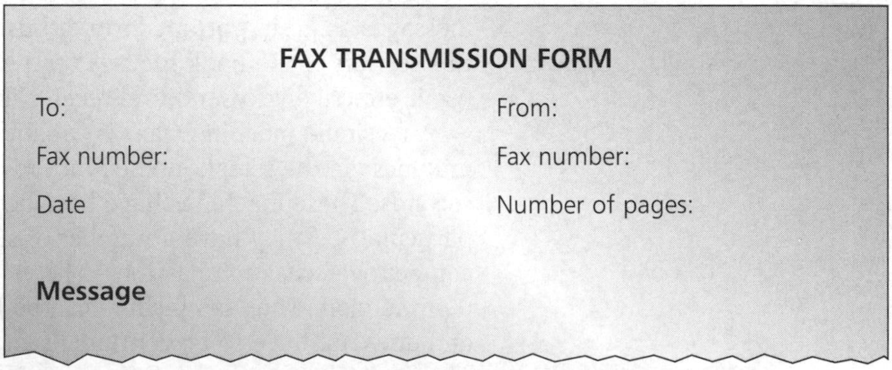

FAX TRANSMISSION FORM

To:	From:
Fax number:	Fax number:
Date	Number of pages:

Message

Figure 4.4 *A typical fax cover sheet*

Following instructions for use of equipment

Fax machines are not complicated, but they are electrical, so everyone using them have to be aware of health and safety considerations. The fax machine will have its own manual or handbook to which you can refer. The information contained in the manual or handbook is likely to include suggestions about the machine, such as:

- Where it should be placed – electrical equipment should not be placed near heaters, water or in sunlight and should be kept as dust-free as possible.
- How to set the machine up when it is first received – although often the manufacturer will send an engineer to do this for you.
- How to keep the machine clean – this will include the type of cleaning materials recommended, for both the outside and the inside of the machine.
- How to operate the fax machine – for instance where and how to insert more paper and what type of paper to use.
- How to replace the printer cartridge – also the type of cartridge needed and where they can be ordered.
- How problems are indicated – these may be signals, such as flashing lights or bleeping noises, which highlight that a problem has occurred with the machine.

Build-up Exercise

Obtain a copy of the manufacturer's manual or handbook for the fax machine that you operate on a regular basis. Take a photocopy of the pages that you need to complete this qualification. Remember you will need to provide evidence of the fax messages you have sent and received while doing the course.

In the same way that you designed a photocopying log sheet, now design one for the times you send or receive faxes. Include all the headings that were included for the photocopying log, because things like reporting problems and ensuring the minimum wastage of paper are just as important for the fax.

Checking confirmation reports

When you send a fax you can check that it has gone to the right fax number by looking at the transmission report your fax machine prints for you. This, however, only confirms that the document has reached a certain number. You could still have to confirm that the document has reached the right person, is readable and has arrived on time. Your fax machine cannot do this automatically. If you are in any doubt about the quality of the document, or whether the right person has received it, you should telephone and ask for confirmation of receipt.

Try it out

Imagine that part of your job is to fax your company's office in the USA every day. One day you encounter the following two problems. For each of the problems say what you would do. ▶▶

1 The document you have been asked to fax is extremely urgent, but every time you key-in the number you get the engaged tone. Your team leader, who asked you to fax the document, has gone to a meeting in London so you cannot ask them for help.

2 It is 5.30 in the afternoon and everyone has gone home except you and the cleaners. You have to send one last fax off to the USA before you can go home. You felt sure you had the fax number of the Santa Barbara office, but when you double-checked you discovered it wasn't their fax number but their telephone number.

Logging and distributing incoming faxes

If someone from outside your business sends a fax, then it is fair to assume that it is reasonably urgent otherwise they would have posted it to you in the mail. It is important, therefore, that all faxed documents are dealt with as a matter or urgency. You can do this by:

- listening for the fax to start up if it is in your office
- checking the fax machine regularly for new faxes
- making sure the fax is not placed somewhere where the messages are likely to get lost, for example by slipping off the machine into the bin, or getting picked up with lots of other paperwork
- stapling together the pages that make up the fax message so they don't get separated while you are delivering them
- putting the cover sheet on the top of the rest of the pages in the document
- delivering the messages immediately to the person concerned.

If, as is often the case, the person to whom the fax is addressed (the recipient) is not in their office, you should not just leave the fax message lying around. Better to:

- check with others in the recipient's office where you should leave it to make sure they see it
- check with your supervisor, team leader or manager where you should leave it
- use your commonsense and leave it somewhere very obvious – don't let it get lost in the pile of paperwork on their desk.

Logging incoming faxes might be one of the organisational procedures you have to follow when dealing with this method of communication. If not, you might consider doing so for faxes you deal with personally. This will allow you to identify the number of incoming faxes you have dealt with. It will also help you to get evidence from the recipients of these faxes to show that you have dealt with them in the required way, following the organisation's procedures. Designing another fax log, but this time for incoming faxes, would be a good way to keep a record of those you have received and distributed personally.

Build-up Exercise

Imagine that you are alone in the office and the following situations occur.

1 You are in the middle of receiving a fax which should be 12 pages long when your machine runs out of paper. What do you do now? If necessary consult the manufacturer's handbook or manual to find out.
2 You can't read one of the pages of a five-page fax you have received from your Santa Barbara office because your cartridge is running out. How do you get them to re-send the page? Refer to the manufacturer's manual to find out how to change the cartridge, or say who you should contact if you are not authorised to do this.
3 There are two pages missing from a 25-page fax you received from one of your suppliers. What action do you take?

Controlling stock

Businesses use stock control systems designed to ensure that stock is ordered, delivered and handled efficiently. It is also essential that stock control allows the business to deal with demand for office items in the most cost-effective manner. Good stock control incorporates re-ordering systems. The main focus of stock control is on the re-order quantities and re-order levels, which determine the level of stock when a new order is placed and how much is ordered.

Build-up Exercise

What kind of stock do you use personally? Do you have an office stationery cupboard? What does that cupboard contain? Whatever is in there can be regarded as stock.

Maintaining stock records

Stock records are essential. They not only list the types of office stock normally held by the business, but also include the following:

- ideal stock levels
- minimum stock levels
- maximum stock levels
- preferred suppliers
- specification (size and weight of envelope, size and colour of staples, etc.)
- procedure for re-ordering (whether the supplier needs to be called or whether they routinely visit to check stock).

Minimum/maximum levels

The minimum level of stock is often referred to as the 'buffer stock'. A business will know from experience how long it normally takes to replace the stock of consumable items in the office (such as paper and envelopes). It will not want to run out of stock while the stock is on order from the supplier. The business will therefore set a buffer stock level, that is sufficient stock to last until the supplier can send the order.

There are obviously some advantages and disadvantages related to holding too much, or too little, stock. Here are some of the key points about holding too much stock:

- storage costs will be high
- stock will need to be insured
- stock will take up more space
- the business will have spent money on stock that it can't use for other purposes
- unused or out-of-date stock may be wasted.

In the case of too little stock, the following apply:

- the business could be caught without enough stock if demand increases.
- employees may have a problem carrying out their work if supplies run out.
- order costs may be higher because the business will need to make quick orders and require the suppliers to express deliver the stock to them.

Receipt and issue, running balance and issuing stock requisitions

Stock control of consumable items will be the responsibility of one or more individuals. The following list covers the duties of stock control assistants who are responsible for stationery supplies:

- They receive orders for stationery from different departments within the organisation.
- They book out stationery stock against orders which have been received.
- They adjust relevant stock record cards to take account of the stock which has been issued.
- They order new or additional stock, either directly from the supplier or by raising a stationery requisition form to instruct the purchasing department to order stock from the supplier.
- They make sure that the stock does not fall below the recommended minimum level.
- They ensure that the area or areas in which the stock is kept is maintained, tidied, organised logically and safe from hazards.
- They carry out periodic stock checks to ensure that the amount of stock 'on paper' is the same as the actual stock level in the stock area.

Maintaining stock levels

The maintenance of stock levels begins with a delivery of stock, e.g. stationery. The first job is to ensure that the boxes of stationery delivered correspond to the actual order. The next steps include:

- The delivery is unpacked and the amount delivered is checked to make sure it is the same as both the amount on the delivery note and the original order.

- The stock is then counted and carefully checked so that no damaged or faulty items are accepted.

- If some items are missing this may be because the supplier is out of stock. Normally, such items would be marked on the delivery note as 'out of stock'. There may also be a note saying 'to follow'. The person checking the order should make a record of this and tell either the accounts or the purchasing department when the items are due. This should also remind the person doing the checking to contact the supplier if necessary to see when the missing items will be delivered.

- Some items may be marked as 'discontinued'. This means that the supplier is no longer able to supply these items. In cases like this the supplier may deliver a replacement or substitute item. These replacements should be similar to what was originally ordered, but if they are not suitable they should be returned to the supplier.

- Occasionally the supplier may forget certain items, despite their being on the delivery note. If this happens the supplier should be contacted immediately and told about the short order.

- Whenever items that have been delivered do not match the delivery note or the original order, the accounts department should be informed so that it does not pay the invoice when it arrives.

- Sometimes the supplier may incorrectly add items to the delivery. These may or may not be on the delivery note. In any case, it is advisable to inform the supplier about the additional items before they contact you. If they are included on the delivery note and were not ordered, the accounts department will need to know so that it does not pay for them when the invoice arrives.

- On other occasions the supplier may deliver the wrong order; the items may bear no resemblance to the original order. The supplier needs to be told about this and so too does the accounts department.

- Deliveries may also include items which have been damaged in transit. The packaging may have been inadequate or the boxes broken during transportation. There is also the possibility that some items do not work (particularly in the case of equipment or delicate items, such as printer cartridges or computer disks). The supplier should replace these but will need to be informed immediately.

- The supplier, following your order correctly, may have sent items which you ordered by mistake. Most suppliers will take these back, but you should be honest and inform them immediately.

When stock needs to be issued to a particular individual or department this should occur only when an authorised stock requisition order has been placed. Many businesses operate on the basis of charging the appropriate individual or department so that the cost of the stock will be set against the appropriate budget. Some organisations only allow stock to be ordered at a particular time of the week. This is to ensure that a member of staff is not constantly occupied getting orders together for different parts of the business. It also ensures that individuals and departments take care in planning their stationery needs.

From time to time it is necessary to check that the amount of stock matches the amounts which are on the stock records. This is known as 'stock reconciliation'. Unfortunately there is no way of doing this other than counting the stock which is held and checking this against the amount that is supposed to be there according to the records. Assuming that all the items are stored correctly and only one box of each type is opened at a time, this job may not be as difficult as it sounds. If there are differences (known as discrepancies) the person checking the stock should inform their manager or supervisor. Provided the person checking the stock has made sure that all items issued have been entered on the stock record cards, the task of stock reconciliation should be relatively easy.

Sometimes there are other reasons why the stock record cards need to be adjusted, these are:

- when stock has been damaged
- when stock has become out of date (such as a business's change of logo or address making its headed paper obsolete).

However, the person responsible for looking after stock should not throw stock away because even damaged stock may be worth keeping or using. Out-of-date paper and forms can be used as scrap paper and large quantities of it can be recycled.

Try it out

Consider the following cases and suggest a solution to each of problem.

1 You have just received a delivery of staples which are the wrong size for the staplers that the business uses. When you check the order you discover that the supplier has sent the ones you ordered. You realise that you must have misread the appropriate line in the price list and written down the wrong order number.

2 A large order of photocopy paper arrives. You check the number of boxes and know that there are five reams of paper in each box. The number of boxes ties up with the number ordered. Five days later, having used some of the boxes, you discover that one of them contains five reams of pink photocopy paper instead of white.

▶▶

3 The business has decided to change its supplier of photocopy paper. You are told to order photocopy paper from a new supplier. The paper is cheaper and it arrives the following day. Unfortunately by the late afternoon several people have complained to you that the paper jams the copiers and that the quality of the paper is poor. You compare the paper to the stock delivered by the old supplier and realise that there is a major difference in quality.

Processing incoming and outgoing post

Incoming post is the mail the business receives each day; outgoing post is the mail that leaves the business each day. The mail, both incoming and outgoing, consists of any number of letters, parcels and special items such as cheques, as well as registered and recorded letters, packets and parcels. Valuable items are usually sent via one of the Royal Mail's special services, such as Special Delivery, or a courier.

Sometimes businesses choose to centralise their mail room activities. This means that all mail coming into or going out of the business is dealt with by one department. Other businesses leave the responsibility for incoming and outgoing post to an individual in each of the departments or functional areas of the business.

Following procedures for handling different types of incoming mail

Whether the responsibility for handling mail is centralised or dispersed, the business will have procedures that need to be followed.

Some documents are delivered between departments by the business's own messengers; this inter-departmental post does not leave the organisation at all. Such documents are sometimes referred to as internal mail, and often consist of memoranda or reports sent from one department to another. Items of internal mail are placed in large envelopes which have space on them for the names of all the recipients to be listed. After the document has been opened the name is crossed off and the envelope is ready to be used again.

The incoming mail to a business may include many different types of documents, including:

- letters for specific members of staff
- general letters
- invoices
- quotations
- estimates
- job applications
- orders
- statements
- advertising material
- parcels
- payments from customers in the form of cheques.

It is important that the mail is opened and distributed as quickly and efficiently as possible so that office staff can begin their work immediately. It may be that one particular member of the mail room staff is responsible for distributing the mail – this is often a junior member of staff. They need to have a good knowledge of the layout of the organisation, particularly if it is large and spread over an extensive area.

An organised routine is important if the mail is to be opened, sorted and distributed quickly. The following list is a guideline to the steps needed to ensure an efficient routine:

■ Sort the mail first – this means taking out any envelopes marked 'private' or 'personal' as these will not be opened but delivered sealed to the individual to whom they are addressed.

■ Open the rest of the mail using a letter knife or letter-opening machine.

■ Date stamp each document as it is opened.

■ Check the mail for enclosures. An enclosure is an item which has been sent with the letter. It could be a cheque, leaflet, photograph or catalogue. Any paperclips should be removed and the enclosures stapled to the accompanying documents. This ensures that the items are not parted during the distribution of the mail.

■ Some organisations record the receipt of cheque payments at this stage in a remittances book. This gives the date the remittance (amount of money) was received, from whom, the amount received and the signature of the person opening the mail. Some businesses also keep a register of all incoming mail.

■ The recipient of each item should be identified where possible, for example on mail marked 'For the attention of' and on mail bearing a subject heading or a reference at the top of the letter.

■ If it is not clear who the mail is for, the person sorting the mail needs to quickly read the letter through to determine who within the organisation should receive it. It may be that more than one person needs to see the letter. In this case it should be photocopied and sent to all concerned. Alternatively a circulation slip or routing slip could be attached to the document so it goes to each person in turn. The most common use for one of these slips is on books or magazines which are to be seen by several people. The circulation slip lists the names of those who need to see the document, their department and a column for them to initial once they have seen it. The slip should also state the name and department of the person to whom the document should finally be returned.

■ Distribute the mail. In a small organisation a person may only have to walk from one room to another with the post. It is, however, more involved in larger organisations. Distributing mail in a very large organisation can be a full-time job for several employees. Trolleys may be used to carry the vast amounts of mail to different floors, with pigeon holes for individual members of staff, or groups of staff.

Figure 4.5 *Trolley for distributing internal mail*

Often the person delivering the incoming mail to each department or section also collects their outgoing mail at the same time. This is taken back to the mail room for sorting and sending. We will look at the procedures for dealing with outgoing mail a little later in this assessment objective.

Some mail, such as recorded and registered mail, must be signed for when delivered by the postman. This provides proof that items have been delivered and received. These are usually urgent or valuable items and may be delivered by either Royal Mail or couriers. Other parcels and packets may also have to be signed for.

There may be an organisational procedure for the way parcels are opened. This may require the mail room, or the individual responsible to:

- open the parcel to check that the contents are not damaged and that everything is there
- not open the parcel at all, but deliver it, unopened, to the recipient named on the parcel
- report any damaged items
- report any suspicious items.

There are certain procedures attached to the handling of suspicious parcels. A parcel may be regarded as suspcious if it is not expected by anyone, and for instance:

- the address is incomplete or it is not addressed to any particular employee
- the parcel is discoloured or has an unusual smell
- the parcel has an unusual postmark
- the value of the stamps don't tally with the weight of the parcel
- there are obviously worrying signs, like a wire sticking out or a noise coming from inside the parcel.

Following instructions for use of equipment to process incoming post

The only office equipment you have to consider for this assessment objective are date stamps and letter openers. Date stamps are simple, hand-held pieces of equipment. They are used with an ink pad. Sometimes the time will also appear on the stamp. Care should be taken not to stamp over the top of any typed or written information. Personal or private mail is date stamped on the envelope.

Date stamps have to be changed every day so that the correct date appears on all incoming mail. The date is important, particularly for legal documents, as it identifies when the business actually received the document.

Letter opening knives are often used to slide along and cut the edge of envelopes. This ensures that the contents are not damaged. Sometimes electrically operated letter openers are used – these remove a tiny strip of paper from the edge of the envelope. The edge of the envelope is placed into the letter opening machine, which looks like a small guillotine and the handle is pressed down to remove a fine strip.

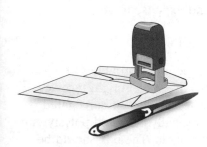

Figure 4.6 *Equipment for date stamping and opening post*

Build-up Exercise

You are to be away from the office for a short time on a training course. A temporary employee will be doing your job in your absence. Write him or her a list of procedures for dealing with the incoming mail on a daily basis, including instructions for dealing with any suspicious or damaged items which may arrive. Make sure you include any of your job or college procedures if you feel they are more appropriate.

Following procedures for different types of outgoing mail

Some smaller organisations keep a record of outgoing mail in the same way as for incoming mail. This log allows them to keep a check on the amount of money spent on postage, and to establish when mail was actually despatched. The recording of postage would normally be one individual's responsibility and allows the ongoing monitoring of costs.

Letters can be sent either first or second class, Recorded or Special Delivery; they may be either stamped manually (by sticking on stamps) or by using a franking machine. We look at the franking machine a little later in this section.

Another duty of the mail room assistant is to weigh any parcels which have been prepared ready for despatch. This is normally done within the department and the parcels are then taken to the post office with the rest of the mail at the end of each day. Alternatively, parcels can be collected and delivered by couriers. However, these parcels still have to be weighed as the couriers charge according to the weight of the parcel. Manual or electronic scales are used to weigh items and calculate the postage due on each.

Parcels should be wrapped sensibly, taking care to ensure that the contents are secure and not likely to be damaged during transit. The Royal Mail and courier services deal with thousands of parcels each day, and although they take every possible care, it is inevitable that parcels will meet with some knocks and bumps on their way. Any damage to parcels can cause delay, loss and expense to your organisation.

Parcels should be packed as follows:

- If items are fragile it is important to use plenty of suitable soft cushioning which will absorb any knocks the parcel might receive. Packing such as crushed newspaper, tissue, kitchen or corrugated paper can be used as inner packaging. Specially designed polystyrene chips or air-bubble polythene are also available. The box should be filled with the inner packing so that the contents do not move around. If the items are not fragile but are awkward shapes, make sure that no parts of the items project through the packaging. Even non-fragile items like sheets and clothing can be damaged in transit, so care must be taken when packing these too. Corrugated paper can also be used as a protective layer under strong brown paper, sealed with self-adhesive tape and tied with string.

- It is advisable to use a strong box, for example one that can be used to carry groceries from a supermarket. Postal boxes are supplied by the Royal Mail in various sizes; they can be bought at most post offices. As an alternative to boxes, padded envelopes can be used – these are often known as 'Jiffy bags'. Where these are not necessary, it is still advisable to use a layer of corrugated paper before wrapping in strong brown paper.
- If a box is being used it should be sealed firmly along each of its edges with self-adhesive tape.
- When just corrugated paper and strong brown paper are used, the parcel should be sealed with tape and then tied with string, knotting the string tightly where it crosses.
- Tie-on tags can be used for parcels, and care should be taken to make sure these are attached securely. The name and address of the sender should also be written clearly on the parcel so that it can be returned should there be a problem with delivery. A further precaution is to include the name and address of both the sender and the recipient inside the parcel.
- Weigh the parcel using manual or electronic scales. Some electronic scales will automatically calculate the postage due. When using manual scales the operator needs to refer to the Postal Rates Guide issued by the Post Office.
- Frank the label with the necessary amount of postage and stick it to the parcel.
- Stamp the parcel with any necessary stickers, for example, 'fragile', 'urgent' or 'handle with care'.

The parcel is now ready to be taken to the post office for handing over to the counter clerk, or for collection by the courier service.

All parcels and packages that are being sent overseas, whether by airmail or surface mail, need a customs declaration label which describes the contents. This is to inform the customs officers in the country to which the parcel is being sent of the parcel's contents. The recipient may have to pay tax (also called duty) on some articles. Duty is put on some goods to discourage their import. Gifts up to a certain value may be allowed in duty free to certain countries if described on the label as 'gifts'.

Special outgoing mail items, such as those which are urgent, important or valuable, can be sent via a courier service. Courier services guarantee time of delivery, very often stating that the item will be delivered the next working day by a certain time. The faster the delivery the dearer the service tends to be.

Important or valuable mail can be sent via Royal Mail's recorded or registered services. If the contents are valuable the sender can take out extra insurance to cover loss or damage of the contents while in transit.

Build-up Exercise

Go to your local post office and collect some of the booklets they provide showing details of the different posting methods available. Find out which of their services you would use for the following items that need mailing:

1 A well-packaged parcel needs to go to Oxfordshire by tomorrow. It must be signed for and it weighs 5 kg.
2 Your team leader wants to send a birthday card to her nephew in Greece. His birthday is in five days' time.
3 You have to send your original birth certificate, an application form, a cheque and photographs to the Passport Office to apply for a passport.
4 You need to send a delicate wall tile to Leicester as a sample for a customer.
5 You need to send new price lists to several new customers. They don't come into effect until next month.

Following instructions for use of equipment to process outgoing post

For this part of the assessment objective you need to know how to follow instructions for using the equipment for processing outgoing post in a mail room. Your organisation or college will have its own equipment and if possible you should take the opportunity to learn how to use it if you haven't already done so.

Franking machines

Unless the organisation is very small, it is usual for a franking machine to be used instead of stamps. A franking machine prints in red the value of the postage required either directly onto the letter or the parcel or on a sticky label that can be attached to the parcel. In addition, it allows space for an advertisement by the organisation, and the time and date of franking. Obviously this avoids the somewhat tedious task of licking and sticking stamps, and recording their use.

A franking machine can be rented or purchased from the manufacturers, although a licence has to be obtained from the Royal Mail before it can be used. There is no charge for this licence, but Royal Mail sets the meter on the machine to record units bought, used and still in credit to the organisation. Since 2002 the replenishment, or topping up, of the credits can be done automatically without needing to take the machine to the Post Office.

The value of the postage being franked can be changed very easily, in much the same way as a date stamp is changed. More sophisticated franking machines incorporate scales which weigh the item, calculate the postage required and print out a franked sticky label.

Each day the person dealing with outgoing mail has to follow the guidelines given below:

- Sort the mail into first and second class.
- Change the date on the franking machine unless the machine does this automatically.
- Check the value of the postage on the franking machine.
- Check the quality of the print on the franking machine. They use cartridges just like photocopiers and if the ink is running out then the machine will print too light an impression to be read properly.
- Check the credit left in the franking machine – once this reaches a certain pre-determined level, the machine will have to be re-credited. This can be done via the telephone or via a computer modem on more sophisticated machines. They are fitted with a mini-modem which is linked to the franking machine via the telephone. With these more sophisticated machines it is no longer necessary for you to take the machine into the Post Office. However, machines which are not linked to the telephone line will still do the same job, although it is more time consuming having to take them to the Post Office to be credited.
- Regular envelopes can be franked directly by feeding them into the franking machine. More bulky items need to be franked by feeding an adhesive label into the machine. This is then stuck onto the parcel or packet.
- Add any adhesive stickers to the mail, for example the words 'urgent' or 'fragile'.

Once the mail has been franked it can be handed over the post office counter before going to the Royal Mail sorting office. It is usually either tied in bundles or placed in a special bag designed for this use.

Packing machines

We looked in some detail at how to pack a parcel ready for the outgoing mail in the last section of this assessment objective. Some organisations, however, such as those that distribute many parcels on a daily basis, use a machine to do this job. For sending out bulky (large and heavy) items, some larger organisations have automated packing machinery which can stuff envelopes with documents or letters, laser print addresses onto the envelopes, seal them, then sort them into appropriate postbags according to postcode.

Some large organisations that routinely send out products to customers use machines with scanning equipment to select the appropriate size box and required packing materials for the product. They can seal the box, weigh it and bind it, as well as print the appropriate address label adding 'fragile' or 'urgent' as required.

Scales

Some smaller businesses may still use the older style of scales, which require you to place the item on the machine and then find out the postal rates from Royal Mail leaflets. Others, however, prefer to use electronic scales which contain a chip programmed to identify the postal charges from the weight of the letter or parcel being weighed. If you use these electronic scales you must remember to set the rate required. This can be either first class, second class, overseas rates, recorded or special delivery rates. Obviously, when the postal rates change (as they frequently do) the electronic scales have to be reprogrammed with the new rates. This often involves just plugging in a new chip.

Use of marking stamps to indicate status of post

Post leaving the business takes a variety of different forms. It can be non-urgent post, which can be sent second class or first class. It can be a letter which must only be seen by one particular recipient. In these cases the address on the envelope should include what is known as a 'For the attention of' line. This means that the envelope would be addressed as shown below.

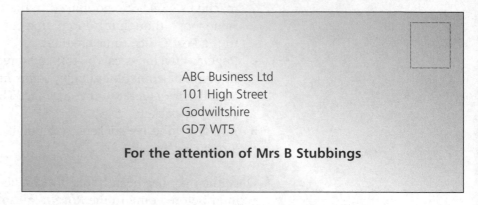

ABC Business Ltd
101 High Street
Godwiltshire
GD7 WT5

For the attention of Mrs B Stubbings

Figure 4.7

The mail could be urgent, confidential, private and confidential or personal, in which case the appropriate wording will be added to the envelope.

If the mail is going overseas, by air to another country, then the word AIRMAIL should be added to the envelope.

Mail which may have to be handled a little more carefully by the Royal Mail or the courier service could be marked with the words 'FRAGILE' or, in the case of photographs, 'PLEASE DO NOT BEND'.

Try it out

You have to make sure the following items are marked up properly before they go in the post tonight. What would you print onto each one?

1 A letter that is going to Japan.
2 A letter that is going to your American branch, but must be seen by Mr Brian Farrow.
3 A set of illustrations that are to be used in the business's new brochure and are being posted to the printers.
4 A letter that has to be read tomorrow, but only by one person, Mrs Shirley Conway.
5 A large box of glass bowls that the business's branch in Nottingham is going to put on display in reception.

Review the ways in which procedures are implemented and their effectiveness

To provide evidence for this assessment objective you will have to review and evaluate the way in which your office duties are carried out following your business's (or college's) procedures. Obviously it is impossible to give you specific guidelines here because different students will be working on different tasks and following different procedures. To help you with this assessment objective, therefore, some broad guidelines are provided here, showing why a business might review or change its procedures and how you can help to evaluate the ones you have to follow.

Whenever a business decides to implement a new procedure it is not sufficient to simply send a memorandum or manual around the business and expect everyone to understand precisely what is required of them. Any new procedure, or indeed an existing procedure which is being ignored, has to be supported and promoted to ensure that everyone complies with it. Businesses need to be practical about putting in place procedures and need to explain these procedures clearly, provide training when necessary, provide supporting documents and forms and have a clear timescale for implementing the procedures.

Whenever new procedures are implemented there will be teething problems and management must be aware that they may have to amend the procedures if there are difficulties.

In your review of the procedures for the routine office activities, you need to focus on how the procedures are implemented and supported, along with the effectiveness of those procedures and support.

You will need to identify at least two ways in which each of the procedures (your two office-based activities) are supported and whether or not this support has been effective.

For the majority of business organisations, procedures are usually introduced by the creation of a manual, which is then used to form the basis of either individual or team training, to make sure that employees understand and follow the set procedures in the manual.

There are, however, other ways in which a business supports the use of procedures at work, including:

- **Mentoring** – when a senior (or long-serving) member of staff shows a new employee how to follow the procedures. This draws on the experienced member of staff's knowledge of the procedures. This is a useful form of individual training, as the new employee can ask the mentor for help or to explain procedures if they come across any problems. The main advantage is that the experienced member of staff has a thorough, practical working knowledge of the procedures and can alert the new employee to potential difficulties, as well as give them tips on how to deal with problems encountered using the company's procedures.
- **Tracking documents** – these are used to note down progress during a particular procedure, or just the fact that the procedure was completed. In the case of fax transmissions, for example, it is normal to print out the transmission reports. These show the date,

time, duration of the call and the number of pages sent to a particular fax number. Other tracking documents, for example in stock control, include spreadsheets that show minimum and maximum levels of stocks, receipts for issues of stock, requisition forms and running balances of stock.

Another way in which procedures are supported and monitored is to include the tasks as part of an overall plan, or project, which has been broken down into different parts (the series and order of tasks involved). Each of the tasks (which involve following procedures) are timetabled for completion at particular points in the overall project. When a task has been completed, it is noted on the timetable, so that the team responsible for the project can chart the progress. At all stages of the project the team will know what has to be done (following the set procedures) and whether they have met the deadlines along the way.

Procedures are also supported by regular internal communications, in the form of memos and e-mails. These inform members of staff of the following:

- that procedures exist to carry out particular tasks
- that the procedures need to be followed by all staff
- the name of the member of staff responsible for monitoring the procedures
- whether there are training sessions for staff relating to the procedures (refresher courses, amendments to procedures and training for new staff)
- whether there have been slight changes to the procedures (for example, following a review of the procedures better ways may have been found to carry out the work)
- whether the procedures have been completely changed (for example, as a result of new equipment systems in the business, such as computerising stock control).

Businesses are concerned with making sure that the procedures are not causing difficulties. Possible reasons for difficulties could include the following:

- **The procedures are unclear** – members of staff are having difficulty in following the procedures as they do not cover all events and problems that could occur. They may not understand why the procedures follow the pattern they do, or that the procedures were written by someone with a greater technical knowledge than the normal users. This means that the procedures are written in a way that is difficult to understand or follow.
- **Others may not know the procedures** – the people who are expected to use the procedures may not have been properly trained, or their training may have covered a previous set of procedures. New members of staff may have missed the training for some reason. Other members of staff may not have had to carry out the procedures in the past (perhaps they have transferred from another part of the business). They may have used different procedures and

not be aware of the new procedures they must follow. People cannot be expected to know the procedures if they have not been informed about them, also the training manuals or procedure handbooks may have been lost, have pages missing or be out of date.

- **The procedures are breaking down** – if a business does not regularly update its procedures then there is every chance that the steps to be taken are no longer relevant to the task. This can also happen when equipment or machinery has changed and the business has not amended the procedures to take the changes into account. It is also likely that the procedures will break down if, after complaints, problems, difficulties and even reviews, it has been established that the procedures do not work but the business has not taken steps to amend the handbook or update the staff training.

- **Lack of tracking systems** – without a tracking system that allows people to see whether a procedure has been carried out correctly, it is unlikely that it can be checked. If, for example, transmission reports are not attached to faxed documents, then no one knows whether the documents have actually been sent or not. In the case of stock control, if members of staff simply help themselves to stationery when they need it, then it is impossible to know where the stock has gone and whether there is enough left to last until the next order. If stock does run out, then members of staff and teams may be held up simply because they don't have one item of basic stock.

  Not having a systematic tracking system means that only the person actually carrying out the task knows whether they followed the correct procedure, or actually carried out the task at all. If that person is not available to ask (for example if they are ill or on holiday), there is a chance it will get forgotten or carried out again by mistake.

  Tracking systems, therefore, are vitally important, not only to check that procedures have been followed, but also to ensure that vital tasks are done. Without a tracking system a business cannot hope to be as efficient as they would want.

There are instances, particularly when using machinery that even the most precise set of procedures cannot hope to cover. Sometimes there may be an electrical fault with the machine, perhaps there is a fault within the machine itself or the electricity supply to the machine may have failed because of a power cut. Most organisations will have procedures to deal with what could be termed as 'critical faults' to their machinery. Many machines may be under a maintenance and repair agreement with the manufacturer, or a contractor who can be called in to deal with electrical problems. Particularly important machines, such as faxes, computers, printer and photocopiers, need to be regularly maintained and checked and replaced at frequent intervals in order to reduce the number of problems that could disrupt the normal procedures of using these machines.

You will also be expected to suggest where improvements can be made to procedures. A good place to start is to consider whether you encountered any difficulties yourself whilst following the procedures. Possible things to think about in relation to improvements are:

- Were there steps that did not make sense?
- Were there steps that were not relevant to what you were doing?
- Did the procedure match the equipment and machinery (were you able to do what the procedure instructed you to do with the relevant machinery or equipment?)
- How old were the instructions (or the procedures manual)?
- Were there any updates put into the procedures manual?
- Were the updates inserted in the right place?
- Did following the procedures slow you down in completing the task?
- Was there somewhere to put the tracking documents?
- Does anyone look at the tracking documents?
- If you did encounter a problem, was there somewhere to log it?
- If you did encounter a problem, who did you have to tell?
- When you told that person, what did they do about it?
- Were all the resources you needed available to carry out the procedure?
- If resources were not available, did you know where to get them?
- If you had to suggest an order for the procedures, how would it differ from the procedures manual?

You also need to think about the effectiveness of each part of the procedures. If you have considered some of the questions in the list above, then you have already begun thinking about this. Other things to consider include:

Storage and retrieval of information

- Was the existing filing neat and accurate?
- Were files and folders correctly ordered (either numerically, alphabetically or chronologically)?
- Were the resources available to create new files?
- Did you know how and where to archive documents and files?
- What were the procedures for handling confidential information?
- Did you know whether or not the information was confidential?
- Were the filing systems lateral or vertical?
- Where, if any, were the card indexes?
- Were the drawers easy to open?
- Could you open more than one drawer in a cabinet?
- If you needed a stapler, was it to hand?
- Did the stapler need reloading, if so where were the staples?

Reproduction of information

- Did the photocopier have paper already loaded?
- Was the photocopier out of order?
- Was the photocopier's toner out or running out?
- If the photocopier was out of order, had the fault been reported?
- If it had not been reported, did you know who to report the fault to?
- Were there spare toners nearby?
- Did you know how to replace the toner?

- Was the toner replacement someone else's responsibility, if so who was it?
- If the photocopier had little or no paper, was there a supply to hand?
- Did you know how to refill the paper?
- If there was no paper, where did you have to go or who did you need to ask to get some?
- Were the instructions clear on how to do multiple and duplex copying?
- Were the instructions clear on how to reduce or enlarge?
- Were different sizes of paper available to you? If not, where did these have to be collected from?
- Did the photocopier collate and fasten for you?
- Did you have to collate and fasten manually? If so where was the stapler and was it loaded?
- Did you have to log into the photocopier, or note the number of copies you made?
- Did you check or test print a copy before making multiple copies?
- Did the photocopier jam?
- Did you know what to do if the photocopier jammed?
- How much paper did you waste?
- Where did you put the wasted paper?
- Was the photocopier safe or did you feel in danger using it, and if so why?

Sending and receiving information

- Did templates exist for fax cover sheets?
- Were you expected to complete the cover sheet by hand or using a computer?
- Had you ever used this type of fax machine before?
- Did the procedures manual match the machine you were using?
- Was there any point, while you were following the procedures, when the fax machine did not respond to what you were trying to do?
- Was there any problem in loading or sending a fax?
- Did your original copy jam in the fax machine?
- Did you automatically receive a confirmation report that you had transmitted the fax?
- When receiving a fax was there sufficient paper in the fax machine?
- Did you know where to get more paper from and how to refill the fax machine?
- When you received a fax did it automatically produce a transmission report, stating the number of pages and the source of the fax?
- Where did this transmission document have to be filed, or did it have to be stapled to the faxed document?
- When sending a fax, where did the log have to be placed to record that a fax had been sent?
- Did the fax machine have sufficient toner?
- Did you know where to get more toner from and how to replace it?
- Did you have to use special paper for the fax machine?
- Was this special paper actually being used regularly?

- Did the fax machine stop, jam or pause when receiving or sending your fax?
- Did the fax machine give you an error report as to what the problem was?
- Did you understand the error report?
- What did you do about the error?
- Who was responsible for carrying out basic maintenance on the fax machine?
- Had the fax machine been recently maintained?

Controlling stock

- Was the stock secured?
- Was it in a cupboard or a cabinet?
- Was it neat and tidy?
- How was the stock organised?
- Could you immediately find what you were looking for?
- Did the description of the stock match what was in the cupboard?
- Where were the minimum and maximum stock levels kept?
- Who was responsible for maintaining the stock cupboard?
- Were the requisition forms correctly filled out and signed?
- Could you easily find what was required from the requisition form and was it in stock? If not, why wasn't it in stock?
- Where did the requisition forms have to be stored?
- Where were running balances recorded?
- What was the procedure if a stock item had reached its minimum stock level?
- How many different stock items did you have to count when you checked the stock levels?
- How many of these stock levels were wrong compared to the running balances?
- Where were the purchase requisition forms or orders kept?
- Who had to authorise these documents?
- What was the procedure for contacting suppliers?
- Did the supplies arrive on the day they were expected?
- Did you check the delivery against the purchase requisition or order?
- Was it correct and if not, what were the procedures for reporting to the supplier that the order was incorrect?
- Could you find where the delivered stock items had to be stored?
- Was there sufficient space to store these items?

Processing incoming and outgoing post

- How many letters in total did you distribute?
- How many parcels did you distribute?
- How many special items did you distribute?
- Did any of the delivered post have to be signed for?
- Were the delivered items opened prior to distribution or opened by the named recipient?
- Did letters and other documents have to be date stamped?
- Did you check that the date stamp had been changed to the correct date?

- If you opened letters, did you do this manually or with an electric letter opener?
- How many letters did you personally despatch?
- How many parcels did you despatch?
- How many special items did you despatch?
- How were the special items marked? Were they urgent or valuable, and were they sent by a particular type of postal service?
- What was that postal service?
- Could you do it at the business premises or did you have to visit a post office?
- Did the business have its own franking machine?
- Was there sufficient credit on the franking machine?
- Did the franking machine have sufficient ink?
- Who was responsible for basic maintenance on the franking machine and topping up its credit?
- Did the business have packing machines?
- What were the procedures for using these?
- Did you have to weigh any items before sending them?
- Were the scales electric or manual?
- Were there stamps to mark mail as being urgent or first class?
- Where did you have to place the outgoing mail for collection, or did you have to deliver it to a post office?
- Were there clear procedures for all different types of mail?

Supporting and promoting procedures

Most businesses create procedures by talking to those who carry out the duties which the procedures will cover. These individuals are aware of the difficulties and potential problems, and of the best ways of carrying out a particular type of task. By asking the experts how they would ideally do a particular job, the business can begin to create a document which outlines desirable procedures. This document forms the basis for a manual that can then be used as a reference for individuals who come to carry out these tasks in the future. The manual can be updated as procedures change or are amended for various reasons.

Businesses do not usually circulate copies of a general manual, nor do they expect people to read it from cover to cover and understand everything that is required. New procedures are often supported by training events, or individuals who were involved in the writing of the manual provide support to others who were not so directly involved. This is known as mentoring. The mentor is considered an expert in the new procedures, and goes on to help other employees through the difficult process of understanding them.

To see whether the new procedures are being used properly, and to track their effectiveness, a business may create a series of new documents or forms. These forms need to be completed by those using the new procedures. They confirm that particular steps outlined in the procedures have been followed and can also serve as a useful way of highlighting difficulties with the new procedures.

Where new procedures are being put in place within larger organisations it may not be possible for those using the new procedures to contact those who have designed the new procedures. Such organisations need to provide support and normally this is achieved by encouraging individuals who encounter difficulties to send memos or e-mails to named people responsible for dealing with the problems.

Identification of the possible difficulties in following procedures

Businesses may spend considerable amounts of time and money designing new procedures, printing manuals, organising training and mentors, nevertheless the new procedures may still cause difficulties. Procedures may still be unclear and there may be many people (such as new members of staff) who have missed the training events. Equally, some people may not realise that the procedures apply to them, but in later weeks or months find they do need to use the new procedures and therefore need support.

There may also be aspects of the procedures which the business had not considered when they were written. A vital stage in the procedure may have been left out. The business may also have forgotten to include useful and vital tracking documents, which again could cause problems.

Identification of possible improvements

Procedures are rarely absolutely foolproof or ideal for every situation. There will always be a need to interpret procedures in certain cases, as circumstances may arise which the organisation had not thought about. The procedures may have been designed to apply to the most common situations, but unusual circumstances always seem to arise for which the procedures are not entirely suitable. This means that there is always room for improvement in any procedure. This is one of the main purposes of a tracking document.

It is vital that users of the procedures are encouraged to contact those responsible if they have any serious suggestions about improvements from a practical point of view.

Procedures develop gradually rather than being set in stone. Businesses want their procedures to work in all circumstances and for employees to be sure of how to act in any event.

Evaluation of effectiveness of specific procedures when completing tasks

In the majority of business situations you will be completing a task according to a series of set procedures. It is therefore vital that the business learns if you have had any difficulties completing the task using these procedures.

Sometimes the procedures may be difficult to follow or, under certain circumstances, inappropriate. It is not suggested that you continually question procedures, but when you can identify a better way of doing things which is more efficient and effective, then you would be expected to inform those responsible for writing and updating the procedures.

Create, manage and integrate files

The sample files referred to in the chapter can be downloaded free of charge from the publisher's website at www.nelsonthornes.com/ ocradmin

Five key assessment objectives

- Manage files and directories/folders
- Enter data accurately from data input sheets and amend existing data
- Create and print an integrated document
- Format page layout and manipulate text according to a house style
- Format tabular data

Each of these broad objectives covers a number of specific skills relating to the creation and management of files. A complete list of the individual skills for each objective can be found in Appendix 1.

In this unit you will learn how to:

- create, name, rename, move, copy and delete files and folders
- understand file types and formats
- open, close and save existing files
- print a file structure
- format a page layout and set text according to specified requirements
- apply a house style
- enter text, numbers and dates accurately and in a specified format
- move and delete text
- use headers and footers
- use automatically generated fields, such as dates
- create bullet and number lists
- amend a document and understand the uses and limitations of the spell checker
- use special symbols and characters
- use the search and replace function
- insert a table, set column/cell widths and alignment
- format table borders and shading
- apply table gridlines and alignment
- specify date formats
- import and manipulate images, charts and data files into a document
- use codes for efficient data entry.

Managing files

Being able to manage the storage of your data effectively and efficiently within a well mapped out file structure is arguably the most important lesson to learn when using a computer in either a business or the home environment. Having spent time and effort creating files, the essence of good file management is arranging them so they can be found quickly when you need to use or amend them. Amongst other requirements, which will be covered as you go through the unit, is the ability to access files that have been previously stored. You will need to be able to open and amend files from different applications and then integrate them into a single document. The files you use in exercises and the assessment are, generally, provided for you.

Consider a situation where you have been working on a document or report for weeks, or even months. The document may include extracts of spreadsheets, databases or graphical files. It is important for you to know where these files are kept, particularly if they are to be regularly updated. A logical file structure will help. There are no hard and fast rules about how folders should be arranged in your file structure, but they should be organised in a way that suits your work.

Viewing file structures

You can view and manipulate files and folders using Windows Explorer, which can be accessed through the Start menu or by selecting the My Computer shortcut on the desktop (see Figure 5.1).

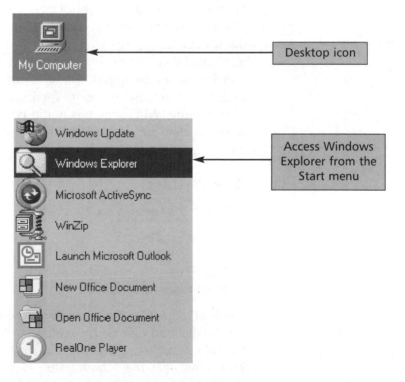

Figure 5.1

Which you choose is very much a matter of personal preference. The way in which you view the files can be altered depending on the options selected. For example, you may just wish to see the structure or folders in a particular area. Alternatively you may want to see the details of a file, such as its name, type, size or the date it was last modified. Figure 5.2 shows two fairly standard options. On the left of the picture is the Large Icon view and on the right the Details view allows more details of files contained in each folder to be seen.

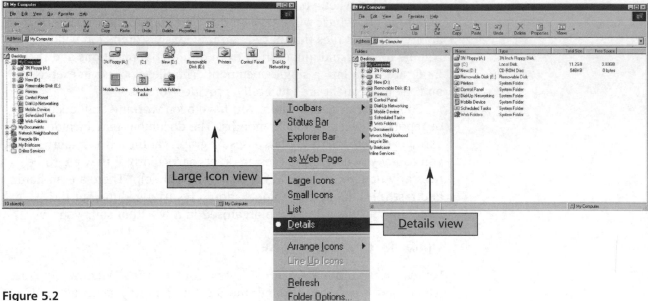

Figure 5.2

On the left-hand side of both views you can see the drive/folder structure for the whole computer. The view for your computer will differ depending largely on how it is set up and whether you have additional drive letters on your hard disk, or other external drives attached to the computer. The plus sign on the left side of the drive or folder indicates that there are further folders within that part of the file structure. Where there is a minus sign, or no sign at all, this indicates that the structure is fully expanded or there is nothing else to view.

Drive letters

In Figure 5.2 you can see four drive letters:

> 3½ Floppy (A:)
> (C:)
> New (D:)
> Removable Disk (E:)

The 3½ Floppy (A:) relates to the standard floppy disk drive and the (C:) to the hard disk on the computer. New (D:) is the CD drive where the CD currently inserted into the drive contains data, but the disk itself simply has the default name 'New'. If there were no disk inserted in the drive you would just see (D:), the drive letter. Removable Disk (E:) refers, in this instance, to an external Zip drive. You may have a number of other letters depending on how your hard disk has been configured and what devices there are attached to your computer. For example, large hard disks are often divided into two or more drives and each would have its own drive letter, assigned at the time the disk was partitioned.

Folders

You can think of the drives as buildings housing your data. As with organisations, different functions can be carried out in different buildings and so it is with drives, each performing a similar but different task. In a building you would expect to see offices with filing cabinets. These hold folders that themselves contain files holding important information about the business or organisation. Folders in a file structure carry out virtually the same function where folders are created and named according to how you want to access your files. When your computer is set up a number of folders containing a variety of files will automatically form part of the folder and file structure on your hard disk. For example, when Windows is installed it creates a number of default folders such as:

- My Documents
- Program Files
- Windows

There are a number of others that you don't need to worry about now. As the name suggests, the Program Files folder contains folders for each program installed on your computer. The Windows folder similarly contains files associated with the Windows operating system. Many of the folders will have sub-folders, which in turn may have further sub-folders. In other words the structure is hierarchical. Have a look at Figure 5.3.

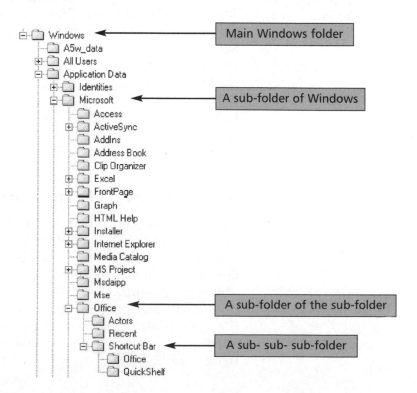

Figure 5.3

Here you have the main folder Windows and a number of sub-folders. Some of these will themselves have a number of sub-folders. The figure shows clearly the hierarchical nature of the structure. It is important that you do not try to alter, move, delete or otherwise tamper with files in these folders as you could prevent either a program, or Windows, from working properly. Most of the files in these folders are known as either program or system files and should be treated carefully if you are not familiar with how they work.

Designing a file structure

For the most part you will only be interested in managing your own data files. These are the files you create using one of the Microsoft or other software applications. Windows Explorer provides the basic folder for you to start developing your structure and this is called My Documents. You do not have to use this folder as the starting point for your file structure but you will find it much easier if you treat the My Documents as the top of your structure.

As mentioned above, how you develop your structure depends largely on your organisation, the type of data files you use and any system you design that helps you to find files quickly.

The following is offered simply as a guide on how you might approach the task of building a structure. There are no hard and fast rules. You might choose to have a structure that relates simply to topics and subject matters or you might decide that files should be separated depending on the application they are associated with or indeed a mixture of both. In Figure 5.4 the example structure is based on data separated by application and then subject. Your wordprocessing files may have a folder for financial matters called simply 'Finance', one for 'Insurance', 'Maintenance', 'Meetings' and so on. Each folder would possibly have sub-folders, similar to those shown in the 'Meetings' folder.

The system is flexible and can accommodate almost any structure or naming convention you need. However, you should also be careful that your structure does not cause the very problem you are trying to avoid by having too many folders. This can lead to difficulty in finding a file when you are unsure which folder it belongs in. As in all things, there is a balance to be struck.

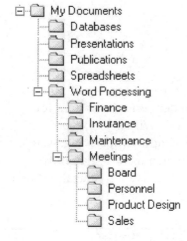

Figure 5.4

How to create a file structure

To create a folders structure start at the top of the hierarchy. In this case My Documents will be at the top of the structure. You can check that the My Documents folder has been selected by clicking on My Documents and then looking at the Address box at the top of the window: see Figure 5.5.

Once My Documents is selected a new folder can be added by choosing File, New, Folder from the main menu. When Folder is clicked, Windows Explorer creates a new folder with the default name 'New Folder' New Folder .

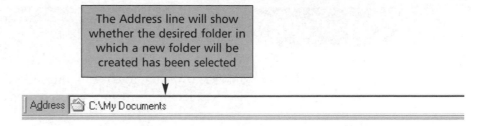

The Address line will show whether the desired folder in which a new folder will be created has been selected

Figure 5.5

Notice how the lettering of New Folder is already highlighted ready for you to overtype the personalised name you want for the folder. If for any reason you click outside the folder box before overtyping the name it is easy to rename the folder by placing the cursor over the folder and clicking on the right-hand mouse button. This will bring up the menu list shown in Figure 5.6.

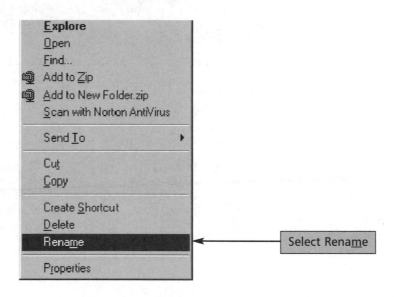

Select Rename

Figure 5.6

Select the Rename option and notice how the New Folder name is once again highlighted ready for you to type in the required name for the folder. By typing 'Wordprocessing' over the name New Folder a new folder has been created in My Documents called Wordprocessing. From here you can either create another sub-folder in My Documents or a new sub-folder of Wordprocessing.

Adding additional folders is equally straightforward. First ensure that the place you want to create the folder is shown in the Address box at the top of the window. If My Documents is showing and you want to create a folder in Wordprocessing simply click on Wordprocessing and when you see it showing in the Address box, repeat the same process as before.

By now you should have the general idea, so have a go at creating a new folder using a floppy disk. The principle for creating a structure on a floppy disk is exactly the same as on the hard drive.

Try it out

Scenario

Assume you have decided to set up a structure for exercises on subjects you want to cover in this unit. For the purpose of this exercise you will set up a structure that contains the following folders:

Folder hierarchy

Main folder: CLAIT Plus

Sub-folders: Computer Art; Databases; Managing Files; Spreadsheets.

Insert a new floppy disk into your disk drive.

Click Windows Explorer (or My Computer if you prefer).

Click on 3½ Floppy (A:).

Note: if you use My Computer instead of Windows Explorer you will need to double-click on 3½ Inch (A:) Floppy Disk.

Select File, New, Folder.

Type 'CLAIT Plus' over the name New Folder.

Click outside your new folder to accept the change.

Click on your new folder CLAIT Plus.

Select File, New, Folder.

Type 'Computer Art' as your sub-folder of CLAIT Plus.

Now repeat this exercise to make new sub-folders in the CLAIT Plus folder for Databases, Managing Files and Spreadsheets.

Your structure should now look like Figure 5.7.

Figure 5.7

You now decide to change the Managing Files folder name to File Management.

Move the cursor so that it is over the folder Managing Files.

Click on the right-hand mouse button.

Select Rename.

Type 'File Management' as the new name for your folder.

In order to complete the remaining exercises in this chapter, you should now create two subfolders, entitled 'Managing files' and 'Sample files', in the My Documents area of the (C:) drive on your computer, and then download the files accompanying this book into these folders. To download the files, go to the book's website at www.nelsonthornes.com/ocradmin, then for each file right click on the file title, select 'Save link as' and save the file to the relevant folder.

How to copy, move and delete files

In the previous section you learnt how to create and rename folders. The process for copying, moving and deleting files is virtually the same as that for renaming a folder or file. There are, however, certain aspects of these processes about which it is useful to know. For example, when you copy a file from one folder to another you will end up with two versions of the same file but in different folders. The original version will still be available in the folder from where the file was copied and there will also be a copy in the folder it was copied to. What you cannot do is have two files of the same name in the same folder. When you move a folder or file, you physically move it from one location to another and therefore you end up with the same folder or file but put in a different location on your hard or floppy disk. When you delete a folder or file from your *hard disk* it is first sent to the recycle bin which gives you an opportunity of restoring it at a later date, providing the recycle bin has not been emptied. If you delete a file from a *floppy disk* you cannot recover it easily as it does not go to the recycle bin.

Try it out

Insert the floppy disk containing the folder structure completed in the previous Try it out exercise.

Open Windows Explorer.

Locate the file named Computer Art in the sub-folder Managing Files in My Documents.

Click on the file Computer Art using the right-hand mouse button so that the file is highlighted (see Figure 5.8).

From the menu list that appears:

Select Copy.

Open the folder called File Management on the 3½ Floppy (A:).

Click on the right-hand mouse button.

Select Paste from the menu list (see Figure 5.9).

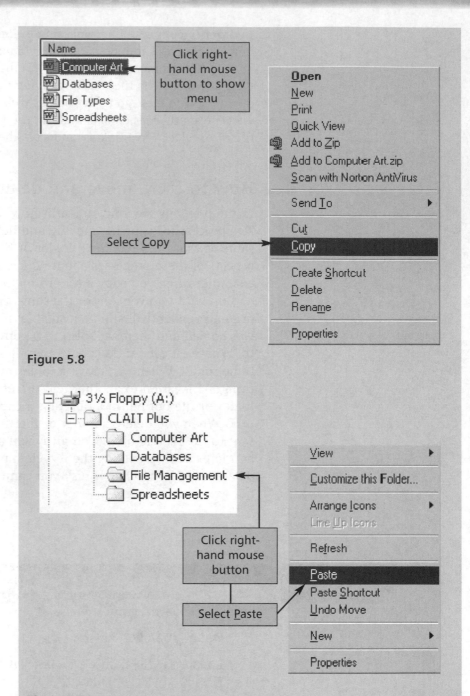

Figure 5.8

Figure 5.9

If you have the File Management folder selected you should see that the file Computer Art has been copied.

Note: remember that when a file is copied from a CD it may have a *read-only* property. In this case if you want to use and change the file you must open it and use the Save As... feature. Alternatively you can change the file's property in Windows Explorer by clicking on the file using the right-hand mouse button and selecting Properties. In the dialogue box uncheck the Read-only property and select the Apply button.

Copying multiple files in one move

Copying more than one file at a time is more or less the same as copying a single file. The benefits are mainly that if you have a number of files to copy you need only go through the copy and paste process once.

First select the files that are to be copied. If the files are all together you can use the lasso approach. Click the left-hand mouse button outside the first file to be copied and then drag the cursor over each file in turn before releasing the button. This will highlight all the files. If the files are not together in the folder then you can select the first file and with the Ctrl key pressed down select each file to be copied in turn (see Figure 5.10).

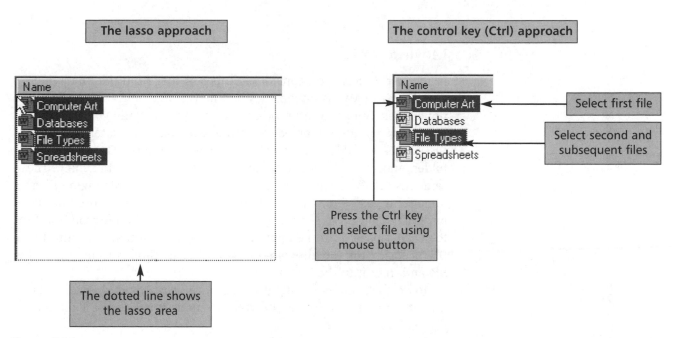

Figure 5.10

The files are then copied in exactly the same way as a single file and also pasted to their destination in the same way. When there are a number of files to be copied you will see a dialogue box that tells you the progress made in the copying cycle, and also both where the file is being copied from and to: see Figure 5.11.

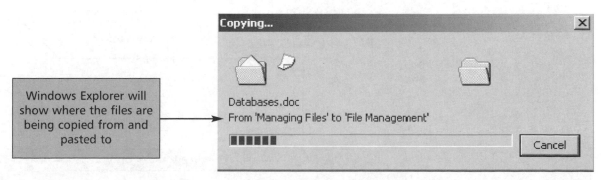

Figure 5.11

Try it out

Open the folder called Managing Files in My Documents.

Copy the files called:

> Databases
>
> File Types
>
> Spreadsheets

to the folder called File Management on your floppy disk.

Moving a file

In the last exercise you copied a number of files from the Managing Files folder in My Documents to the File Management folder on your floppy disk. Suppose you now decide that you actually want each file in the appropriate folder. For example, you want the Databases file in the Databases folder and the Computer Art file in the Computer Art folder, and so on. There are a number of ways you could achieve the same result. You could copy the respective file in the Managing Files folder and paste it to the new folder and then delete the original file, but this would be time consuming. You could cut the file from the first folder and paste it to the appropriate folder, but you always run the risk of losing the file altogether. The easiest method is to highlight the file and drag it to the folder you want it to reside in.

To do this, simply highlight the file you want to move and literally drag it across to the folder you want to move it to. Have a look at Figure 5.12.

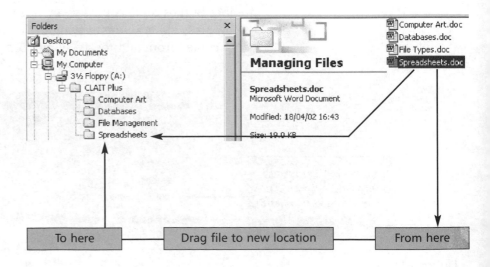

Figure 5.12

Try it out

Move the files in the File Management folder on your floppy disk so that each file is placed within the appropriate folder: see Figure 5.13.

Close Windows Explorer.

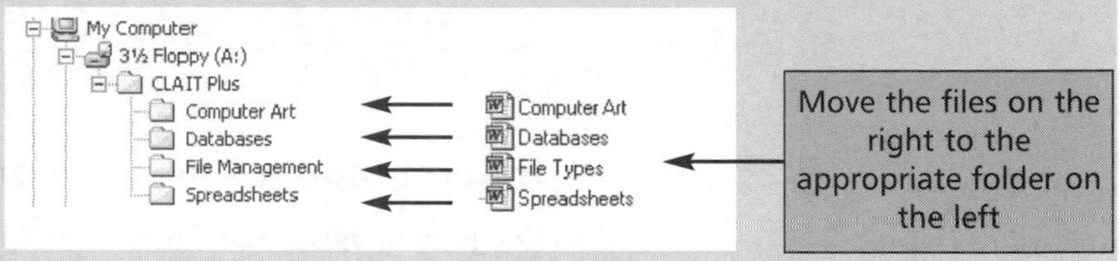

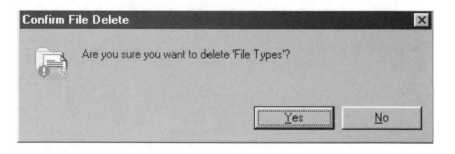

Figure 5.13

As was the case for copying files, if you have a number of files to move, and provided they are all going to the same folder, you can highlight all or selected files and drag them to their new destination.

Deleting a file or folder

To delete a file (or folder) place the cursor over the file/folder to be deleted and then press the right-hand mouse button. A menu list will appear. Select the <u>D</u>elete option. If it is a folder you are deleting and there are currently files in the folder, Windows Explorer will ask if you wish to delete the folder and all its contents. If it is simply a single file Windows Explorer will still offer you the chance of changing your mind by displaying the dialogue box shown in Figure 5.14.

Figure 5.14

Press the <u>Y</u>es button to continue with the deletion and the <u>N</u>o if you want to check if you have the correct file. Remember if you are deleting from the floppy disk you cannot reverse the process once you have confirmed the deletion.

Restoring a deleted file

To restore a deleted a file from your hard disk simply double-click on the Recycle Bin on the desktop, highlight the file that you wish to restore and then select the Restore button.

Try it out

Create a new folder called Test on your floppy disk.

Copy the file **Test File** 1 located in the Sample Files sub-folder in My Documents, to the new folder Test on your floppy disk.

Delete the folder and file **Test File 1** on your floppy disk.

Understanding file types and formats

Files have a variety of functions. Some deal with the systems in your computer whilst others have specific functions in running and managing programs. The majority of files you will have direct dealings with are ones that contain information relating to a particular application, such as a wordprocessor, spreadsheet or database type of file.

All files can be identified by file extensions. These extensions help to identify the type and function of a file. Extensions come at the end of a file name, separated from the name of the file by a dot similar to a full stop. An example of this may, for instance, be a wordprocessor data file such as **MyLetter.doc**. Here 'MyLetter' is the name given to the file, while the '.doc' signifies that the program associated with the file is Microsoft Word. Knowing what the file extensions of individual files mean can be useful in helping you to locate a file (or groups of files) of a particular type or program. The list of file types is virtually endless but some will become more familiar than others. Table 5.1 shows the extension identifiers for some Microsoft programs that you may come across in the course of your studies.

Table 5.1

File or application type	File extension
WORD	.doc
ACCESS	.mdb
EXCEL	.xls
POWERPOINT	.ppt
PUBLISHER	.pub
PAINT	.bmp
OUTLOOK	.pst
WEB PAGE	.htm
NOTEBOOK	.txt
WORDPAD	.rtf

As a general rule most modern, generic software packages can either read each other's formats or they will convert them into a form that can be read. For example, probably the most common type of file for the average user is the text file. Each proprietary wordprocessing package will have its own file extension. As you have already seen Word has the file extension '.doc'. WordPerfect, another popular wordprocessing package, uses a file extension '.wpd'. Most modern processors will read either format, but you also have the option of using simple text files formats such as:

- Rich Text Format (.rtf)
- text files (.txt).

Rich Text Format

Rich Text Format (.rtf) files will save your work with its formatting, and allow users of different programs to open and read or amend your document with the format you created in the original file.

Text files

Saving your work as text (.txt) files means that users of other programs will be able to open them, but none of the formatting (such as bold, underlining and so on) will be saved with the file.

Opening, closing and saving files

Opening a file

One of the benefits of understanding extensions, as has already been mentioned, is the ease with which you can identify the type of file and hence its associated application. In Figure 5.15 you can see a selection of different file types as shown in Windows Explorer. Some are graphic files and have an extension of .jpg or .gif which identifies them as pictures. A file with .sys identifies it as a system file and these should not be tampered with. The file with the extension .exe shows it is an application file; double-clicking on this type of file will open the related application.

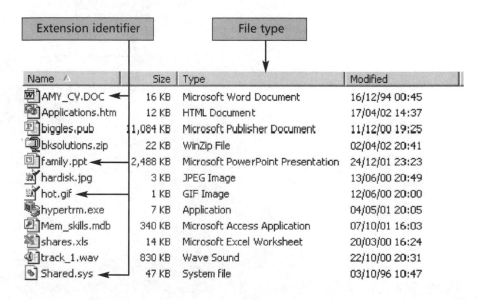

Figure 5.15

Where the file is a data file, with an extension such as .doc, .mdb or .xls, it is related to an application. By double-clicking on it the data file will be opened in the relevant application.

Normally you will open a data file from within the application to which it is related. All applications within the Microsoft Office suite of applications have a main menu bar similar to that shown in Figure 5.16.

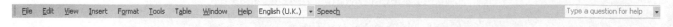

Figure 5.16

By selecting the File option on the main menu and then Open (Figure 5.17),

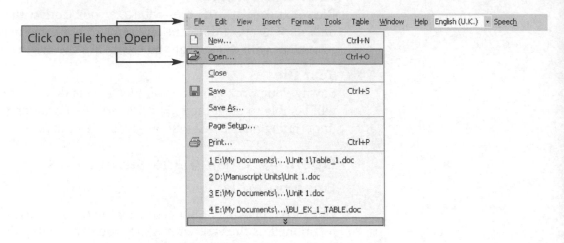

Figure 5.17

the Open File dialogue box will appear as shown in Figure 5.18. This allows you to locate and open the required file. First, the appropriate folder is selected by pressing on the down arrow to the right of the Look in: box. Next the required file from those shown in the main part of the window is highlighted and finally the Open command button located on the bottom right is pressed.

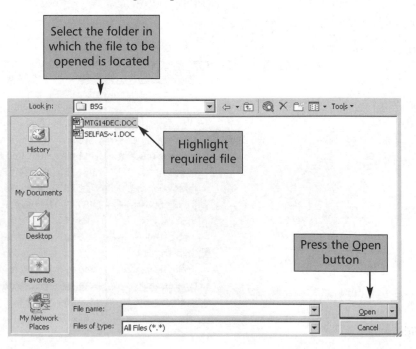

Figure 5.18

Closing a file

Generally speaking the procedure to close a file in any of the Office applications is the same, although there are minor variations for Access and FrontPage. These are covered later in the book. For programs such as Word, Excel and PowerPoint there are three standard options.

Option 1
Select <u>C</u>lose from the <u>F</u>ile option on the main menu.

Option 2
Press the close icon on the standard toolbar.

Option 3
Press the close window button (the cross) in the top right of the screen shown in Figure 5.19.

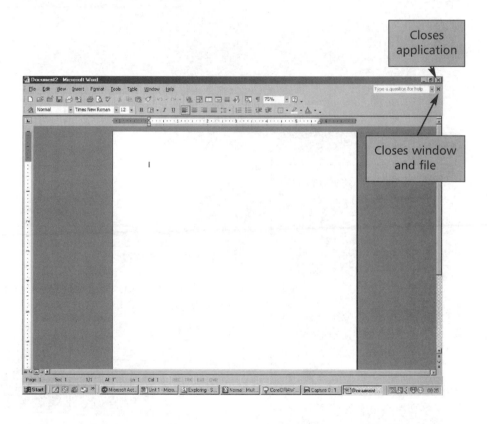

Closes application

Closes window and file

Figure 5.19

Saving files

If you have used computers previously, opening, closing and saving files will not be new to you. However, being able to save files properly and in such a way that they are easily located for future use is probably one of the most important skills to learn. The importance of setting up your folder structure was emphasised earlier in this unit. When you start saving files the need for this becomes very apparent.

Files can be saved and stored on a number of devices:

- the hard disk
- a floppy disk

- a CD (if you have a CD-write facility)
- a zip or tape drive.

For this unit you will only be expected to know about saving files to a hard or floppy disk. Although the procedure for saving files in most of the Office applications (with the exception of Access and FrontPage) is the same (or similar) this unit concentrates on saving files for Microsoft Word.

Save and Save As

To save a newly created document the <u>S</u>ave option is selected from the main menu. This opens the Save As dialogue box shown in Figure 5.20.

Figure 5.20

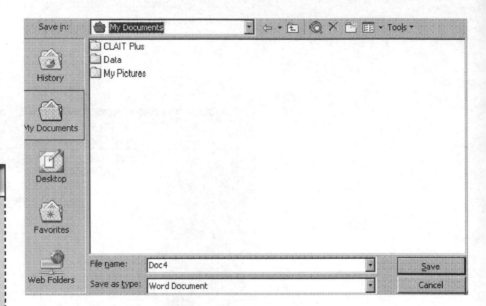

Word will, by default, offer the My Documents folder as the starting point to locate the folder you want to save your document.

SAVING TIP

You can always change the default folder by selecting <u>O</u>ptions... from <u>T</u>ools on the main menu. The Options dialogue box will appear as in Figure 5.21.

Select the File Locations tab and press the <u>M</u>odify... button. Using the arrow to the right of the Look <u>i</u>n: box select the folder you want Word initially to offer for saving your documents.

Note: If you are saving to your hard disk, the folder names, other than My Documents, will be different to those shown in Figure 5.22 as they will represent whatever folder structure you have set up for your own computer.

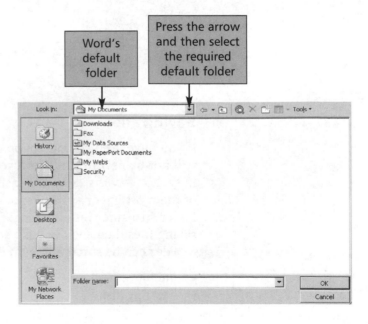

Figure 5.21

To save your file to a floppy disk, simply select 3½ Floppy (A:) from the drop-down menu shown in Figure 5.22.

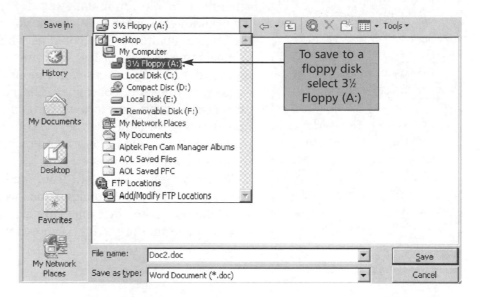

Figure 5.22

Once a file has been saved, Word will always remember its location. You should get into the habit of saving your work regularly. There is nothing more frustrating than spending a long time on a piece of work only to lose it because of a computer 'hang up' or a power failure or some similar catastrophe. To save new work on a file once it has been initially saved, simply click on the save icon 🖫 or select <u>S</u>ave from the <u>F</u>ile option on the main menu. You will not be shown the Save As dialogue box again,as Word is already aware of the file's location.

Note: If you are saving to a floppy disk keep the disk in your 'A' drive until you have finished and closed the file on which you are working.

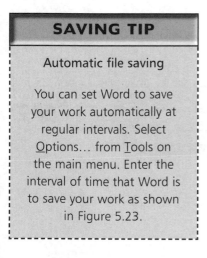

SAVING TIP

Automatic file saving

You can set Word to save your work automatically at regular intervals. Select Options... from Tools on the main menu. Enter the interval of time that Word is to save your work as shown in Figure 5.23.

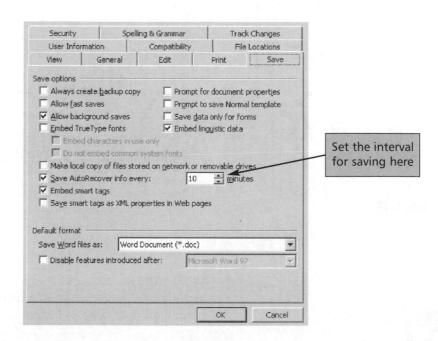

Figure 5.23

TIP

Opening generic files

Generic files such as '.txt' (text) or '.rtf' (Rich Text) files are opened in exactly the same way as any other file. Simply select File, Open… on the main menu. When the Open dialogue box appears make sure the Files of type: field at the bottom of the dialogue box has the relevant generic file format selected, e.g. Text Files or Rich Text Format.

Save As

There will be occasions when you wish to save your file as something other than the file you initially saved. For example, you may want to make minor changes to a document you use on a regular basis but keep the original unaltered. This could be where the main text of the original remains more or less the same with only changes to dates or figures; this may be the case for a monthly report or a repetitive message to friends or colleagues. Alternatively you may want to save a document in a different format. For example, if you opened or imported a generic file such as a text or Rich Text formatted file you may wish to save the file in a Word or other wordprocessing software format or an html web page.

To do this select Save As… from the File option on the main menu. You will see the Save As dialogue box as you did when you initially saved the file for the first time. You can now select another location or change the format of the file as shown in Figure 5.24.

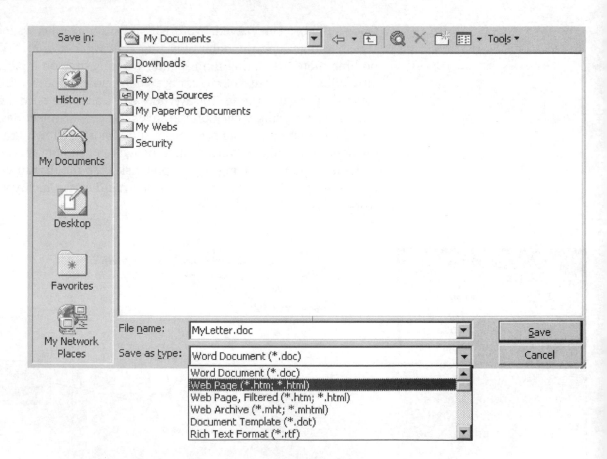

Figure 5.24

Notice how the file name now appears in the File name: box. Here you can give the file a different name from the original. If you are changing the format you can keep the original name if you wish.

Try it out

Insert the floppy disk with your file structure into the A: drive.

Create a new sub-folder called My Exercises in the File Management folder.

Copy the file **The_Village_Web_Site.rtf** from the folder Sample Files in My Documents to your new folder My Exercises.

Open the file **The_ Village_Web_Site.rtf**.

Save the file as **Village_Web.doc** (i.e. as a Word document).

Close the file.

Delete the file **The_ Village_Web_Site.doc** from the folder My Exercises.

Re-open the file **The_Village_Web_Site.rtf**.

Save the file with an html (webpage) format in the same folder (My Exercises).

Close the html file **Village_Web.htm**.

Printing a file structure

For this unit you will be expected to produce a printout of your folder structure or the contents of your folders. Unlike printing a normal document there is no facility to print the structure directly using a print function in Explorer. To overcome this you can use the PrtScn button that is found on the keyboard. Pressing the PrtScn (short for 'print screen') copies an image of the complete window to the clipboard. Once the screen has been copied, the image can be pasted into a document and printed off.

As you may have found before, the image can then be manipulated in the same way as any graphic can be modified. The easiest way to find out how this works is to have a go.

WINDOWS TIP

To move between open applications press and hold down the Alt key and then use the tab key to move between the windows. As a window is shown release the Alt key and that window will become the active window.

Try it out

Insert the floppy disk containing your file structure into the A: drive.

Create a new document in Word.

Open Windows Explorer.

Make sure that all of your file structure is fully expanded. For example, if there is a + sign against a folder, click on it to expand and show the sub-folders.

Click on the sub-folder named My Exercises to view the files **Village_Web.doc** and **Village_Web.htm**.

Press the PrtScn button on your keyboard.

Tab back to your new Word document.

Select <u>P</u>aste from the <u>E</u>dit option on the main menu. (Alternatively press the right-hand mouse button to show the menu list and select <u>P</u>aste or press the Ctrl+V keyboard keys to paste the image.)

The screen dump picture of the file structure should look similar to that shown in Figure 5.25.

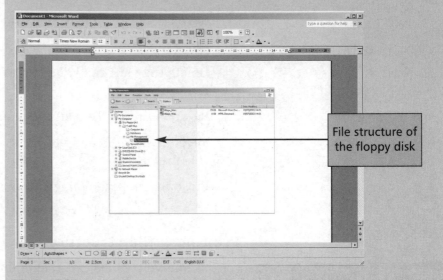

File structure of the floppy disk

Figure 5.25

Note: your structure will be slightly different to that shown in Figure 5.25, but the structure for the floppy disk should be the same.

Cropping a picture

Whilst this printout is perfectly acceptable it includes more of the structure than is required, so for clarity it is better to crop the image to show just the relevant information. By clicking on the graphic, the Picture toolbar will activate as shown in Figure 5.26.

Crop tool

Figure 5.26

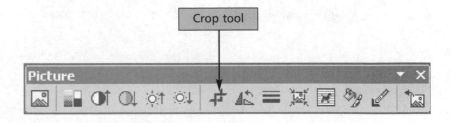

This toolbar allows you to edit a picture's contrast, brightness, orientation (rotate it), and a number of other features that you may wish to look at when you have time. However, also included on the toolbar is the crop tool which looks something like a square with overlapping sides. By highlighting the graphic and then selecting the crop tool you can adjust the area of the picture to be viewed. If you place the cursor over one of the picture's size handles and drag in the desired direction you can crop the image to suit your needs. Have a look at Figure 5.27.

Click on graphic to view the picture toolbar

Select crop tool and place cursor over one of the picture handles and drag to required size

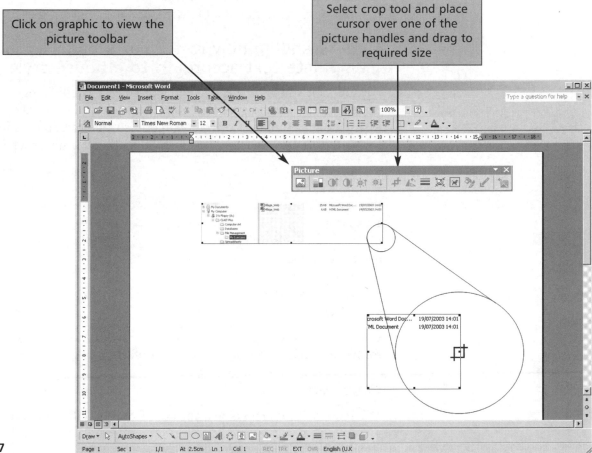

Figure 5.27

Here you can see that the picture has been cropped to show just the file structure of the floppy disk.

Try it out

Crop the file structure image so that only the floppy disk file structure and the files **Village_Web.doc** and **Village_Web.htm** can be viewed.

Print the document.

Save the document and image on your floppy disk as **My_Files**.

You should now be able to:

- create a folder structure
- rename a folder or file

- move and copy files to different locations
- delete a file or folder
- understand about different file formats
- open and close a file
- save a file in a required location
- save a file with a different format
- print a screen dump of a file structure and relevant files.

Understanding how to format a page layout and manipulate text according to a house style

For this unit you will be expected to produce a single integrated document based on a specified house style. House styles are instructions describing how a document is to be presented and formatted. House style instructions will include formats such as:

- paper size
- orientation
- margin sizes
- spacing
- font type, style and size
- text alignment
- required headers and footers
- page numbering
- table formats.

In the next part of this unit you will learn how to use the page setup and format text and numbers facilities to conform to a given house style.

Page setup

The Page setup dialogue box, selected from the <u>F</u>ile option on the main menu, allows you set the basic format parameters for your document. Have a look at Figure 5.28.

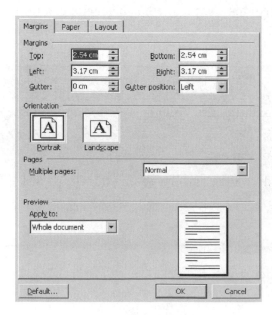 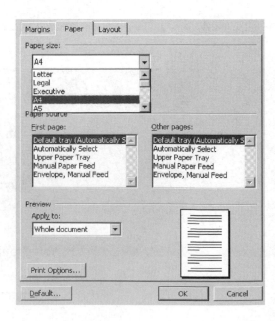

Figure 5.28

The picture on the left under the Margins tab, not surprisingly, allows you to set the top, bottom, left and right margins, the orientation (i.e. portrait or landscape) and a number of other features you do not need to worry about at this stage. The picture on the right under the Paper tab allows you to set the paper size and other features, which again you need not worry about for now. Similarly you can ignore the Layout tab for the time being.

To set a page to a required format for text which has already been prepared you must first open the document. Once the document has been opened you can use the Page setup dialogue box to set the required margins, orientation and so on.

Try it out

Scenario

You are going to apply the following house style details to a pre-prepared text document.

Paper size:	A4	
Orientation:	Landscape	
Margins:	Top	3 cm
	Bottom	2 cm
	Left	2.5 cm
	Right	2.5 cm

Open the file **Random_Text** in the sub-folder called Sample Files in My Documents.

Select Page Setup… from the File option on the main menu.

Set the page size (under the Paper tab) to A4.

Set the margins (under the Margins tab) as shown above.

Set the orientation (under the Margins tab) to Landscape.

Press OK.

Save your file as **Random_Text_1**.

Close the file.

Styles and formatting

Modifying the body text style of a document

Word provides a number of built-in styles which automatically set the format of a document's text, numbering, colour, paragraph, line spacing and so on. However, these formats can be amended for individual aspects of the document. In addition you can add your own, new styles.

There are a number of options to change the format of a document's text. The option you choose largely depends on what it is you want to format – the whole document, a paragraph, just a line or individual words.

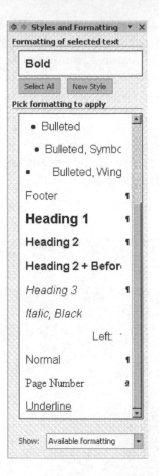

Figure 5.29

When you create a new document it is based on a template (normally the 'Normal' style template). All templates available are shown in the Styles and Formatting task pane which can be seen by either selecting Styles and Formatting... from the Format option on the main menu or pressing the Styles and Formatting... icon on the formatting toolbar . The style currently selected for the document is shown in the styles box, normally immediately to the right of the Style icon.

If the text for the whole document is to be reformatted then simply click on the arrow to the right of the Normal template in the Styles and Formatting task pane and select Modify... from the drop-down menu list. In the Modify Style dialogue box choose the font, font size, weight etc. that is required: see Figures 5.29, 5.30 and 5.31.

The font for the whole document will then follow the amended style for the template, in this case the 'Normal' template. The changes will only apply to the active document unless the formatting for the underlying template is changed by checking the Add to Template check box.

If only a paragraph is to be reformatted, then the cursor is placed in front of the first word of the paragraph and an appropriate text template selected. For example, using the Normal template will change the font for the whole document, body text templates are based on paragraphs and will reformat only the paragraph.

Alternatively, reformatting can be achieved by using the toolbar formatting icons. The text to be changed is first highlighted and the relevant toolbar icon used.

Try it out

Open Lost_Opportunities.doc from the Sample Files sub-folder in My Documents.

Select Page Setup... and apply the following settings:

Paper size:	A4	
Orientation:	Portrait	
Margins:	Top	2 cm
	Bottom	2 cm
	Left	3.5 cm
	Right	2.5 cm

Click OK.

Now you are going to format the font for the whole document.

Select Styles and Formatting... from the Format option on the main menu.

(See note below if you are using an earlier version of Office.)

Place the cursor over the Normal style.

Press the arrow to the right of the box: see Figure 5.30.

▶▶

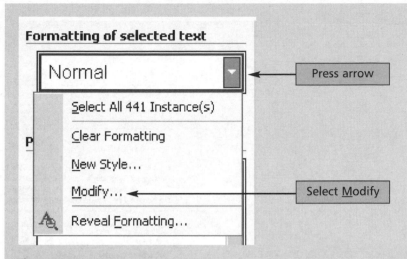

Figure 5.30

Select Modify... and the Modify Style dialogue box shown in Figure 5.31 will appear.

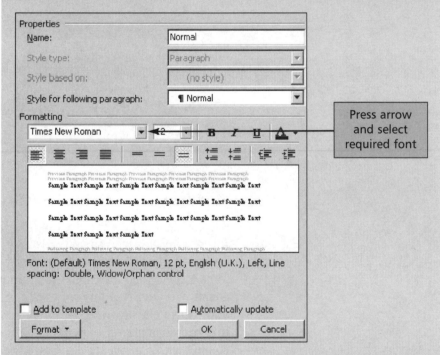

Figure 5.31

Note: if you are using an earlier version of Office to XP then select Style... from the Format option and the styles dialogue box will open. Press the Modify... button and a Modify Style dialogue box will open. It will look slightly different to Figure 5.31 (see Figure 5.32) but the principles for modifying styles are exactly the same. In Office XP there is a Formatting option on the main dialogue box to modify the font, but you can equally use the Format button to bring up the Font dialogue box. From here both versions of Office are more or less the same.

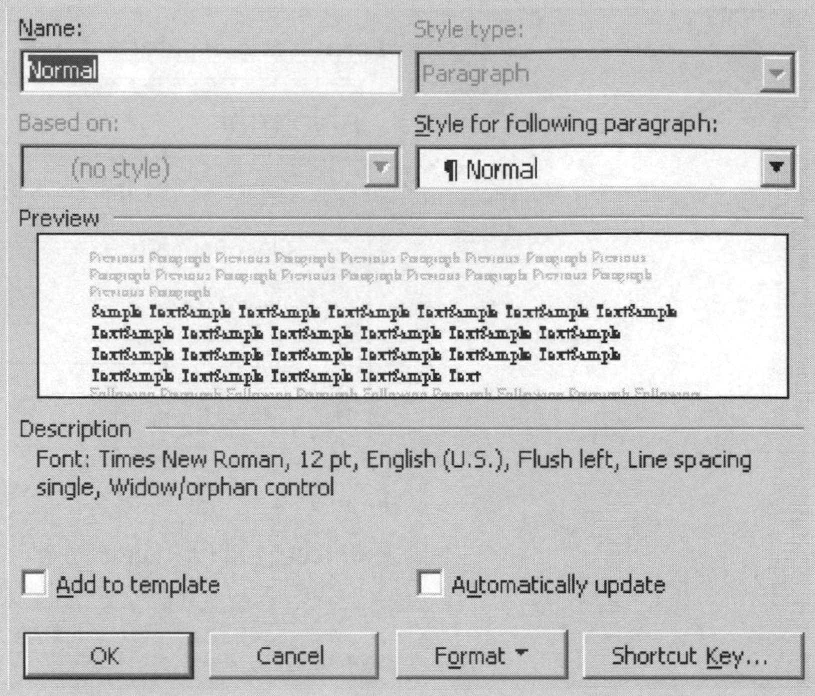

Figure 5.32

> **Select** Arial as the font and 12 points as the font size.
>
> **Save** the file as '**Lost_Opportunities**' on your floppy disk.
>
> **Close** the file.

Modifying or creating heading styles for a document

For this unit you are required to follow the house style for headings and sub-headings as well as body text. Although text formats, whether body text or headings, can be reformatted using normal formatting options for fonts available on the toolbars or menu options, it is invariably easier to create your own heading styles or modify those offered by Microsoft. By doing this you can ensure you have consistency throughout a document. It is entirely a matter of personal preference how you format text to comply with a given set of house styles and using the toolbar formatting icons or options on the main menu under Format are both valid ways. However, the built-in styles do provide you with a better opportunity of maintaining consistency. The following section gives guidance on how to create (or modify) heading and text styles.

Creating a new heading style

As you learnt in the previous section, formatting text can be achieved by using the Styles and Formatting... option on the main menu or with text-related icons on the formatting toolbar. Microsoft provides a number of solutions to complete most tasks. However, students are not required to complete tasks in any specific way providing the outcome meets the OCR's standards. That said, some solutions are considered to be more appropriate than others depending on the tasks to be undertaken. Formatting headings is an example where using a built-in style may provide more benefits than simply formatting the text using the formatting toolbar icons.

For example, in a long document with many main and sub-headings it would help the reader if a table of contents were placed at the beginning of the document. A table of contents is simply a list of the headings used in the document. This book has a contents page at the beginning based on the unit and paragraph headings. By using recognised styles you can insert a table of contents. For this unit you are not expected to know how to do this but if you learn to format your headings using styles you may find creating tables of contents easier in the future should you wish to do this.

To create a new heading style use the Styles and Formatting task pane by selecting Styles and Formatting… from the Format menu.

Click on the New Style button to bring up the New Style dialogue box.

In the Name: box a new heading name is entered e.g. Main Heading. The font is changed to the specified style, size and weight and when the OK button is pressed the new heading style is created: see Figure 5.33.

New style is added to the list

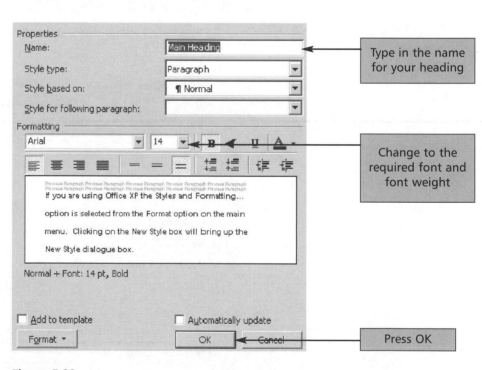

Type in the name for your heading

Change to the required font and font weight

Press OK

Figure 5.33

Figure 5.34

Once the new style has been created it is added to the Styles and Formatting list (see Figure 5.34) and can then be selected from the styles list icon on the formatting toolbar.

The new style that is created will only be available in the active document. If you want to add this to the Styles and Formatting task pane list for new documents then select the Add to template check box. The new style will then be available for all new documents.

To modify existing styles simply select the style from the list, press the arrow to bring up the drop down-menu list and select <u>M</u>odify... . Changes to the existing style are then made in exactly the same way as if you were creating a new style.

Now create three new heading styles.

Try it out

Open Lost_Opportunities.doc.

Place the cursor in front of the 'C' of Chapter 1.

Select <u>S</u>tyles and Formatting... from the F<u>o</u>rmat option on the main menu.

Press New Style in the Styles and Formatting task pane (or select <u>S</u>tyle... and <u>N</u>ew... from the F<u>o</u>rmat menu if using an earlier version of Office).

Type 'Main Heading' as the name of your first new heading.

Select Font type as Arial.

Select Font size as 14.

Select Font weight as bold.

Press OK.

Select Main Heading as the heading style from the styles option on the formatting toolbar: see Figure 5.35.

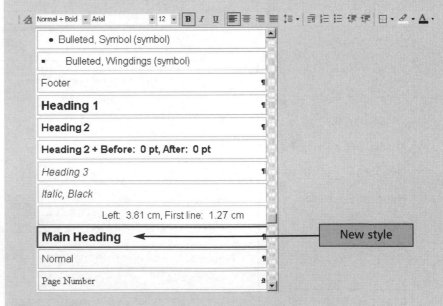

Figure 5.35

The heading 'Chapter 1' will now assume the format of your new style heading and you can then use the same style for any main heading.

Now **create** two further headings based on the following styles:

Name: Sub-heading 1
Font: Arial
Size: 12
Style: Bold, italic

Name: Sub-heading 2
Font: Times New Roman
Size: 12
Style   Bold

Modify the heading 'Lost Opportunities' to the Sub-heading 1 style.

Save your file.

Close the file.

Moving, inserting and deleting text

There will be occasions when having completed a document, either for yourself or someone else, amendments will need to be made. You may already have learned these useful functions so this section is included here as either a refresher or an introduction to understanding how to amend a document.

Moving text using cut and paste

To move either a single word or a paragraph using cut and paste you must first highlight the text in question. Having highlighted the text you can cut it out of the document by using Cut from the Edit option on the main menu or alternatively use the cut icon ✂ on the formatting toolbar. Cutting data from any document sends it to the clipboard – an area of memory that allows you to keep objects or data until you want to use them again; but once the computer is switched off everything on the clipboard is lost. To view what is being stored on the clipboard, select Office Clipboard… from the Edit option on the menu (alternatively press Ctrl+C twice).

Once the item to be moved has been cut, place the cursor at the point to which the data or object is to be moved and then either select Paste from the Edit option on the menu bar, or press the paste icon found on the formatting toolbar 📋. The object or data will then reappear.

Try it out

Open the file **Precinct_Society.doc** in the Sample Files folder in My Documents.

Move the final paragraph so that it becomes the second paragraph.

Reminder:

Highlight the final paragraph that starts with Professor Willow... .

Cut the paragraph using either the menu or toolbar options.

Place the cursor on the line immediately below the first paragraph.

Press the Enter key to create a new paragraph.

Paste the paragraph back into the document using either the menu or toolbar options.

Save your amendments as a new file on your floppy disk.

Close the file and application.

Deleting and restoring text

To delete text from a document first highlight the text to be deleted and then press the delete button on the keyboard. Remember that deleting text does not send it to the clipboard and therefore if you find that you have made a mistake by deleting the wrong text you will need to undo that last action. To undelete a deletion, select the Undo option from Edit on the main menu or alternatively press the undo arrow on the Standard toolbar ↰ .

Using automatically generated date fields in a specified format

To enter a date into a document select Insert, Date and Time... from the main menu. The Date and Time... dialogue box will appear, offering you a variety of formats for the date such as:

22/06/04
22 June 2004
22.06.04

You can also select the country format. The English format is always in the order of day, month, year. Date format codes are often shown 'dd/mmm/yy' or 'dd/mm/yy' or 'dd/mmm/yyyy' where the d is the day, m the month and y the year. American date formats reverse the month and day so 22/06/04 becomes 06/22/04. You can easily spot this where the day is greater than 12, as in the case above, but it can be easily missed if the date was, say, 05/06/04.

The date and time dialogue box also offers you the opportunity to update the date (or time) automatically. This is done by clicking in the Update automatically box in the bottom right corner of the dialogue box. If this is checked, every time you open the document the date will automatically be updated to the current date.

Once you have selected the date and country format required, simply press the OK button and the date will be inserted into the document.

Using headers and footers

Some documents need specific information on every page, such as page number, date, file information and so on. Using headers and footers allows you to include information throughout a document without the need to retype the same information onto each page of the document. Also, bearing in mind the need for accuracy and consistency, if Word reproduces repeating data, the likelihood of mistakes is reduced. Word, and for that matter most modern wordprocessing packages, provides a headers and footers function.

Headers and footers are placed in the top and bottom margin spaces of the page. You can insert text, numbers, data fields or graphics as a header or footer. Common examples of standard headers or footers are:

- page numbers
- dates
- author details
- book details
- company logos
- file names and location paths.

To insert a header or footer simply select the Header and Footer menu item found under the View option of the main menu. Alternatively, click on the header and footer icon ▦ ; it can be placed on the toolbar using Customize... from Toolbars, under View on the main menu.

Once Header and Footer has been selected you will see the header box and the header and footer toolbar displayed as shown in Figure 5.36.

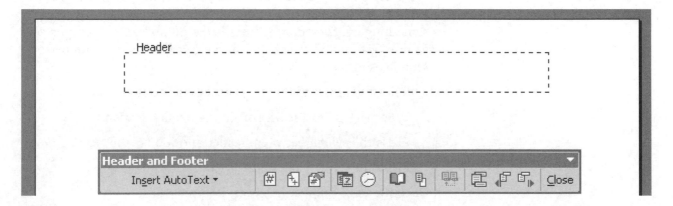

Figure 5.36

It is worth having a more detailed look at the options available on the toolbar itself, as shown in Figure 5.37.

Figure 5.37

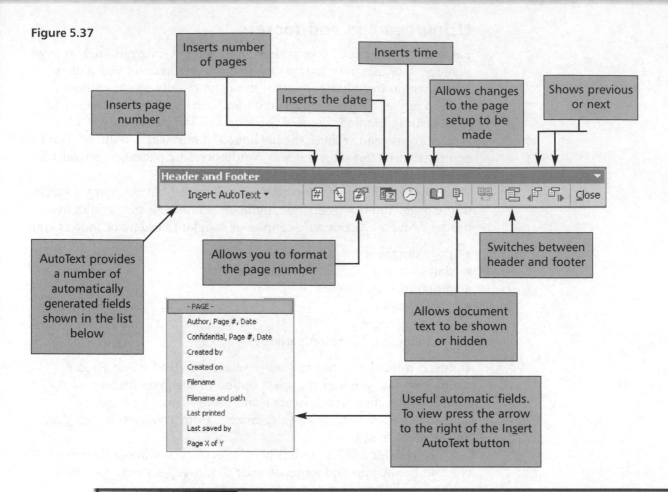

Inserts number of pages

Inserts time

Inserts page number

Inserts the date

Allows changes to the page setup to be made

Shows previous or next

AutoText provides a number of automatically generated fields shown in the list below

Allows you to format the page number

Switches between header and footer

Allows document text to be shown or hidden

Useful automatic fields. To view press the arrow to the right of the Insert AutoText button

Try it out

Open a new Word document.

Type '=Rand(10,10)'.

(**Tip:** the Rand formula allows you to generate random text to avoid the need to type a lot of text when you want to try something out. The first number is the number of paragraphs you want to create and the second number represents the number of sentences in the paragraph.)

Select Header and Footer from the View main menu.

Type 'The Quick Brown Fox' in the header section.

Press the switch between header and footer icon.

Press the insert page number icon.

Once the page number has been inserted

Press the centre icon on the formatting toolbar.

Press Close.

Notice how the heading appears on both pages and that page numbers have been inserted with 1 on the first page and 2 on the second.

As you can see from the above exercise in addition to using the built-in functions such as date, time, filename etc., you can type your own text into either the header or footer. For example, you can type your name or address.

Now test your knowledge and understanding of the skills learnt so far in this unit by completing Build-up Exercise 1.

Build-up Exercise 1: Stage 1

Scenario

You are the administrative assistant for an antiques and auctioneering company called Bellings. You have been asked to prepare a leaflet on a forthcoming auction. The leaflet is also an opportunity to let people know other details about Bellings, the services they offer and events they organise.

Open the document called **Bellings**.

Set the page format as follows:

Paper size: A4
Orientation: Portrait
Margins: Top   2 cm
                Bottom 2 cm
                Left   3 cm
                Right   3 cm

Set the text styles as follows:

Table 5.2

Feature	Font	Type size	Style	Alignment	
Body text	Sans serif	12 point	Normal	Left	
Bullet text	Sans serif	11 point	Normal	Left	
Headings	Sans serif	14 point	Bold	Centred	
Sub-headings	Sans serif	12 point	Bold, italic	Left	
Tables	Sans serif	12 point	Gridlines	Column heading	Centred, bold and shaded
				Row heading	Left
				Text	Left (wrapped)
				Numbers	Right
				Date	Right
Imported data	Sans serif	12 point	Gridlines	Column heading	Centred, bold and shaded
				Text	Left
				Numbers	Right

Note: some of the features in this table will be covered later in the unit.

Create a new main heading to the house style specification.

Create a new sub-heading to the house style specification.

Amend the Normal style to reflect the house style specification.

Apply house style to the headings and text as per the house style.

Insert the graphic file **Belling_Logo.jpg** as a header.

TIP
Inserting graphics

Inserting graphics as a header is executed in exactly the same way as a text or automatic header. Select Header and Footer from the View menu to bring up the header box. When the header box and toolbar come into view select Insert, Picture, From File... on the main menu. When the Insert Picture dialogue box appears as in Figure 5.38, locate the folder on the website (Unit 5, Sample Files) where the graphic is stored, select the graphic and then press the Insert button at the bottom of the box.

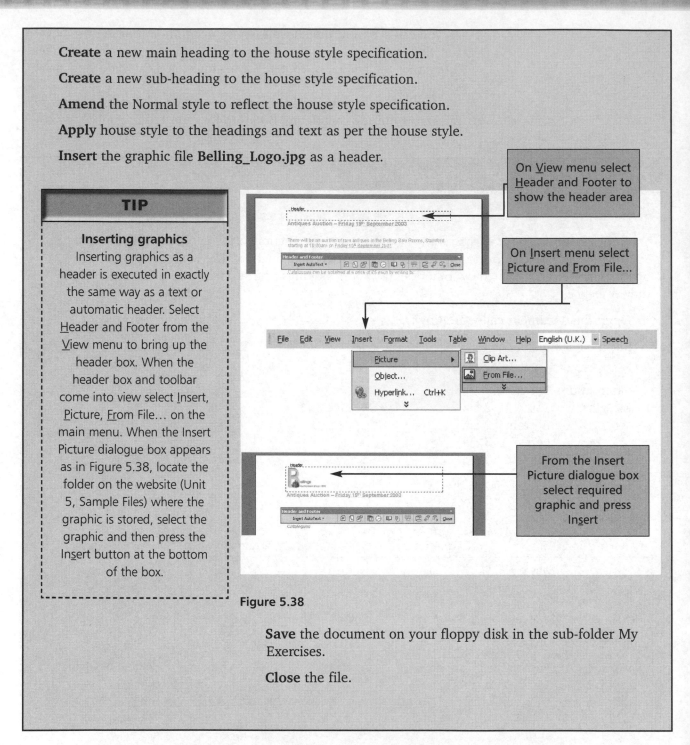

On View menu select Header and Footer to show the header area

On Insert menu select Picture and From File...

From the Insert Picture dialogue box select required graphic and press Insert

Figure 5.38

Save the document on your floppy disk in the sub-folder My Exercises.

Close the file.

Creating bullet and number lists

Word offers a variety of ways to enhance documents to emphasise major points or lists. Bullets and lists come in a number of formats. The easiest way to start a bullet or numbered list is to click on the appropriate icon on the formatting toolbar: see Figure 5.39.

Figure 5.39

Alternatively you can select Bullets and Numbering… from the Format option on the menu. By choosing this method you can select the bullet or number style that is appropriate for your work. Have a look at Figure 5.40.

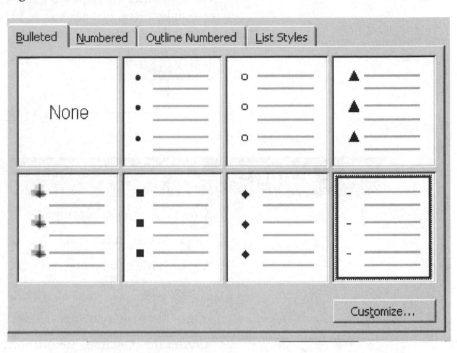

Figure 5.40

You can also convert text to a list after the text has been entered. Now have a look at Figure 5.41.

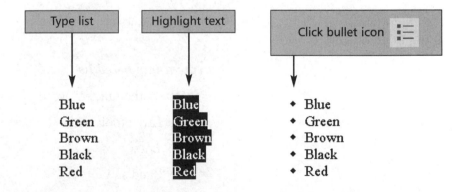

Figure 5.41

First the text for the list is typed, then the whole text is highlighted and once the bullet icon is pressed the text is converted into a bullet list. The bullets can still be reformatted by using the Bullets and Numbering… option from the Format option on the menu.

Numbered lists are created in a similar way. The cursor is placed where the list is to start. When the number icon is selected Word will start the list with the first number. After the enter key is pressed Word inserts the next sequential number. If a line is wanted between the numbers then by pressing the Shift key and then, whilst still holding the Shift key, pressing the Enter key a line will be inserted without starting a new sequence in the list. Pressing the Enter key will insert the next number on the following line. A number list can also be created by typing the number one at the beginning of a line and entering text for that line. Word will automatically assume that a number list is required and once the enter key is pressed the next number will be inserted.

Where sub-lists are required these can be achieved by pressing the increase indent icon or back to the primary number by pressing the decrease indent icon: see Figure 5.42.

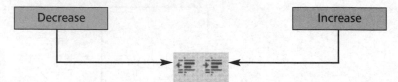

Figure 5.42

Try it out

Create a bullet list

Open a new Word document.

Click on the bullet icon.

Type 'Garden' following the first bullet.

Press Enter.

Type 'Tools' after the next bullet.

Create the remaining items in the list with:

Plants
Bulbs
Seeds

Press Enter twice.

Create a numbered list

Click on the number icon.

Type 'Large tools' after the first number.

Press Enter.

Type 'Band saw'.

Press the increase indent icon.

Press Enter.

Type 'Circular saw'.

Press Enter.

Type 'Small Tools'.

▶▶

Press the decrease indent icon.

Notice how the primary series is returned to with the next sequential number.

Press Enter.

Type 'Screwdriver'.

Press the increase indent icon.

Press Enter twice.

Close the document without saving it.

Amending documents and using the spell checker

However careful you are in preparing and presenting documents for yourself or other people, there will inevitably be a need to review the document and make amendments. These can be as a result of spelling errors, punctuation mistakes, inaccurate or changing data, inserting new information or simply the need to move text from one location in the document to another. In this section you will learn how to:

- use Word's built-in spell checker
- use search and replace data
- insert and delete text
- copy and move text from one location to another.

The spell checker

Word provides a powerful spell checker to assist you in ensuring spelling errors are minimised. The spell checker can be used in a variety of languages, although those available on your computer will depend on options selected when the software was installed. Despite the power of Word's spell checker there are a number of points you will need to consider when using it. The first is to check what default language was set when Word was first loaded. Microsoft is an American product and therefore often you will probably find that the dictionary's language is set to English (US). To reset the default language to English (UK) either select <u>T</u>ools, <u>L</u>anguage, Set <u>L</u>anguage... on the main menu or alternatively use the language drop list on the formatting menu. Both these options are shown in Figure 5.43.

Using the menu option allows you to set the required language as the default.

The second point to watch is the actual use of words. The spell checker will look for the correct spelling of a word. It does not determine whether the word chosen is correct for the context of the work. So, for example, if you use 'there' rather than 'their' or 'week' as opposed to 'weak', Word rightly sees no spelling error.

Menu option

Toolbar option

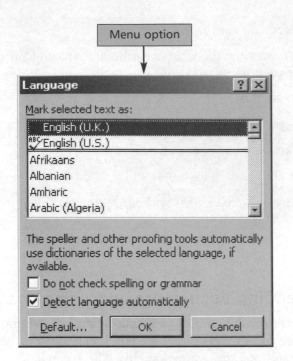

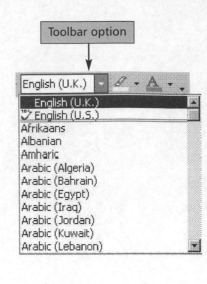

Figure 5.43

Word checks both spelling and grammar. Incorrectly spelt words will have a wavy red line underneath while questionable grammar is underlined in green. To use the spelling and grammar checker select Spelling and Grammar... from the Tools menu option. You will be shown the spelling and grammar dialogue box. At the top of the box you can see the default language. Now have a look at Figure 5.44.

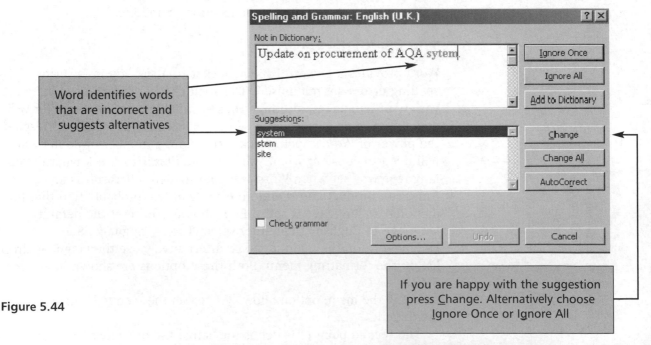

Word identifies words that are incorrect and suggests alternatives

If you are happy with the suggestion press Change. Alternatively choose Ignore Once or Ignore All

Figure 5.44

The spell checker gives you the option of accepting suggestions from a list of alternative words, or ignoring it. If you wish to accept a suggestion offered simply select the appropriate word in the Suggestions: box and then press the Change button. If there are a

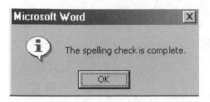

Figure 5.45

number of occurrences of the word then you can choose whether to change them all at once by pressing the Change All button or one at a time by pressing Change. Occasionally Word may display a word that appears to you to be correct. This will happen if the word itself is not in Word's dictionary. In this case you can choose to ignore or add the word to the dictionary for future use.

Once the spell checker has finished checking the document a dialogue box as shown in Figure 5.45 indicates the check has been completed.

Try it out

Open the file **Company_Performance.doc** in the Sample Files folder in My Documents.

Select Spelling and Grammar, from the Tools option on the menu.

Press Change to accept the suggested replacement words. There should be three in total.

Once the check has been completed

Close the file without saving.

Build-up Exercise 1: Stage 2

Open Bellings.doc.

Format the list of services to become bullet points as shown below:

- Best trade prices

- Valuations

- Packing and shipment of items anywhere in the world

- Insurance arranged

- Export advice and documentation

- Storage

Select Spelling and Grammar from the Tools option on the menu and spell check the document.

Note: where the spell checker highlights a word which is correct, but not in the dictionary (e.g. proper names such as Bellings), **press** the Ignore Once button.

Save the file.

Close the file.

You should now be able to:

- format the page layout of a document according to a given house style
- create and modify headings and body text styles for a document
- insert a date in a specified format
- insert headers and footers
- create bullet and number lists
- check a document for spelling mistakes using the spell checker.

Using special symbols and characters

In addition to the bullets shown in the bullets and numbering dialogue box in Figure 5.40 above, Word provides a wide range of symbols and special characters that can be used in a document's body text or alternatively used to customise bullet points. To view the characters and symbols available select <u>S</u>ymbol… from the <u>I</u>nsert option of the main menu. A dialogue box similar to that shown in Figure 5.46 will appear.

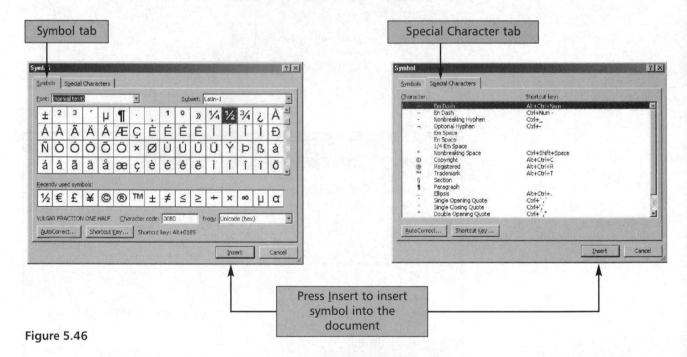

Figure 5.46

This dialogue box has two tabs. The first, <u>S</u>ymbols, allows you to select from a wide range of symbols. By pressing down on the arrow to the top left of the box you can select from the list of fonts available; the arrow on the right helps you to select the style of symbol you want to use. To insert the symbol into a document simply highlight the required symbol and then press the <u>I</u>nsert button.

The second tab allows you to select from a range of special characters. A selection of these is shown in the list below:

© copyright
¶ paragraph symbol
® registered trade mark
™ trade mark

Inserting a special character is carried out in exactly the same way as a symbol, by pressing the Insert button.

Earlier you learnt how to create bullet lists using the default bullets in the bullets and numbering box. You can also use this dialogue box in conjunction with the available symbols to customise bullets.

Open a new Word document.

Open the Bullets and Numbering dialogue box (see Figure 5.40).

Select one of the bullet boxes to be customised.

This will then enable the Customize… button.

Press the Customize button and you will be shown the Customise Bulleted List dialogue box shown in Figure 5.47.

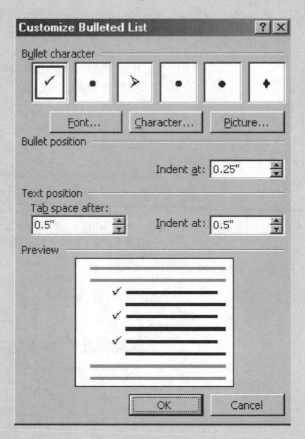

Figure 5.47

Here you have a choice of selecting the Font button to format the font of the existing bullet shape, the Picture button to select a picture as a bullet or the Character button. Pressing the character button will bring up the symbol dialogue box from which you can select the style of font and character or symbol required for the bullet.

Press the character button.

Select Wingdings from the font drop-down list.

Select a suitable Wingding to replace the bullet style.

Press OK three times to return to the active document.

A bullet to start the list will be inserted.

Type the list:

Coffee
Tea
Water
Orange juice

Close the file without saving.

Using the find and replace function

Two extremely useful functions available to you in Office applications are the Find… and Replace… options. These functions allow you to look for specific words in a document and then replace them with another word or phrase.

Have a look at the following paragraph:

John returned to the centre of the town with his bicycle. The bicycle was bright red but his recent accident had severely scratched the paintwork and he wanted to find a suitable colour match to repaint the bicycle frame.

For the sake of argument let us say you want to change the word 'bicycle' to 'cycle'. Clearly in this short example it would not be difficult to find all the occurrences of the word 'bicycle'. However, had this been part of a long story then making sure you changed *all* the occurrences would have been more difficult.

Under the Edit option on the main menu is a menu item called Replace… and selecting this option will bring up the dialogue box shown in Figure 5.48.

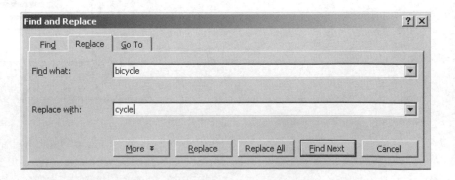

Figure 5.48

Type in the word to be replaced in the Find what: box, and the new word in the Replace with: box, and Word will find each occurrence and, depending on whether you select Replace or Replace All, change it to the new word. Once Word has changed all the words to be replaced it helpfully tells you it has finished and the number of occurrences it has changed: see Figure 5.49.

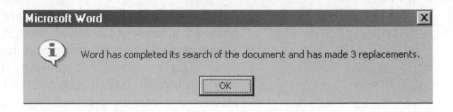

Figure 5.49

The example paragraph will now reflect the changes as shown below:

John returned to the centre of the town with his cycle. The cycle was bright red but his recent accident had severely scratched the paintwork and he wanted to find a suitable colour match to repaint the cycle frame.

Try it out

Open the file **Conference_Centre.doc** in the Sample Files folder in My Documents.

Replace the words 'No. 24' with 'The Business Café'. There should be three occurrences in all.

Close the file without saving it.

Creating and using tables

Tables have a variety of uses, but predominantly they are used to organise and present data in an easily understandable format. Tables are made up of *rows* and *columns*. Where a row intersects a column a *cell* is formed in which data can be placed and stored. Have a look at Figure 5.50.

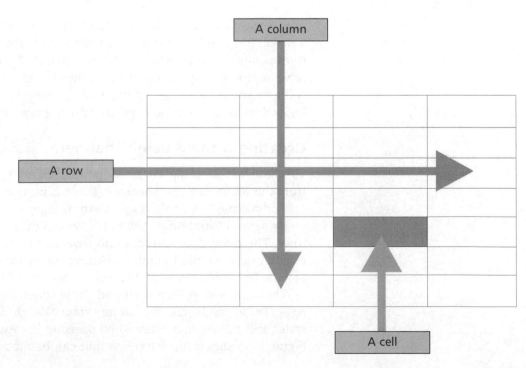

Figure 5.50

For this unit you are required to create a table from a given set of data, change a number of the table's properties (column width, cell alignment, etc.) and insert it into a document.

Creating a basic table is simplicity itself. There are a number of ways in which this can be achieved but the two most common ways to create tables are to use the menu option or toolbar icon.

Creating a table using the toolbar

On the standard toolbar you should see the insert table icon ▦ . By clicking on the icon a table-shaped box will appear with 20 squares. By selecting the first box and dragging the cursor over the number of rows and columns required, and then releasing the cursor, a table is automatically inserted into your document at the point where the cursor is positioned: see Figure 5.51.

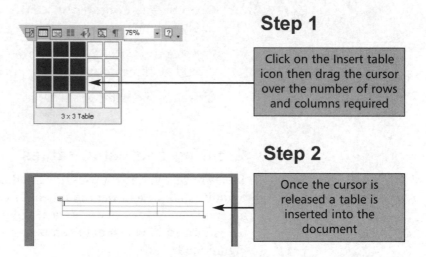

Step 1

Click on the Insert table icon then drag the cursor over the number of rows and columns required

Step 2

Once the cursor is released a table is inserted into the document

Figure 5.51

This is without question the simplest way of creating a table. However, as you will have noticed, the toolbar option limits the size of the initial table to five columns and four rows. Whilst you can add columns and rows to a table at any stage, you may prefer to dictate the number of rows and columns you want at the beginning of the process – that is providing you know the size of the table required, which is not always the case.

Creating a table using the menu

To create a table using the main menu click on Table, Insert, Table... from the menu options. Once the Table... item is selected the Insert Table dialogue box appears as shown in Figure 5.52.

By default Word offers the initial option of five columns and two rows. The number of columns and rows can be adjusted by simply typing in the required number or using the arrows to the right of the column or row boxes to add or reduce the default settings.

The default AutoFit format and Table style: are set to automatic. Again these can be changed at any stage. Word offers a wide range of styles and these can be viewed by pressing the Autoformat... button. Figure 5.53 shows the selections that can be made.

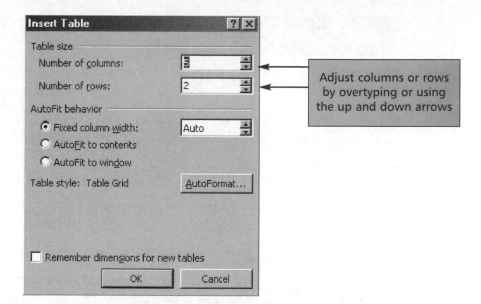

Figure 5.52

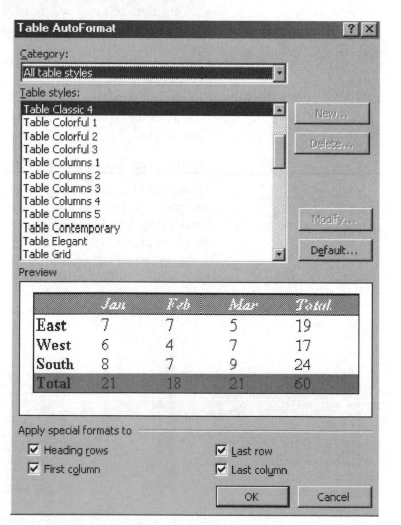

Figure 5.53

Once you have determined the size and format of the table, pressing OK will insert the table into the document.

Try it out

Open a new Word Document.

Select T<u>a</u>ble, <u>I</u>nsert, <u>T</u>able... from the main menu.

Amend the default table size so that it has four columns and ten rows.

Press OK.

Print the table.

Save the file as **Table 1.**

Close the document.

Setting a table's column widths

When a new table is created and inserted into a document, Word automatically sets the column width. However, it is seldom that a table with multiple columns will need the same column widths throughout. For example, a column of text is likely to be wider than one containing numerical data.

As you will now appreciate there is more than one method available for amending the column and row widths for a table. Column widths can be changed either by amending the table properties in the Table Properties dialogue box, or alternatively by using the mouse and the drag method.

Using the Table Properties dialogue box

All objects in a Windows environment have properties, and tables are no exception. By placing the cursor over the object and pressing the right-hand mouse button the drop-down menu provides the range of options shown in Figure 5.54.

Note: for pre XP versions of Office select Table on the main menu and then T<u>a</u>ble P<u>r</u>operties... from the list offered.

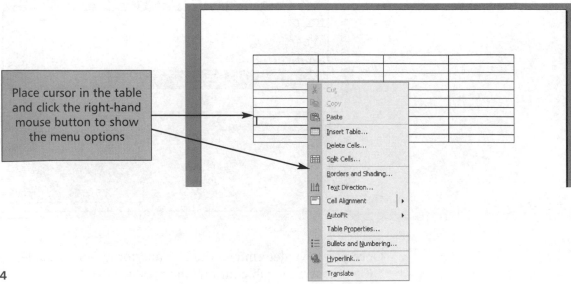

Place cursor in the table and click the right-hand mouse button to show the menu options

Figure 5.54

To change the properties of the table the Table Properties... item is selected and the dialogue box shown in Figure 5.55 appears.

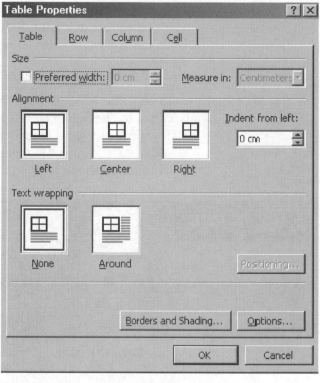

Figure 5.55

Each tab allows you to format different aspects of the table, from its columns and rows to borders and shading. To change the column width the Column tab is selected as shown in Figure 5.56.

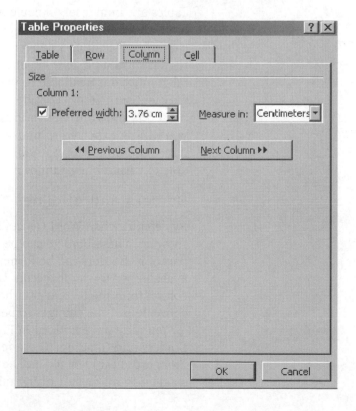

Figure 5.56

With the Column tab selected the width of the table columns can be changed. The width of the column is measured either by using a width measurement or as a percentage of the rest of the columns in the table. To change the width simply type in the required width in centimetres (or other measurement depending on the default setting) or alternatively type a percentage value (e.g. 20%) for that column.

Using the drag method

To alter the width of a column using the drag method, place the cursor over the line between the columns, and pressing and holding down the left-hand mouse button, drag the column out to the required width. As the cursor is moved over the line between the columns it will change shape to ◄‖►.

Try it out

Open Table 1.

Using the Table Properties dialogue box method

Format the column widths as follows:

Column 1   5 cm

Columns 2–4   2 cm

Save the table.

Close the file.

Table borders, gridlines and alignment

Tables are immensely flexible and useful tools for presenting data in many different ways. However, the sheer range of formatting functions can in itself lead to a danger of making the end result less readable than it should be. It is beyond the scope of this book to review all the table functions available to you but having understood the basics you may feel sufficiently confident to try practising with some of the functions shown in the various dialogue boxes and menus. For this unit you will be expected to understand how to align text and numerical data in columns, format table borders and cell borders, and also be able to turn table gridlines on and off.

Borders and gridlines

By default, when Word creates a table it does so with the borders showing. These borders can be shown either for the whole table or any part of it. Borders can be formatted using either the menu options available, or the toolbar icon. Using the dialogue box gives you greater control than the toolbar but the toolbar is perhaps easier to use and more convenient if the changes to be made do not call for complex formatting.

You may have noticed in Figure 5.55 that there was a button for Borders and Shading. These features allow you to format the borders around the table or for individual cells. They can also introduce shading to all or part of the table. Now have a look at Figure 5.57.

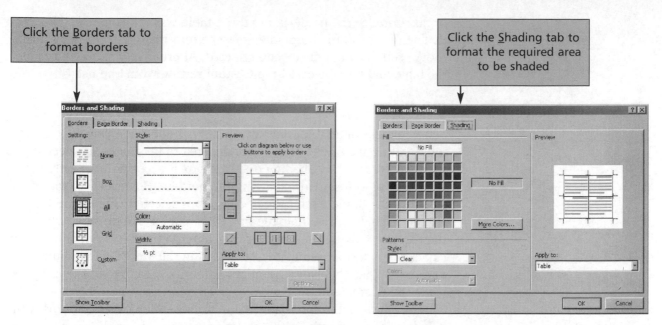

Click the Borders tab to format borders

Click the Shading tab to format the required area to be shaded

Figure 5.57

Pressing the Borders and Shading button brings up the Borders and Shading dialogue box. However, before accessing this you will need to highlight (or select) those areas of the table which are to be formatted. Have a look at Figure 5.58.

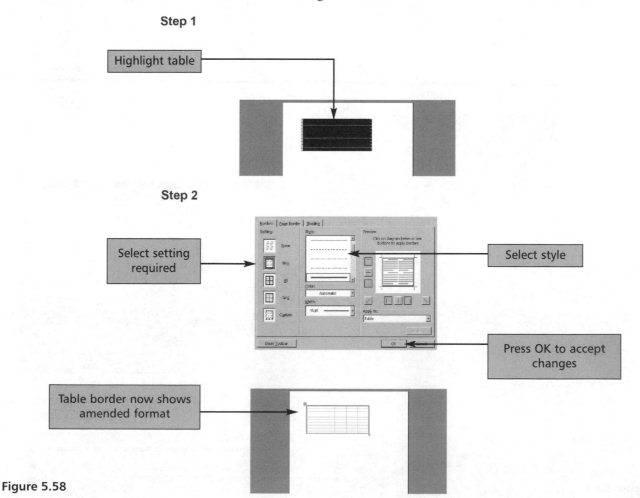

Step 1

Highlight table

Step 2

Select setting required

Select style

Press OK to accept changes

Table border now shows amended format

Figure 5.58

In this instance the border around the table was reformatted to a double line. If all the borders were to be reformatted in this way then the Al̲l setting could have been selected. Alternatively, if only parts of the table had been selected the Cu̲stom setting would be used.

Shading

Shading areas of a table is achieved in much the same way as reformatting the border style. First the area to be shaded is selected, then the Borders and Shading dialogue box is accessed in exactly the same way as you saw for changing the borders. However, instead of selecting the B̲orders tab the S̲hading tab is selected (see Figure 5.57). On the left side of the dialogue box is the colour palette from which the required colour is selected. If the colour you want is not shown you can create a customised colour by selecting the Mo̲re Colours button and then either choosing a standard colour or creating your own by using the Custom tab.

Beneath the Fill colour palette is a further option called Patterns with a Sty̲le box underneath. In this selection you can either choose a percentage shade or a pattern: see Figure 5.59.

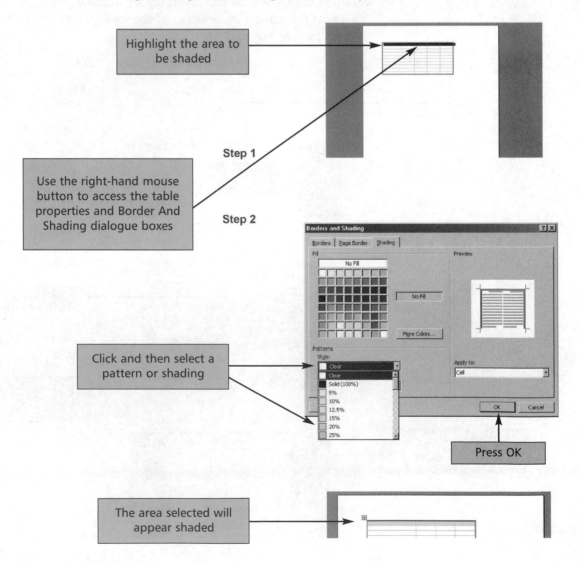

Highlight the area to be shaded

Use the right-hand mouse button to access the table properties and Border And Shading dialogue boxes

Step 1

Step 2

Click and then select a pattern or shading

Press OK

The area selected will appear shaded

Figure 5.59

Using the toolbar

On the formatting toolbar you will see the borders icon, shown in Figure 5.60.

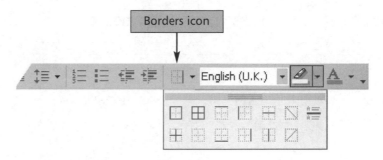

Figure 5.60

Essentially this toolbar is a facility for you to show or hide the borders for specific areas of a table. It does not provide a facility to format the lines of a border (i.e. weight, double line, etc.) and is therefore slightly less flexible than using the options within the <u>B</u>orders and Shading dialogue box.

To use the borders icon, first either place the cursor where you want to make changes or, if the whole table or multiple cells are to be changed, they all need to be highlighted. In Figure 5.61 notice how the border to the right of the first cell in the table is to be removed. To reinstate the border simply click on the appropriate border in the toolbar.

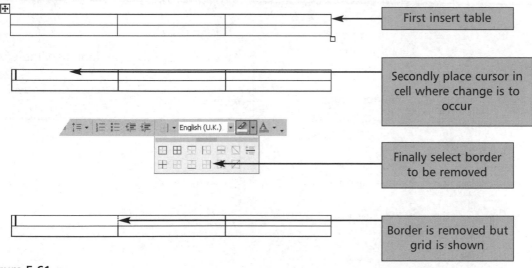

Figure 5.61

Gridlines

In some documents you may want to import a table but make it seem as if it is not a table but a part of the typed document. To achieve this you may want to remove all the printable borders, but still see the gridlines while working on the document. Gridlines help you to navigate around the table you are working on but will not print when the document is completed. Have a look at Figure 5.62.

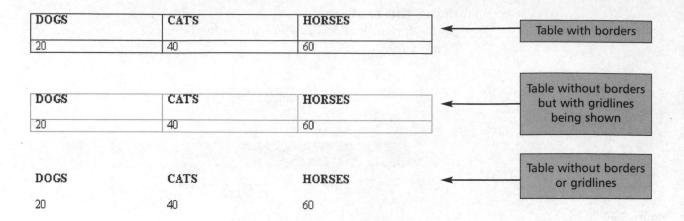

DOGS	CATS	HORSES
20	40	60

Table with borders

DOGS	CATS	HORSES
20	40	60

Table without borders but with gridlines being shown

DOGS   CATS   HORSES

20   40   60

Table without borders or gridlines

Figure 5.62

The first table above has all the borders and these will be printed. The second table has all the borders removed, but you can still see the cells, which helps you navigate round the table. The third table is how it would appear in a printed document. In fact you can also turn the gridlines off while working on the table, but this does make it more difficult to work on the table.

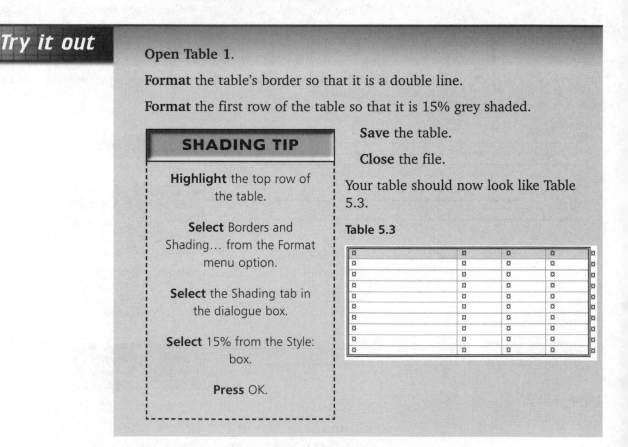

Try it out

Open Table 1.

Format the table's border so that it is a double line.

Format the first row of the table so that it is 15% grey shaded.

SHADING TIP

Highlight the top row of the table.

Select Borders and Shading... from the Format menu option.

Select the Shading tab in the dialogue box.

Select 15% from the Style: box.

Press OK.

Save the table.

Close the file.

Your table should now look like Table 5.3.

Table 5.3

Aligning text and numeric data

By default, Word aligns both text and numeric data to the left of a cell. Data can be aligned in much the same way as normal text is in a document.

There are two main ways to set the alignment for a column, row, group of cells or a single cell.

Option 1: using the toolbar

To align data in a column using the toolbar, first select the column and then press the appropriate alignment icon on the formatting toolbar (see Figure 5.63).

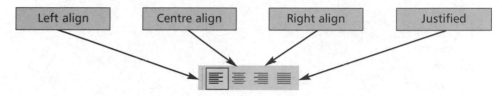

Figure 5.63

A column can be selected by placing the cursor in the first cell and while holding the left-hand mouse button, dragging down the column. More conveniently, if it is a large table, place the cursor above the column to be highlighted and, when you see an arrow appear, click on the left-hand mouse button (see Figure 5.64).

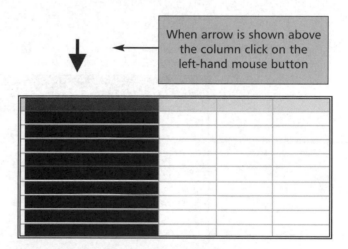

When arrow is shown above the column click on the left-hand mouse button

Figure 5.64

Option 2: using the menu option

To use this option, again highlight the column or cells to be aligned, but this time use the right-hand mouse button and you will see the drop-down menu shown in Figure 5.65 appear.

By selecting the Cell Alignment menu item the alignment options are displayed. Select the required alignment and any text or data placed in cells in that column will be aligned according to the selection that has been made.

Try it out

Open Table 1.

Highlight the second and third columns and using either of the above options

Format the cells so that they are right-aligned.

Figure 5.65

Enter the following data:

Table 5.4

Visitor categories	Qtr 1	Qtr 2	Qtr 3
Japanese	560	853	1025
French	212	198	350
German	364	520	569
American	1525	1487	1920
Chinese	105	114	96
Dutch	56	41	78
Swedish	26	45	26
Italian	115	140	267
Total	2963	3398	4331

Save Table 1.

Close Table 1.

Build-up Exercise 1: Stage 3

Open Bellings.doc.

Replace the word 'events' with 'shows' wherever it appears (four occurrences in all).

Save the file.

Close the file.

Build-up Exercise 1: Stage 4

Open a new Word document.

Create a table with three columns and six rows.

Set column widths as follows:

Column 1   5 cm

Column 2   2.5 cm

Column 3   5 cm

Insert the following data into the table:

Table 5.5

Venue	Date	Type
Birmingham	27/10/02	General
Glasgow	15/12/03	Specialist antique
Exeter	20/2/04	Specialist antique
London	24/5/04	Specialist antique
York	9/8/04	General

TABLE TIP

You may have noticed that when you draw the cursor over the table a handle similar to this ⊹ appears. By clicking on this handle you can select the whole table. This allows you to format all text and data at one go. You can also still use the drag method by clicking in the first cell and, with the left-hand mouse button held down, dragging across the range of cells to be highlighted.

Format the first row with 10% shading.

Format the date column (column 2) to be right-aligned and columns 1 and 3 left-aligned.

Format the heading row as bold.

Format the font style for all data to Arial 12.

Save the file as **Venues**.

Close the file.

You should now be able to:

- use special symbols and characters
- find and replace words and phrases
- create and use a table
- format borders and align data in a table
- understand about gridlines in a table
- shade columns, rows and cells in a table.

Importing and manipulating images

A wide range of packages and techniques exist, in which data files, images and charts can be created. You may already know how to use some of these, but for this unit the files, images and charts are provided and all you need to do is import and insert them at a specified point within a document.

In this section of the core unit you will learn how to import a picture into a particular location of your document and then resize the image to meet specified formatting requirements.

Inserting an image

First put the cursor at the point in the document where you want to place the image. As you learnt in the headers and footers section, images can be imported directly into any document using the option Insert, then Picture on the main menu. Clicking on the Picture option produces a further menu list. The one you will be concerned with for this unit is the From File... option. Selecting this opens the insert picture dialogue box shown in Figure 5.66.

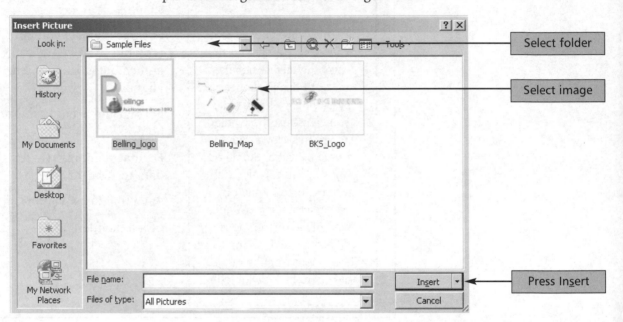

Figure 5.66

Once you press the Insert button the image is inserted into the document at the point where the cursor has been placed. By default Word imports the image so that it moves in line with the text. In this format the image will always stay with text associated with it. This is useful when you have additions to make in an earlier part of the document, since the image will then move with the text to which it applies. Clearly, when you add a new line or paragraph, text below the new insertion will move down.

Formatting an image's layout

The image can be relocated by clicking on it and dragging it to another location where it will again become locked to the text at its new position. The layout of images can be changed in a variety of ways depending on how you want them to behave with text. By pressing the right-hand mouse button with the cursor over the image that is to be reformatted, and selecting Format Picture... the formatting dialogue box will appear. If you select the Layout tab you can see the various options that are available and how these options change the way the picture behaves with any text around it: see Figure 5.67.

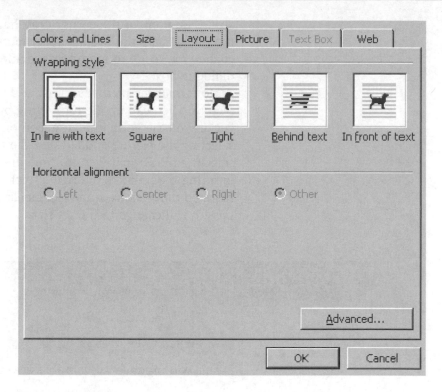

Figure 5.67

Image editing

Although Word is not designed as a graphics editing package it does offer some remarkably useful editing functions using the Picture toolbar. The toolbar can be viewed either by selecting the picture or selecting View, then Toolbars, then Picture from the main menu. This toolbar allows you to adjust the brightness, contrast, rotation, format (i.e. layout, size, etc.) and a number of other aspects of the image. Figure 5.68 shows the Picture toolbar and some of the functions available.

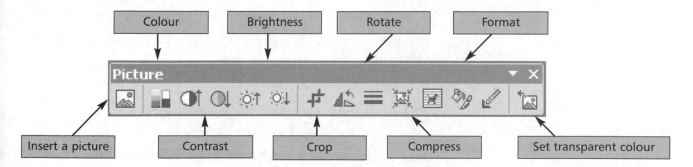

Figure 5.68

Whilst this is not a requirement for this course, you may wish to experiment with some of these options. You will, however, be required to ensure an image is sized correctly, maintaining the original proportions of the image.

To resize an image without changing its proportions can be achieved in two ways. First, if the precise size is not defined you can use one of the corner drag handles to drag the image to the required size. Using one of the corner drag handles will ensure that changes to the image keep the proportions the original image. If you need to change an image to an exact, specified size, use the format picture dialogue box.

To format the picture size using the dialogue box, first select the picture. Then call up the formatting picture dialogue box either by clicking on the Format picture icon on the Picture toolbar, or by selecting the picture and clicking the right-hand mouse button and selecting the Format Picture... menu option. Press the Size tab and, ensuring the Relative to original picture box is checked, enter the required dimensions in the Height: and Width: boxes. Press OK and the picture will change to the set size.

Try it out

Create a new Word document.

Type '=rand(10,10)'.

Press the Enter key.

This will produce random text as described earlier in the unit.

Place the cursor after the last word of the second paragraph.

Press Enter twice to create a new paragraph and line.

Select Insert, Picture, Clip Art... from the main menu.

Press Search to show all pictures available in the gallery.

If you see the Add Clips to Organizer dialogue press the button which says Later.

Select one of the pictures from the clip art gallery. It is not important which picture is used.

Press the arrow to the right of the selected image to view the menu list.

Select Insert.

(Alternatively, to insert the image double-click on it.)

Changing the size using the format picture dialogue box

Click on the image using the right-hand mouse button.

Select Format Picture... from the list.

Select the Size tab.

Making sure the Relative to original picture size box is checked,

Type 14.5 cm as the width of the picture.

Press OK.

The image will automatically resize, keeping its original proportions, based on the width selected. You could equally have inserted a height.

Press the undo icon on the toolbar to undo the resizing.

Changing the size using the drag technique

Click on the image to make drag handles appear.

Place the cursor over a corner handle (usually the bottom right handle) until you see the cursor change shape to a double arrow.

Click and hold down the left-hand mouse button.

Drag the image to the required size.

Close the document without saving.

Importing and formatting charts

Charts are a particularly useful feature made available in most Microsoft applications. Charts show a pictorial view of data and help the viewer understand the story behind the figures. For this course, unless you choose to complete the unit on graphs and charts as one of the optional units, you are not expected to be able to create a chart. However, you are expected to understand how to import and place charts (as well as datafiles and images) and also ensure that the imported object is legible. On occasions this may mean you will need to change the size of text or to alter a fill colour/pattern where, for example, a clear distinction cannot be made between two data series when the chart is printed in black and white.

Importing a chart

In this section you will learn how to import a chart pre-prepared as part of an Excel worksheet and to change a number of its properties.

Again, as with most application functions there are a variety of ways you can import chart objects. For this core unit you will use the Insert, Object... option on the main menu. Since this option is relatively straightforward it is easier to understand by doing it rather than reading detailed explanations. Have a go at following the Try it out exercise below.

Try it out

Open a new Word document.

Type '=rand(10,10)'.

Press Enter to generate random text.

Place your cursor at the end of the last word in paragraph 2.

Press the Enter key twice.

Select Insert, Object... from the main menu.

Select the Create from File tab on the Object dialogue box.

Press Browse: see Figure 5.69.

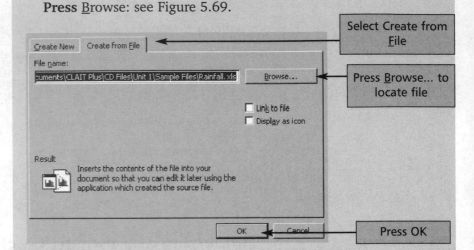

Select Create from File

Press Browse... to locate file

Press OK

Figure 5.69

Select Rainfall.xls from the Sample Files folder in My Documents.

Press Insert.

Press OK.

The chart from this worksheet is inserted into the document. You will notice that the size is not appropriate for the page orientation.

Click on the chart to show the size drag handles.

Reduce the size of the chart so that it fits between the margins of the document by clicking on and dragging one of the corner drag handles.

Your document should now look similar to Figure 5.70.

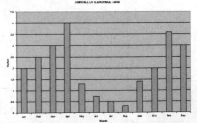

Figure 5.70

Save the document as **Chart_1**.

Formatting a chart

Once a chart has been created, irrespective of the application in which it was created, its properties will be set to the default of that application. Amongst properties included are:

- font colour, size and style
- scale
- colour and pattern fills.

Any of these and other formats relating to the chart can be changed to meet any given house style. Because the size of the chart you imported in the previous exercise was reduced to fit between the margins it is possible that the detail of the chart may not be clearly legible and to make the label or axis fonts easier to read it may be necessary to change their size.

Changing a heading, data label or axis font size

To change a chart's formatting, first double-click on the chart itself. Doing this allows Word to recognise that the chart was created in Excel and so change the toolbar to access the Excel menu. To change the font size, type or colour of the chart's axis heading, data label or other aspect of the chart, the relevant part of the chart has to be selected. For example, if you want to change the font size of the X-axis double-click on one of the axis labels and a Format Axis dialogue box will appear, with the font tab already selected as shown in Figure 5.71.

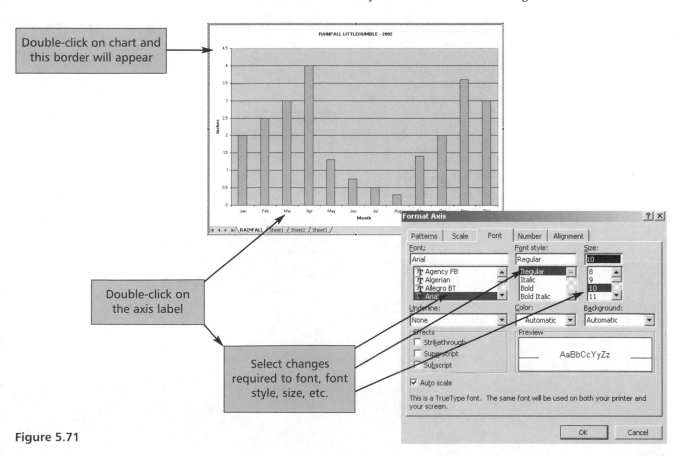

Figure 5.71

Try it out

Open your document **Chart_1** if it is not already open.

Double-click on the rainfall chart.

Double-click on the X-axis data label (any of the months will do).

In the Formatting Axis dialogue box:

Change the size of the font to 16 point.

Repeat this exercise for the Y-axis data label with a font size of 16 point.

Change the X- and Y-axis titles (Month and Inches) to font size 18 point.

Change the main heading to font size 22 point.

Save your document as **Chart_2**.

Have a look at Figure 5.72 and see how the change makes the detail of the chart more legible.

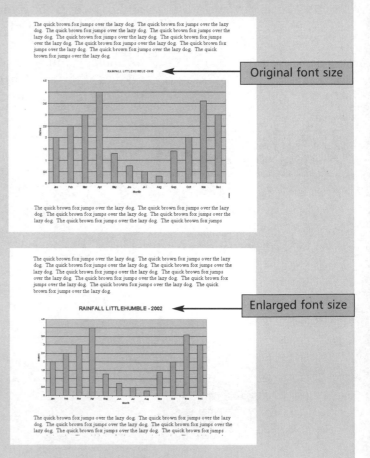

Figure 5.72

If your chart has labels attached to the data itself then the same procedure should be followed to change the properties of the data labels.

Formatting a chart's data series

The data series of a chart can also be formatted using similar techniques to those outlined above. Format a series of data (in the previous example the series would be columns in the rainfall chart) by double-clicking on the series; the dialogue box shown in Figure 5.73 now appears.

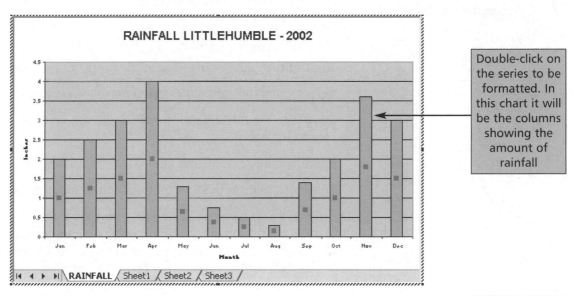

Double-click on the series to be formatted. In this chart it will be the columns showing the amount of rainfall

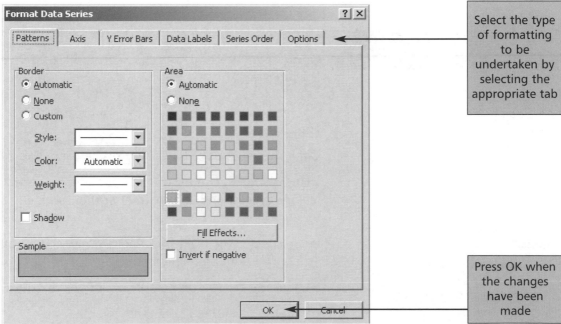

Select the type of formatting to be undertaken by selecting the appropriate tab

Press OK when the changes have been made

Figure 5.73

Where there are two sets of data and the chart is to be printed with a black-only printer it can be useful to change the colours to patterns so that the data sets are easily distinguishable from each other.

Importing datafiles

Since OCR does not prescribe any specific software for you to use to complete this unit, the data files provided for you to use in assignments are in .csv (comma separated values) format. This simply means that instead of, say, having an Excel file saved in its normal .xls format the file has been saved in a way that the data is separated by commas. You will not notice any significant difference, but using a generic format such as .csv allows the file to be opened and used by a variety of packages other than Microsoft software.

The simplest and most effective way of importing a datafile is to follow this procedure:

Open the file to be imported in Excel.

Highlight the data range (or all the data) to be imported.

Select Copy from the Edit option on the main menu.

Switch to the document into which the file is to be imported (normally Word).

Postion the cursor at the point where the file is to be placed.

Select Paste from the Edit options on the main menu.

The file will now be pasted as a table into the target document. Being a table all normal formatting on the table, such as column widths, borders and shading, fonts sizing etc., can be carried out on the imported data table. Now have a go at importing a simple .csv datafile from Excel into a Word document.

TIP

Opening files in Excel

First select Microsoft Excel from the programs list on the Start menu. Select File, Open…. Locate the file from the website, or your hard disk if you have already transferred the website files. Make sure the All Files option is selected in the Files of type: box at the bottom of the Open dialogue box. Click on the .csv file to be used and click OK.

Try it out

Open Car_Sales.doc from the Sample Files sub-folder in My Documents.

Open Car_Sales_July.csv in Excel.

Highlight cells A1:D9.

Copy the contents of these cells to the clipboard.

Insert the datafile after the first paragraph of **Car_Sales.doc** leaving at least one line space after the last line of the paragraph.

Paste the datafile from the clipboard into the document using Edit, Paste from the main menu.

Format the heading row in the datafile with 10% shading.

Format the heading in the table to bold.

Adjust the width of the table so that the heading is not word wrapped.

Save the file as **Car_Sales_July** on your floppy disk.

Close both working files (Word and Excel).

Your document should look similar to Figure 5.74.

TIP

Copying to clipboard

After highlighting the data

Select Edit on the main menu.

Select Copy.

You will notice an animated dotted line around the highlighted cells.

RESULTS OF THE CAR SALES COMPETITION FOR JULY

I am delighted to announce the winner of the sales competition for July. As you can see from the table below July was a good month for all the sales team but Andy managed to pip Peter to the post by one.

CAR SALES COMPETITION - JULY 2003		
CHARLIE	14	
PETER	16	
ANDY	17	
JOAN	15	
JONATHAN	10	
JED	12	
SUSAN	14	

Again many congratulations to you all and Andy in particular. The prize for this month's competition is an all expenses paid trip to Venice for a long weekend. There will not be a competition next month as a number of the team will be away on holiday and others are attending the sales convention in Brighton. Competitions will start again in September and run through to December.

Figure 5.74

You should now be able to:

- insert an image into a document
- format the layout properties of an image
- resize an image
- import a chart and change its properties
- import a datafile.

Now put together some of the skills learnt in the last section by completing the following build-up exercise.

Build-up Exercise 1: Stage 5

Open Bellings.doc in Word.

Insert Belling_Map.jpg in the Catalogues paragraph after 'A map showing how to find us is shown below.' Ensure that the size of the picture is contained within the margins of the document.

Insert the bar chart **Repeats.xls** (from sample files) in the About Bellings paragraph after '....through repeat business shown in the chart below' ensuring that the chart is within the margins.

Format the data and axis fonts as follows:

X- and Y-axis titles	14 points
X- and Y-axis labels	14 points
Chart title font	18 points

Insert the following paragraph with a sub heading 'Range of Items' after the Catalogues paragraph:

'For this September's sale we are pleased to announce that the range of antiques on offer is excitingly broad and there should be something for most collectors and enthusiasts. The information below shows the range of antiques currently in the catalogue with a guide to the anticipated prices they may attract.'

Insert the datafile **Antiques.csv** (from the Sample Files folder in My Documents) immediately below the last sentence of the paragraph Range of Items.

Insert the table 'Venues', created in Stage 4, after the last paragraph.

Finally ensure that no datafile crosses the page boundaries and that there is no more than a two-line space at the bottom of each page.

Your final document should look similar to Figure 5.75.

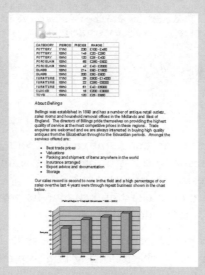
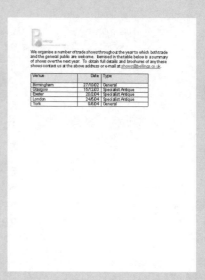

Figure 5.75

You have completed all the requirements of OCR for the core unit on creating, managing and integrating files.

Now have a go at the full practical assignment below. A solution to this assignment can be found in Appendix 2.

Practical assignment 1

Create, manage and integrate files

Scenario

You are the secretary for the senior partner in a motorcycle training company called BKS. Your boss has noticed that there is a backlog of students awaiting training because the pass rate for the theory test has reduced dramatically. He has been carrying out some analysis of these results and decided to offer additional training for the theory test. Those students who decide to take up this offer will be given a discount. You have been asked to prepare a brief on the proposals for all the instructors.

To produce this brief you will need the following files:

	File location	
■ A text file that forms the basic brief to which you will need to make a number of am endments and also import a variety of files.	Folder: Filename:	Sample Files **Theory_Test.doc**
■ An Excel spreadsheet containing a chart showing the student pass rates over a six month period.	Folder: Filename:	Sample Files **First_Passes.xls**
■ The company logo	Folder: Filename:	Sample Files **BKS_Logo.jpg**
■ A datafile containing details of student bookings for the month of January 2003.	Folder: Filename:	Sample Files **Student_Bookings.csv**

In carrying out this exercise you should consult the house style sheet to ensure the document layout is as required.

Part of this exercise requires you to create a table with certain data and format. To include the relevant data you will need to consult the student booking sheets.

You will use the following software to complete this exercise:

■ Word

■ Excel

■ Access

Your work should be saved on a new floppy disk or your hard disk.

Practical assignment 1

House style sheet

Page setup

Orientation		Portrait
Margins	**Top**	2.5 cm
	Bottom	2.5 cm
	Left	3.0 cm
	Right	3.0 cm

Header BKS_Logo   Left-aligned

Footer Date   Left-aligned   Page number   Right-aligned

Spacing Single spacing

Text styles

Text	Font	Text size	Style	Alignment
Heading	Sans serif	16 point	Bold, capital	Centred
Sub-headings	Sans serif	14 point	Bold, capital	Left
Body	Sans serif	12 point		Justified
Bullet text	Sans serif	12 point		
Tables	Sans serif	12 point	With gridlines	Column heading – centred, bold, 10% shading Text – left Numeric data – right-aligned Dates – right-aligned
Imported datafile	Sans serif	12 point	With gridlines	Column heading – centred, bold, 10% shading. Text – left Numeric – right Dates – right
Graph/chart	Text sans serif	Legible		

Note

Spacing between headings, sub-headings and paragraphs must be applied consistently.

Avoid widows and orphans.

Text, images, graphs and lines must not be superimposed.

Imported data is not to be split across pages.

Graphs and charts must be positioned within the margins of the page.

Spell check the document.

Practical assignment 1

Exercise brief

Assessment objectives	Stage	
		In completing this exercise you will be working with a number of files so you will need to setup a folder either on a floppy or your hard disk.
1a	1	On your floppy or hard disk create a new folder and call it BKS.
1e	2	Copy the files:
		Theory_Test.rtf
		First_Passes.xls
		Student_Bookings.csv
		BKS_Logo.jpg
		From the Sample Files folder in My Documents to your new folder:
1b	3	Open the file called **Theory_Test.rtf** and save as a Word document.
2e	4	Using the spell checker check the document for spelling errors.
2a 2b 2c 3b 2d 2e 3c 3d 3e 4c 4d 4f 5a 5b 5c 5d	5	Referring to the draft document on pages 71–2 make the changes indicated.
4h	6	Using the search and replace function replace Theory Test with Theory Exam wherever it occurs (six occurrences in all).
4a 4b 4e	7	Apply the page layout and house style as indicated on the house style sheet – Practical assignment 1.
2e	8	Recheck for any spelling errors.
1b	9	Save your document to the newly created folder BKS using the **Theory_Test** name.
3e	10	Print the document.
1b	11	Close the document and application.
1f	12	Rename the BKS folder **BKS_Bike_Training.**
1a	13	Create a new folder in the working folder and call it **Dumps.**
1d	14	Move the files **First_Passes**, **Student_Bookings**, **BKS_Logo** to the Dumps folder.
1h	15	Produce a screen printout of the folders and the files they contain.

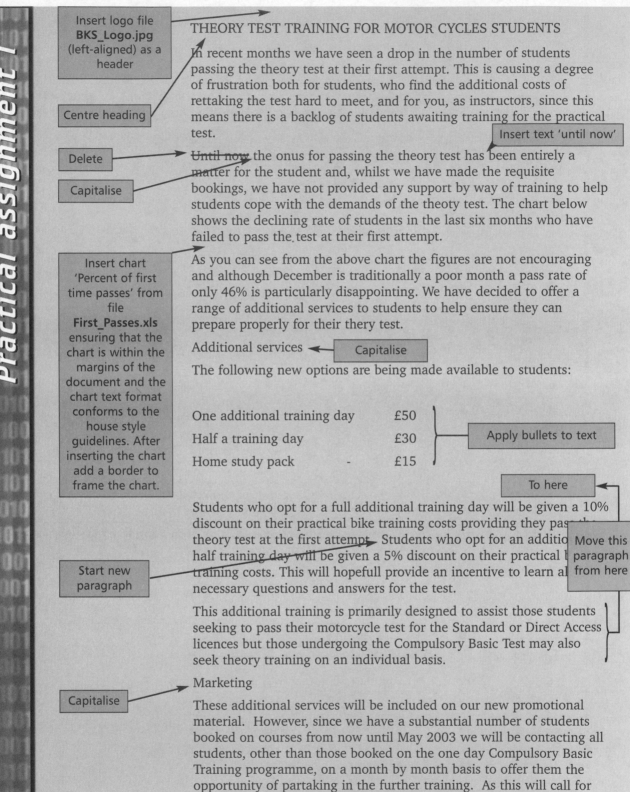

Practical assignment 1

THEORY TEST TRAINING FOR MOTOR CYCLES STUDENTS

[Insert logo file **BKS_Logo.jpg** (left-aligned) as a header]

[Centre heading]

In recent months we have seen a drop in the number of students passing the theory test at their first attempt. This is causing a degree of frustration both for students, who find the additional costs of rettaking the test hard to meet, and for you, as instructors, since this means there is a backlog of students awaiting training for the practical test.

[Delete] [Capitalise]

[Insert text 'until now']

Until now the onus for passing the theory test has been entirely a matter for the student and, whilst we have made the requisite bookings, we have not provided any support by way of training to help students cope with the demands of the theoty test. The chart below shows the declining rate of students in the last six months who have failed to pass the test at their first attempt.

[Insert chart 'Percent of first time passes' from file **First_Passes.xls** ensuring that the chart is within the margins of the document and the chart text format conforms to the house style guidelines. After inserting the chart add a border to frame the chart.]

As you can see from the above chart the figures are not encouraging and although December is traditionally a poor month a pass rate of only 46% is particularly disappointing. We have decided to offer a range of additional services to students to help ensure they can prepare properly for their thery test.

Additional services [Capitalise]

The following new options are being made available to students:

One additional training day   £50
Half a training day   £30
Home study pack   -   £15

[Apply bullets to text]

[To here]

Students who opt for a full additional training day will be given a 10% discount on their practical bike training costs providing they pass the theory test at the first attempt. Students who opt for an additio half training day will be given a 5% discount on their practical training costs. This will hopefull provide an incentive to learn al necessary questions and answers for the test.

[Move this paragraph from here]

[Start new paragraph]

This additional training is primarily designed to assist those students seeking to pass their motorcycle test for the Standard or Direct Access licences but those undergoing the Compulsory Basic Test may also seek theory training on an individual basis.

Marketing [Capitalise]

These additional services will be included on our new promotional material. However, since we have a substantial number of students booked on courses from now until May 2003 we will be contacting all students, other than those booked on the one day Compulsory Basic Training programme, on a month by month basis to offer them the opportunity of partaking in the further training. As this will call for setting up a completely new programme the theory training will be offered from week one of the new training year in January. Our booking schedule for weeks 1 - 4 is shown in the table below:

> Insert a table containing five columns with the headings of Course, Course No, Start, End and Students. Include data contained in the sheets named BOOKINGS FOR JANUARY 2003. Only include records for Direct Access Licence and Standard Licence courses. Direct Access courses should be coded as DAS and Standard Licence courses coded as SLC. Date format should be English (short date format). Gridlines and borders on the table should be shown. Ensure that only the data asked for is included and that all data is visible and that column widths are sufficient to ensure words are not split.

As will be appreciated the extended programme will call for amendments to made to the schedule and final details will be advised to all trainers once the January uptake has been evaluated. However, it is likely that three day programes will now run from Monday to Thursday and from Tuesday to Friday.

New Booking Dates ◄—— Capitalise

Some students may wish to change their booking dates and you should contact your individual students, once they have decided whether or not to opt for additional training, to see whether their current booking is still acceptable. A list of students and the courses they are currently booked on for January is shown in the following table.

You will be advised in the next couple of weeks whether students, once contacted, wish to undertake additional training. The central office will not be asking students whether their present booked dates are still acceptable. This will be left to individual trainers to arrange with students.

> Insert here the datafile **Student_Bookings.csv** found on the website.

BOOKINGS FOR JANUARY 2003

Serial: 1   **Training Week:** 1

Date: 30/12/2002	**Day:** Monday		**Duration** 3		**End:** 1/1/2003	
Course: Direct Access Licence		**Course No:** 1201				
Bike (cc): 500	**Cost:** 300					
Students: 3	**Trainer:** BC					

Serial: 2   **Training Week:** 1

Date: 1/1/2003	**Day:** Wednesday		**Duration:** 3		**End:** 3/1/2003	
Course: Standard Licence		**Course No:** 1123				
Bike (cc): 125	**Cost:** 250					
Students: 2	**Trainer:** KL					

Serial: 3   **Training Week:** 2

Date: 6/1/2003	**Day:** Monday		**Duration:** 3		**End:** 8/1/2003	
Course: Direct Access Licence		**Course No:** 1202				
Bike (cc): 500	**Cost:** 300					
Students: 4	**Trainer:** BC					

Serial: 4   **Training Week:** 2

Date: 8/1/2003	**Day:** Wednesday		**Duration:** 3		**End:** 10/1/2003	
Course: Direct Access Licence		**Course No:** 1203				
Bike (cc): 500	**Cost:** 300					
Students: 2	**Trainer:** MH					

Serial: 5   **Training Week:** 2

Date: 8/1/2003	**Day:** Wednesday		**Duration:** 1		**End:** 8/1/2003	
Course: Compulsory Basic Training	**Course No:** 1118					
Bike (cc): 125	**Cost:** 60					
Students: 3	**Trainer:** HI					

Serial:	6	Training Week:	3			
Date:	13/1/2003	Day:	Monday	Duration: 3	End:	15/1/2003
Course:	Direct Access Licence	Course No:	1204			
Bike (cc):	500	Cost:	300			
Students:	2	Trainer:	BC			

Serial:	7	Training Week:	3			
Date:	13/1/2003	Day:	Monday	Duration: 1	End:	13/1/2003
Course:	Compulsory Basic Training	Course No:	1119			
Bike (cc):	125	Cost:	60			
Students:	3	Trainer:	HI			

Serial:	8	Training Week:	3			
Date:	15/1/2003	Day:	Wednesday	Duration: 3	End:	17/1/2003
Course:	Standard Licence	Course No:	1124			
Bike (cc):	125	Cost:	250			
Students:	3	Trainer:	KL			

Serial:	9	Training Week:	4			
Date:	20/1/2003	Day:	Monday	Duration: 3	End:	22/1/2003
Course:	Standard Licence	Course No:	1125			
Bike (cc):	125	Cost:	250			
Students:	3	Trainer:	KL			

Serial:	10	Training Week:	4			
Date:	20/1/2003	Day:	Monday	Duration: 3	End:	22/1/2003
Course:	Direct Access Licence	Course No:	1205			
Bike (cc):	500	Cost:	300			
Students:	3	Trainer:	BC			

Serial: 11   **Training Week:** 4

Date: 22/1/2003	**Day:** Wednesday	**Duration:** 1	**End:** 22/1/2003

Course: Compulsory Basic Training   **Course No:** 1120

Bike (cc): 125   **Cost:** 60

Students: 3   **Trainer:** HI

Serial: 12   **Training Week:** 4

Date: 22/1/2003	**Day:** Wednesday	**Duration:** 3	**End:** 24/1/2003

Course: Direct Access Licence   **Course No:** 1206

Bike (cc): 500   **Cost:** 300

Students: 3   **Trainer:** DT

Serial: 13   **Training Week:** 4

Date: 27/1/2003	**Day:** Monday	**Duration:** 3	**End:** 29/1/2003

Course: Standard Licence   **Course No:** 1126

Bike (cc): 125   **Cost:** 250

Students: 2   **Trainer:** KL

Serial: 14   **Training Week:** 4

Date: 27/1/2003	**Day:** Monday	**Duration:** 3	**End:** 29/1/2003

Course: Direct Access Licence   **Course No:** 1207

Bike (cc): 500   **Cost:** 300

Students: 1   **Trainer:** DT

Serial: 15   **Training Week:** 4

Date: 27/1/2003	**Day:** Monday	**Duration:** 1	**End:** 27/1/2003

Course: Compulsory Basic Training   **Course No:** 1121

Bike (cc): 125   **Cost:** 60

Students: 2   **Trainer:** HI

Serial:	16	**Training Week:**	4				
Date:	29/1/2003	**Day:**	Wednesday	**Duration:**	3	**End:**	31/1/2003
Course:	Standard Licence		**Course No:**	1127			
Bike (cc):	125	**Cost:**	250				
Students:	21	**Trainer:**	HI				

Serial:	17	**Training Week:**	4				
Date:	29/1/2003	**Day:**	Wednesday	**Duration:**	3	**End:**	31/1/2003
Course:	Direct Access Licence		**Course No:**	1208			
Bike (cc):	500	**Cost:**	300				
Students:	3	**Trainer:**	BC				

Assessment

This assessment section is designed to help you understand what is required for each of the units. Each of the units are dealt with by looking at:

- the assessment criteria – what do they mean and how are they structured
- the type of assessment – whether it is an examination or a locally assessed assignment or series of tasks
- how to go about completing what is needed for the unit, or how to prepare for the examination
- what you need to look out for and ensure that you have done
- what the examiners or assessors are looking for from your work

Each of the units has a theme of assessment, which can be best described as:

- **Unit 1 – Preparing business communications**: asks you to create business documents by looking at provided information. You are expected to use the correct style and tone, understand why you are creating the documents (their purpose and audience) and use accurate English.

- **Unit 2 – Maintaining effective working relations with colleagues and customers:** this unit has two elements, the first of which needs you to take part in two different team activities. You have to meet the first six objectives, whilst involved in the activities, and then use your own experience of the activities to tackle the last two objectives (which are the reviews). The second element requires you to interact with customers on two different occasions. On both occasions you need to cover objectives 1–5 and 7 and 8. On one of the occasions you need to cover objective 6.

- **Unit 3 – Working in business organisations:** this asks you to look at how businesses are organised, how they develop and operate, their different working practices and working conditions and the rights and responsibilities of employers and employees. The examination targets each of the four sections of the unit.

- **Unit 4 – Following office procedures to complete tasks:** this focuses on office procedures (rules, guidelines, best practice) and requires you to understand the procedures and identify any problems encountered, as well as suggesting improvements. You will need to complete two tasks in each of the five different office-based activities, following the procedures to complete the tasks. You will also need to have witness statements completed to back up your own work.

- **Unit 5 – Create, manage and integrate files:** this is also a part of the OCR Level 2 Certificate for IT Users (CLAIT Plus). It is assessed by a three-hour practical examination, covering the five main areas, including the use of software to create and manage files and directories, using input devices to enter data, working with data files (using spreadsheets and databases), creating and printing integrated documents and formatting page layouts to match house styles.

Three of the units (Units 1, 3 and 5) are externally assessed by examination and the remaining two units (Units 2 and 4) are locally assessed and externally moderated.

We will now look at the five units in greater detail.

Unit 1 – Preparing business communications

Method of assessment: Written examination of 2.5 hours, plus 10 minutes reading time.

What you need to do

Above all, you will need to demonstrate your ability to handle complicated information. You will often be asked to find, in a complex series of documents, particular information and then present just that information in the correct format. If, for example, you were asked to suggest the travel arrangements for a manager at work, which meant they had to stay over at a hotel for the night, you would not simply hand over a train timetable and a copy of the *Yellow Pages* for that area, with the hotel section book-marked. Ideally you should suggest an appropriate train time, tell them the approximate length of the journey (in hours and minutes), how to get to the hotel and the telephone number and address of the hotel. This would be everything the manager would need to make the appropriate bookings,though you may have to suggest two or three hotels in case the first one is fully booked.

Obviously, whenever you take information from another source, you will be expected to make sure it is correct and that you have not made any mistakes. You will also have to make sure you choose the right format for the information you are presenting (such as a memo or a business letter). In most cases, you will also have to ensure you have used the correct vocabulary and style of language for the situation. Most communications need to be formal, but not unfriendly. The last thing to remember is to check your spelling, the length of the sentences and the grammar used. Neither you nor your business would wish to give a poor impression to the reader of the communication.

The assessment objectives for this unit are:

1 **Use accepted formats and conventions when preparing routine business documents.**
   This means you should know what a standard letters, e-mails, faxes, memos, forms, agendas, business notes, reports, articles, job descriptions, leaflets, notices and advertisements look like. As

outlined in the textbook, each of these forms of communication have 'conventions', which means they have standard formats, as well as ways of addressing the person it is aimed at and of closing the communication.

2 **Analyse, extract and adapt information to meet a given purpose.**
This means reading the information you have been given and then identifying what is relevant to what you have been asked to find out. It often means that some of the information, although important, may not be relevant; this should be left out of your communication. If there are contradictions in the information, you need to make sure you present the right information. Once you have found what you need, you should then put the relevant information into one of the formats described in the first assessment objective. Above all, the presentation of your information must be clear; using sub-headings and paragraphs to break it up.

3 **Use of appropriate tone and style for different purposes.**
There are times when you can be casual and use normal speech, but in most business communications you need to choose the right tone, style and words. You would not write to a customer and open the letter with 'Frankie old mate', but use the more formal 'Dear Ms Smith'. An examiner would not be pleased if you used slang words, abbreviations or were casual in the way in which you wrote your communications. Remember that tone and style are as important as what it is you are saying.
You may need to be tactful or diplomatic in your presentation, and you may also need to be persuasive (in other words, put forward your view in order to persuade someone to do something). Remember that the wrong style and tone reflects badly on you and on your employer.

4 **Use English correctly.**
You should always check what you have written and make sure there are as few spelling and grammar mistakes as possible. Pay attention to your punctuation and do not be tempted to leave out full stops – long, single-sentence paragraphs are very off-putting to the reader. If you do use complicated sentences, look out for places where commas or semi-colons should go. Above all, think about how your presentation is structured and organise it properly into paragraphs.

Areas to focus on

- Revise the standard formats of business documents and their conventions (including headings, methods of addressing the addressee and methods of closing).
- When you are asked to produce a named type of business document, make sure you use that format and no other.
- Read magazine articles or newspaper features, and write down the key points as practice in summarising information and identifying important information.

- Don't be tempted in the examination to pad out your business documents with irrelevant information. Remember the key is to put in only the relevant information, in the right format.

- When you are using two or more sources of information, check that the facts are correct and tally with one another. Make sure you check all the information in these sources very carefully.

- Make sure your documents are easy to follow and read. Don't be frightened about using paragraphs and sub-headings in the right format if you think it will be easier to follow.

- Make sure that everything you put into the document has a logical sequence. Think about the beginning, the middle and the end of the document.

- Use the right words; don't forget you can take a dictionary into the examination with you.

- Remember that you are writing a business document and not a chatty letter to a friend. Make sure your style and tone reflect this fact.

- You may need to deal with a complaint or other non-routine situation. Again your style and tone may need to be adapted for this.

- Remember that you will be asked to write to a particular person, or a particular audience. Adapt the contents of your communication to reflect this. Don't use technical terms in a general letter in case the reader would not understand them. You may need to be tactful (careful and thoughtful), you may need to be diplomatic (being careful not to upset or annoy), or you may need to be persuasive (not aggressive, but assertive).

- Your dictionary should help you with words that are difficult, but keep an eye on how your sentences look. Overly long, complicated sentences, like this one, with plenty of commas, and separate ideas may (in some cases) be very difficult to follow, for most people anyway. Avoid them if you can. If you do need to use long sentences, break them up at the appropriate places with semi-colons. Semi-colons are used to pause a sentence before another, additional (but related) thought is written.

- Use paragraphs for each different point in your presentation. In a letter, for example, the opening paragraph should say clearly why the letter has been written. The following paragraphs then deal in turn with the various points you need to make. The last but one paragraph sums up the content of the letter and the final paragraph tells the reader what they need to do (if anything).

What the assessors and examiners are looking for

The examination is usually broken up into four different questions, each of which will ask you to read and use the information to present a particular type of business document. Usually, but not always, the questions are equally weighted (worth 20 marks each). In other cases, some are worth more (up to 24 marks) with others worth less (15 marks). Take a note of this when you are reading the paper and make sure you split you time on each question according to the value of that question. The total marks available are 80, so as a guide this means just under 2 minutes per mark.

For each question the examiners look at the four assessment objectives, so they will be marking you on:

- layout (have you used the right format and style?)
- content (have you put in what is required and left out what is not needed?)
- tone and style (do these match the purpose of your letter?)
- Use of English (have you structured your sentences correctly, used the right grammar and punctuation and used the correct spelling?)

Usually, the bulk of the marks are awarded for the content, but you could lose up to three quarters of the marks if you ignore the other three things examiners are concerned with in marking your paper. Here is a checklist of what the examiners will be looking for:

- that you have used the format asked for in the question
- that you have used the right conventions for that format
- whether you have identified and included relevant information and excluded irrelevant information
- whether you have checked your sources of information carefully and not made a mistake in putting the information you've chosen into your presentation
- that you have adapted the information for the presentation (and not just copied it, without changes, from the source(s))
- that your presentation is easy to follow, doesn't jump around and is logical
- that you have used paragraphs and sub-headings where appropriate
- that you have used a wide enough vocabulary to suit the purposes of the document
- that your style and tone are generally business-like and polite.
- that you have checked your spellings, punctuation, sentence structure and overall layout.

Normally you would need to achieve a 50% grade to be awarded a pass, between 65 and 74% for a credit and 75% or more for a distinction.

Finally, the tasks required in the examination are set in a scenario. You will be given all of the information needed to complete these tasks and you do not have to invent information. If there are links between the questions (for instance they may refer to the same background information or scenario), you may have to use information from one question in another.

Unit 2 – Maintaining effective working relationships with colleagues and customers

Method of assessment: Locally assessed and externally moderated.

What you need to do

As there are two elements in this unit, we will deal with them separately. The first element, 'Working with colleagues', asks this of you:

You will need to be involved in two different team activities in order to meet the assessment objectives 1 to 6 (we will look at these shortly). Each of the assessment objectives needs to be met in both of the team activities. During the team activities you will need to:

- Carry out a task which contributes to the work the team has been set. An acceptable task can include collecting information from different sources, liaising with the other team members, reporting back your findings and solutions, or progressing follow-up activities.
- Show that you have liaised with at least two other members of the team during the work you have carried out for each of the tasks.
- Report back to the person who has set you the tasks.

Let's turn our attention to the six assessment objectives:

1 **Contribute to the work of a team.**
   Show you understand the importance of teamwork and how different team members have different roles. You should focus on target setting (what you have to do), planning (how you will do it and when), clarifying your objectives (being clear about what is required), identifying resources and timescales (what information or items you will need and when), exchanging information (sharing information with others) and cooperating with others (being useful, adaptable, understanding and doing what is expected of you).

2 **Confirm own responsibilities, including working arrangements.**
   You will need to show that you have thought about a number of things, these include:
   - what you need to do
   - what resources you (and the team) will need
   - setting a timetable for the activities (this is vital as some things will need to be completed early so that later tasks can be started on time)
   - what to do if you fall behind with the work (what can be done to catch up again)
   - who in the team should do particular tasks according to their skills and what they will need in order to carry out the task
   - what you should do and what you should not get involved with or worry about.

3 **Carry out tasks allocated.**
   You will need to show your own personal abilities to plan and prioritise your work, show that you have followed instructions (or

agreed ways of doing things). You must also prove that you have worked safely (used machinery and other equipment correctly), that you have respected confidentiality and security (remember at work you may be working on documents that are either confidential or secret), and that you have met your deadlines. You will also need to show your ability to solve any problems you may encounter.

4 **Work with others to complete tasks.**
This objective focuses on your ability to cooperate as a team member. You should make sure that you report your progress. Whenever you find out vital information that could be useful to the team, you should pass it on straight away. You should also offer help to other team members and not be too proud to accept help yourself. Remember that as a team you will encounter problems; you will be expected to deal with them together.

5 **Communicate effectively with others.**
During the team activities you will be expected to show your verbal and written communication skills. Make sure you use the right style and manner in work that has to be submitted and that you use the right language and tone during the activities. Remember you may have to deal with difficult situations (such as a team member not contributing enough), so tact and diplomacy are also important.

6 **Maintain effective working relationships.**
Remember that you are a team and that you cannot possibly hope to complete all of the activities on your own. You need to demonstrate that you understand your role and that you are an effective team member. Teams work best by cooperating, making joint decisions (democracy), negotiating rather than arguing and being able to work with people that have very different characters to your own. If there is conflict and misunderstanding you will need to be able to deal with it.

In addition to these six assessment objectives, which, as we will see, are dealt with by witness statements, you will have to write a report (which can be handwritten or word-processed) on your view of how the team worked. You will need to include thoughts on the following two assessment objectives:

7 **Review your contribution to the team activity.**
Think about your own work and whether the tasks given to you were completed and any personal objectives were met. Think about your own performance. How did you contribute to the team? What was your relationship like with the other team members?

8 **Review the overall performance of the team.**
You now need to turn your attention to the team as a whole. Did you, as a team, successfully complete the activity and meet your objectives? What was the performance of the other team members like? What strengths and weaknesses were obvious in the team? What helped you either to succeed or meant that you failed to complete the activity or meet the objectives?

Areas to focus on

Remember that you need to do the following in both of the team activities:

- show you are aware of the importance of teamwork and the importance of individuals in the team
- show that you know what the objectives are
- take part in the planning, and take an active role in deciding what has to be done, the order in which it needs to be done and when it needs to be done by
- show you understand what is required of you as an individual
- show you understand what steps you have to take to complete your tasks
- make sure you ask for and receive any resources needed to complete the tasks
- make sure you know when your tasks have to be finished by, how long you have got to do the work and what is your deadline
- show you know what to do if there is a problem and you cannot finish your tasks
- make regular reports back to the team on your progress
- know what is expected of you and what is not
- plan your work and prioritise your activities
- write down any instructions given to you and stick to them
- follow any agreed procedures
- make sure you work safely
- pass on any information you think the other team members might need
- ask for help if you need it and offer help if someone else is struggling
- make a statement about how you think you performed
- say something about your contribution to the activities as a whole
- mention how you got on with the other team members and how you dealt with problems
- show you understand the purpose of the team activity
- state whether the objectives were met
- briefly, rate the other team members in terms of their performance
- recognise the strengths and weaknesses of the team
- mention what helped in making the activities a success or what made them a failure.

What the assessors and examiners are looking for

Your centre will have devised the team activities and will be watching what you do during the activities. The task supervisor will prepare a witness statement for each of you, which contains the following sections, that are to be completed, about your performance:

- Communicate effectively with the other team members – make sure they understand what you mean.
- Show you understand your role and how it fits into the work of the team.

- Show you are an effective team member by being committed to the activities and to the team.
- Negotiate, cooperate and make democratic decisions in the team.
- Show you can work with different people, even if they have very different personalities from your own.
- Be understanding and helpful if there is conflict in the team.

The checklist above shows what you need to think about during the team activities. It is also very useful to be thinking out the review you will be asked to do after the activities. The assessor will be looking for about two pages of A4 (approximately 500 words). If you think about what you will need to say afterwards in the review whilst you are doing the activities, this will be quite an easy job to complete. You should include the following:

- evidence that you have understood the purpose of your tasks
- a description of what you did to complete the tasks
- a statement on your communication skills
- evidence of your ability to work with others
- the outcome of the work your carried out
- confirmation that you did carry out the work
- a statement as to whether or not you behaved in a business-like manner throughout the activities.

This witness statement will be compared against evidence checklists for each assessment requirement, to make sure you have covered all of the aspects of assessment objectives 1–6.

Assessment objectives 7 and 8 require you to write your review. You will need to make sure that:

- your work is neat
- there are no spelling mistakes
- punctuation and grammar are acceptable
- you have been clear
- your statements are logical and linked.

Above all, you must not be vague about your contribution and thoughts. Here are some acceptable examples:

- 'I have completed my tasks by the deadline.'
- 'I have contributed as a team member.'
- 'The team did not work well and we did not finish the activity.'

Here are some better ways of saying similar things in your review:

- 'After I had been given my tasks, my first job was to work out what I needed. I checked that the stationery was available and that the library had copies of the magazine for the past six months. I also checked that I did need to complete my research by 3.00 p.m.'
- 'I attended all of the team meetings which took place every hour for five minutes. We shared our information and made sure that we were all up to date. When one of us had fallen behind we helped them catch up.'

- 'Two of the team members did not seem to be interested and one of them left in the afternoon as she had a headache. We did find it difficult to agree on most things, which meant that although I had finished my tasks, the rest of the work was not completed by 4.00 p.m.'

Element 2 of this unit, 'Working with customers', also has eight assessment objectives. This, too, is locally assessed and externally moderated.

You will need to be involved in two situations in which you communicate with customers to standards that would normally be acceptable at work. Assessment objectives 1 to 5 and 7 to 8 must be met on both occasions, whilst assessment objective 6 needs to be met at least once. The customer communication situations should include:

- a telephone conversation with a customer
- a situation where you have to find out or check information for a customer
- identify and begin follow-up action on behalf of a customer.

Let's turn our attention to the seven assessment objectives:

1 **Present a positive image to customers.**
   You need to be aware that there are many different types of customers, both within the organisation and outside of it. In work you will be expected to take note of your style of communication, personal presentation and body language towards these customers. You will also need to be aware that the way in which you present yourself to a customer can reflect well or poorly on the business for which you work. You will also need to ensure that whatever the enquiry or problem presented to you by a customer, it needs to be dealt with in an effective manner.

2 **Follow company procedures for communicating with customers.**
   Many organisations have preferred ways in which you should deal with customers, either face-to-face or on the telephone. Most of them will require you to deal with customers promptly and not make them wait for answers or help. Businesses will expect you to address the customer correctly, such as calling them 'Mr' or 'Mrs' or 'Sir' or 'Madam'. There will be ways in which the business prefers to deal with complaints from customers and these procedures should always be followed. There may also be circumstances when you must not pass on confidential information that is not supposed to be told to anyone outside the organisation.

3 **Interact effectively with customers.**
   You will need to show that you understand the importance of communication and how to use verbal and non-verbal communication skills. In order to find out exactly what a customer needs, you will often have to ask questions. Sometimes you may need to ask further questions in order to be absolutely sure what the customer is asking for. There are circumstances when communication is difficult with certain customers; perhaps they are

hard of hearing or English is not their first language? You will need to 'think on your feet' about how best to deal with these situations.

4 Use appropriate tone and manner.
Apart from making sure that you use the appropriate tone and language with customers at all times, you will also need to be aware of the importance of being helpful, polite, calm and confident.

5 Convey information clearly and accurately.
Many customers will expect you to have all the answers, and the answers that you do give them must be accurate, clear and concise. There are times, however, when you may not have the necessary information at your fingertips and you may need to refer to someone else who can help you. Remember, though, that you have to be careful what information you give to customers, as some may be restricted to within the organisation.

6 Resolve difficulties using organisational procedure.
Most businesses will have set procedures to deal with particular situations, such as problems, queries and complaints. In order to deal with these effectively, you need to recognise what the customer is asking and to explain to them clearly what will now be done for them. Some minor problems, queries and complaints can be dealt with immediately, but others will need to be referred to more senior members of staff who have more expertise in dealing with such issues. Whatever the problem facing the customer, you should always apologise, though not admit on the business's behalf that it is the fault of the business.

7 Record information accurately.
It is of vital importance that records are kept of most of the interactions you have with customers. Most businesses keep records of enquiries and requests for information. This enables the business to follow up any customer contact and evaluate the way in which they dealt with particular customers in particular circumstances. You will need to show that you understand how to record interactions with customers and how to follow up complaints.

8 Ensure customers' requirements have been met.
This means you will have to show that you can summarise a situation and confirm to the customer that particular decisions have been made. In order to do this it would be normal procedure to keep a written record and to check with the customer that the details are correct. Above all, you will be expected to show that you know that the customer must be told about any further action and what will happen next.

Areas to focus on

Remember that you will need to show on two different occasions that your ability to communicate with customers is of an acceptable business standard. You will be expected to show the following:

- that you have identified whether the customer is an internal or an external customer (and then acted appropriately)
- that you have presented yourself well and given a good impression of yourself and of the business
- that you have had a positive and friendly attitude towards the customer
- that you have shown support and cooperation towards colleagues whilst the customer has been present
- that you have used appropriate body language
- that you have dealt promptly with the customer
- that you have followed company procedures in greeting the customer
- that you have followed company procedures for dealing with complaints and confidentiality issues
- that you have listened to the customer and clarified what they have said by asking questions and checking that you have understood what the customer wants
- that you have been tactful and used the appropriate language and tone
- that you have been confident and in control of the situation
- that you have double-checked information either given to you by the customer, or required by the customer, and made sure that they have the correct information
- that you can handle simple problems, but recognise when the situation requires you to refer it to a relevant individual in the business
- that you have apologised on behalf of the business, without admitting liability
- that you have recorded the information accurately so that the information can be referred to in the future and any follow-ups can be made
- that the conversation with the customer ends in an appropriate manner, with them knowing what has been decided, what further action will be taken and when it will be taken, and that a written record has been made

What the assessors and examiners are looking for

The key to achieving this element is to make sure that you interact with the customers on both occasions in a business-like and efficient manner. The supervisor will complete a witness statement that confirms that you have carried out these interactions and behaved in an acceptable manner. Remember that the assessor will be looking to ensure that you have met assessment objectives 1 to 5, 7 and 8 on both occasions and assessment objective 6 (resolving difficulties using organisational procedures) on at least one occasion. You will need to demonstrate the following:

- that having identified the type of customer, you deal with them in the appropriate manner, whilst maintaining a good impression, being friendly, positive, cooperative and using the right body language

- that you follow business procedures and deal with customers promptly, greet and address them correctly, use procedures to deal with complaints and maintain confidentiality
- that you interact well with the customer and listen, ask questions, check their understanding and use appropriate body language or use of language on the telephone whilst being tactful
- that you use the right language and tone, that you are polite, helpful and confident
- that you pass on and receive accurate information by repeating details, checking understanding and maintaining confidentiality
- that you can resolve simple problems and are able to identify who needs to deal with the situation if you cannot
- that you are able to apologise or express regret without admitting liability
- that you record your interaction with the customer in an accurate manner, which allows follow-up and evaluation
- that you have ensured that the customer is happy with the outcome of the conversation. You will need to make sure that they are clear about what has taken place, what will be done and when, and that you have kept a written record of the interaction.

Unit 3 – Working in business organisations

Method of assessment: Written examination of 2.5 hours, plus 10 minutes reading time.

What you need to do

This unit tests your understanding of how business works and what happens in business organisations. It also looks at the importance that a business places on having clear aims and objectives, which can assist it in planning its future activities. There are many different roles or jobs within a business organisation and each of these roles plays a part in making sure that the organisation's objectives are met. You will also be expected to understand how the working environment affects both employers and employees.

The assessment objectives are:

1 **Describe and compare business organisations.**
   As this assessment objective has three sub-sections, we will look at each of these in turn.
- You will need to know the difference between the various organisations in either the private or public sectors, with particular reference to who owns them, controls them and decides on their objectives, and the limits of their liability. You will also need to know about the advantages and disadvantages of the different types of organisations and why the different forms of ownership may change over a period of time.
- The second part of this assessment objective requires you to understand how businesses develop. You will need to understand what is meant by terms such as capital, liability, specialisation,

diversification, mergers, de-mergers and takeovers. You will also need to appreciate how changes in any of these can have an impact on the organisation itself.

- In the final part of this assessment objective you need to show an understanding of mission statements, objectives and strategic plans and how these determine the way in which a business operates.

2 **Explain how business organisations are structured.**
This assessment objective is split into four areas, which will bedealt with one at a time:

- You will need to understand and identify the different parts of a business organisation, such as accounts, human resources, marketing and administration.

- The second part of the assessment objective requires you to understand that most businesses are different from one another and organise themselves in different ways, according to the markets they serve, the type of products or services they sell, where they are located and whether they have a centralised headquarters or not. You will also need to understand how the different areas of the organisation, which you looked at in the first part of the learning objective, interact with one another.

- The third part requires you to understand the function of different job roles within an organisation and how responsibility and the ability to make decisions is dependent upon how senior a member of staff is within the overall organisation.

- The fourth part requires you to understand that administrative duties are carried out at almost every level of an organisation and that effective administration often underpins the success or failure of a business.

3 **Identify and explain effective working practices.**
This learning objective is also split into five different areas. Again we will look at them in turn:

- Part 1 requires you to show that you understand how important planning is in a business. Businesses need to prioritise what they do, make sure they have enough resources to carry out different activities, ensure that the progress of activities is reported back, meet deadlines, and be aware that every activity consists of a number of individual tasks, each of which has to be tracked. You need to understand that planning is vital to ensure success and that the business needs to make best use of its time and its employees. You will also need to appreciate issues such as confidentiality, and the needs and commitments of others within the organisation (who may not have the same set of priorities as yourself).

- The second part requires you to appreciate the importance of keeping your working area well organised and neat. This means that any equipment you use regularly, resources that you need, and probably individuals with whom you work, are close at hand. You will also need to understand that many businesses take the question of wasted resources very seriously and have put strategies in place to reduce wastage.

- The third part requires you to understand that in all working environments you need to be flexible. You will need to be able to monitor your progress and head off potential problems before they occur. No matter how well organised you are, you will be expected to deal with unexpected problems as they arise and cope with the fact that deadlines and targets are often changed.

- Part 4 of this assessment objective requires you to show that you understand that many things can affect your efficiency. You should understand that in order to carry out particular tasks, you do need to listen to the instructions. You should also be aware that you need to use your own time as efficiently as possible and not waste other people's time. This means that you must be aware that in a busy office you will be distracted and that effective communication is the only way in which people will respond to what you are asking or telling them. You must also be aware of the importance of following business procedures in all that you do at work.

- The final part of this assessment objective is to understand that no matter how perfect your own performance may be, there is always room for improvement. Obtaining feedback on what you have done is useful, as is setting targets and plans to improve your performance. You should also be aware that training opportunities are often available and that not only self-assessment is valuable, but also the opportunity to review your work with a manager.

4 **Identify and explain issues affecting working conditions.**
   This learning objective is also split into five sections:
   - The first section asks you to consider the importance of office layout and the way that equipment, individuals, lighting, noise, heating, ventilation, décor and working space can impact upon efficiency.

   - The second part asks you to appreciate the basics of health and safety, including the Health and Safety At Work Act (1974). You should be aware of potential hazards, how to take precautions, how to follow safe working practices and how to deal with low-risk issues. You will also need to be aware of how accidents and hazards are reported, what to do in the case of accidents, emergencies and fire, be aware of first-aid requirements and law relating to the use of computers and monitors.

   - The third part requires you to understand that employers have responsibilities under health and safety legislation. They must provide a healthy and safe workplace, have a health and safety policy, make risk assessments and take preventative measures. They must also train, appoint and consult safety representatives.

   - The fourth part asks you to state the main obligations an employer and employee have towards one another, which can be found in a contract of employment. You will need to be able to list, and possibly explain, the importance of issues such as working hours, job requirements, disciplinary issues and codes of behaviour.

The final part requires you to remember that there are other types of legislation that aim to protect both the employer and the employee at work, including issues such as unfair dismissal, discrimination and equality.

Areas to focus on

Although there are 17 different parts to the four assessment objectives in this unit, many of them are interlinked and lead on from one another. You should ensure that you:

- can remember the differences between the public and private sectors and the types of organisations that form part of these two groups, as well as their advantages and disadvantages, ownership, control, objectives and liability
- can understand that the type of ownership changes, or may change, over time as a business grows, or adapts
- review why organisations develop, primarily because they need more capital, wish to change their liability, specialise in certain area or diversify (get involved in new areas of activity). These can be achieved in a number of different ways, including mergers and takeovers. You should also be aware that any changes will affect both the business and its employees
- understand why businesses have mission statements and objectives and the purpose of strategic plans. You also need to remember that a business's objectives have a direct impact on the way that business operates
- review your notes regarding the different parts of most medium to large organisations and be able to explain briefly what different departments do and how they are expected to cooperate and support one another
- following on from your revision of the 'functional' areas of the business, understand that different organisations organise themselves in different ways, for a variety of reasons, but that the functional areas or departments still need to interact, cooperate and communicate with one another
- are clear that you understand what a typical organisation looks like, remembering that many of them look like a pyramid, with a handful of senior staff at the top and more members of staff as it broadens out towards the base. You will need to remember what a managing director, a manager or team leader does
- appreciate that nearly all organisations rely on an effective administrative system and that its effectiveness can have a positive impact on the organisation's overall performance
- review the importance of planning and how this helps a business clarify what has to be done, by whom, when and how. This means that a business prioritises and makes sure that they have sufficient resources at the right time
- review the best practices in organising your own work area and how poor organisation can affect your ability to carry out work efficiently

- understand that, increasingly, businesses are looking for a flexible workforce that can respond quickly to problems and deal with them in an efficient manner
- understand and list factors that could have a negative impact on efficiency and how you, as an individual, could improve your own work performance (such as training, reviews and self-assessment)
- remember that businesses will attempt to organise their office layout in the most efficient manner, taking into consideration what is being done, as well as health and safety issues
- remember the basics of the Health and Safety At Work Act, safe working practices, first aid, accident reporting, emergency procedures, as well as employee rights and responsibilities in these areas
- review what an employer is expected to do in relation to health and safety and the legally binding contract which is signed between the employer and the employee in relation to the terms and conditions of employment
- finally, understand the fundamentals of laws that protect employees, as well as equal opportunity legislation.

What the assessors and examiners are looking for

The examination is broken down into four separate questions, with three to four sub-questions each. You will notice from any sample papers you may have seen that each set of questions has an equal weighting, in other words they are all worth 20 marks. The important thing to note, however, is that some of the individual questions are worth up to 10 marks, whilst others are only worth 3 or 4. When you read through the examination paper for the first time, make sure you give yourself sufficient time to spend on the questions that are worth more marks. You should probably spend about 35 minutes on each set of questions; this will give you around 10 minutes at the end of the examination to read through what you have written.

When the examiners are offering 8 marks, for example, a question will probably ask you for 8 points. In other cases, when they offer 9, they may ask for 3 points in more detail.

The examiners will be working from a checklist that suggests the type of answer you should give. They will award you a mark for each point if you are asked to list, for example, advantages and disadvantages, and additional marks if you explain what you mean (this is true in cases when they ask you for three points and nine marks are available).

The four questions will each target one of the four sections in the specification. In other words, you can expect a question on different types of business organisation, the structure of organisations, working practices and working conditions. As with Unit 1, in order to achieve a pass, you will need to have reached 50% of the marks. A credit is awarded if you achieve between 65 and 74% and those achieving 75% or more will receive a distinction.

Unit 4 – Following office procedures to complete tasks

Method of assessment: Locally assessed and externally moderated.

What you need to do

This unit requires you to understand why office procedures are carried out and their importance in the office environment. Above all, this is a practical unit, which requires you to show that you can complete office procedures alone and then review and evaluate both your own work and the procedures themselves. There are four assessment objectives. These are:

1 **Identify and describe a range of office-based activities requiring procedures.**
   This means that you must be aware of the main office procedures, including the storage and retrieval of information, the reproduction of information, the sending and receiving of information, stock maintenance and post processing and all of the individual steps within these procedures.

2 **Explain the purpose of procedures.**
   This means that you should be aware that all of the different activities have different procedures and that the procedures have a purpose, such as quality assurance, ease of access and safe working.

3 **Follow procedures to carry out office tasks.**
   This may appear to be a very long and daunting list of office tasks, but essentially you will need to remember the basic procedures for the storage and retrieval of information, the reproduction of information, the sending and receiving of information, the control of stock and the processing of post. Each of the activities has procedures for clear reasons, such as being able to find information when required in the case of storage and retrieval, or an accurate record of stock in the case of stock control.

4 **Review the ways in which procedures are implemented and their effectiveness.**
   Many businesses do not rely entirely on procedures being passed verbally from person to person; they also produce manuals and provide training. Office procedures allow a business to track documents, and set timescales and standards for internal communication. You should be aware of the fact that some office procedures are incomplete – they may be unclear, employees may not be familiar with them, they simply do not work, or there are no tracking systems in place. You should be able to suggest how office procedures could be improved in order to improve efficiency.

There are three parts to the assessment. Often you will be given a choice as to which office procedures you wish to focus upon. In the first part of the assessment you will need to identify and explain the purpose of two different office procedures relating to each of the following activities:

- storage and retrieval of information
- reproduction of information
- sending and receiving information
- controlling stock
- processing incoming and outgoing post.

Having identified and explained the purpose of the two different office procedures, you should now complete two tasks in each of two different contexts. You will probably be offered the opportunity to choose two office-based activities from the list in the first part of the assessment. Here is some guidance on what you will be expected to carry out:

Storage and retrieval of information

- Carry out filing on at least two occasions.
- On each occasion file at least six different documents or files.
- On each occasion file at least one document in each of the main systems (alphabetical, numerical, chronological).
- Over the two occasions create three new files.
- Over the two occasions archive three documents or files.
- Retrieve at least six documents or files.

Reproduction of information

- Carry out photocopying on at least two different occasions.
- On each occasion copy and assemble at least three documents in the correct order.
- Over the two occasions you must carry out single copying, multi-copying, back-to-back copying, enlarging and reducing, as well as using different types of paper.

Sending and receiving information

- On three occasions send a fax.
- On one occasion send a fax with three or more pages.
- On one occasion log, then distribute, at least five incoming faxes.

Controlling stock

- On two occasions issue stock against three requisitions.
- On at least one occasion check stock levels, reorder, take delivery of stock and store.
- On each occasion update the stock records.

Processing incoming and outgoing post

- On two occasions distribute at least ten items of post, which includes routine and non-routine items (including registered post or cheques).
- On two occasions despatch at least six items of post.
- On at least one occasion despatch an urgent item, a valuable item and a parcel.

The final part of the assessment requires you to review the procedures that you have followed. You will be required to produce around two sides of A4, in other words around 500 words. You should:

- include two ways in which each of the procedures you have used are supported and promoted, as well as commenting on their effectiveness
- identify any difficulties you encountered
- suggest any improvements to the procedures
- comment on the overall effectiveness of the procedure that you followed.

What the assessors and examiners are looking for

The evidence for the first part of this assessment requires you to clearly identify and describe procedures related to office-based activities. You must also explain the purpose of each of the procedures and how they benefit the organisation. The information that you provide will be entered onto an evidence sheet.

In the second part of this assessment, which is a practical one, your task supervisor will complete a witness statement that confirms that you have carried out the work to an acceptable standard and followed procedures. The task supervisor will be looking to ensure that you have carried out the following tasks, dependent upon the office-based activity that you have chosen:

- **Storage and retrieval of information** – that you have followed procedures on at least two different occasions. That on each occasion you have stored and retrieved six documents, files or pieces of information. That you have filed at least one document alphabetically, numerically and chronologically. That you have created three new folders or files and archived three documents or files. That you have worked safely (open and closed drawers with care and used the stapler correctly).
- **Reproduction of information** – that on at least two different occasions you have copied and assembled three documents to a required standard. That you have used different forms of copying, including reduction and enlarging, that you have collated and fastened pages, that if necessary you have replaced the paper in the photocopier, you have kept appropriate records, minimised waste, reported any problems and worked safely.
- **Sending and receiving information** – that you have followed procedures for sending and receiving information by fax on three different occasions. That on one occasion you have transmitted a fax of three pages or more, that you have prepared and completed cover sheets as required, checked the confirmation reports, logged and distributed five incoming faxes, replaced paper as required and reported any problems encountered.
- **Controlling stock** – on two occasions you must have issued stock against three or more requisitions. You must have maintained stock records (receipt and issue, running balance, minimum and

maximum levels). That on one occasion you have checked the stock levels and completed a purchase requisition or order as required. On one occasion you must have taken delivery of stock and stored it appropriately in a safe manner.

- **Processing incoming and outgoing post** – that on at least two occasions you have distributed at least ten items of post, including those requiring special attention. That on at least two occasions you have prepared at least six items of outgoing mail (including an urgent item, a valuable item and a parcel). That you have worked out the postage required on each occasion, kept records as appropriate and used relevant machines and equipment, such as letter openers, date stamps, franking machines and scales, in a safe manner.

The third part of the assessment requires you to write a review, where the assessor will be checking to see that you have carried out the following:

- provided a description of two ways in which each procedure is supported and promoted
- assessed the effectiveness of each of these procedures
- identified at least one difficulty with each procedure
- suggested at least one improvement to each procedure
- evaluated the effectiveness of each procedure.

Again, the examiners are looking for either handwritten or word-processed reviews that have been checked for spelling, punctuation and grammar. You should be clear about your statements and put your ideas down in a logical manner. Simply saying that a procedure was not effective and that you had problems is not enough. You should say, perhaps, that the manual was not clear, and that you suggest producing a flowchart, which shows each step involved.

Unit 5 – Create, manage and integrate files

Method of assessment: Practical assignment with a duration of three hours.

What you need to do

You may well have already completed Unit 5 if you have studied the OCR Level 2 Certificate for IT Users (CLAIT Plus). There are five major areas that require you to show that you can use software safely and securely to create and manage files, directories and folders, that you can use input devices to enter data, work with data files (database and spreadsheets), that you can create and print integrated documents that combine text and tables, images or charts and that you can format pages and manipulate text to adopt particular house styles.

The specific assessment objectives are:

1 **Manage files and directories/folders.**

You need to show that you can access files, directories and folders. You will also be required to show that you can create, name and rename these files, directories, sub-directories and folders. You need to understand the difference between Copy, Move and Delete when dealing with files. You should be able to Save files and documents and then access these existing files, which may be text, database, spreadsheets, images or charts. You need to be able to choose and then access the right software for a particular task. You should be able to produce printed evidence of a directory or folder's contents and also know the difference between documents, files and applications and know the purpose of file extensions.

2 **Enter data accurately from data input sheets and amend existing data.**

You should be able to understand the purpose and limitations of grammar and spellcheckers. You need to understand how to insert, delete and edit data and appreciate that accurate data entry is of vital importance and that you should proofread your work on screen, as well as the hard copy. You should also be able to understand how to encode data and how to incorporate any amendments to the text.

3 **Create and print an integrated document.**

You need to understand the procedures when transferring data between files and know the need for presenting documents. You need to be able to import and place data files and charts, how to save documents and print the integrated document.

4 **Format page layout and manipulate text according to house style.**

You need to understand why it might be necessary to change the orientation of a page and the layout. You need to understand the purpose of and to use headers and footers. You should understand that many businesses use particular house styles, such as font size and type, and be able to use them. You need to understand and use automatic fields in headers and footers and be able to use page breaks, paragraph breaks, line spacing and margins, as well as page formatting, special symbols, bullets and numbering, and the search and replace function to amend documents.

5 **Format tabular data.**

You need to know how to indent text and the methods used to achieve this. You need to know how to create a table, then alter the column width and cell alignment. You also need to be able to use different types of border and shading to aid the readability of the table.

Areas to focus on

- Practice creating and naming directories and folders.
- Practice opening, closing and saving existing files.
- Practice deleting and moving files, directories and folders.
- Practice copying, renaming and printing file, directory and folder structures.
- Practice entering text and numerical data into documents using dates in different formats.
- Practice encoding data.
- Practice using checkers, such as grammar and spelling.
- Using an existing file, import data into it, such as text, tables, images or charts. Check how the document looks and then print it.
- Using an existing document, change the page orientation and layout.
- Insert automatic fields in your header and footer and then amend them.
- Choose a house style and apply a particular font and size to the document.
- Break down paragraphs by using bullet points or numbering.
- Practice inserting special symbols, such as the © copyright symbol.
- Use the search and replace facility to change every occurrence of a particular word or statement.
- Create a table in a document; change the column widths and the cell alignments. Insert data into the table and then apply different types of borders and shading to the table.

What the examiners and assessors are looking for

The examiner will be looking to make sure that you have followed the instructions as outlined in the series of activities that make up the final assignment. Normally, the examination paper consists of a scenario, with supporting information for you to amend, and other information that you will have to reproduce and later import. There may be as many as 14 different steps and it is important for you to make sure that you have covered all of the tasks required.

Examiners will be looking for evidence that you have carried out particular objectives, such as moving, editing, deleting or resizing. Therefore it is vitally important for you to print out everything you produce at each stage. They will look for what they call 'critical errors'. These are serious problems that make a document unfit for its purpose. If, for example, an image is missing from a document, you will be penalised. If documents do not link together you will also lose marks.

In creating, managing and integrating files in particular, the following are considered to be critical errors:

- a missing data file
- a missing image
- a missing chart
- an incomplete document.

In addition to critical errors, they will also be looking for accuracy errors. These fall into two different categories:

- you may have not completed one of the assessment objectives
- you may have made a data entry error, such as spelling a word incorrectly, not putting a space between two words, or putting in the wrong figure in a table or database.

In each of the five sections of this unit, the examiner will penalise you for the following:

- **Manage files and directories/folders** – for not creating files, directories/folders and not using specified names. For opening, closing or saving files at the wrong time. For not deleting files, directories or folders when required. For failing to move files to particular directories or folders. For copying files you were not required to copy or failing to copy files you were required to copy. For not renaming files, directories or folders or using their right name. For not printing out the file structure.
- **Enter data accurately from data input sheets and amend existing data** – for not using a specified format. For not having a single line space between paragraphs. For not using the English (UK) spellchecker. For not using upper and lower case when required. For not using the correct English format for dates (DD/MM/YY). For not using specified codes. For failing to make amendments or not amending the document correctly. For incorrect spelling of words.
- **Create and print an integrated document** – for not creating a new document using a specified file name. For failing to import specified data files, images or charts. For not printing out the integrated document.
- **Format page layout and manipulate text according to house style** – for not using a specified page orientation. For not following a specified layout. For failing to insert headers and footers. For not using automatic fields for headers and footers when instructed. For not using bullets or numbering if requested. For either not inserting special symbols or using the wrong symbols when required. When an amended word (in search and replace) has affected the text or spaces and this has not been dealt with.
- **Format tabular data** – for not inserting a table where required. For not setting column widths to display all of the data in the table. For not setting the column or cell alignment as required. For not using grid lines, borders and shading when required.

In order to achieve a pass in this practical three-hour assignment, an examiner will expect you to have made only a limited number of errors. There is no possibility of achieving a credit or distinction as this unit is either passed or failed. Additional opportunities will be given to you if you fail to pass this unit at the first attempt.

Index